Children's sexual thinking

By Ronald Goldman

Angry Adolescents

Religious Thinking from Childhood to Adolescence

Readiness for Religion: A Basis for Developmental Religious
Education

Breaththrough (ed.)

Children's sexual thinking

A comparative study of children aged
5 to 15 years in Australia, North America,
Britain and Sweden

Ronald and Juliette Goldman

Routledge & Kegan Paul
London, Boston, Melbourne and Henley

First published in 1982
by Routledge & Kegan Paul Ltd
39 Store Street, London WC1E 7DD
9 Park Street, Boston,
Mass. 02108, USA and
Broadway House, Newtown Road,
Henley-on-Thames, Oxon RG9 1EN
Set by Hope Services, Abingdon
and printed in Great Britain by
T.J. Press (Padstow) Ltd
Padstow, Cornwall

Library of Congress Cataloging in Publication Data

Goldman, Ronald.
Children's sexual thinking.

Bibliography: p.
Includes indexes.
1. Children and sex – Cross-cultural studies.
2. Children – Attitudes – Cross-cultural studies.
I. Goldman, Juliette.   II. Title
HQ784.S45G64   305.2'3   81–15353

ISBN 0-7100-0883-X   AACR2

This book is dedicated to Sylvia and Vivian who endured and enjoyed the six childhoods of five daughters and one son

'. . . the misinformed mislead the naive, and almost everyone pretends.'

from W. H. Masters and V. E. Johnson,
The Pleasure Bond

Contents

CONTENTS

CONTENTS

Preface

Nothing in human life is more basic than sex. It was classified by earlier psychologists as one of the major fundamental human drives (McDougall, 1908) and later described, somewhat loosely, as one of the primary instincts humans share with all mammals (Trotter, 1919). Undoubtedly, sexual thinking, that is thinking about sex in all its forms, occupies an enormous amount of human energy and time.

These statements appear to be widely accepted today in the light of such dated documents as the Kinsey Reports (Kinsey, 1948 and 1953) and the well publicised researches of other sexologists in the USA (Masters and Johnson, 1966, 1970 and 1975). Yet this universal acceptance would appear to exclude children, despite Sigmund Freud's work on infantile sexuality and the popularisation of his ideas over the last fifty years. Children are still largely regarded as asexual creatures, in thought and behaviour, and childhood remains characterised as the age of innocence unaffected by any interest in sex. No doubt Freud in some ways, perhaps unwittingly, strengthened the age of innocence concept by his hypothesis of a childhood latency period when the child, educated into inhibition by taboos, punishments and more subtle social sanctions, ceases to be overtly interested in sex (Freud, 1908; Erikson, 1963) at least until the arrival of puberty.

Whether or not the Freudian hypothesis of latency can be substantiated is a matter we shall return to in later discussion. Sex and sexuality are clearly more in evidence to children today than ever before. Newspapers, magazines, even children's comics, television, films and advertisements have overt sexual references. In some countries sex education begins in first school, well before the onset of puberty, and sexual differences, often strongly stereotyped, are evident in children's language and behaviour.

This book will demonstrate not only that children are aware of sex during the so-called latency period, but that they are active sexual thinkers also. That is, they observe sex and sexuality in the world around them and seek to understand it, to integrate it into their scheme of things, and if satisfactory explanations or theories are not forthcoming they will invent intellectually satisfying ones for themselves. Nowhere is this more apparent than in the attempts of children to understand and explain the origin of babies. What we mean by the terms sex, sexual and sexuality will be clarified in the next chapter, but what we do wish to state in this preface is that sexual thinking, according to the broad definition we use, is an appropriate term to be applied to children and is not the exclusive domain of adolescence or adulthood.

The research described in this volume is part of a larger study of 5- to 15-year-olds in four countries: Australia, North America, Britain and Sweden. The larger and more extensive study began as 'Children's Conceptualisation of Development': an attempt to discover how children understand, misunderstand or only partially understand their own physical development. The term children is used throughout this book, occasionally 'teenagers' being used to denote the 13- to 15-year-olds separately. The area chosen was a broad one covering body functions, the process of ageing, expectations of body growth and change, and included the topics described here by the term 'sexual thinking'. Other sections of the more comprehensive research will be published in articles in professional and learned journals. The items dealt with here have a commonality, as a scrutiny of the contents pages will reveal.

The idea for the larger project came from three sources. The first came from an examination of Piaget's publications and the surprising discovery that, despite his considerable interest in biology, neither Piaget nor his colleagues in Geneva had examined thoroughly children's concepts of human biological growth. About that time, we had read a stimulating paper by a La Trobe University colleague, Dr Peter Langford, on a similar theme (Langford, 1975) called 'The Development of the Concept of Development'. We had discussions with another colleague, Professor Stewart Fraser, whose interesting book we had read describing sex education in several countries (Fraser, 1972) encouraged us to think of the research in comparative terms. The Dean, Dr Malcolm Lovegrove, enabled us to use an extended period of study leave to complete the work in Europe and North America. We are indebted to all these colleagues for encouraging us to undertake such a complex and stimulating study.

During 1978 we reviewed the literature and discovered there were many pieces of research which covered parts of the area we wished to investigate. Overall however, the paucity of published articles reinforced our conviction for the need to undertake what was to prove a difficult and demanding project for the next two years. The initial trial interviews, constructing a suitable interview schedule and testing out ideas, were made possible by the enthusiastic participation of La Trobe University Education students, Bruce Watkinson, Tom Kent, Charles Parkinson and Gordon Nolte, the latter providing a large number of pen-and-ink drawings used in the trial interviews, two of which were retained in the final interview schedule (see Figures 4.1 and 4.2).

We are also indebted to our Australian colleagues, Dr Glenn Rowley, Dr Bob Montgomery, Diane Worrell, and members of the Centre for the Study of Urban Education at La Trobe University for providing help, advice and constructive criticisms, especially in the early stages. We are grateful to Ben Karlsson, Lecturer in Swedish Studies at the University of Melbourne for backtranslation of our interview schedule from Swedish into English to check possible inaccuracies. In addition, although they must remain nameless in order to safeguard the identity of schools and the children interviewed, we wish to acknowledge the help of many district inspectors, school principals, deputy principals and staff in the urban-suburban schools of Melbourne.

There were many colleagues at the State University of New York at Buffalo to whom we must record our gratitude, including the Dean, Dr Bob Rossberg, Dr Philip Altbach, Chairman of the Department of Social and Philosophical Foundations, Dr Charles Fall and Dr Ron Gentile, who provided encouragement and contacts in gaining entry to schools to conduct the interviews, which proved a difficult and often frustrating process. We are also grateful to Dr Peter Atherton, Dean of the School of Education at Brock University, Canada, for support in contacting education officials of several areas in Ontario adjacent to the Niagara and Buffalo conurbation. The invaluable help of school superintendents, school principals and staff in Upper New York State and in the southern part of the province of Ontario made the North American sample possible.

The School of Education at the University of Reading in England was the base for a considerable part of our sabbatical year and we wish to record our gratitude to members of staff, particularly Professor Jack Wrigley, Dean of the School, Paul Mercier, Maurice Rolls and Dr Chris Gayford for professional advice, and Yvonne Lowe and Ann McCord for administrative assistance. The Director of Education for Berkshire and his senior education advisor, Peter Coles, granted us access to schools, enabling us to receive the support of many school principals and staff in urban-suburban areas of the county. The initial statistical work and computing of the first results were done through the Department of Applied Statistics at Reading University, where we received invaluable help from Professor Robert Curnow, Chairman of the department, Keith Freeman and Joan Knock.

PREFACE

We are particularly grateful to Professor Torsten Husen and Dr Ingemar Fagerlind of the University of Stockholm, Department of International Studies and Professor Ingvar Werdelin of Linköping University, who encouraged us to begin negotiations with the Swedish National Board of Education, where Ulla Riis and Lars Naeslund enabled us to include the Swedish collection of the data in their ongoing project, 'Stages of Maturation and Concept of Self' at the Stockholm Institute of Education. At the Institute we were helped by the interest and co-operation of its head, Professor Bengt-Olov Ljung, and the Swedish project leader Dr Gunilla Westin-Lindgren and her interviewers, Lars Hagerstrand, Rose-Marie Ahlgren, Lennart Johansson and Inger Klingensjö. We record our gratitude for their cheerful work not only in organising, and interviewing the children in Swedish, but also translating the responses into English, a long and complicated task.

Except in Sweden where the Swedish Board of Education gave financial help in the Swedish interviewing, no government funding in any of the countries involved was directly available to support the research. However, we are indebted to generous funding from the Centre for the Study of Urban Education, and to La Trobe University for release on an Outside Study Program scheme for a full year to collect the overseas data.

Last, but certainly not least, our heartful thanks go to Pauline Church, our indefatigable amanuensis, who has over two years handled the enormous amount of filing, telephone calls, correspondence and manuscript typing required for the project.

The area researched and reported here is, of necessity, delicate and sensitive and we will no doubt receive some criticisms once the work is published. In thanking all who have helped in this complex and fascinating study, we wish to state that we accept sole responsibility for any errors or problems which have arisen in the course of this project. Our hope is that the hundreds of children who shared so freely their insights and problems in this sensitive area will be the major benefactors.

1 The theoretical background to the research

Despite the enormous volume of literature and the increasing research in the last thirty years about human sexuality, our knowledge of this basic area of human experience, thought and behaviour remains astonishingly incomplete. Perhaps this can be explained by the fact that the universality of sexuality is accompanied by a universality of sexual taboos in every society. One example is self-stimulation, or masturbation, which is accepted as universally practised but universally disapproved, and condemned under the misnomer of self-abuse.

Reporting on their cross-cultural and cross-species survey of sexuality, Ford and Beach (1951), in their classic book, *Patterns of Sexual Behaviour*, state (p. 287):

> It is most regrettable that an area of inquiry having such fundamental importance in both its practical and its theoretical aspects should have been so inadequately studied and so incompletely understood. Hesitancy to attack basic problems in this field cannot today be excused on grounds of public disapproval or moral censorship. Intelligent people everywhere are eager for information that will help them to understand their own sexual lives and those of their associates.

In the twenty years since that was written there has been a considerable increase in the number of objective studies into human sexuality, and opposition to such enquiries has tended to lessen. Nevertheless strong taboos still operate to limit enquiry in the form of public and private protest, political and institutional obstruction and the exercise of moral censorship.

Nowhere are these more obvious when the field of study focusses upon children and their developing sexuality. Despite a greater apparent openness about sex in our society, sometimes characterised as 'the

1

permissive society' and sometimes described by a change from 'hot' to 'cool' sex (Francoeur and Francoeur, 1974), there appears to be strong resistance to the recognition of children's growing sexual awareness and knowledge. Hostility to adolescence is one manifestation of this resistance, where even the word 'adolescent' is frequently used negatively and insultingly (Eppel and Eppel, 1966). Adolescents may be seen to be sexual rivals to older groups and sexual challenges have always been resisted, rather like animals with territorial possession; invading predators have to be fought off. Their sexuality is also diminished by referring to adolescents, even those fully post-pubertal and with obvious primary sex characteristics, as 'children'. 'Schoolchildren' is still a classification covering young men and women up to 18 years of age as well as those in the younger age groups. In some countries school uniforms are the vogue; Britain and Australia are examples of this, and appear to be designed in part to eliminate sexual identity for as long as possible.

Childhood itself, which we define as the period from infancy to the beginning of puberty, is subject to even more social taboos where sexuality is concerned than is adolescence. All investigators testify to the problems they face when trying to gain access to children for the purpose of studying the genesis of sexuality and the extent of children's growing sexual awareness. Visits by the police, telephone calls by irate parents, stone-walling letters from school administrators expressing a wish to help but voicing fears of dismissal are commonplace (Schofield, 1968). Certainly, in carrying out the study described in this volume, we encountered similar difficulties.

Psychologists have long been interested in children's sexuality, not only because of Sigmund Freud's theories, but also because developmentally it has been recognised as a key area for understanding child growth. Yet psychologists also reflect the taboos and limitations imposed by society, sometimes even perpetuating myths about the sexuality of childhood themselves. More than fifty years ago the Child Study Association of America published a guide to Childhood and Youth (Gruenberg, 1926) containing statements such as 'In the ordinary sense of the word "sex", the infant would seem to be entirely free of desires or interests that are strictly sexual' (p. 238). In another section it is stated that a special danger of masturbation is 'the possibility that impotence may result' (p. 241).

More recently the *American Psychologist* published a special issue (1979) entitled 'Psychology and Children — Current Research and Practice' to commemorate the International Year of the Child. Although intended as a survey of Child Psychology and Child Development a thorough reading reveals nothing on the normal sexual development of children and no mention of sexual thinking, despite several informative sections on children's cognition. One would at least expect in the section headed 'Identifying the Problems and Needs of Our Children' there would be some recognition of the area of sexuality. The nearest reference is in the article on 'Child Abuse' which mentions the sexual abuse of children in defining the terms used, but concentrates the discussion entirely upon physical violence. An examination of the bibliography confirms this tunnel vision. The only other allusion to children's sexual development is in the article on 'Divorce' (pp. 851-8) quoting Wallerstein and Kelly (1974): 'Perhaps because of their own awakening sexuality pre-adolescents and adolescents are particularly distressed by an increased awareness of their parents as sex objects, first when both parents are dating and then when parents remarry.' Yet there is no sustained discussion or examination of children's normal sexual development not even in the following section 'Improving Our Knowledge of Children's Thinking'. The focus here is upon the competence of pre-school children, early intervention programmes, the teaching of reading and the effects of families upon children's intellectual development. In introducing this section the editor states (p. 893) 'In this year of celebrating children it is appropriate to take stock of where we are and to renew our commitment to the pursuit of fundamental research in such areas as children's thinking'. Again, the area of children's sexual thinking is conspicuous by its absence.

A perceptive comment is made by the author of *Sexually Victimised Children* (Finkelhor, 1979) who points out that 'we know more about sexual deviance than we do about sexual normality or ordinariness' and that 'all theories about children's sexual victimisation must be viewed against their true backdrop: a vast ignorance of the forces governing the development and expression of sexual behaviour in general' (p. 20). Plainly there is a pressing need to combat this ignorance by investigating key areas such as children's sexual thinking, to develop realistic norms of how children perceive and generalise about sexual matters. An exploratory article (Breese, 1978) suggested Piagetian theory might be applied to sexuality as knowledge and suggested sexual cognition of children might develop in stages, but no evidence was advanced to support this interesting speculation.

The sexual thinking of children

When terms such as sex, sexual and sexuality are used they are often associated with coitus that is, the act of copulation or sexual intercourse. This is why many may feel the term 'sexual' applied to children is inappropriate or even repulsive. Most dictionaries, however, define sex as 'being male or female'; sexual as 'pertaining to being male or female'; and sexuality as the sexual identity and activities of males and females. (Some definitions include also the term hermaphrodite, the rare condition

3

of possessing both male and female sex organs.) The *New World Diction-ary* defines sexuality simply as 'the quality of being sexual'.

As Unger (1979a) has pointed out, the word 'sex' can be used to describe the chromosomal composition of individuals, the reproductive apparatus and secondary sex characteristics. It also covers, she adds, intrapsychic characteristics presumed to be characteristic of males and females, and all behaviours differentially expected. Unger prefers to use the word 'sex' to describe the biological differences and 'gender' as the social label by which we distinguish two groups of people. 'Gender may be used for those traits for which sex acts as a stimulus variable indepen-dently of whether those traits have their origin within the subject or not.' These terms clearly have a much wider meaning than sex identity and the sex act, about which, incidentally, many younger children appear to be completely ignorant. But it is obvious that the world children experience from the moment of birth is a sexual world gradually dis-covered experientially and cognitively as they develop. In a later work (1979b) Unger enlarges on her theme, pointing out that fewer and fewer sex differences are being confirmed and that many sexually differentiated characteristics and behaviours can be said to be socially learned.

Although concerned with sexual deviancy, Plummer (1975) supports this view (p. 29):

> the sexual motives which human beings have are derived from the social roles they play: like all other motives these would not be possible were not the actions physiologically possible, but the physiology does not supply the motives, designate the partners, invest the objects with preformed passion, nor even dictate the objectives to be achieved.

This is not only an interactionist view but is supported by many investi-gators into sex differences with varying theoretical approaches (Bee, 1974; Maccoby, 1967).

Where children's sexual thinking is concerned it has been thought that their biological maturing stimulates a curiosity and a desire to explore sexuality. Hence, the general tendency to leave sex education programmes until the onset of adolescence. However, small numbers of children with hormonal anomaly have been studied (Hampson and Money, 1955). These are children who are post-pubescent in early childhood, due to early hormonal changes. Their sexual thinking, according to theories making biological assumptions, would be ex-pected to be in advance of their peers as an automatic or instinctive product of the body achieving sexual maturation. Yet the investigators found that psychosexual maturation, including sexual thinking, appeared to be determined by the experiences they encountered and had to deal with. For example, the sexual dreams and fantasies of a 6-year-old who had completed puberty were much more congruent with his age than with his physical maturity. Eroticism was not associated with copulation. As Bernstein (1973) has pointed out, this supports the view that a child's understanding of procreation is more a function of cognitive than physiological development.

It is the broader meaning of 'sexual' that has been used in planning and completing the research outlined in this book. The term encompasses the identity and roles of mothers and fathers, reflecting differences and similarities of men and women generally; the child's own identity and sex preferences as a boy or girl; the family, and marriage in particular as a sexual, not only a social, institution; the growing and changing physical differences between girls and boys; the origin of babies and how their sex is determined, including their conception, gestation and birth. The wider meaning also includes what the growing child experiences and observes about 'not having babies', sex education and sources of sex information, and the social convention of clothing the sexual organs. In addition the vocabulary used to describe sexual organs, behaviour, experience and matters associated with sexuality is included.

We therefore define children's sexual thinking as 'thinking about' the broader area described above. It is evident from previous research and our own findings that children from a very early age are, by this definition, active sexual thinkers.[1] They 'think about' mothers and fathers, differences between men and women, their own identity as boys or girls and the sexual role of other persons whom they encounter in the long process of socialisation within the family and in society. This is similar to Kohlberg's (1969) use of moral thought. Children's sexual thinking, learning and behaviour may be described as subject to sexual socialisation from the moment of birth. This process will be examined in more detail later and the most recent studies will be reviewed.

We prefer to use the more popular term sexual 'thinking', rather than psychosexual development or even cognition. While 'psychosexual' may appear to be appropriate in terms of one dictionary definition as 'relating to sexuality as it manifests itself in the mind in contradistinction to its physical or somatic manifestations' (Hinsie and Shatzky, 1947), developmentally it is a term which has been used more widely 'as the development in the individual of the various aspects of sex during his life history' (Dorland, 1948). 'Cognition' on the other hand we recognise as a more precise term as the means by which an individual comes to possess organised knowledge and how that knowledge can be used to guide behaviour. We include cognition, in this sense, within the term 'thinking'. By thinking, we mean the processes originating in sensation, percepts developed through the senses, the development of symbols to retain percepts in memory, and the development from perception to conceptualisation. This includes the normal process of generalisation, the identifying of common elements which go together, and the process of abstraction, the separating of unlike from like. As Glick (1975) points out: 'The category or concept describes an organisational feature of cognitive process whereby objectively discriminable stimuli are treated as being similar. This has the adaptive consequence of reducing the amount of complexity that must be dealt with' (p. 596). According to these inclusive categories the study could alternatively have been called Children's Sexual Cognition or Children's Sexual Conceptualisation, but the more widely used word 'thinking' has been retained for the non-technical reader, to include both cognition and conceptualisation. It will be noted that the word 'process' has been used frequently. As Cole (Cole *et al.*, 1971) has pointed out, cognition, previously synonymous with thinking, has gradually been extended to include thought processes. He supports Bruner's view that cognition is present whenever the subject 'goes beyond the information given'. Included in this view of cognition is the process of 'theory building'.

In their development, children seek to understand their sexual world, evidence of which is visibly present in their own bodies and in the members of their own family. Not only do they seek sexual knowledge but they strive to understand it, to make sense of it, and to do this they develop theories or hypotheses to explain what they observe. These complex processes are, however, made more difficult by the operation of taboos, enforced by evasive, repressive and even coercive actions on the part of the adult world. Guilt and inhibition are soon acquired from the child's earliest enforcers, the parents, who reflect not only their own personal restraints but those of the society in which they have been reared. In other words, culture plays a considerable role in how children's sexual thinking develops.

Cultural influence on thinking

As Bruner (1966) has stated, 'there is no "standard child" and "natural childhood" is hard to imagine outside a cultural context.' That is, while there are considerable variations between children in any one society, what is accepted as normal or natural for children is determined by the culture to which they belong. There are approximately 150 possible definitions of 'culture': we accept Kroeber and Kluckhohn's (1952) as the one most widely accepted (p. 180):

> Culture consists of patterns, explicit and implicit, of and for behaviour acquired and transmitted by symbols, constituting the distinctive achievement of human groups, including their embodiments in artifacts; the essential core of culture consists

of traditional . . . ideas and especially their attached values; culture systems may on the one hand, be considered as products of action, on the other as conditioning elements of further action.

Comparing Americans, which they use as representative of Western cultures, with 185 'primitive' cultures, Ford and Beach (1951) classify societies sexually into three categories as restrictive, semi-restrictive and permissive. Western societies tend to be nearer to restrictive sexual societies in viewing the acquisition of sexual knowledge and experience by young children. For example, masturbation is often severely punished. Western cultures and less technically developed cultures alike maintain a public conspiracy against the acquisition of sexual knowledge. In some societies it is forbidden for children to watch the birth of animals. In others, boys of 4 or 5 years old are removed from their homes to bachelor accommodation for the specific purpose of preventing them witnessing parental sexual behaviour. Many of these restrictive practices are reflected in a British study of 4-year-olds (Newson and Newson, 1968) where the negative attitudes of their mothers to the sexual exploration of their children is described.

What is permissible for children to know, explore and practise varies considerably between restrictive, semi-restrictive and permissive societies. Homosexuality, for example, receives repressive treatment in restrictive societies but is permitted, and sometimes seen as a necessary sexual induction process for boys, in the other two categories. Courtship behaviour, pre-marital sex, the circumstances and frequency of coitus and allowable sexual partnerships, all vary according to the cultural values placed upon such matters.

D'Andrade (in Maccoby, 1967) states that anthropologically sex differences are seen as social and cultural institutions. They are culturally transmitted patterns of behaviour, determined in part by the functioning of a particular society. These differences can be seen cross-culturally in the performance of daily tasks, in ascriptions of social status, in interpersonal behaviour, in gender identity and in fantasy productions. In the same volume, Kohlberg elaborates the theory 'which assumes that basic sexual attitudes are not patterned directly by either biological instincts or arbitrary cultural norms, but by the child's cognitive organisation of his social world along sex-role dimensions'. Serpell (1976) provides a useful summary of cultural influences upon thought and behaviour. Where cognitive skills are concerned he draws attention particularly to field dependency (Witkin et al., 1974) across cultures. Field dependency theory is of particular interest, especially where explanations of sex differences are examined. Although Witkin has pointed out that sex difference in field-dependent scores may have a genetic basis, most research relates it to different patterns of child-rearing. Girls, it is suggested, are more protected by their mothers in Western cultures, who encourage their daughters to be less assertive and aggressive than their sons.

Whatever the theoretical explanation there is no dissent from the view that culture strongly influences sexual behaviour, and by varying child-rearing practices provides a cognitive framework, both negative and positive, within which the child has to operate intellectually. It follows from this that children in differing cultures may pursue different strategies in sexual thinking and achieve varying levels of knowledge and insight about sex at differing ages.

The importance of comparative studies

The influence of culture upon thinking has, over the last twenty years, caused cognitive psychologists to check their generalisations about children in Western-type societies, by the inception of cross-cultural studies. It is significant that the largest number of cross-cultural studies so far completed have been in the area of cognition, and by far the most numerous of these have been mounted to test Piagetian hypotheses. It is significant for this present study because much of the data has been subjected to Piagetian scoring and analysis, and children's responses in four countries have been compared.

Piaget himself has asserted (Piaget, 1972) 'the need and significance of cross-cultural studies in genetic psychology'. But it should be pointed out that both Piaget and his followers who carried out this cross-cultural work, were motivated by the desire to confirm the universality of Piaget's operational stages of thinking. As Cole and Scribner (1974) have written: 'Cross-cultural research is like virtue – everybody is in favour of it, but there are widely differing views of what it is and ought to be.'

One issue is the definition of the term cross-cultural. Jahoda (1970) maintains that his usage is confined to the study of peoples contrasting sharply in modes of life and ecology, such as the Scots and the Ashanti. He excludes comparative studies of culturally similar populations like the French and the English which he suggests are more properly called 'cross-national'. On the other hand, Lloyd (1972) while agreeing that comparisons among Western groups are usually termed 'cross-national', suggests that this should not be a hard and fast rule, simply because within Western societies there are varying cultures and sub-cultures, such as working-class and professional groups. Lloyd adds 'often a combination of comparisons between and within societies is most conducive to a fuller understanding of psychological processes' (p. 18).

Concerning the question of the purpose of cross-cultural studies there are those who see their primary objective to be the testing of

8

hypotheses. A prime example of this is Berry and Dasen (1974) who review the testing of Piagetian hypotheses about operational thinking in several differing cultures. Strodtbeck (1969), however, states quite strongly 'From the viewpoint of the logic of discovery it is expressly in the generating of new hypotheses that the cross-cultural method has its particular strength.'

Despite these differing views, comparative studies are seen to be beneficial, as the results of cognitive researches have demonstrated, for by making inter-group comparisons, whether cross-national or cross-cultural, assertions of universality about children can be tested and new theories or hypotheses generated (Cole and Scribner, 1974). It can, of course, be contested that Western-type societies can all be lumped together under one cultural umbrella. Members of the Laboratory of Comparative Human Cognition at the University of California at San Diego in contributing to an interesting paper (Laboratory, 1979) wrote: 'No context of observation, despite the care taken in its construction, is culturally neutral. Settings for behaviours are culturally organised and they are embedded in larger systems of social organisation which influence them' (p. 829). Although written in the context of discussing Pitt-Rivers's anthropological expedition to Torres Strait in 1901, it could equally apply to differing Western-type countries; certainly the four countries represented in this investigation, Australia, Britain, North America and Sweden. There are subtle and sometimes pronounced cultural differences, especially in the area of sexuality, which may account for differences in children's sexual thinking in those countries.

One of the few comparative sexual studies is that of Williams, who compared sex-trait stereotypes in France, Germany and Norway (Williams et al., 1979) following a similar comparison of England, USA and Ireland in 1977. University students were administered the Adjective Check List of 300 items, indicating which they thought were predominantly male or female. The results proved to be relatively similar. The authors suggest that while the six countries chosen do not represent all Western countries 'for the present we believe the stereotype similarity found in the six countries studied is sufficient to propose the hypothesis that there are general similarities in the patterns of traits differentially ascribed to men and women in all Western countries' (p. 155). This is a rather sweeping generalisation, especially when 'Western' as opposed to 'European' can often be taken to include Latvia, Greece, Japan and New Zealand.

A political scientist (Lipset, 1963) has argued in a paper comparing Canadian, Australian, American and English societies, that all four countries are urban, industrial and stable democracies, but that culturally the USA is egalitarian and populist, England is deferential and elitist, and that Canada and Australia fall somewhere in between. Unfortunately,

9

this is not a research-based article but conveys only impressionistic estimates of differences, based upon a value analysis from the perspectives of Talcott Parsons. It is interesting to speculate, from the standpoint of this study, where Sweden would fall on such a value scale. But Lipset's article does highlight some of the subtle but important differences in societies with several important commonalities which might account for differences in behaviour and thinking among their populations. We shall return to this issue in chapter 3 when the four countries chosen for the sample will be discussed.

Omissions in Piagetian research

Despite the fact that Piaget was trained as a biologist, that his dominating interest was genetic psychology and that he has pioneered an unprecedented range of research into children's thinking, the major focus of his work and that of his colleagues appears to be fixated upon the physical and mathematical sciences and particularly how children think about problems suggested by these disciplines. One would expect in a volume titled *Biology and Knowledge* that Piaget (1967) would have tried to outline the child's discovery of biological knowledge, particularly the child's own physical and sexual growth and identity. The book, however, is a theoretical discussion about 'the problem of intelligence and of knowledge in general, in particular logico-mathematical knowledge, in the light of contemporary biology'. It contains nothing, not even a question, about children's biological knowledge and understanding. This blind spot is repeated in a later work, *Behaviour and Evolution* (Piaget, 1976), another theoretical discussion, about the relationship between behaviour and biological evolution, Piaget arguing for his own theories after reviewing those of Lamarck, Baldwin, Weiss and others.

It could be argued that these were books with a specific purpose and could not contain such matters not directly germane to the central arguments. Yet further illustrations of the blind spot abound. In a UNESCO publication (1972) Piaget draws attention to the small proportion of students choosing scientific as opposed to liberal arts careers. He goes on to say how education's aims, goals and methods should be revised to rectify this balance. All the illustrations used are from the physical and mathematical sciences. For a paper called 'A Structural Foundation for Tomorrow's Education' no mention whatever of biological science, human biology and the need for children to understand biological and sexual processes is a singular omission.

A systematic search of Piaget's earlier works, and that of the 'Geneva school' generally, indicates a similar gap. A survey of 1,500 Piaget-related studies (Modgil, 1974) shows that the vast majority, which replicate or extend Piaget's work, are concerned with the growth of logic largely in relation to mathematical and physical science problems, the most popular being conservation, seriation, spatial and geometrical concepts. This is marked in all sections including research related to handicapped children, curriculum studies and cross-cultural and cross-national studies.

The evidence in comparative studies of Piaget's theories appears to indicate two major conclusions. The first is that in non-Western societies the population does not appear to progress beyond concrete operational thinking to formal operational thinking. The second is that there appears to be a time-lag for arriving even at concrete operational thought. But the content of all the studies leading up to these conclusions is again focussed upon number and physics (Dasen, 1972). There are many criticisms voiced of Piaget's work. These include objections that Piaget has always been ethnocentric (European based with logico-scientific assumptions about thinking), has neglected cultural factors in pursuit of his genetic-maturational theories, and even within one culture his samples have always been socio-economically biased (Vernon, 1969; Heron, 1974; Dasen, 1972; Buck-Morss, 1975; Greenfield, 1976).

Yet it is the neglect of biological conceptualisation by children which continues to surprise. Reviewing the 'Geneva school' research to that date, Piaget and Inhelder (1966) provide a summary of the stages of genetic development. In this review practically all the illustrations are from the physical and mathematical sciences. Despite books with titles such as *The Child's Conception of Physical Causality* (Piaget, 1927), there is nothing on biological causality. The nearest is to be found in *The Child's Conception of the World* (1929) where several anecdotal discussions with children are reported about the origin of babies (p. 362):

Q: 'Where is the baby now that a lady is going to have a baby next summer?'
A: 'It's inside her.'
Q: 'Has she eaten it then?'

Piaget suggests that by looking chronologically at the questions children ask about the origin of babies, in terms of age sequences, we can obtain some idea of the process of logic involved. From the questions noted, he deduced a threefold sequence.

Stage 1: Babies have always pre-existed.
Stage 2: Babies are artificially made and are the results of production (Artificialism).
Stage 3: Material for the production of babies comes from the parents' own bodies, without children knowing precisely how and what.

Without any demonstrable evidence Piaget suggests that these questions and theories lead to wider questions about the first man on earth, and the growth of artificialism by stages.

We are prompted by this paucity of material on biological thinking to make two observations. The first is that the focus so far emphasised shows a serious defect in the content of Piagetian-type investigations, a bias towards technological science which is of no more importance than science applied to the human condition, particularly to human biology and sexuality. The second observation is that what biological thinking content is present is superficially researched and presented, not followed through in later studies, and relegated by inference to an unimportant position in the scale of values such as to discourage future researchers from venturing into the field of biological or sexual thinking.

To be fair, it should be stated that no one person, not even a prodigious and prolific researcher of Piaget's stature, can hope to encompass encyclopedically the whole universe of children's thinking. What we have attempted to do here is to point out the imbalance in cognitive studies unwittingly created by the 'Geneva school', and to underline the need for investigations in the other scientific areas, particularly the biological and sexual. It is the intention of the authors to begin the process of rectifying the imbalance by this present research. Maybe, in so doing, by the process of 'equilibrium' over many years a proper balance may emerge. As will be seen, we have used certain criteria, frequently adapted from Piaget or adjusted from Kohlberg and others, to score children's responses on sequences from pre-operational to formal operational thinking. The paucity of studies in the area of biological and sexual thinking has made this task extremely difficult, although similar difficulties were experienced in an earlier work on children's religious thinking (Goldman, 1964).

The authors are well aware of other more recent criticisms of Piaget, for example, Brown and Desforges (1979) who maintain that some of Piaget's theories are as yet untested, much has been tested and found wanting, and that many aspects of his theories appear to be untestable. It is not, however, the purpose of this study to enter into this debate, but rather to examine the biological-human relations areas relatively unresearched by Piagetian theories.

Freudian theories of children's sexuality

The most controversial of Sigmund Freud's pronouncements in the early days of psychoanalysis was not the centrality of sex in human thought, motivation and behaviour, but the assertion of infantile sexuality (Freud, 1908). It was primarily based upon free-association, abreactive memories of childhood by Freud's first patients, who frequently recollected incestuous relationships with a parent, sexual jealousies of one parent or the other, narcissistic love of the self, repressed sexual desires fixated upon the sexual organs, and many other related areas of the body. 'Sexual life does not begin only at puberty but starts with clear manifestations soon after birth' (Freud, 1940), and 'Sexual life comprises the function of obtaining pleasure from zones of the body — a function which is subsequently brought into the service of that reproduction' (*ibid.*). It is little wonder that these assertions have been distorted and dramatised, such as Brophy's (1968) statement that 'The quality Freud said is supposed to be characteristic of infantile sexuality is polymorphous perversity.'

Freud's pronouncements frequently had the capacity to shock, particularly the prudish middle-class society of Vienna of which he was a member. Many examples can be cited, but it is sufficient to quote only two: 'We say that the human being has originally two sexual objects — himself (sic) and the woman who nurses him — and in doing so we are postulating a primary narcissism in everyone' (Freud, 1914, p. 88); 'Children have, to begin with, no idea of the significance of the distinction between the sexes; on the contrary, they start from the assumption that the same genital organ (the male one) is possessed by both sexes' (*ibid.*, p. 55).

Such statements were the beginnings of an elaborate theory, or a series of *ad hoc* theories, developed by psychoanalysts, as Maslow (1963) points out, 'in the effort to order their clinical findings'. And indeed, the theories were subject to considerable change when it was realised that what patients reported were not actual happenings of childhood but the sexual fantasies of adults projected regressively into their earliest years. Not until the psychoanalytic approach was applied to play therapy with children by Anna Freud and Melanie Klein were theories of infantile sexuality more precisely formulated and systemised (Klein, 1932). Even so, the theories are still imprecise and the basic hypotheses largely untested and unproven. To complicate matters further, post-Freudian analysts have advanced differing theories and interpretations; both cultural revisionists such as Fromm, Horney and Kardiner, and anthropologists, such as Benedict and Mead.

Since some of the Freudian theories are relevant to our study, we describe below what we consider to be the major Freudian concepts of infantile sexuality, and how they would appear to affect children's thinking about sex in later years. Later we shall attempt to show how our findings may be relevant to these theories. Because this overview has to be compressed it is necessarily somewhat oversimplified, and the reader who wishes to explore further is referred to the works of Sigmund and Anna Freud, Melanie Klein and others. An admirable summary is provided by Brown (1961) in his *Freud and the Post Freudians*.

Freud's use of the word 'sex' developed it from a narrow copulation-based definition to a broader meaning which included any pleasurable sensation experienced physically by the child, and also those sexually sublimated feelings such as pleasure to be found in eating and drinking and evacuating and in the emotions of tenderness and friendship. This definition included sensuous experiences the child may enjoy, from being fondled, stroked and comforted, as well as feelings towards members of the same sex. Genital activity therefore is not an essential ingredient of Freud's broader meaning, although it was included in it, particularly early pleasurable explorations of the genital organs. In other words, infantile sexuality does not necessarily include copulation or even the genital organs, but rather the broader world of relationships and feelings. This concurs with our own definition. Among the informed, infantile sexuality has ceased to be an expression narrowly focussed upon coition and its wider meaning is generally accepted. The general public, however, does not always understand or accept this; this is symptomatic of the still widespread ignorance of and resistance to the word sexuality, particularly when associated with children.

The most important aspect of Freudian child theories, for the purposes of this study, is the developmental stages posited by Freud as being related in the early years of life to the three apertures of the body, the mouth, the anus and the genitals. The oral, anal and genital stages, it is asserted, represent the dominant interest and pleasure experienced by the infant from the moment of birth in an unmistakable chronological sequence. The oral stage is characterised by the pleasure of feeding and is sexually significant because of breast-sucking (or its bottle substitute) and the sensuous warmth and comfort of the mother's body. This oral pleasure is never lost and is even heightened in the later years by the activity of the mouth in sexual activity. Weaning to the cup and more solid food is the first training requirement and carries with it possibilities of increased pleasure or trauma associated with the mouth.

Next comes the anal stage when pleasure is dominantly focussed upon the experience of expelling excreta and later learning to retain it. The proximity to the sexual organs and later associations of sex activity with this area of the body are again seen, as in the oral stage, as being of considerable sexual significance. Toilet training consequently is viewed as another important developmental event in which approval and disapproval are voiced by parents, often the reward coming from mothers in a hug or a kiss. Approval provides the pleasure of receiving adult support and also of physical achievement. Adult disapproval and expressions of disgust create feelings of guilt and associations of 'dirtiness' with sex due to the proximity of the sex organs to the excretory organs. Since in Western countries toilet training begins towards the end of the baby's first year of life and continues well into the second year, and longer in many cases, this stage overlaps with the oral stage. However, once successful weaning occurs the child's anus becomes the dominant area of interest. With greater flexibility and control of limbs the growing infant discovers the genitals. Pleasurable stimulation at bathing and cleaning times is experienced, and in some cultures mothers are observed actively to caress and tease the penis of male infants in cuddling and play situations. Erections are in fact observed in male infants in the first few days of life and female babies lubricate vaginally in the first four to six hours of life. Less is known of female genital activity and one weakness of Freudian theory is its early obsession with male development. Clearly touching, exploring and stroking the genital area becomes evident in the third year of life for both girls and boys. This begins the genital stage, interestingly called the phallic stage by Freud, since he asserts that it is the penis, and in the female, the penis-less condition, which is the object of interest and pleasure. It is natural then for children to increase their pleasure by stroking and stimulating their own sex organs, this being their earliest overt directly sexual activity, and the beginnings of masturbation. It is known in many cultures that this pleasurable practice is discouraged, if not severely punished, from an early age. In America, Sears, Maccoby and Levin (1957), in England the Newsons (1968) and Ford and Beach (1951) provide evidence from several cultures that the genital stage is terminated by strong disapproval and discouragement. The fear by adults of infantile overt sexual activity is widespread, so that what is called the latency period intervenes, when sanctions and taboos force the child to repress sexual curiosity and activity.

The latency stage or period is said to begin about 5 years of age and continue until 10 or 11, or whenever pre-pubertal developments begin to occur. The latency period does not mean that all interest and activity concerned with sexuality disappears, but because of the onset of the Oedipal phase, so Freudians assert, there is no further sexual development apparent. Like most developmental stages, one stage does not replace the preceding stage, but previous stages continue alongside the current dominant stage. Consequently oral, anal and genital interest continues in the latency period, but the child learns to control and repress too overt an expression of it. The final stage of sexuality comes with pubertal development involving the glandular changes which lead to adolescence and full adult genitality.

Since this study is concerned with children aged 5 to 15 years we shall be dealing, according to Freudian theory, with those mainly in the latency period and those older ones moving towards or having attained full genitality. This aspect of Freudian theory is of particular interest in chapter 9, which deals with how children perceive sexual differences between newborn babies, and later sexual differences as they grow older.

There are two other Freudian theories which are relevant to our study, the Oedipal phase and Freud's view of children's theories of childbirth. On this last area, Freud has posited a 'cloacal' theory whereby young children hypothesise that conception is caused by the mother eating food, the food becomes the baby and the baby is evacuated through the anus. This will be discussed fully in chapters 10 to 11, where children's concepts of the origin of babies, and of gestation and birth processes are presented.

The Oedipal phase, or complex, as it is often called, is named after the king in the Greek play, *Oedipus Rex*, whom Sophocles dramatises as killing his own father and marrying his mother – although he does not know them to be his parents at the time. In brief, this theory applies to the genital stage, or the phallic period (3 to 5 years) when the boy sees his father as the rival for mother's affections. Feelings of jealousy and sexual rivalry are directed by the boy against his father, but these come to an end when taboos on illicit feelings are recognised, and the boy, it is said, fears punishment by castration from the father (the castration complex). This is repressed during the latency period, but is said to affect relationships within the family and attraction to the parent of the opposite sex in later years. For girls there is an equivalent situation named the Electra complex, derived from the Greek myth in which the daughter Electra plots the death of Clytemnestra who was responsible for the murder of her father Agamemnon. Freud's theory is much less clear here but it consists of the girl being attached to her father, with accompanying jealousy and sexual rivalry with the mother. The girl conquers her complex only by acceptance of her feminity and not having a phallus, and by renouncing all hope of becoming a male. The difference between the boy and the girl apparently is that both have to wrestle with the castration complex, but the boy resolves his problem by fear of castration, whereas the girl does so by accepting castration as having happened. As Brown (1961, p. 25) states, 'The fact that the girl thinks "I have been punished" while the boy fears "I may be punished" is believed to have important consequences for their later development'. Freud (1924) claimed quite specifically that the Oedipus complex is 'smashed to pieces by the shock of threatened castration'. We shall discuss the relevance of this in chapter 7 when the roles of mothers and fathers and preferences for a favourite parent are presented. A very full description of the Oedipal phase can be read in Machtlinger (1976) and Bronfenbrenner (1960). There has been a recent interest in, and a series of investigations into the role of father in the family (Lamb, 1976), mainly because of the growing incidence of divorce, the increase in single-parent families and a growing awareness of incest.

What might be called a classical statement of a later and more developed Freudian theory can be quoted from Melanie Klein (1932) in a chapter entitled 'The Sexual Activities of Children' (p. 164):

> One of the important achievements of psycho-analysis is the discovery that children possess a sexual life which finds utterance both in direct sexual activities and in sexual fantasies . . . . We know that masturbation occurs in general in the sucking stage and that it is very commonly prolonged, in a less measure, right up to the latency period . . . In the period before puberty and particularly during period itself, masturbation becomes very frequent again. The puberty in which the child's sexual activities are least pronounced is the latency period. This is because the decline of the Oedipus complex is accompanied by a diminution in the force of instinctual trends.

One of the major problems of Freudian theories of child development is the difficulty in testing the hypotheses advanced. Although developmental stages have been elaborated by Erikson (1959) into 'Eight Stages of Man', beginning with the oral, anal, genital and latency stages, it is very difficult to ascertain the validity of these theories from experimental research. The authors, for example, took Erikson's stages and tried to devise scoring codes which might yield a developmental scale of children's responses. But the vague and anecdotal descriptions of each stage were so imprecise that such scoring attempts had to be abandoned. This is not without precedence, since many attempts have been made to validate or invalidate Freudian claims. Psychoanalysts themselves have paid much attention to children raised in kibbutzim in Israel, to observe whether or not the Oedipal phase is seen in children raised with minimal contact with their parents (Rabin, 1965; Bettelheim, 1969).

One would expect a book called *The Experimental Study of Freudian Theories* (Eysenck and Wilson, 1973) to provide some solid evidence which might cast more empirical light on Freudian theories. Unfortunately, the articles chosen are those 'which are widely believed to be the most convincing, the best designed and the most conclusive among those which confirm Freudian theories' (p. xii). The reports contain only those persuasive to the Freudian viewpoint, as judged by Freudians. These are justified by the rather specious argument quoted from Kline (1972), 'Failure to confirm the theory can always be blamed on the test. Test validity, on the other hand, automatically implies the validity of the theory.' The Eysenck and Wilson book is disappointing from our viewpoint since it contains nothing on the latency period, nor on children's stages of development.

Kline's own book *Fact and Fantasy in Freudian Theory* (1972) contains a much wider selection of research concerned with the testing of Freudian theories, including Freud's child development theories with some discussion of the latency stage. Pointing out the many poor research designs and difficulties inherent in evaluating psychoanalytic theories, his overall findings can be summarised as follows. There is some evidence for the oral stage, strong evidence for the anal stage, good evidence for the Oedipus complex and for the widespread existence in many cultures of castration fears in children. Among the most convincing evidence for the Oedipal situation he cites the results from Rabin's study of kibbutzim boys and for castration fears Stephens's (1962) cross-cultural study of more than sixty societies. The point is well taken that studies, such as ours, which include an examination of children's preferences for one parent or the other, provide no evidence for accepting or rejecting Oedipal theories since processes of repression, sublimation and rationalisation may mask children's choices. Two matters, however, are relevant when examining theories of the Oedipus complex. The first is that research is focussed almost exclusively on boys, and the Electra complex tends to be ignored. The girl's sexual development is, in fact, the least convincing of Freudian developmental theories. The second is that the theory that the latency period or stage is the result of the boy repressing his Oedipal complex because of fear of castration, cannot really be proved or disproved. That is, while a latency stage, in which there is a diminution of sexual interest and activity, may be discerned in children, and Oedipal situations and castration fears may be similarly identified, the causal connection between latency and Oedipal-castration factors cannot. The latency stage may be accounted for by simpler social learning theories as the result of severe taboos and the sanctions imposed by an inhibited and sexually repressive society. As Broderick (1966) noted, there is little evidence for a latency period in childhood in which sexual interest and activity actually abates. He adds that there is also little evidence that activity is dramatically higher in one phase of the period than in another.

Freud and Piaget

It is of interest to us to see what connecting ideas and theories there are between Freud and Piaget. During his formative years Piaget worked in Bleuler's psychiatric clinic, reading Freud and listening to lectures on psychoanalysis by Pfister and Jung. He apparently found psychoanalysis interesting 'but highly speculative and nonscientific' (Cowan, 1978). There are many references to Freudian theories in Piaget's writing, and there is a recognition that while Freud's thrust was in terms of children's libido, instincts and emotions, Piaget's own thrust was in terms of

18

children's cognition, intellect and reasoning. It is in the relationship between affect and cognition that the major differences can be seen. Whereas Freud saw emotion and cognition as separate systems, with the emotional as primary and dominant, Piaget saw them as two aspects of the same system, co-equal and one dominating the other at any time. As Cowan points out (p. 52), 'Piaget stresses the complementary rather than the conflict relation between cognition and emotion.'

Anthony (1970) has provided a useful comparison between Freud's psychosexual stages, Erikson's psychosocial stages and Piaget's psychocognitive stages although this is a speculative exercise and is not based upon any empirical findings. (See Table 1.1. We have adapted the table and excluded Jersild's psychoaffective stages as interesting but not immediately relevant to our study.)

TABLE 1.1 *Schema for various developmental stages*

Ages	Educational status	Psychosexual stages (Freud)	Psychosocial stages (Erikson)	Psychocognitive stages (Piaget)
0–18 months	Infancy	Oral	Basic trust v. Mistrust	Sensori-motor
18 mths– 3 years	Nursery	Anal	Autonomy v. Doubt, shame	Symbolic
3–5 yrs	Pre-school and kindergarten	Genital Oedipal	Initiative v. Guilt	Intuition, representational
6–11 yrs	Elementary school	Latency	Industry v. Inferiority	Concrete operational
12–17 yrs	High school (junior and senior)	Adolescent recapitulation	Identity v. Role confusion	Formal operational

Freud's and Erikson's stages, not surprisingly on Anthony's interpretation, correspond closely since the latter originates from the former, but the correspondences seen by Anthony between Freud's and Piaget's stages are of interest. One possible and important connection between the two is that with concrete operational thinking there comes a capacity to formulate generalisations based upon concrete experience and observations, faulty at first, but becoming more accurate with increasing age. We suggest that the child's concrete experience of sexual taboos, the consistent inhibitions enforced by parents and a growing awareness of the unspoken embarrassments about sex in the adult

19

world, hastens the process of social conformity, hence the latency period. Another possible connection is that if puberty in Freudian terms corresponds with Piaget's formal operational thinking, then the sexual drives requiring an object of love may have the potential for diminishing the natural egocentricism of the child. The altruistic need to give as well as to get provides a means of moving beyond concretisms or more abstract thinking. In each case the connection could be causal, one appearing to cause the other; or it could be interactive, the two factors, psychosexual and psychocognitive, interacting upon each other to cause development to the higher stages. The former view would in some cases appear to support a Freudian interpretation and the latter view would appear to support Piaget's. Readers may wish to refer back to this discussion after reading the final assessment of our results in chapter 17.

Moral, religious and sexual thinking

No discussion of the theoretical background of this study can be complete without reviewing theories concerning moral thinking, and their possible relationship with sexual thinking. Similarly, since religious values are still maintained by many in Western societies as the basis of moral and sexual judgment, and as such are taught to children, we shall also examine the relationship between religious and sexual thinking.

Moral thinking and the identification of stages of moral judgment in children have been the focus of research for a long time. Piaget himself (1932) stimulated a new interest in this area with his examination of 'the rules of the game' and his rough distinction of the child's progress from heteronomic to autonomic judgments. However, it is the work of Kohlberg (1969) and his colleagues which has produced a more precise theoretical structure of the development of moral thought. Kohlberg's three levels of pre-conventional, conventional and post-conventional moral judgment, each level divided into two stages, will be discussed in more detail in later chapters where relevant. What is of interest here is that moral thought and judgment have extended to specific sexual areas such as the sex-role attitudes of children (Kohlberg and Zigler, 1967), stages in the development of psychosexual concepts and attitudes (Kohlberg and Ullian, 1974) and moral reasoning about sexual dilemmas (Gilligan, Kohlberg et al., 1971). The last mentioned article was, in fact, a report to the United States Commission on Obscenity and Pornography.

Previous work done on sexual dilemmas had been rather anecdotal (Clark, 1968) or had been concerned with the content of sexual attitudes and behaviour rather than with the structure or processing of reasoning about the morality of sexual relationships. The Gilligan study

(1971) concentrated upon late adolescents, 15 years and older, and raised with them a series of issues on pre-marital sex, the relationship between love and sex, honesty and trust, personal conscience, civil liberties and other matters. The level of moral reasoning was scored according to the subjects' answers to the various sexual dilemmas posed. In discussion based upon the Kohlberg criteria, the authors point out three possibilities to explain the results. Many of the subjects tended to resolve dilemmas by low-level arguments. It is conceivable, they suggest, that in the realm of sex the culture predisposes young people to a lower level of sexual reasoning. The second possibility suggests that 'the affective involvement of the adolescent with sex depresses his ability to reason at a level comparable to that shown in more abstract issues' (p. 149). Thirdly, it is noted that regression of thinking may be interpreted as a rejection of conventional morality, preceding the attainment of principled thinking: 'That this regression should manifest itself in the sexual area may be indicative of the fact that this is an important area of confrontation between the individual and the culture' (p. 150). In other words, sexuality may be an area where young people begin to question conventional definitions of right and wrong.

An interesting speculative article by Martinson (1976) reviews the contributions of Freud and Piaget to the area of children's sexual knowledge, comparing the early capacity for sensate experience with the fact that 'the full range of cognitive capacity in humans does not emerge during childhood and is not available until adolescence at best' (p. 251). This is due, he maintains, to the secretive and repressive moral sanctions imposed by our society, initially mediated through non-permissive mothers, highlighting the Gilligan study of low-level problem solving evident in addressing sexual dilemmas. It also underscores the gap between the secular trend in physical maturing and sexual experiences 'allowable' by society, a fact we review in the next chapter.

Clearly the moral and sexual domains overlap, affecting each other. Popular assumptions would appear to make the terms 'moral' and 'sexual' almost synonymous. We have therefore included in this study adapted forms of Kohlberg's levels of moral thinking to score some of the items on which children's views were ascertained. Moral inhibitions did vitiate the behaviour and responses of children in the interview situation, and certainly did restrict the authors' decision to include items in the interview and to exclude items from it.

Religion and morality, particularly sexual morality, have a long association, religious leaders frequently making the assertion that religion is the foundation of moral values, and there can be no morality without religion. This fallacy has been demolished by philosophers (Wilson, 1965), who demonstrate that moral values may be formulated

21

without a belief in the supernatural, a necessity in many increasingly secular modern societies. Nevertheless, religious groups frequently treat religious and sexual morality as intertwined if not identical; religious education programmes frequently emphasise the one as the basis of the other. In several countries religious opposition to sex education in schools is marked by appeals to dogma and low-level logical arguments (Fraser, 1972).

Religion as an area of psychological research has been given some attention (Cattell, 1938; Allport, 1951; Argyle, 1958) and occasionally its moral aspects explored (Flugel, 1945), but research into children's religion and how children come to develop religious concepts has been rather sparse. A notable book by Bovet (1928), a predecessor of Piaget in Geneva, entitled *The Child's Religion* called attention to it as an important field for investigation. (The date of publication, incidentally, is misleading since it was first published in 1902.) The evidence produced by Bovet was anecdotal and speculative, and Piaget later (1930) explored the child's explanations of physical causality in terms of artificialism, often religious in content. Piaget further explored children's concepts of justice (1932), children progressing from retributive to distributive justice, often using religious grounds to support their arguments.

This was the finding of one of the authors of this present study (Goldman, 1964) in investigating children's religious thinking, using Piagetian criteria to assess the responses of children aged 5 to 17 years. It was evident that moral concepts, particularly in relation to justice, were dominated by religious assumptions, even in children who came from non-religious families. However, no thoroughgoing investigation into the relationships between religious thinking and sexual thinking has to our knowledge been undertaken. Our study does not cover the association between the two, primarily because of the complexity of research design in a four-country comparative study. The theoretical importance of the relationships between religion, morality and sexuality should, however, be noted.

Having outlined the theoretical background to this study, in the next chapter we address ourselves to the practical manifestations of sexuality in Western-type societies, the empirical research which illustrates the practical issues they reflect, and how they form an essential background to this study of the development of children's sexual thinking.

Summary and discussion

Sexuality in children is comparatively unresearched largely due to the cult of childhood innocence, usually defined as meaning sexual innocence, and a reluctance to admit sexuality as part of child development before the pubertal period. Freud's theory of 'latency' tended to strengthen taboos about childhood sexuality, and psychologists generally have for various reasons been inclined to avoid this area. The one exception is child abuse but there the focus tends to be upon violent physical assault against children, rather than incest or the sexual victimisation of children. In cognitive studies few focus upon the sexual thinking of children and then only in a fragmentary manner.

Sexual thinking is defined for the purpose of this research as thinking about that broad area of sex and sexuality which impinge upon the child's world from birth: the sex identity of self, mother and father, siblings and friends; the sexual bond of marriage, the identity and roles of males and females generally, the child's own sexual organs and the biological functions of their bodies; the origin and sudden appearance of babies and many other related matters. Sexual thinking is not confined narrowly to thinking about sexual intercourse but embraces a much broader universe of experience. In this sense a child is a sexual thinker from birth.

Much of this sexual thinking is biologically based but much is socially induced in terms of gender roles. Hence, different cultures induct children into varying sex-typing behaviours and cognitive frameworks, so that comparative studies are important in investigating children's sexual thinking. The bulk of cross-cultural studies, however, with children's thinking based mainly upon Piagetian theory, has been in the areas of mathematics and the physical sciences. Little has been researched into children's biological concepts; surprising in view of Piaget's own initial training as a biologist and his lifelong interest in the genetic basis of intelligence. This omission is to be seen in the Geneva school generally, and reasons for this serious gap in our knowledge of children are explored.

Freud's theories of children's sexuality have been widely disseminated but their validity and universality relatively unresearched. These theories and their attendant researches are reviewed in this chapter, the Oedipus and latency period theories in particular, as relevant to this currently reported study. A comparison between Freud's and Piaget's theories of developmental stages is discussed, and the relationship of sexual thinking on the one hand to moral and religious thinking on the other is examined in the light of Kohlberg's and others' work.

This forms the theoretical basis of the extensive cross-national research into children's sexual thinking reported in this volume.

2 The practical background of the study

In the first chapter we discussed the theoretical background to studies involving children's sexuality, the relative nature of sexuality in varying cultures, the need to look cross-culturally and cross-nationally at the problems raised, the two major theories of child development — Piagetian and Freudian — most relevant to our study, and the relationship between moral, religious and sexual thinking. Such a study as this, however, should not be viewed solely in theoretical terms, but must be seen in the light of the many practical issues involving sexuality which face Western societies. These issues focus mainly upon adolescents and adults but they are also projected onto childhood and infancy, affecting child-rearing practices, the confidence of parents, curricula in schools and education generally.

Controversy, confusion and uncertainty are the hallmarks of these sexual issues. This is well illustrated by Suehsdorf (1964) in her introduction to the Child Study Association of America's publication *What to Tell Your Children about Sex* (p. 4):

> We like and admire the sexy glamor boys and girls of our movies, TV, and books, and yet we disapprove of youngsters or adults who behave the same way 'in real life.' We believe in lasting marriages, and yet we have a high divorce rate. We like to think we are wise and up-to-date in our ideas about sex, and yet we are often fumbling, tongue-tied, and untruthful in the way we prepare our youngsters for the sexual side of life. We have too many tots whose natural interest in sex is discouraged. Too many tense little grade-school girls worried about menstruation. Too many adolescents baffled and upset by the surging changes going on within their bodies. Too many emotionally childish adults. Too many parents passing on the mistakes of their own sexual upbringing to the children coming along.

THE PRACTICAL BACKGROUND OF THE STUDY

The major practical issues which are seen as a background to our study are the earlier sexual maturing of children, the greater incidence of sexual activity in the young and especially pre-marital sex, an increase in teenage pregnancies, questions raised by divorce, abortion, rape and child molestation, venereal disease, pornography, homosexuality and prostitution, and the continuing controversies about sex education. While many regard these issues as problems to be solved or accommodated, there are many who refuse to recognise that they exist. If they do admit to their reality many are confused and uncertain about how they should be resolved. These are not so much issues as dilemmas, requiring a choice between alternatives which are equally unpalatable for some. For example, if teenage pregnancy is increasing should the present restrictive practice of limiting access to contraceptive information and devices continue, or should they be made more available at a much earlier age? In the sections which follow, figures cited are taken wherever possible from surveys in the four countries covered by this study — Britain, North America, Australia and Sweden.

Earlier physical maturing

The earlier physical maturing of children, often termed 'the secular trend in physical growth', has been noted over the last twenty years, and authenticated in Britain by Tanner (1961 and 1978), in Sweden (Ljung et al., 1974; Westin-Lindgren, 1976 and 1979), in Australia (Harper and Collins, 1972a) and in many other countries. More recent data from Britain (Fogelman, 1976) from the follow-up study of children born in 1958, indicated that 2.2 per cent of all girls had menstruated by the age of 10, 15.2 per cent by the age of 11 years, 39.2 per cent by the age of 12 years, and over 73 per cent by the age of 13 years. The onset of menstruation was reported by these girls when interviewed at the age of 16. It is significant to note that only 2 per cent had not yet reported menstruation by that age. Data for the boys concerning their pubertal development are much more difficult to assess, but Fogelman reports that at 16 years 85 per cent reported their voices to have broken, 7 per cent that their voices had not broken and 8 per cent were unsure; 50 per cent of the boys had developed pubic hair considered to be adult, 39 per cent were intermediate and 10 per cent were considered to have sparse pubic hair.

All this appears to confirm Tanner's basic premise that the age of puberty has been falling each generation; the girls normally a year or more lower than the boys. There are a few contrary pointers such as Roberts and Dann's (1975) twelve-year study of menarcheal age which appeared to indicate that 'the downward trend in menarcheal age ceased in girls born about 1946', and added that an upward swing may have since occurred. This was based upon the 1965 student intake at the University College of Swansea, and as such represents a somewhat biased socio-economic sample compared to the wider and more typical population surveys previously cited. The figures advanced as evidence also appear to be marginal.

Hunt's Population Report (Hunt, 1976) for the United States Department of Health, Education and Welfare is worth quoting: 'The trend towards earlier menarcheal age appears to be universal, although it seems to have levelled off in a few developed countries. Today girls everywhere are sexually mature at an earlier age than previous generations.' Citing various researchers, Hunt reports the trends shown in Table 2.1.

TABLE 2.1 *Estimated mean menarcheal age and trends in several countries*

Country	Estimated mean age	Reported trend
Japan	13.2	Decreasing
Finland	13.2	Decreasing
Europe	12.0	Decreasing
USA	12.8	Stable

(Adapted from Hunt, p. 7.)

Given the fact that earlier maturing is a phenomenon to be recognised in the countries cited, the average age of the first menstruation of girls is from 12 to 13 years and the equivalent pubertal event in boys is between 13 and 14 years. This means that most girls and boys have the capacity to procreate, to engage in overt sexual activities and experience sexual urges at a much earlier age. Not only is sexual maturation taking place earlier but the age of marriage is increasing, thereby extending the period of nonmarital fecundity. Boys and girls are spending a longer time at school, enter employment later and marry later. As Hunt (Figure 2.1) shows, there is a widening gap between sexual and social adulthood.

The issues this raises are several. The major one is in what ways has society and its institutions, particularly family and school, adjusted to this situation? There are indications that such an adjustment is feared and resisted. While token adjustments have taken place, such as the age of majority reduced from 21 to 18 years, the age of consent (for intercourse) still remains, in most countries, at 16 and considerable penalties are attached to its violation. Has the age for providing sex education earlier, to prepare children for their earlier maturing, been lowered? The indications are that such an adjustment has not been made in most countries faced with this issue.

26

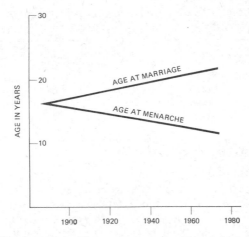

*Figure 2.1   Increasing gaps between sexual and social adulthood
(indicated by declining age at menarche and rising age at
marriage. From Hunt, 1976, p. 8.)*

Sexual experience of the young – Britain

Earlier maturing has raised the question whether earlier overt sexual activity including sexual intercourse on the part of the young has occurred. Schofield's (1968) well-known survey of *The Sexual Behaviour of Young People* was based upon a national random sample of young people aged 15 to 19 years in England. Married young people were excluded from the sample. In assessing what kinds of sexual experience the respondents had known, he defined three categories – the Non-experienced, the Inceptives (a term meaning 'beginners') and the Experienced. The Non-experienced he categorised as sexually innocent (Stage 1) and those who had experienced only kissing and fondling (Stage 2). The fondling at Stage 2 was over garments, not under them. The Inceptives were those who had engaged in breast and genital stimulation, but had not had sexual intercourse (Stage 2). The Experienced were those who had had sexual intercourse with one partner (Stage 4) and with more than one (Stage 5). The widespread use of genital apposition was reported in Stage 3, that is, the stimulation of sex organs without entry as a form of birth control. For example, a girl might encourage a boy to orgasm before full sexual intercourse can occur. Table 2.2 summarises some of the results.

Breaking down those categorised as Experienced into two age groups, the 15 to 17 year group revealed 11 per cent of boys and 6 per cent of girls to be experienced and the 17 to 19 year group revealed 30 per cent

27

TABLE 2.2   *Stages of sexual experience* (in percentages of totals
N = 1,873)

Category of experience		Boys	Girls
Non-experienced	Stage 1	16	7
Non-experienced	Stage 2	35	46
Inceptives	Stage 3	29	35
Experienced	Stage 4	5	7
Experienced	Stage 5	15	5

(Adapted from Schofield, 1968, p. 53.)

of boys and 16 per cent of girls to be experienced. This category, however, tends to minimise the extent of sexual experience. If, for example (see Table 2.2) the figures for Inceptives and Experienced are combined, the total for boys is 49 per cent and for girls 47 per cent. Schofield reports that middle-class girls were more likely to be 'Inceptives' and working-class boys were more likely to be 'Experienced'.

Patterns of early sexual activity are also described by Schofield. By the age of 13 years, 25 per cent of boys and 33 per cent of girls had dated; before 16 years, 75 per cent of boys and 85 per cent of girls had dated. Most teenagers appear to have had their first serious contacts with the opposite sex between 12 and 14 years, the girls earlier than the boys. This would be consistent with the figure cited previously on earlier maturing, see Table 2.1. In a later section Schofield presents some facts about the first experience of sexual intercourse by the respondents. Girls who were Experienced before 17 years old invariably had an older partner. Overall, one-third of boys and two-thirds of girls were introduced to sexual intercourse by an older partner. Of those experienced, 45 per cent of boys and 85 per cent of girls claimed they were going steady with their sexual partner; 35 per cent of boys and 16 per cent of girls maintained their sexual partner was an acquaintance; 16 per cent of boys and 4 per cent of girls maintained their sexual partner was a 'pick-up'. Other important features of Schofield's report is the characteristics of the Experienced, who tended to be 'early starters' (p. 70) and the place of any first intimacy tended to be the home of either the boy or the girl (p. 75).

Two other British surveys of a later date give somewhat different figures about the incidence of sexual activity in the young. Farrell (1978) based on a wider area sampling and using a 16 to 19-year-old sample reports that ten years after Schofield's survey 51 per cent were sexually experienced (55 per cent boys; 46 per cent girls) compared with Schofield's earlier figure of 16 per cent. While recognising that the comparison is not a clear one because of the inclusion of the

16-year-old age group she comments 'there has obviously been an increase in the numbers of teenagers saying that they have had sexual intercourse' (p. 21). On 'Early Experience' Farrell reports that nearly half of those sexually experienced (Stage 4 and 5 of Schofield's scale) nearly half said their first experience was before the age of 16. 'This means that a fifth (21 per cent) of the whole sample had had at least one sexual experience by the time they were 16; three quarters of them were boys' (p. 21). In other words, 12 per cent of all the girls and 31 per cent of all the boys by the age of 16 were fully sexually experienced. These figures must be accepted with caution since what teenagers say is their experience is not necessarily the case; as Collins (1974) points out in his Australian study, many teenagers may only be conforming to what they think is the teenage norm, and by making the assertion wish to be seen as 'normal'.

A more recent study *Pregnant at School* (National Council, 1979) using as a sample 3,600 pregnant schoolgirls under 16 years in Britain, reports that 81 per cent of the pregnant girls were known to have a steady relationship with their boyfriends.

Sexual experience of the young – America

In the USA a useful study was conducted by Venner, Stewart and Hager (Venner *et al.*, 1972) providing comparisons with the British study by Schofield as Table 2.3 indicates. The American sample, however, is not a national one. The age was 15 to 19 years, being 81 per cent of the enrolments of three high schools. Moreover the instrument was an opinionnaire not a personal interview. Any comparisons therefore with Schofield must be viewed with caution. The categories used by Venner and his colleagues were somewhat different to Schofield's but the comparisons have some correspondence; the Inceptives and the Experienced may be reasonably identified in the USA study. The results and comparisons are much too complex to report here, but two features stand out. One is that American young people are sexually much more active ('precocious' is how the American authors describe it) than their British peers. This can be seen in Tables 2.4 and 2.5 taken from Venner (1972). The second feature of the Venner study is that this sexual precocity stands out somewhat starkly when Venner's figures of the 'Experienced' are compared with Schofield's but illustrate that British adolescents are 'catching up' in the older age group (see Table 2.6).

These comparisons must be viewed warily due to differences in sampling, since lower working class, non-Caucasians and regions other than Michigan are not included in the American sample. It does, however, illustrate that the degree of pre-marital coital activity can vary at different age levels in different societies.

TABLE 2.3 *Categories of equivalent sexual experience: Venner and Schofield*

Venner *et al.*, stages	Schofield stages	
1 Held hands	Not Experienced	1
2 Held arm around or had been held	" "	1
3 Kissed or have been kissed	" "	2
4 Necked (prolonged hugging and kissing)	" "	2
5 Light petting (feeling above the waist)	Inceptives	3
6 Heavy petting (feeling below the waist)	"	3
7 Gone all the way (coitus)	Experienced	4
8 Number of coital partners (coitus with more than one partner).	"	5

The American results are confirmed in general by Selnik and Kantner (1972) whose evidence is based upon a national (USA) probability sample survey of females aged 15 to 19 years. Discussing 'The Probability of Premarital Intercourse' they conclude that it is 'beginning at younger ages and the extent of premarital intercourse is probably on the increase' (p. 335). In a parallel article Kantner and Selnik (1972) from a similar survey predict the likely percentage of young unmarried women in the USA to have experienced coitus can be calculated as 14 per cent at 15 years, 21 per cent at 16 years, 27 per cent at 17 years, 37 per cent at 18 years and 46 per cent at 19 years. The higher numbers than Venner's are no doubt due to a more typical USA sample, especially when racial, educational and other variables are considered.

Wiseman's book *The Social Psychology of Sex* (1976) contains accounts of several surveys which also confirm Venner's assessment, particularly Broderick's study of the heterosexual attitudes and activities of 10- to 17-year-olds. Another interesting survey in this publication (Wiseman pp. 108–42) is Macklin's research into unmarried heterosexual cohabitation on university campuses. Macklin's evidence reveals a considerable increase in this and, more revealingly, that such cohabitation is not now regarded as immoral or as grounds for discipline or expulsion on many American campuses. Indeed, many colleges and universities in America and Australia currently provide accommodation such as dormitories, flats and houses requiring no assurance of legal relationships between members of the opposite sex who wish to occupy them. It has long been the practice of Swedish and British universities to provide mixed halls of residence, on a non-sexually segregated basis, rooms being allocated as in hotels.

Sexual experience of the young — Australia and New Zealand

There are no comparable data for Australia based upon national sampling,

TABLE 2.4 *Incidence of heterosexual activity for males by age* (in percentages): *Venner et al.*

	Percentage of boys who have participated in an activity at least once					
Levels of sexual activity	13 and younger (N=313)	14 (N=458)	15 (N=424)	16 (N=451)	17 and older (N=415)
1 Held hands	79.1	84.4	90.5	90.3	94.4
2 Held arm around or had been held	63.3	79.2	82.9	88.9	92.0
3 Kissed or have been kissed	64.0	73.0	77.7	85.8	88.9
4 Necked (prolonged hugging and kissing)	46.1	56.8	62.7	75.1	81.1
5 Light petting (feeling above the waist)	36.1	48.7	53.7	67.9	74.1
6 Heavy petting (feeling below the waist)	27.8	33.8	39.7	54.8	64.7
7 Gone all the way (coitus)	19.6	18.0	21.2	28.4	33.4
8 Coitus with two or more partners	12.3	12.7	10.9	14.4	16.0

31

TABLE 2.5 *Incidence of heterosexual activity for females by age (in percentages): Venner et al.*

Levels of sexual activity	Percentage of girls who have participated in an activity at least once					
	13 and younger (N=433)	14 (N=449)	15 (N=399)	16 (N=416)	17 and older (N=392)
1 Held hands	78.4	87.8	89.7	96.2	96.2
2 Held arm around or had been held	67.7	79.5	87.7	93.8	93.1
3 Kissed or have been kissed	64.9	75.5	83.2	91.8	92.6
4 Necked (prolonged hugging and kissing)	43.7	55.5	67.9	79.6	83.9
5 Light petting (feeling above the waist)	22.3	33.0	45.4	61.3	70.2
6 Heavy petting (feeling below the waist)	16.3	15.8	27.1	41.1	54.3
7 Gone all the way (coitus)	6.8	7.1	12.3	18.3	25.8
8 Coitus with two or more partners	4.4	2.0	3.5	6.5	7.1

TABLE 2.6 *Coital experience (Schofield and Venner) of those who experienced coitus at least once* (in percentages)

Age	Schofield (UK)		Venner (USA)	
	Male	Female	Male	Female
13 years and younger	1	0	20	7
14	2	0	18	7
15	6	2	21	12
16	14	5	28	18
17 and older	26	10	33	26

although there are some comparisons possible from studies with regional samples. One example is Collins (1974), an investigation into the norm and peer expectations concerning dating intimacy among Australian adolescents. Further investigations (Collins, Kennedy and Francis, 1976; McCabe and Collins, 1979) confirm these earlier findings. The sample is restricted to 110 males and 207 female students aged 17 to 19 years attending an introductory course in the behavioural sciences at a university in Sydney. Some of the results are shown in Tables 2.7 and 2.8 which we have adapted from Collins (p. 31).

TABLE 2.7 *Percentages of Australian male respondents in sexual behaviour categories* (N = 110)

Level of intimacy	1st date	After several dates	Going steady	Marriage considered
Kissing	71.8	89.1	90.9	90.9
Necking	52.7	80.9	87.3	87.3
Light petting	39.1	71.8	83.6	83.6
Heavy petting	20.0	41.8	64.5	65.4
Petting to orgasm	9.1	25.5	52.7	54.5
Intercourse	10.0	16.4	42.7	44.5

TABLE 2.8 *Percentages of Australian female respondents in sexual behaviour categories* (N = 207)

Level of intimacy	1st date	After several dates	Going steady	Marriage considered
Kissing	74.9	87.4	90.3	90.8
Necking	39.6	70.0	87.0	87.9
Light petting	23.2	55.1	84.1	85.0
Heavy petting	6.3	27.5	69.0	72.9
Petting to orgasm	3.4	10.6	49.3	55.0
Intercourse	1.9	8.2	28.0	34.3

Although these are not broken down by age groups they may represent a time continuum from first date to a relationship where marriage is considered. As Collins points out (p. 325), 'The results show an initial tendency for males to be more experienced sexually than females, with the behaviour of females approaching that of males as the commitment in the affectional relationship increased.' He draws the conclusion, from the data on peer expectations not included here, that 'there is tremendous pressure on both adolescent boys and girls to conform to behaviour that they think is the norm, rather than to what is the norm'. This concurs with Schofield's view, says Collins, that many teenagers 'think their friends are more sexually experienced than they are themselves'.

From a New Zealand sample of 2,175 first-year students with a general age level of 17 at the University of Canterbury and the nearby Teachers' College, Irwin reports (in Stewart, 1976) that 25 per cent of these young people were sexually experienced, 27 per cent male and 22.5 per cent female. However, the category is not precise and includes 'attempted intercourse'. Only 14 per cent answered 'Yes' to the question 'Have you been sexually active in the last three months?' Of those reporting active sex 76.7 per cent said it was with a steady boy- or girl-friend. These figures would appear to be consistent with Collins' findings in Sydney, but they are not strictly comparable.

Sexual experience of the young – Sweden

A Swedish State Commission reporting on Sex and Personal Relationships (Current Sweden, 1974) reports, 'A common belief is that almost all 16 and 17 year olds have intercourse. Studies suggest that the majority of young people make their sexual debut after Basic School (16 years), and that one fifth wait until after their teens'. The commission warns against misconceptions concerning the sexual habits of young people, particularly caused by mass media programmes selecting and interviewing promiscuous young people and presenting them as typical. The commission does acknowledge a considerable variation in the sexual behaviour of the 15- to 21-year-old.

Specific studies indicate that the age of first sexual intercourse has dropped over the last twenty years. A comprehensive investigation was made of high school students in 1964, whose average age was slightly under 18 years. This study revealed that 57 per cent of the boys had experienced intercourse, the median age for first coitus being 16 years. The figure for girls was 46 per cent and the median age 17 years. As in other cultures the vast majority reported that first intercourse was between those 'going steady' (Linner, 1971). A 1967 study of 3,000 Stockholm youths aged 15 to 25 years revealed the not very surprising fact that two-thirds of them had had first intercourse before the age of 20. It was noted that the traditional Swedish attitudes of accepting pre-marital sex relations but expecting sexual fidelity after marriage were expressed in the attitudes of the respondents (Linner, 1971). The first study in any country of sexual behaviour conducted on a national scale of all age groups was carried out by the Swedish Institute for Public Opinion Research in 1967. It was made for the Royal Commission on Sex Education, the findings of which form the basis for current programmes in Swedish schools. Based upon face-to-face interviews, over 90 per cent of the randomly selected respondents aged 18 to 60 years old were successfully interviewed. Tables 2.9 and 2.10 are from Holmstedt (1974).

TABLE 2.9 *Estimated average age of first intercourse in Sweden* (in percentages)

Age	Male	Female
13 years and under	2	1
14–15 years	17	7
16–17 years	38	36
18–19 years	28	38
20–4 years	13	17
25 years and older	1	1

These correspond more closely to the American figures (Venner, 1972) than to the British (Schofield, 1968).

The Swedish report also compares median ages for first intercourse between the older and younger generations. The older generation men reported a median age of 17.4 years and the younger generation men 16.6 years. The older generation women reported a median age of 18.5 years and the younger generation women 17.2 years. The continuous decrease in age of sexual debut can be seen in Table 2.10.

TABLE 2.10 *Estimated median age of first intercourse in Sweden by decreasing age*

Age now	Age of first intercourse
51–60 years	18.6 years
41–50 years	17.7 years
31–40 years	17.4 years
26–30 years	17.3 years
21–5 years	17.0 years

A more recent report (Sundström, 1976) confirms the continuance of these trends, estimating that the average age for first intercourse for girls, as well as boys, is now around 16 years, compared with the late 1960s when the girls were 17 and the boys 16 years.

The overall picture reveals in most countries a considerable amount of sexual activity on the part of the young from the age of 13 years, and in some countries evidence supports the view that first sexual intercourse is occurring earlier. The evidence does not support the view that there is widespread or increasing promiscuity among the young but rather that the majority of young people appear to uphold the traditional view of faithfulness within an on-going steady relationship. This issue is well argued in Reiss' early work *Premarital Sexual Standards in America* (1960) and his later writing (Reiss, 1967; 1970) where he observed a shift in attitudes towards a shared standard of 'permissiveness with affection' away from the previous double standard tradition of 'permissiveness without affection'. Schofield (1976) in *Promiscuity* commenting on his earlier survey, points out that this revealed only 12 per cent of the boys and 2 per cent of the girls aged 15 to 19 had experienced sexual intercourse with more than one partner. 'The original percentages are very small,' he comments, 'and it is probably still true to say as I did then that "promiscuity, although it exists, is not a prominent feature of teenage sexual behaviour"' (p. 37). Hunt (1976), surveying many countries, comments: 'Earlier sexual maturity, later marriage and greater opportunities for sexual contracts due to urban life-styles suggest that developing countries will be increasingly confronted with the problems of adolescent sexuality.'

The issues raised by these facts are many. Should sex education be introduced much earlier than is normally judged suitable in most countries to prepare children for earlier experience? Is there any substance in the accusation that sex education encourages the young to experiment and 'try it out for themselves'? Should contraceptive advice and devices be available for the young much earlier than is currently in practice? What kind of content is suitable in sex education programmes to meet both the sexual and cognitive needs of earlier maturing youth?

Teenage pregnancies

The fact of earlier physical maturing, the possibility of earlier and increasing sexual activity by the young, involving an earlier age for first sexual intercourse, would lead us to expect an increasing incidence of teenage pregnancy, sometimes termed 'teenage exnuptial conception'. This is based upon the assumption that contraceptive services are not readily available to teenagers below the age of 18. In some Western countries it is still illegal to advertise birth-control aids, to advise young people unless they are married or preparing for marriage, and even in some areas to set up birth-control clinics or family planning centres at all (Hunt, 1976). Contraceptive services are often affected by moral considerations on the part of those providing them, and many young people are inhibited from asking for advice or help. Cartwright (1970) has described in some detail some of the obstacles to the use of effective contraception in England.

The two factors of teenage pregnancies and availability of contraception are closely related. The lack of provision or obstacles to the use of effective contraception may lead to pregnancy particularly when the average age of first intercourse is decreasing. They are also connected with the availability of legal abortion. The outcome is frequently tragic, not readily reflected in the statistics, as the following letter to the British newspaper the *Guardian* reveals (23 July 1979):

Clinics that ward off tragedies

Sir, — The tragic death of a 16-year-old girl was recorded at an inquest in Droitwich, Worcestershire, last week. The press reported that the girl had kept her pregnancy secret, that the baby was born prematurely, and that its body has not been found. Medical experts said she had lost nearly half her blood at the birth.

Days later she collapsed and died. Her mother had noticed she was putting on weight and 'I even asked her if she was pregnant. . . . She told me not to say such terrible things.'

The reason for repeating this sad story is that there is now a lobby seeking to prohibit family doctors, and doctors in family planning clinics and Brook Advisory Centres, from using their discretion in prescribing contraceptives for girls under 16 without first obtaining a parent's consent. This young girl may well have been under 16 when she conceived, and was obviously reluctant to ask her mother for help.

To avoid more tragedies, such girls need to know that doctors will help them in confidence when they summon the courage to ask for contraception, abortion, or antenatal care. The help they get will usually include encouragement to confide in their family. — Yours sincerely,

Caroline Woodroffe,
Brook Advisory Centres,
233 Tottenham Court Road,
London, W1.

Teenage pregnancies or teenage exnuptial conception must be seen against the broader background of increased exnuptial conception in the population generally. The statistics available conceal the true figures since many such pregnancies are not brought to full term because the foetus is aborted or lost from other causes. But the statistics unmistakably indicate a general rise in exnuptial births. Latest figures from the Australian Bureau of Statistics (1978) indicate that what are termed 'illegitimate births' have risen to the highest level this century. In 1978 out of 224,000 live births in Australia, 25,000 were 'illegitimate', that is, approximately 11 per cent. This represents a rise of 1,430 or 6 per cent on the previous year.

Comparative and up-to-date figures are difficult to obtain, but some other figures indicate this to be probably a world-wide trend. In an article 'Unwed Motherhood — a Continuing Problem', Friedman (1972) cites the USA Bureau of Statistics as showing illegitimate births rising from 7.1 per 1,000 of live births in 1940, to 21.8 per 1,000 of live births in 1960. By the late 1960s the figure was 23.5. Friedman's study also reveals that the characteristics common to the 200 unmarried women he interviewed were defective ego functioning, denial of interest in their sexual lives and unawareness of the possibility of pregnancy. Smyth (1976) in New Zealand reports that exnuptial births rose from 8 per cent of live births in 1962 to 15 per cent of live births in 1973. These statistics represent both Caucasian and Polynesian populations in an undifferentiated total. In his Population Report Hunt (1976), after reporting earlier sexual maturity, later marriage and greater opportunity for sexual activity in most urban-industrial type countries, goes on to produce the following interesting figures in Table 2.11.

TABLE 2.11 *Trends in percentages of total births to mothers under 20 years in selected countries (1962–73)*

Country	Previous data		Current data
Canada	9.0 (1963)	11.5 (1967)	12.0 (1973)
USA	14.5 (1963)	17.1 (1969)	19.3 (1972)
Australia	8.9 (1963)	10.8 (1967)	11.0 (1971)
USSR	3.3 (1963)	6.7 (1967)	8.8 (1973)
W. Germany	13.6 (1963)	16.3 (1968)	23.0 (1972)
Denmark	11.8 (1963)	11.5 (1966)	6.8 (1972)
Sweden	11.7 (1963)	11.4 (1967)	7.5 (1973)

(Adapted from Hunt, 1976, p. 6.)

With the average age of marriage rising in these countries it can be assumed that a large proportion of these figures represent exnuptial conceptions and births. Commenting on this, Hunt says, 'With few exceptions, unmarried adolescents are excluded from official family planning programs and find it difficult to obtain safe and effective contraception or abortion services.' Our comment, since the countries cited include some in our comparative study, is that all countries indicate a rise in these births to women who are technically still 'teenagers', except the two Scandinavian countries, both of which have a more liberal policy in sex education and in making available contraceptive and abortion services to teenagers. It may be argued that this statement might also apply to the USSR but other factors may be operating there contributing to the rise in these births.

In studying pregnancy problems in teenage girls in Aberdeen, Scotland, Gill, Illesley and Koplik (Gill *et al.*, 1970) point out that in England and Wales over a number of years the number of maternities to women aged under 20 had more than doubled (from 31,148 in 1950 to 82,284 in 1965). Part of this rise included a more than three-fold increase of births to unmarried teenage mothers.

Perhaps the most convincing evidence concerning the high rate of teenage pregnancy in Britain can be seen in *Pregnant at School* (National Council, 1979) reporting an investigation into girls pregnant at the age of 16 years and under. Discussing its incidence in Appendix I, the report establishes the following facts. In 1977, the date of the investigation, 3,625 girls under 16 or 1 in every 500 girls of 11 to 15 years were known to have become pregnant. This represents, the report asserts, 2.4 per cent of known conceptions to single woman of all ages. Of these 3,625, 63 per cent (2,300) resulted in legal terminations, 36 per cent (1,299) in live births and 1 per cent (26) in stillbirths. Of those aged 16 years, 8,424 or 1 in 44 single girls were known to have become pregnant in 1977. This represents 5.6 per cent of known conceptions to single women of all ages. Of these 8,424 pregnancies, 49 per cent (4,100) resulted in legal terminations, 34 per cent (2,681) in live births outside marriage, 17 per cent (1,430) in pre-maritally conceived live births and 0.4 per cent (33) in stillbirths. It is interesting to note the changes over the previous six years. The rate of known conceptions per 1,000 girls aged 11 to 15 increased by 19 per cent between 1971 and 1973 and has remained stable since then. The rate of known conceptions per 1,000 single girls aged 16 years increased by 11 per cent between 1971 and 1973, but since then there has been a slight decrease.

The report comments that this increase since 1971 'certainly reflects more sexual activity amongst the young'. The decline among 16-year-olds since 1973 'is likely to be accounted for by an increased used of efficient contraceptives' (p. 57). Nevertheless, the report comments that it is still 'widely believed that you cannot "get caught" the first time', or 'if you do it standing up', or 'if you don't enjoy it'. In addition many girls find it difficult to realise that they are already 'fertile' (p. 10).

Figures from New Zealand (Stewart, 1976) and from the United States (Rauh *et al.*, 1973; Wallace *et al.*, 1973) confirm a high incidence of teenage pregnancy; the figures spanning different age groups are, however, difficult to present in comparative terms.

The situation in Sweden may be misunderstood when it is stated in official statistics (Fact Sheet, 1979) that 'a third of all children born in Sweden have unwed parents'. This must be seen against the new law effective from 1977 which makes the sole legal reference 'to children, with no qualifying adjective or clause', granting all children full legal rights, the same legitimate status to inheritance and name, irrespective or whether they are born within marriage or not (Linner, 1977). Table 2.12 shows rapid increases in the proportion of exnuptial births since 1968, although the figures are inflated from 1977 due to the inclusion in this category (the right-hand column) of births to divorced or widowed women, who may well have conceived within marriage.

TABLE 2.12   *Total nuptial and exnuptial births in Sweden (1968–78)*

Year	Nuptial births	Exnuptial births
1968	95,196	17,891
1970	89,895	20,255
1972	84,131	28,142
1974	75,423	34,451
1976	65,689	32,656
1978	59,736	33,512

(Adapted from *Swedish Statistical Yearbook*, 1979, p. 83.)

In a society where the stigma of illegitimacy has been removed it is not surprising that the figures show such a high proportion of exnuptial births. Previous to these changes in the law the wedding ceremony in Sweden since the Middle Ages had been considered more or less as the formal confirmation of an existing relationship. The right to sex was often connected with engagement, a recognition sometimes ritualised by ceremonies.

In terms of teenage births, reference back to Table 2.11 will be useful as also to Table 2.13. It will be observed from an examination of these two tables that in 1978 there was a total of 5,035 live births to mothers below the age of 20 years out of a total of all live births of 93,248. This is 5.4 per cent of all live births, compared with 7.5 per cent in 1973 (see Table 2.11). Secondly, since 1970 the greatest incidence of birth is to be seen in the 25 to 29 year age group due to later marriage. In 1978 there were only 1,828 marriages in Sweden of brides below the age of 20 years, but 12,928 in the 20 and 24 age group and 11,162 in the 25 to 29 age group. All these figures would appear to indicate a similar increase in teenage pregnancies from the 1950s but a considerable decline to the present time, perhaps for the same reasons advanced in Britain (National Council, 1979).

The issues raised by these facts seen in many Western countries are

TABLE 2.13 *Total live births by age of mother in Sweden (1956-78)*

Dates	Age 10-14	Age 15-19	Age 20-4	Age 25-9
1956-60	13	9,215	29,067	30,823
1961-5	17	13,179	35,388	32,929
1966-70	17	11,802	40,708	36,058
1971-5	31	9,252	39,716	41,527
1975	17	7,503	31,861	39,866
1976	14	6,489	29,417	37,421
1977	10	5,737	28,427	36,095
1978	16	5,019	26,578	34,611

(Adapted from *Swedish Statistical Yearbook*, 1979.)

similar to those raised in connection with earlier physical maturing and earlier sexual experience. The figures from Sweden in particular highlight the possible relationship between the provision of contraception and abortion services and lower rates of exnuptial pregnancies and births. The choices open to sexually inclined or active adolescents can be seen in Figure 2.2.

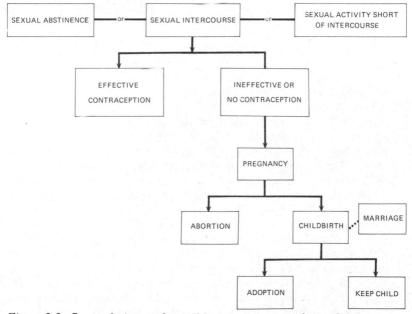

Figure 2.2 Some choices and possible consequences of sexual intercourse for adolescents (for a more detailed fertility decision-making model see Hass (1974, Figures 1-4))

41

Divorce

Research already cited in several countries emphasises that the earlier the marriage, particularly teenage marriages and those entered into because of exnuptial conception, the greater the risk of marital failure. The high incidence of divorce in these groups may be due to many factors including over-hasty decisions to marry, succumbing to family or other social pressures, low economic earnings before career or job opportunities are developed, and sexual tensions if a pregnancy is experienced prior to marriage. Again, the incidence of divorce among the young must be seen against the background of a greater divorce incidence in the general population. In Australia, for example, the increase can be seen in Table 2.14.

TABLE 2.14 *Divorces in Australia (1971-6)*

Year	Decrees granted	Divorces per 10,000 mean population
1971	13,002	10.05
1972	15,707	11.92
1973	16,266	12.15
1974	17,744	13.05
1975	24,307	17.65
1976	63,267	45.46
1977	45,175	32.00
1978	40,633	29.00

(Australian Bureau of Statistics, 1979.)

In 1976 the new Family Law Act (1975) was implemented and accounts for the high figures in 1976, since the grounds for divorce were liberalised and legal procedures became less expensive. Many people delayed divorce to await the new act; consequently 1977 and 1978 figures reveal a decrease but it will be some years before clear trends can be seen. More revealing figures can be found in Divorce Statistics for 1978 (Australian Bureau of Statistics, 1980) where the tables on 'the ages of parties at separation and interval between date of separation' are given. The highest number of legal separations granted is in the 20 to 24 age group of husbands after less than one year, and between one and two years of marriage. The number drops until after 10 to 14 years of marriage when the separation again increases. The figures for wives follow a similar pattern, the high figures for separation being up to 3 years of marriage and a similar new peak after 10 to 14 years of marriage. This is the kind of evidence supporting the assertion 'the earlier the marriage, the greater risk of marital failure'.

These figures could be replicated, with variations, from the Census returns of most Western countries particularly the USA, Canada, England and Sweden. Sweden in particular deserves special mention. Raw figures for divorce in Sweden are to be seen in Table 2.15 and show an actual decline.

TABLE 2.15   *Divorces in Sweden (1974-8)*

Year	Number of divorces	Per 10,000 of mean population
1974	27,208	33.34
1975	25,751	31.43
1976	22,411	27.26
1977	20,994	25.44
1978	20,599	24.89

(*Swedish Statistical Yearbook*, 1979.)

A comparison of Table 2.15 with Table 2.14, showing Australian divorce figures, indicates that while Sweden's incidence of divorce has been higher until 1976 (if we compare the incidence per 10,000 of the Mean Population) it has consistently decreased and Australia's has consistently increased in the 1970s; Sweden's divorce rates are currently less than Australia's. Another interesting Swedish statistic giving figures from 1966-77 shows a steady increase in the mean average length of marriage from 9.72 years to 11.11 years. Unfortunately, there are no comparable statistics available in Australia or other countries.

The issues raised by the increasing incidence of divorce in most Western countries raise questions of the effects of this upon children (see *Journal of Social Issues*, 1979) and whether divorce should be made more accessible or not. From our viewpoint by far the most important question is what kind of education is needed to prepare people to think of marriage realistically, to find in sexual partnership a continuing fulfilment and to develop mature concepts of what marriage is and might be, whether legalised or not.

Abortion

Accurate figures for the incidence of induced abortion are impossible to obtain, simply because it is not feasible to assess the number of self-induced, illegal or 'back street' abortions. It is reasonable to assume that the more liberal abortion laws are in a country in providing ease of availability for legal abortion, the fewer illegal abortions will occur. In an illuminating discussion on this point, Wainer (1979, p. 1) notes that 'even countries with the severest laws report tens of thousands of illegal abortions per annum' (Tietze and Murstein, 1975, pp. 26-7). However, this does not solve the problem of assessing the total number of induced abortions, legal or illegal, in any given year. All that can be assessed and compared is the incidence of abortions legally induced. Even this may be misleading, since often no figures are available to compare legal abortions allowed and legal abortions requested. In other words, the refusal rate may be high or low, reflecting the liberality or illiberality of the law, but few countries keep statistics of this kind. Some comparative figures are available as we can see from Table 2.16.

TABLE 2.16   *Trends in percentages of total legal abortions to women under 20 years in selected countries (1968-73)*

Country	Previous data		Latest data
Australia	NR	15.0 (1970)	26.3 (1971)
USA	29.1 (1971)	32.0 (1972)	31.5 (1973)
England and			
Wales	21.6 (1971)	22.7 (1972)	24.0 (1973)
Denmark	16.8 (1970-1)	14.2 (1971-2)	15.2 (1972-3)

(Adapted from Hunt, 1976, p. 16.)

Of all the women in the countries shown in Table 2.16 who have had legal abortions in the stated year, the percentages shown are of those under 20 years. Again it can be seen in a country such as Denmark, where contraceptives are more readily available to adolescents the figures are considerably lower. Figures are not available from Sweden for 1968-73 but are for 1975-7 (see Table 2.17).

TABLE 2.17   *Totals and percentages of legal abortions to women under 20 years in Sweden*

Year	Total number of abortions	Abortions to women below 20	Percentages under 20 years
1975	32,526	6,000	18.44
1976	32,351	7,394	22.86
1977	31,462	6,778	21.54

(Adapted from *Swedish Statistical Yearbook*, 1979, p. 292.)

It should be noted that the figures for each age group from 16 years to 19 years are fairly constant at about 1,500 per age group, for each year 1975 and 1976. The Swedish figures are higher than the Danish, but lower than the latest figures for Australia, USA and England and Wales.

Unmarried adolescents often have difficulty obtaining abortions, since many abortion laws require parental consent. In only a few countries is abortion easier for young or unmarried women to obtain, as in Finland where the Abortion Act allows abortion without a doctor's certificate for women under 17 and over 40 years. In Hungary minors do not require parental consent and unmarried status is a legal justification for abortion. In some developed countries the trend appears to allow adolescents greater access to both contraception and abortion services, and to avoid setting age limits. In the USA the picture is uneven, since only half the states allow services to under 18s (Hunt, 1976).

The issues raised by induced abortions involve religious and moral questions, responsibility both to the pregnant mother and the unborn child, and far-reaching social questions about the use of taxpayers' money in services provided by the State. The debates generated by these issues are usually emotive and bitter, and frequently conducted without regard to the antecedents of abortion, particularly those affecting children and adolescents.

Rape and child molestation

So far we have dealt with sexual activities or their outcomes which are the result of mutual interest between male and female. We now discuss sexual activity conducted against the will of one party, sometimes accompanied by violence and terror.

The overwhelming majority of rapes are of a male upon a female, a few are of a female upon a male. Rape also can be homosexual, that is by a member of one sex upon the same sex. Many dictionaries are misleading; for example, Webster's in defining rape as the 'illicit carnal knowledge of a woman without her consent, effected by force, duress, intimidation or deception as to the nature of the act', and the Oxford dictionary defines rape as 'ravishing or violation of a woman'. There are also pack rapes or 'gang' rapes and prison rapes, the latter usually of a homosexual character. A much broader definition of rape is 'any sexual intimacy, whether by direct physical contact or not, that is forced on one person by another' (Medea and Thompson, 1974, p. 50).

As in other areas of sexuality statistics are difficult to determine. Even a statement such as, 'Crime statistics show clearly that reported rapes have been on the rise. FBI uniform crime reports show that both the number of rapes and the rate per 100,000 inhabitants increased dramatically in recent years' (Holmstrom and Burgess, 1978), must be accepted cautiously in view of many rapes going unreported, failures to detect and prosecute rapists, cases dismissed by courts or verdicts of not guilty, none of which may appear in official statistics (Amir, 1971).

45

One of the most detailed statistical analysis of rape was conducted by Amir who collected data on all cases of forcible rape listed by the police in Philadelphia in 1958 and 1960. The foreword to Amir's book contains the statement, 'Statistically, among all crimes, or even among all major crimes, rape is a relatively infrequent phenomenon', the writer estimating it to be about one per cent of all serious crimes. Amir's study analyses the characteristics of rapists and their victims, examining many variables — age, time of crime, vicinity, race, incidence of alcohol and many other factors. Practically all publications on this subject dismiss the stereotype of the victim as 'sexually provocative' and 'asking for it' as unjustifiable inversion. Blaming the victim is a common rationalisation in a number of crimes and has little foundation. In sexual crimes, however, where the victims are mainly women, blaming the victim is seen as a natural projection of sexism (Holmstrom and Burgess, 1978; and Thompson, 1975).

From the viewpoint of our study the age of the younger victims and offenders recorded by Amir is of some interest and relevance. It will be seen that 52 per cent of the victims are 19 years or below and 65 per cent of them are below the age of 25. The offenders reveal similar percentages, 44 per cent of the offenders are 19 years or under, and 70 per cent of them below the age of 25. This is a sad commentary about society's handling of sexuality and the young, especially when it can be seen that 7.9 per cent of all victims of rape in that city were 10 years or younger.

In Sweden the incidence of sexual offences 'known to the police' (which include attempted crimes, as well as completed, and those not brought before the courts) is given in Table 2.19 in total numbers from a population of approximately 8 million people. Where rape is concerned we have no breakdown by age of victims and offenders. All we can comment is that the figures are very low in relation to the total population.

Child molestation involves rape in a small number of cases, but it is a term used to describe children who in various ways may be sexually used or victimised. Unlike rape, many of the child victims molested are frequently boys as well as girls, and usually less force and violence is involved. Finkelhor (1979) indicates that the usual sexual act that occurs in the sexual abuse of children is not intercourse but rather fondling of genitals, masturbation and exhibitionism. The stereotype of 'blaming the victim' by suggesting that adults may be tempted by sexually precocious children and teenagers (the Lolita syndrome) is reflected by Finkelhor and some blame for this myth attributed to Freud. An earlier work (Burgess et al., 1978) supports Finkelhor's evidence that a sizeable proportion of the offenders come from the child's own family, and that they are known to the child. Most of these therefore involve incestuous relationships.

TABLE 2.18   *Rates of recorded rape by percentage of total rapes commited per 100,000 population (City of Philadelphia, USA)*

Victims				Offenders			
Age-year	Number	%	Rate per 100,000	Age	Number	%	Rate per 100,000
0–10	51	7.9	27.6				
10–14	123	19.9	158.4	10–14	47	3.6	59.0
15–19	161	24.9	232.3	15–19	521	40.3	796.8
20–4	87	13.5	133.4	20–4	332	25.6	566.4
25–9	68	10.5	110.1	25–9	207	16.0	340.0
30–4	50	7.7	74.2	30–4	98	7.7	153.5
35–9	44	6.8	59.8	35–9	37	2.8	55.5
40–5	21	3.3	28.5	40–4	21	1.6	32.6
45–9	18	2.8	25.1	45–9	8	0.6	12.5
50–5	9	1.4	1.6	50–4	11	0.8	18.7
55–9	1	0.2	7.5	55–9	5	0.3	9.3
60 & over	13	2.0	62.0	60 & over	5	0.3	5.9

(Adapted from Amir, 1971, p. 52.)
The figures show the number of offenders to be greater than victims by 2 to 1. This can be explained by the incidence of pack or gang rape.

TABLE 2.19   *Incidence of sexual offences in Sweden: total figures (1973–8)*

Offence	1973	1974	1975	1976	1977	1978
Rape	597	684	769	773	800	851
Carnal abuse of children (under 15)	352	566	277	227	267	272
Other carnal abuse	79	91	101	63	74	70

(From *Swedish Statistical Yearbook*, 1979.)

Summarising his findings, Finkelhor (p. 71) states that sexual molestation probably occurs for about one in every five girls (20 per cent) and one in every eleven boys (10 per cent); that peak vulnerability for the child falls prior to puberty, between the ages of 10 and 12; that coercion is present in over half of the experiences and only a tiny fraction are initiated by the children themselves; that only a minority of incidents are ever reported, even to parents and friends, let alone police; and that girls had particularly strong and consistently negative reactions to the experiences but the boys less so. If Finkelhor's figures are at all typical, the incidence of child molestation would affect the sexual lives of considerable numbers of people.

The incidence of rape and child sexual molestation in Western societies, whether on the increase or not, involves more than the terror and trauma caused to the victims over a long period of time. They are indicators of sexual immaturity and maladjustment on the part of offenders; in the case of rape, the majority are under 25 years of age, and in the case of child molestation are often members of the child's own family. This raises questions not so much of punishment but of prevention and remediation and the whole question of educating the young towards a wholesome, mature and healthy view of sex. Where victims are concerned, particularly children and adolescents, it raises questions of how they can be mentally as well as physically protected or prepared for such eventualities. How can a child of 10 who knows nothing of sexual intercourse, who has received no sex education, and who trusts most adults and members of his own family, be made aware and told what to do in such circumstances? Evidence provided in our study may help to supply some answers to these difficult questions.

Venereal diseases

Earlier sexual maturation and consequent increased incidence of sexual intercourse by the young would appear to indicate an increased risk of venereal diseases among the young, particularly if the contraceptive pill is used extensively by females and many males do not use a condom, one of the better known prophylactics against the venereal diseases. Ignorance about venereal diseases and their prevention are indicated by many researches, typical of which is Holmes, Nicol and Stubbs (1968) who took a sample of 152 young people under the age of 20 attending a VD clinic at a London hospital. Compared with a control group, there was no evidence that these young people came from lower socio-economic or broken homes (a common stereotype), but their major characteristics were that they were early school-leavers and that 63 per cent of the boys and 43 per cent of the girls appeared to have had no sex education at school. Seventy-six per cent claimed to have received no information or education about venereal diseases in school. Another study, fairly typical of American researches, is that of Arafat and Allen (1977), taking a sample of students from four New York City colleges aged 17 to 22 years. They found that the majority lacked adequate knowledge of venereal diseases (see also Arnold, 1972; Brown *et al.*, 1970; and Webster, 1972).

Assertions are frequently made that venereal diseases have reached epidemic proportions and that this is due to the permissive society and

THE PRACTICAL BACKGROUND OF THE STUDY

largely to the increase of promiscuity in the young. These assertions must be treated with caution and the facts looked at objectively. In assessing the situation it should be borne in mind that statistics of the incidence of venereal diseases are of 'reported cases' and that in many countries, due to more tolerant social attitudes, the incidence of 'reporting' or attendance at clinics may have increased rather than the actual incidence of the diseases. We also observe that to discuss venereal disease in the singular, as one generic component, can be misleading. When, for example, we separate the statistics for the most common venereal diseases, syphilis and gonorrhoea, a somewhat different picture emerges for each of them.

TABLE 2.20   *Reported cases of syphilis in five countries (1955-73)*

Year	Canada	USA	England and Wales	Australia	Sweden
1955	2,401	122,588	4,983	646	–
1965	2,560	122,842	4,075	–	–
1966	1,969	105,159	3,678	798	–
1967	2,385	102,581	3,603	955	–
1968	2,233	96,271	3,741	840	268
1969	2,395	92,162	3,413	1,072	379
1970	2,501	91,382	3,267	947	322
1971	2,489	95,997	3,139	1,077	332
1972	3,065	91,149	3,051	1,217	371
1973	3,771	87,469	–	1,433	431

(Adapted from *World Health Statistics Annual* WHO, 1979, 'Infectious Diseases' volume, pp. 116–18.)

Examining comparative figures on syphilis in Table 2.20 it can be seen in some countries that the incidence appears to be fairly stable, with only slight increases or decreases in the last few years, allowing for population increases. The figures for the USA show an actual decline and later Swedish statistics also (in 1978 there were 385 reported cases of syphilis in Sweden). In all countries quoted the incidence of syphilis is only a very small proportion of the population, far less than one-hundredth of 1 per cent in most cases.

The figures for the incidence of gonorrhoea, on the other hand, seen in Table 2.21, are not only much greater but show a considerable and continuing increase in most countries. Later figures show that for England and Wales (*Social Trends*, 1980) the reported cases of gonorrhoea had reached 57,464 by 1978, but in Sweden had dropped to 20,917 in that year (*Swedish Statistical Yearbook*, 1979). It is interesting to note that the date of a widely publicised warning by the

TABLE 2.21   *Reported cases of gonorrhoea in five countries (1955-73)*

Year	Canada	USA	England and Wales	Australia	Sweden
1955	14,300	237,137	17,845	–	13,852
1965	20,453	324,925	36,691	–	24,100
1966	21,479	351,738	37,483	9,036	25,002
1967	22,601	404,836	41,829	9,388	25,974
1968	22,520	464,543	44,962	9,932	30,124
1969	27,164	534,872	51,260	9,648	34,420
1970	31,544	600,072	54,764	9,542	38,885
1971	34,405	670,268	57,571	10,539	38,152
1972	41,467	767,215	54,974	11,037	31,498
1973	45,330	842,621	–	11,337	26,490

(Adapted from *World Health Statistics Annual* WHO, 1979, 'Infectious Diseases' volume, pp. 123-6.)

World Health Organisation that 'gonorrhoea had reached almost epidemic proportions in Europe' was 1963 (Morton, 1971, p. 40). Since then, in the countries providing the sample for our study, there have been considerable increases, with the exception of Sweden noted above. This increase may not be due to greater sexual promiscuity, so much as to changes in contraceptive practices. Juhlin (1968) concluded that pill-taking has probably increased the risk of gonorrhoeal infection since the use of condoms has declined. Morton (p. 90), in a somewhat emotive discussion of the phenomenon, questions the dispensing of contraceptive pills to single women maintaining that 'for the single the pill may be classified as the most dangerous of the polluting pesticides'.

Assertions that it is the under-20s in particular who are responsible for increases in venereal diseases cannot be substantiated. Not all countries report in their medical statistics how the incidence of VD is distributed by age groups, but in those that do the figures for the under-20s of reported cases of gonorrhoea indicate the contrary. Table 2.22 for England and Wales provides one example. Tables 2.23 and 2.24, the latest figures available for Sweden broken down into age groups, provides another. It will be seen that the greater incidence of any age of a four- or five-year age span is the *over*-20s, who have achieved adult status as well as maturity.

Statements such as Morton's (1971, p. 59) that 'It should surprise no one therefore to learn that one third of all gonorrhoea in females in England and Wales occurs among those under the age of twenty, and that the disease is commonest in young men aged between twenty and twenty four years' and Schofield's (1976, p. 163) that 'one sixth of all new gonorrhoea infections are under twenty' should be seen in

TABLE 2.22   *Gonorrhoea in England and Wales: sexually
transmitted diseases – new patients seen at hospital
clinics – by age-years*

Year	Under 16	16–19	20–4	25 and over	Totals
1966	206	5,013	11,407	20,752	37,378
1971	541	10,271	19,209	27,448	57,469
1978	509	11,279	19,543	26,133	57,464

(Adapted from *Social Trends* Great Britain, Central Statistical Office, 1980, p. 177.)

TABLE 2.23   *Gonorrhoea in Sweden: reported cases by age-years*

Year	0–9	10–14	15–19	20–4	25 and over	Totals
1969	7	110	7,842	14,635	11,826	34,420
1970	6	133	9,226	16,311	13,209	38,885
1971	11	157	8,957	15,223	13,804	38,152
1972	9	111	7,039	12,119	12,220	31,498

(Adapted from Sexual-och samlevn ad-sundervisning, USSU., p. 687.)
*There are some slight discrepancies in total figures cited in Table 2.21 due to slightly differing criteria for classifying the disease.

TABLE 2.24   *Sexually transmitted diseases in Sweden reported
for the under-20s*

Disease	1971	1978	1979
Syphilis	28	18	14
Gonorrhoea	9,125	4,226	3,297

(Based upon statistics from the Swedish National Board of Health and the National Bacteriological Laboratory, Stockholm.)

perspective. Schofield writes in his book *Promiscuity* (p. 29):

It is, however, possible to read too much into the rise in the
incidence of VD. In the same period that the VD figures increased
by 47 per cent, hospital admissions for all types of illnesses went
up 34 per cent; some may say that society is much sicker, but a
more feasible explanation is that both rises are due to changes in
medical practices. It is certain that more people who have
contracted a venereal disease now go to a clinic whereas in the
past many of them went to a family doctor, who may not have
reported the disease.

It is reasonable to recognise that adolescents will reflect the practices and attitudes to be seen in adults, and that the increase in a certain kind of VD (gonorrhoea) does not necessarily indicate greater promiscuity in the young. Commenting on his earlier much quoted survey of sexuality in the young (1968), Schofield points out that many of those infected when young are now married and retaining one permanent sexual partner. There were cases, he indicates, of young people who had only ever had sexual intercourse with one person, but were nevertheless infected by their partners. He adds: 'Although it can be shown that the more promiscuous are more likely to get VD, it does not follow from this that the less chance there is of getting VD the more promiscuous people will be' (Schofield, 1976, p. 31).

This highlights the issue raised by this practical evidence, of what children and adolescents should be told about venereal diseases, what they are, how they are transmitted and what preventative measures can be taken. The evidence indicates that much of this information is given certainly too late, and the only preventative measure widely advised appears to be the negative one of abstention from sexual activity. Our concern in this study is to discover not only what information the young have received but how they have received it, namely, how they have assimilated it. This raises not only the moral issue of when the young should be made aware of VD but at what age they would normally be intellectually capable of understanding the dangers and formulating values on which to base their behaviour.

Pornography, homosexuality and prostitution

Government commissions in the last decade or so under various titles, such as 'Human Relations', have reported in Australia, the USA and Britain on the topics of pornography, homosexuality and prostitution. We do not wish to enter into the debate concerning the definition of these terms, but for the purpose of discussion accept what is popularly understood to be their meaning. On pornography, all these commissions report the increase of pornographic publications, which include books, magazines, newspapers and films, not only available at specialist sex shops but over-the-counter at newsstands, stationers and from other sources. Soft-core movies can now be seen on cable television in some countries. A disturbing feature is the use of children and adolescents in some of these publications, including depictions of incest and various sexual situations.

Homosexuality, including lesbianism, has received much greater acceptance in Western societies in the last decade. Considerable publicity is now given to 'gay' activities, news items about them appear in newspapers, magazines, and on radio and television programmes. Government commissions have pointed out the 'normality' of a certain proportion of the population having homosexual tendencies. Rarely, however, is attention given to how this fact may be imparted to children, and especially how the young with emerging homosexual rather than heterosexual desires should be helped. The only attempt known to the authors to include homosexuality as part of a sex education programme for children is in Sweden (Swedish National Board of Education, 1977).

Prostitution, both legal and illegal, has been a social issue over the centuries. Government commissions in recent years have tended to recognise the continuing existence of prostitution as a necessary evil, some recommending its legalisation and control. Little is known, however, about child and adolescent prostitution (where children and adolescents are sold or hired out for sexual purposes), but it is known to exist and suspicion is sometimes voiced that it may be increasing, especially in a period of continuing unemployment.

Our intention in raising these matters, albeit very briefly, is to call attention to the fact that they exist in the society in which the young are reared, that they impinge upon the lives of the young, directly or indirectly, and that social action has to be taken, often by legislation, to protect them from exploitation in these areas. Little is done, or even thought of as needing to be done, to equip the young to know about, to understand or come to terms with these features of Western society. This raises two questions, what should the young know, and what are the young capable of knowing, given their limitations of experience and thought. The second question is more directly the concern of this study.

Sex education

Sex education for the young has developed all over the world in recognition of the need to inform them about sexual matters, but controversies abound about whether it should be the prerogative of home or school, at what age it should be taught and what is a suitable content (Fraser, 1972). Our illustrations of the controversies are confined to the countries upon which this study is based, since they form the context in which the children studied, received or did not receive their sex education.

Nowhere in the vast literature now available on sex education is it suggested that sex education should not take place in the home. Even if the Freudian viewpoint is rejected, it is widely recognised that in attitudes and behaviour towards the child, in exploring his own body, in feeding and toilet training, in trying to answer or avoid the child's early curiosity about sexual matters, parents are home-based sex educators. When a new baby is due to arrive some parents utilise this family experience to help the child grasp what conception, gestation and birth are. Others even encourage older children to witness the birth of the new baby (Mehl *et al.*, 1977). Plainly an increasing number of parents take their task as sex educators of their own children quite seriously.*

* Yet it is because of parental inadequacy, inhibitions and emotionality about the subject that a case for school-based sex education is made, not to supplant but to supplement the teachings of parents (Calderone, 1969; Haimes, 1973)* The opposite view, expressed in many bitter campaigns in the USA, maintains that sex education is a threat to the family as the primary source of sex information and attitudes.*Many antagonists of sex education also assert that it arouses curiosity and desire and encourages children to experiment with sex.* 'Is the Schoolhouse the Proper Place to Teach Raw Sex?' was part of a campaign to prevent sex education in United States schools (Fraser, 1972). The case of the dismissal of the schools' superintendent in Anaheim, California, is well documented (Breasted, 1971). The result is that in some areas in the USA no sex education is taught at all, and where it is taught express permission of parents must be sought. Invariably such courses are only provided towards the end of high school, long after most students have achieved physical maturity.

In Australia opinion has been strongly divided about school-based sex education. A 1970 Australian Gallup Poll reported that 51 per cent of parents favoured sex instruction by specialists in schools (this presumes high schools only) and 37 per cent favoured leaving it to parents (Faust, 1975). Evidence from Queensland and the nervousness of other state education departments about the introduction of courses in sex education and human relations suggests that the picture remains as polarised in 1980 as in 1970. Currently government committees and the Curriculum Development Centre in Canberra are examining proposals and in some cases devising courses, but the prospect for sex education available for all children and adolescents is still uncertain.

In Britain sex education is the scene of controversy also, although the virtual autonomy of local education authorities in curriculum matters leads to much diversity of practices and content. Disagreements exist about what content should be taught, at what age it should be taught and who should do the teaching (Hyde, 1971). The authors saw in one county children of 7 years preparing for a visit to a maternity home, with preparatory and follow-up discussion, but also talked with 15-year-olds who had only recently had their first sex education lessons.

• Sweden is the only country included in the present study which has compulsory courses in sex education and personal relationships in the basic school (7 to 16 years). These began in 1956, and the content was subject to extensive revision in 1977. It has been revised to meet the needs of children in modern Sweden and contains for the 7- to 10-year-old such subjects as external differences between the sexes, the structure and function of the sexual organs, menstruating, intercourse, masturbation, contraceptives, conception, pregnancy, childbirth, sterility, adoption, exhibitionism and pedophilia (Linner, 1978)." This content is interesting in view of the sexual-social problems reviewed earlier in this chapter. Lest readers think that this programme is possible only through a centralised bureaucracy and imposed without heeding public opinion, the new handbook on sex education was introduced only after the widest consultations with parents, church leaders, teachers' organisations and many public groups who supported it. It will obviously be of interest to observe if there are any measurable differences between Swedish children and children in Australia, North America and Britain in this study.

In the light of the practical background of this study outlined and discussed, particularly the social and sexual issues evident in Western societies, it is surprising that sex education still arouses so much opposition and that a consensus about its provision has not evolved, as has occurred in Sweden. Perhaps the results of this investigation may not only contribute to our sparse knowledge of children's sexual thinking, but also[stimulate parents, educators and the general public to require better educational provision than currently exists to guide our children towards sexually mature thought and behaviour.]

Summary and discussion

The practical social background, no less than theoretical consideration, is the concern of the authors in presenting their findings on sexual thinking. "Children are developing in a changing world where many sexual issues are debated and their attendant consequences influence children's thinking directly or indirectly, sooner or later in their development."

Not least is the factor of the secular trend in physical growth, known more popularly as earlier maturing. One feature of this is the lowering of the menarcheal age in girls in the countries examined – Australia, England, North America and Sweden – to a mean average of 12.5 years. Evidence for this from many sources cannot be doubted, but with it also comes evidence of earlier sexual activity in the young, despite exhortations to sexual abstinence by adult society. At the same time the age of marriage has been delayed, largely so that young people may complete studies or become economically independent before beginning a permanent sexual partnership. Consequently the gap between the onset of full sexual capacity and the expression of it in marriage has increased, imposing serious stress on the young. This is perhaps one explanation for the increase in overt sexual activity in a pre-marital context among the very young, which cannot justifiably be labelled 'promiscuous', as the evidence reviewed indicates.

Moral considerations apart; the consequences can be seen in the incidence of teenage pregnancies accompanied by continued restricted access to birth-control resources and information for the young and also the limited availability of legal abortion. An added risk is that of infection. Figures show syphilis to be fairly constant if not declining, but gonorrhoea is reported as reaching 'epidemic' proportions. The evidence indicates that young people are at increased risk of venereal infection due to various social changes. Children, not only adolescents, become aware of these matters, as our study shows, not through sex education programmes which are denied to large numbers because of the polemics surrounding sex education in many countries, but through the magazines and newspapers they see and the television programmes they view daily. They are also increasingly aware, as our study indicates, either from personal experience or through second-hand sources, of such sexual matters as divorce, rape, child molestation, pornography, homosexuality and prostitution.

Whatever moral stand is taken on these matters, children are in need of enlightenment and guidance about sexuality much earlier than was thought necessary. The motive may be to warn, to deter or to prepare children for the sexual world they are already encountering. The authors regard this current study as a necessary beginning to explore and explain what children at various ages have perceived of their sexual world, what sexual knowledge they have and what they are capable of understanding.

3 The research design

Sexual thinking as a broader definition we have described as thinking about gender, physical differences between girls and boys, differences between men and women and those human biological functions with a sexual connotation, and related social associations. Our concern is limited to children's thinking about human sexuality and is confined to their thinking about babies, infants, children, adolescents and adults. Children's thinking about animals and other species would form an interesting focus for research, but it was not the intention of this research to include this. Another limitation, already discussed in chapter 1, has been to focus upon cognition and to exclude sexual attitudes as the emphasis of our research. This is not to minimise the importance of affect, emotion and attitudes towards sex. Far from it. We recognise their importance in development, and ideally our project could profitably have included this vital area. However, all researchers have at the outset to define the area of concern, bearing in mind limitations of the time, personnel and money available. Such a choice had to be made in an earlier study on children's religious thinking (Goldman, 1964) where again the argument can be made that thinking about religion must involve what a person feels and believes about religion. The argument, in a sense, whether applied to religion or sex, is circular, since thinking has an effect upon emotion (cognition influences affect) and emotion certainly enters into all thinking processes (affect influences cognition).

The aims of the research

The authors' aims in this research were to measure the extent of children's sexual knowledge, their sexual understanding at various ages, and to identify what processes of thought they use in trying to explain

57

biological functions and the phenomena of their own bodies as they grow and change. If these could be achieved it would help us to grasp not only what children actually know and comprehend, but would also provide clues about the cognitive difficulties they face in sexual thinking. Most curricula in schools and advice to parents are based not upon research findings but upon intuitive ideas of what children might be capable of grasping, as well as what they appear to need at certain periods of their lives. Sometimes these intuitive ideas can be misleading, as has been shown from the results of varied research into children's mathematical (Churchill, 1958), historical (Coltham, 1960), and religious (Goldman, 1965) thinking which have led to radical reforms of syllabuses and a changed view of the curriculum. If we could find some solid evidence in relation to the questions raised about children's sexual thinking, we believe it might have a similar input into the curricula for health and sex education, human relations and other courses, as well as providing guidelines for parents.

This study has also considerable theoretical interest in the light of Piaget's encyclopedic researches into children's thinking. Despite the extensive range of topics investigated by the Geneva school, there are many important areas uninvestigated, although Piaget as early as the 1920s did look at how children understood 'origins' (Piaget, 1926 and 1927). Nevertheless, as we have already noted in chapter 1, there has been a concentration upon aspects of physical science, the major reason probably being that the research methodology is simpler, and the area of knowledge more tangible. Questions of human biology, as understood by the child, although rooted in physical phenomena, are basically internal and present intellectual problems for both the child and the researchers not evident in other areas investigated. Although the human body can be seen to act and move, the internal processes of growth and function cannot be so readily observed. And although children experience these internal processes personally, and daily live with their outcomes such as urine, excreta, perspiration, digestion and countless other physical sensations, it is difficult for them to reflect upon and understand how they operate and what their significance is. Indeed, this familiarity may be a barrier to understanding, since internal physical processes are there as part of daily life not normally subject to discussion or questioning. Some outcomes of internal body processes are, it is widely recognised, subject to taboos, particularly the excretory and sexual functions, thus making it more difficult for children to explore cognitively their significance. It is therefore of great interest to see what forms of pre-operational and operational thinking are evident when the child attempts sexual understanding, and whether stages can be discerned with increasing age and experience.

We hoped also to throw some light upon Freudian theories, not only the general theory of infantile sexuality but particularly the concept of a latency period. Many sex educators have questioned the validity of a latency stage from about 5 to 10 years (Calderone, 1969), and certainly the Freudian theory for latency and its causal antecedents, the Oedipus complex and castration fears, are open to question. Our study is not intended to provide conclusive evidence about Freudian theories; what in fact emerges is material which may contribute to a modification of current ideas about latency. Another area, not widely known, is Freud's cloacal theory of gestation and childbirth. That is, children believe that babies are formed inside the bowels (curiously 'cloaca' is the Latin name for sewer) and, like excreta, emerge at birth through the anus. This is similar to what we later call 'the digestive fallacy' of children. We are interested to explore what proportion of children provide this explanation and at what ages it appears in their psychosexual development.

Some of the scales we have developed to evaluate the children's responses are concerned with what we term 'biological realism'. This encompasses not only what children know in terms of sexual facts and sexual vocabulary, but what explanations and mythologies they invent to understand what they know. Some of the children's mythologies impinge upon other theorists, Piaget and Freud for example, but many of them are to our knowledge not explained elsewhere in the literature, especially the variations of medical mythologies children devise as explanations.

Our purpose then was to explore the basis of all these practical and theoretical considerations and to examine the following questions. Do children develop a sequential process or a hierarchy of stages in sexual thinking? If stages are evident, can they be approximated to a Piagetian scale from pre-operational to formal operational thought? Are there any significant differences to be found, apart from those between age cohorts, between girls and boys, differing ability levels, different socio-economic groups and between children in large and small families? In addition, to see whether any of the results could be generalised across cultures we sought to discover any major differences and similarities between the children in the four countries from which data were collected. Incidentally, in using the term 'children' we are aware that in covering the age groups 5-15 years we are also including young adolescents. 'Children' is used deliberately, not as a diminutive for the older group, but as a generic term to aid simplicity.

Planning the research

Any research design must begin with a recognition on the part of the researchers of the limitations within which they must work. In our case the time limits were imposed by an eleven-month sabbatical,

59

extended in the event to twelve months, due to the inclusion of Sweden in the project. Planning in mid-1978, we had to allow for a period of pretesting whatever instrument was devised, and to complete the collection of Australian data before we left to work in USA and Britain during 1979. Clear limits of time were also obvious in the return to full university duties of teaching and administration in March 1980.

Within such a time span we recognised that the public school system containing the full age range from 5 to 15 years old, was the obvious institutional structure to use for making contact with children. (The term 'public school system' is used to describe the non-private statutory provision of schooling in each area used. It is not used in the confused British sense of its opposite, the premier private schools as defined by membership of the Headmasters and Headmistresses Conferences in the UK.) Other groups such as families, churches, recreational or leisure clubs were sometimes more accessible to us but considerable variations in the type and diversity of these institutions created other sampling problems. In using schools as our sampling frame we were conscious of the pressures they are subject to in terms of time limits. From past experience we recognised that access to children would have to be limited to a maximum of forty-five minutes to one hour, the most common timetabled unit of teaching. By whatever method we chose to collect our data we determined to restrict ourselves to such a time limit.

Personnel and finance imposed limitations of a similar kind, since limitations of money will restrict the personnel to work on any project. With a year completely clear of regular university teaching and research, both authors were available and so they determined to collect the data themselves, thereby increasing the reliability of the results. International travel expenses were covered in part by the grant normal for university sabbatical leave, leaving only local travel and administrative costs to be covered.

In the light of these limitations, and also the opportunities presented by a sabbatical, we reviewed the research methods available. The first and obvious choice was to opt for a cross-sectional age group type of research, rather than a longitudinal study. It is obviously more rewarding and illuminating to follow the same children over a period of time, but such a longitudinal study, even if it had entailed following children over as little as a two year period, would have made the comparisons between children in different countries impossible.

A further choice had to be made concerning methods of collecting responses, that is by the use of written answers in the form of a 'test' or questionnaire, or by oral answers in the form of a clinical interview based upon a standardised interview schedule. Since the purpose of a cross-sectional age study was to encompass as wide an age range as possible and the public school systems in Australia, Britain and North

America – the three countries initially planned for – included 5- to 15-year-olds, we wished to develop a standardised procedure which was suitable for young children and young adolescent school-leavers. The content chosen had to be neither too difficult for the youngest, nor too childish for the oldest. This almost automatically ruled out written responses or the construction of multiple choice instruments, for the first would require writing skills and the second reading skills beyond the capacity of the five-year-olds and less able children of much older age groups.

An individual face-to-face interview was therefore chosen as the most appropriate method. This clinical interview had several advantages over written response-type methods, apart from questions of literacy. The kind of verbal responses stimulated by a face-to-face discussion are more substantial and varied. Follow-up and 'contingency' questions may be asked by the interviewer, particularly important in such an area under investigation, and the establishment of a friendly rapport with the respondents is of vital importance. Assurances of understanding and anonymity can be given if there is hesitation or difficulties in making a response. Undifferentiated replies at all ages may occur in written responses which could lead to the false assumption that there is no progression or refinement of ideas with increasing age. For example, there were two standard responses to the question 'Why do people get married?'; one of which most children used in reply, 'Because they love each other', or 'Because they want to have children'. The follow-up questions, 'Well, why does loving each other make them want to get married?' and 'Why is it so important to have children?' lead to differentiated replies which could then be scored on a sequence of operational thought (see chapter 6). In addition follow-up questions help to reveal obscurities or confused thinking and give added dimensions to the investigators' assessment of a particular child's conceptualisations.

The clinical interview method also tends to increase motivation; once rapport is established, interest can be stimulated and even many shy and seemingly inarticulate children are flattered to have the undivided attention of a friendly adult for almost an hour. Introduced within the context of children helping the interviewers by providing their views and opinions, involvement and motivation are improved. This personal element is not as evident in requesting a group for written responses since the respondent is only one in a group of twenty or thirty children, whereas in an interview it is a one-to-one relationship. To increase this personal element no tape recorder was used, since it was found that writing down responses word for word (neither interviewer possessed shorthand skills) seemed to impress the children and also gave them time to think and elaborate. It was felt that mechanical devices, unless used very skilfully, can interpose an artificial barrier in

61

an interview-discussion situation. There is also the distinct possibility of a mechanical breakdown and an interruption of the interview flow. It may be argued that older children, particularly young adolescents, might have found the interview too personal and too intense. This was not our experience, possibly because respondents who might be worried by an interview situation had already screened themselves out in the initial stages of selection (see later on 'Selecting the sample'). Hostility to adults by adolescent respondents was experienced only a few times by the interviewers, and was usually handled in a friendly manner without the need to terminate the interview.

One additional advantage in the use of the clinical interview was, for the younger children, the possibility of stopping the interview if the child showed signs of fatigue, then resuming after a rest. As opposed to a written response, an interview can be terminated at any time. Ample evidence exists from Piaget and his colleagues that the clinical interview method is a well-tried technique, particularly suitable for a wider age range of respondents and particularly appropriate for cognitive investigations.

Choice of interview content

Given the method of a personal clinical interview lasting approximately forty-five minutes, the next task was to select a suitable number of items which would adequately cover the broader 'universe' of how children perceive growth and physical development, and the narrower 'universe' of sexual thinking, described in this volume. It may be useful to examine the narrower 'universe' of children's sexual thinking as an example of how the items were selected. Any investigator devising an instrument to explore a given topic must first choose the parameters of his universe, be it 'intelligence' (Peel, 1960), 'politics' (Connell, 1971) or 'prejudice' (Rokeach, 1960). The first task is to collect as many items as possible, either used by other researchers, or suggested by wide reading or invention, and to subject them to 'trial' groups, eliminating those inappropriate on various criteria, retaining those which together appear to cover the universe identified, and which are viable items in terms of the children's responses. In the case of a universe of sexual thinking it was evident at the beginning that some items, which would be suitable with adult subjects, had to be deleted when applied to children. The sensitive and delicate nature of the universe to be covered would appear to us to include, in an ideal situation, such areas as masturbation and homosexuality. Data gathered on the topic of masturbation (Kinsey, 1948 and 1953) indicate it to be an almost universal practice of both sexes for the relief of sexual tension. Information gathered about this would have been extremely valuable, but we judged from trial responses that to have included such items would have gone beyond the limits set by social taboos in home, school and community. Similar taboos in relation to homosexuality and lesbianism led us to exclude questions on these topics. Operating within the constraints evident within public school systems the content had to be adjusted to what was realistically possible and acceptable. The influence of these and other sexual taboos, preventing discussion, exploration or research in certain areas, is in itself an indication of the need for research into sexual thinking.

All this involves the question of ethics in socio-psychological research. The authors, respectively a professional psychologist and a sociologist, and both previously infant and primary teachers observed the normal ethical requirements to safeguard the children. Anonymity of the children, their parents, their schools and school districts were assured by the use of coding devices. Permission of the school administrators and principals was obtained, and the parents of each child selected for interview were sent a letter and asked permission for the interview to take place. The questions to be asked have been vetted by professional university colleagues and the normal procedures required by professional ethics had been observed. In the event only a 20 per cent refusal rate from parents occurred. Frequently, we found, parents consulted their children, almost always the older children, and it was whether or not the children themselves felt they wanted to be interviewed which appeared to be the decisive factor. Occasionally telephone calls were received from parents of 5-year-olds expressing some anxieties, mainly concerned with fatigue or strain. Such fears were allayed in most cases by assurances to parents that interviews of younger children would be arranged early in the school day, and that suitable breaks would be made in the interview if necessary.

Two problems had to be faced early in the project. The first was to notify the schools and parents what the project was about in general terms, without revealing too much detail which might prepare the children in advance for the questions to be asked. To this end we drew up a statement for administrators and schools called 'Introducing the Project', and a sample letter for the schools to send out to parents was submitted to the principal. In both these documents the topic of the research was presented as 'Children's Concepts of Development' and how they look at growing up. The letter to parents invariably included the statement, 'Since the process of growing up includes body growth and physical maturing, some of the questions will be on this topic'. Among the topics mentioned as part of the interview were 'birth' and 'growth'.

The second, and related problem, was to avoid using the word sex, which might invoke all kinds of taboos and invite a veto on the research

63

before it had begun. All questions put by administrators, teachers and parents were answered honestly. Often on meeting with school staff we were asked what sort of questions we were going to ask the children. To this usually three examples were given: questions on ageing; do you prefer being a boy or a girl and why?; and questions on the origins of life. When asked directly, 'Do you ask questions about where babies come from?' we answered 'Yes'. When asked what use the research would be to educators, it was stated that it would be useful in providing general insights for parents and teachers, and valuable guidelines for teachers and curriculum planners of human biology, health and sex education, and human relations courses.

This oblique approach we discovered was necessary in all the countries involved,* including Sweden, which has a long tradition of open discussion on sexual matters and probably has the world's most advanced sex education curriculum.* Its introduction was aided in Sweden by the research being included in an ongoing project concerned with children's maturation. Even so, the Swedish project leader found this low-key introduction necessary.* The greatest difficulty experienced, as outlined later, was in North America. *

At all times we tried to avoid showing the interview schedule itself, since it could be misunderstood if read through without explanation. Many questions listed were contingent upon a child's previous answer and the language of the child was used in phrasing the contingent questions. From the text it could look as though sophisticated and sexually phrased questions were asked of all children when, in fact, many of the questions were asked only of older children who had already introduced the topic themselves. A clear example of this was the question: 'Apart from wanting a baby, why do people want to make love/have sex/have sexual intercourse?' This was asked only of those children who, in discussing the origin of babies, had mentioned quite specifically the sexual activity of parents as a prime cause of conception. In asking this question only the vocabulary actually voiced by the child was used. The three examples mentioned above, to describe the sexual act, were frequently changed to 'rooting', 'having it off', 'humping' or simply 'it'!

This low key approach was felt to be necessary in view of the universe to be researched. As explained in chapter 1 our definition of 'sex' and 'sexual' is in the broadest possible terms. Given this broad definition, about half the content of the larger developmental project was not specifically sexual in the narrower sense. This included ageing, mother and father roles in the family, boy and girl identity and preferences, sex-roles and sex-role stereotyping. Taking the narrower definition of sexual relationships, however, only six or seven questions out of a total of sixty-three questions in the interview schedule can be directly identified within these limits.

Pretesting the interview schedule

Having determined the age range to be covered, 5 to 15 years, the method of investigation by clinical interview, and the approach to schools and parents, there still remained the problem of trying out the universe of questions selected to conform to a period of approximately forty-five minutes. Allowance had to be made for variations in speed of responses of individual children, so that any period between thirty minutes for the fastest child to a full hour for the slowest child was planned for.

The considerations outlined in the previous section had determined the range of ideas to be explored with children in the trial period. In all, five versions of the interview were pretested, individual items being included or discarded on various criteria. For example, we had discarded the technique of a previous researcher (Conn, 1947) who used boy and girl dolls to elicit responses, since it was obvious that subjects 9 years of age and over would find such an approach rather childish. However, working on previous projective techniques demonstrated by The Thematic Apperception Test (Murray, 1943) and used in similar research to ours (Jackson, 1952; Goldman, 1964), we began by including several pictures, consisting of simple pen and ink drawings. We asked children to describe differences between a baby and a child, a child and a teenager, a teenager and an old adult. These pictures were actually retained in another form (see Figures 5.1 and 5.2) but children in the context of this particular question were too distracted by details in the picture. As a consequence the responses were insufficiently differentiated and the item was discarded.

For similar reasons an interesting item on the increasing responsibilities of growing children, showing pictures of a tricycle, bicycle, motor bike and car, was rejected. So also were questions on children's judgment at what age they could be left alone at home, stay out after dark, date, marry and have babies. Another lengthy area on the body functions of digestion and excretory functions based upon an American and Israeli project (Moore and Kendall, 1971) was also discarded on the grounds that our pretest responses confirmed the original research, that although interesting, the results yielded were insignificant. These items were pruned with some regret, since they included how children regarded the process of toilet training, and had potential for testing out Freudian and other developmental theories.

By the fourth and fifth pretest runs the final content of the interview schedule had been decided, to conform to the required time limits and the suitability and variety of the children's responses. An item testing out children's response to vocabulary, for example, was retained but was reduced from 28 to 11 words. The final version of the interview schedule contained a total of 63 questions and in 6 sections titled Ageing and Powers, Parents, Sex Differences and Preferences, Birth and Conception, Sex Education and Body Functions. Time was then spent refining the content to remove ambiguities, developing contingency questions and standardising the procedures between interviewers to improve interviewer reliability. By necessity, all these trials had to be held in Australia, but having a working knowledge of schools in the other countries involved, the authors were satisfied that the interview schedule would be a feasible instrument, apart from slight alterations in vocabulary in the American version, which was vetted by child psychologists at the State University of New York at Buffalo. Overall some 135 Australian children were interviewed in pretesting the interview schedule.

Several other valuable lessons were learned during the trial period. One was that absolute privacy was essential during interviewing and both interviewers when working in the same school had to ensure this requirement. This was difficult in some overcrowded schools, but interestingly no school selected had to be rejected because of accommodation problems. The interviewers talked to children in vacated staff rooms, storerooms, counselling rooms, principals' and deputy principals' offices, gymnasia and changing rooms. Staff were most generous in often vacating their rooms, altering schedules and accommodating us so willingly.

Another lesson learned early in the trial period was the possibility of 'contamination', that is children who had been interviewed early talking to those who were to be interviewed later. To avoid this, which would distort 'natural' responses, wherever possible only one day was spent in each school, arranging interviews in such a way that two children from the same classroom were interviewed consecutively, so that there was no time for respondents to confer with each other. This meant that only four children from one group, two boys and two girls, could be interviewed without contamination occurring. School breaks were used by interviewers to move to another age group in order to minimise contact. Where it was necessary to return to a previously visited school a gap of several days was arranged so that if there had been any contact between a child who had been interviewed and one still to be interviewed, the intervening period would minimise the impression made. In memory tasks retroactive inhibition is reputed to minimise retention of information.

The first and second trials had been conducted by one of the authors and several of his students, but on the third, fourth and fifth rounds, the two authors conducted the testing of the final versions. It was felt that a man and woman team would be more acceptable to schools and to parents, and particularly if the interviewers were a married couple.

Since interviewing in two of the originally planned countries had to be completed in a sabbatical year, desirability and necessity in the choice of the two interviewers happily coincided. Although both authors were trained primary and infant teachers, the male author also had secondary teaching experience. Originally, therefore, the plan was for the woman to interview all younger children and the man the older children. In the event, it was soon evident that above the age of 7, boys were more at ease talking to the man, and girls to the woman interviewer. This was the final pattern adopted and confirmed the experience of other researchers (Schofield, 1968). When Sweden joined the project a similar dichotomy was observed when interviewers, trained by the authors, interviewed in Swedish.

Selecting the sample

To distort a popular political aphorism 'some investigators choose samples, but others have samples thrust upon them'. All well-trained researchers are aware that sound sampling procedures are essential. Yet every researcher knows from experience that sampling is not as simple as the textbook approach suggests, and that various restraints arise to modify what is regarded as ideal. These restraints were encountered by the investigators, many of them caused by cultural differences and many by the nature of the topic being investigated. This will become clear as the sampling procedures are described.

Age groups selected

Within the limits of time imposed the selected age range of 5 to 15 years presented a choice. The kind of statistical analysis envisaged for the results required at least 20 children in each age cohort, for each country. Trials of the interviews, however, indicated that observable differences between 5 and 6 year olds in the responses given were very slight, and similarly between 7 and 8 year olds and the older groups 9 and 10, and 11 and 12. By taking every alternate year it was calculated that the number in each cohort could be considerably increased, at the same time enhancing the sequential analysis.

The intention then was to interview 40 children in each cohort, in each country, 20 boys and 20 girls, aged 5, 7, 9, 11, 13 and 15 years. This would yield, ideally, a total sample of 240 children in each country. This was achieved in Australia and Britain, but as Table 3.1 indicates this was not achieved in North America and in Sweden; the former for mainly political reasons and the latter because of the necessity for completing the Swedish sample within a certain time limit.

TABLE 3.1 *Total number of respondents by age-years and sex in four countries*

Age-year	Country	Boys	Girls	Totals	Mean age
5	Australia	20	20	40	5.64
	England	20	20	40	5.59
	North America	13	11	24	5.66
	Sweden	15	15	30	5.44
7	Australia	20	20	40	7.51
	England	20	20	40	7.52
	North America	15	15	30	7.45
	Sweden	15	15	30	7.63
9	Australia	20	20	40	9.52
	England	20	20	40	9.54
	North America	15	15	30	9.57
	Sweden	15	15	30	9.60
11	Australia	20	20	40	11.50
	England	20	20	40	11.42
	North America	14	16	30	11.50
	Sweden	15	15	30	11.58
13	Australia	20	20	40	13.54
	England	20	20	40	13.41
	North America	16	17	33	13.57
	Sweden	15	15	30	13.49
15	Australia	20	20	40	15.47
	England	20	20	40	15.39
	North America	16	15	31	15.49
	Sweden	15	15	30	15.47
Totals		419	419	838	

A note on statistical tables

All figures in the tables which follow giving percentages, may be rounded to the nearest whole number. Since percentages of zero scores are not normally included the totals do not necessarily come to 100%. Where decimal points are used, figures are rounded to two decimal places.

The countries selected

As Australians themselves the authors were aware that Australians tend to model their school systems and curricula, and their educational assumptions upon British education, stemming from the origins of the country as a series of British colonies. But there has been an increasing practice in recent years of focussing attention upon North America, borrowing ideas from both the USA and Canada as large numbers of Australian academics return home having taught or taken research degrees in North American schools, colleges and universities. As one of the authors (Goldman, 1971) noted elsewhere:

Educationally and emotionally Australia saw itself initially as an island off the coast of Britain referring to it even now . . . as 'home'. With the second World War, the coming of United States soldiers and General Motors to Australia, Australians moved their position to an offshore island just out of sight of California. The emotional towing process has gone on ever since.

Apart from the Australian use of Britain and North America as educational models, all countries initially planned for the project have certain other similarities. They are English speaking although, to parody George Bernard Shaw, they may be three peoples divided by a common language, with some distinct dialect and linguistic usages. All stem initially from the same British colonial roots. Books, journals and curricular materials of all kinds are used interchangeably in educational institutions. Australia with only a small population of 14 million, compared with Canada's 23 million, UK's 54 million and USA's 203 million, looks to Britain and North America for a great deal of its research ideas in education, psychology and the social sciences generally (approximate figures taken from the *Statesman's Year Book*, 1979). Generalisations about children, child development and the establishment of 'norms' have in Australia been largely based upon North American or British samples. Only recently have distinctively Australian samples been used, as research funds and expertise have increased. From an Australian viewpoint it was important to discover in what ways Australian children differed from or had similarities to their Anglo-Saxon and Anglo-American cousins, apart from the intrinsic value of cross-national studies.

Sweden cannot be included in the above historical, cultural, educational and linguistic context. It was included in the study for a quite different reason. The Swedish educational system has long been admired, sometimes envied, by English-speaking countries and quoted extensively in comparative literature as the *avant-garde* if not the *enfant terrible* of the educational world. In the realm of sex and morals, Sweden has also been regarded, well before 'the permissive society' was talked about elsewhere, as socially tolerant about divorce, pre-marital relations, sex films and publications, and other related sexual matters (Linner, 1977). In health and sex education Swedish curricula, when compared with the cautious and controversial approach in Australia, USA and Britain, is markedly advanced, although there are many critics who would characterise it as retrogressive rather than progressive. At the

69

time of the authors' visit to Scandinavia, a new Swedish sex education programme was about to be launched, which had almost universal support from the churches, parental and teachers' groups and the political parties. It is therefore of considerable interest, not least to Swedish educators, to know, after so many years of compulsory sex education in the schools, how Swedish children may differ from their English-speaking peers.

The inclusion of the Swedish sample did mean that these interviews could not be done by the English-speaking authors, since Swedish children had to be interviewed in Swedish. This introduced a variable not present in the other three samples. This was, however, minimised by two measures adapted to meet these problems. The first measure was the close co-operation of the authors with Swedish colleagues, training them in the standardised interview technique required and a thorough briefing in the approach to schools and parents. The second measure, as is normal procedure in cross-cultural studies, was to check the translation of the interview schedule from English into Swedish by 'back-translating' it from the Swedish translation into English, then comparing both English versions, the original and the back-translation to discover possible discrepancies (see Brislin et al., 1973). Only one item, not central to the investigation, was found to have been mis-translated. As scoring of the Swedish children's responses proceeded, several minor verbal discrepancies were discovered. These were noted, their significance discussed with Swedish colleagues, and allowed for in evaluating the results. Campbell (1969) listed fifteen factors which may jeopardise the validity of any explanation of data obtained from different countries, pointing out that 'translation inadequacies constitute instrumentation errors'. All Campbell's factors were covered in this study including translation, principally because the Swedish colleagues involved were experienced Swedish-English bilinguals, not surprising when English is the compulsory foreign language in all Swedish schools, and higher degree dissertations in Swedish universities must normally be presented in English. Consequently, the Swedish interviewers were conversant with the original English interview schedule and were also responsible for translating the children's responses from Swedish into English.

The larger problems, outlined by Goodnow (1969) in a discussion on cross-cultural comparative research into culture and thinking, were faced at the outset of the study (p. 439):

> When we consider intellectual growth or style in different cultures, we are confronted by three requirements. We need to obtain, by combining results from several studies, some picture of skills common to people from many backgrounds, as well as skills that

differentiate among them. At the same time, we need to find the features of milieu that may account for the similarities and differences in skills. And finally, the thorniest requirement of all, we have to ask as we transpose a task from one culture to another, whether the same answer means the same thing in both worlds.

Goodnow's point is well taken, but it also involves looking not only at the differences but at the similarities of the societies chosen for study. Lipset's (1963) comments on the political commonalities he identified in Canada, Australia, USA and England were noted in chapter 1. Another commonality regarded as central by many researchers (Goodnow, 1969; Le Vine, 1970; Lesser and Kandel, 1968) in cross-cultural comparisons of children, is the factor of schooling. This was found to be particularly important in research involving Piagetian-type tasks (Dasen, 1977). It can be claimed that all the countries involved in this study of children's sexual thinking have compulsory universal school provision. Their school systems share several important characteristics such as an emphasis on verbal and spoken activity, the asking of questions, and a problem-solving approach in many subjects. These are, in contrast to many other universal school's systems, not dominated by rote-learning or memory task learning from textbooks, as Goodnow found to be the case in her study of Hong Kong children (p. 457).

The age-structured school system in the areas chosen in Australia, England and North America were almost identical, schooling beginning between years 5 and 6 and comprehensive high schools beginning about year 12. Areas in England which retain selective high schools, that is, the grammar school system, were not used. The major structural difference in the countries selected is in Sweden, where schooling does not begin until year 7 and provides a 'basic school' often called 'comprehensive' from that age until 16. This difference was noted in Husen's (1967) international study. A very large proportion of Swedish 5-year-olds do attend kindergartens rather similar in programme to Australian 'prep' classes, British 'infant' schools and first-year American elementary schools. These different structures can be seen in Table 3.2. Apart from this structural difference, the type of learning emphasis mentioned earlier would appear to be the most vital common schooling factor. A wide variety of schools was chosen in each area selected, and this varied according to all kinds of factors, the nature of the administrative system, the distances to be travelled and the willingness of the school principal involved. An examination of Table 3.2 shows a suitable distribution of schools, with the exception of the North American sample, due to the political problems discussed elsewhere. We have already noted that this was responsible for the difficulty of gaining entry to the schools and

71

TABLE 3.2 *Distribution and types of schools from which children were selected by country*

Schools	Australia	England	N. America	Sweden	Totals
Kindergarten	–	–	–	12	12
Primary/ Elementary	10	9	5	–	24
Comprehensive (Primary and Secondary)	–	–	–	11	11
Secondary	5	4	4	–	13
Totals	15	13	9	23	60

the consequentially less satisfactory nature of the sample. In all four countries all schools used were co-educational.

Selection of geographical areas

One of the thorny problems in cross-cultural sampling is the selection of areas which can be regarded as typical or representative of the countries involved (Brislin *et al.*, 1973). According to orthodox sampling method the sampling to meet this requirement of typicality would be the selection of children in Australia from all six states of the federation, in North America all fifty states of the USA and the ten provinces of Canada, all four countries forming the United Kingdom and all twenty-four counties in Sweden. A national sample should also, theoretically, include a suitable proportion of urban and rural children, and within states, provinces and countries an appropriate 'scatter' of children. This would ensure that all socio-economic groups and, in particular, different ethnic and first generation immigrant groups would be included. An example of an attempt to use a national sampling frame of this rigour can be seen in the latest revision of the Stanford-Binet intelligence scales in the USA. Even here, after the expending of several million dollars, the actual sample achieved falls far short of the ideal. Such an ideal sampling frame was not within our limited time and resources, and it would have required a much larger sample if all the necessary ingredients were to be included. Rigorous sampling was attempted in Husen's (1967) *International Study of Achievement in Mathematics*, which included North America, Australia, England and Sweden but it could not be claimed that with even the most detailed planning and generous financing completely adequate national samples were achieved.

In its place the investigators chose geographical areas which were not untypical and could bear comparison between countries. This may seem a convoluted way of choosing the sample, but it is in fact eminently practicable. For the purpose of controlling the enormous number of variables involved it was decided to exclude country based and inner-city children. Each area selected was urban–suburban, situated near to a large city containing mixed residential socio-economic groups, and within reasonable access of a university to be used as a research base. The following were selected:

Australia	suburbs north of Melbourne city centre and within 24 kilometres (15 miles) of La Trobe University.
England	suburbs within the Reading–Slough conurbations and within 32 kilometres (20 miles) of Reading University.
North America	suburbs in the Buffalo–Niagara area, upper New York State and Ontario Province, Canada, and within 32 kilometres (20 miles) of the State University of New York at Buffalo or Brock University, Ontario.
Sweden	outer suburbs of Stockholm, and within 24 kilometres (15 miles) of Stockholm University. Part of the Swedish 5-year-old sample was taken from a city 80 kilometres (50 miles) west of Stockholm.

It may be argued that these areas are in many ways not typical of the countries involved, and many examples may be cited. When the considerable diversity of North America is considered, for example, the point is well taken. We therefore do not suggest that the samples selected represent national samples, but in claiming that they are not untypical we would argue that they are suitable samples for comparison of Australian, English, North American and Swedish children with certain geographical and ethnic limitations. Such sampling devices have frequently to be used in cross-cultural studies (Price-Williams, 1969).

Political problems in selection

Apart from North America we experienced no problems in approaching administrators and school principals, securing access to schools and gaining the consent of parents through the procedures outlined earlier. On both sides of the Canadian–USA border, despite the continuous efforts of university colleagues to help us make contacts and gain access to schools, we encountered widespread negative attitudes, and considerable opposition. This was so pronounced that after more than a month of fruitless effort, we almost gave up and returned to Britain. However, patient persuasion and persistence succeeded, although the time spent in this process left us less time for the actual interviewing. For this reason the North American sample is the smallest and least satisfactory of the four samples completed.

The overall reason for these difficulties would appear to be the direct political control exercised by elected Boards of Education in the USA, to whom area superintendents of schools are responsible. These Boards are usually composed of lay persons who act as watchdogs, if not leaders, of the community. In Canada committees of professionals, using head teachers, perform this function, and while not as vulnerable as the Boards on the other side of the border, have nevertheless corporate responsibilities and are subject to corporate pressures. By a misfortune of timing, we were trying to gain entry to schools in New York State only a few weeks before the local Boards of Education elections. Administrators were plainly anxious that our project might provide political ammunition during those elections and leave them exposed to public criticism. These anxieties concerned two issues about our project.

The first issue stemmed from an awareness that sexual development was part of our enquiry and, while personally recognising its importance as a research topic, administrators knew it to be, as one put it, 'a red-hot political issue'. While in some parts of the United States sex education has been accepted, the classic case of Anaheim, California, is well known to administrators (see Breasted, 1971; Fraser, 1972). A superintendent of the schools in Anaheim and several teachers had introduced a health and sex curriculum into their schools, having gained the support of the local Board of Education to do so. However, at the next Board of Education election it had become such an issue that vociferous opponents were elected to the Board, who promptly sacked the superintendent and 'offending' teachers. Anaheim, California is famed in educational circles as more than the home of Disneyland. One superintendent said to us he didn't want his home bombed, and another, due to retire shortly, reported that he would not put his pension at risk.

The second issue stemmed from a misunderstanding of what cross-cultural methodology has to ensure. In preliminary discussions with administrators when we outlined the need to control certain variables, it was accepted that like had to be compared with like in each country. Selection of children had to be confined to those speaking the vernacular, the majority indigenous language, and those of similar ethnic, racial and cultural background. Without a large-scale sample, it was impossible to compare differing ethnic and immigrant groups in the four countries chosen. Apart from language problems, how could Indians and Chinese in Canada, Poles and Hispanics in the USA, Pakistanis and Indians in Britain, Greeks, Italians and Turks in Australia, and Yugoslav guest workers in Sweden, be compared with each other? Not to include these and other ethnic groups in our sample on both the USA and Canada was interpreted by some as discriminatory and contrary to human rights. By such arguments research into the characteristics of girls would discriminate against boys; research into working-class characteristics would discriminate against the middle classes; research with the handicapped would discriminate against the healthy. Our concern to ensure no first-generation immigrants and exclude non-vernacular speakers was therefore misinterpreted occasionally and seen as a political issue.

It has been apparent to the authors for some time that worthwhile research in North America is greatly impeded by this kind of political control. Only surveys of the most impersonal kind would seem to be acceptable, and even in these cases records are carefully guarded. Our recent experience confirms this impression and it is our personal view that in particular this kind of political paranoia is disastrous for those who have no say in the matter, the children themselves. This situation accounts for the composition of the North American sample, which led to its being predominantly Canadian children from the southernmost part of Ontario, adjacent to its border with Upper New York State. Although there are historical and subtle cultural differences between the two areas on each side of the border, economically and socially the life-style appears to be almost identical, the same radio and television programmes are experienced by the children, and schooling, in terms of the factors discussed earlier, is similar. Since the total number of children was only 178 from the two areas combined, it was not feasible to break these down into separate USA and Canadian samples since the numbers in each age cohort would be too small for cellular analysis. The 178 children have, therefore, been presented as one North American sample.

Selecting the children

Once access to schools had been agreed, registers were examined so that only the names of children within the age group specified were retained. Then, depending upon the size of school, every second, third or fourth name was selected in strict order. While this is not random but known as systematic sampling, it is thought to be as acceptable as random sampling. After ensuring that only Caucasian children remained on this selected list, the final selection from each school was decided on two criteria. All children had to be living in a two-parent family situation and all children to be interviewed should have at least one younger brother or sister. Despite the large number of divorces and separations in all societies involved, it was felt important to interview children with the best opportunity to observe a parent of each sex at home, to see at first hand a marital relationship and have first hand experience of such

75

a partnership. Surrogate parents and *de facto* relationships were accepted under this category. Screening was assisted by teachers, and by consulting school records when available.

The second criterion to ensure each child interviewed had a younger sibling was again to provide the best possible conditions for children observing and learning about physical development. Such children would have observed a new baby entering the family and both mother and baby undergoing physical changes. This control of birth order and experience has been used in other studies of a similar kind (Bernstein, 1973).

The parents of all children meeting these criteria were then written to and permission to interview requested. The parental refusal rate, as reported earlier, was about 20 per cent, slightly higher with adolescents and varying slightly from school to school. In Sweden the parent refusal rate was about 5 per cent. Acceptances in each school were then examined for father's occupation so that a rough estimate could be made of the socio-economic spread of the sample. Since it was not possible for each interviewer to interview more than eight or at the most nine children in a school day, the selection from the final list tended to eliminate any school bias. Set out in Table 3.3 is the composition of the sample by size of family, birth order, father's occupation and ability estimates. Each variable is analysed and tested to see if there are significant differences between countries and within age cohorts.

TABLE 3.3 *Mean size of family from which children were selected by country*

	Australia	England	North America	Sweden
Mean size of family	3.26	2.80	2.83	2.57
Standard deviation	1.53	1.11	0.98	0.81
Variance	2.35	1.23	0.97	0.66
N	240	240	178	180

When tested by Analysis of Variance for the main effects of country, there were significant differences found between sizes of family in the four countries (with 3 d.f., $F = 13.15$ yielding < 0.001 significance). One would expect such differences to be evident since the average size of families differ from one country's population to another as Table 3.3 indicates. However, an examination of the mean size of family from which the children were selected shows the differences between each country to be minimal, and for the purpose of the research can be accepted as roughly comparable. When tested for differences by age-year the results are again significant (with 5 d.f., $F = 16.12$ yielding

< 0.001 significance). This is not surprising since families which include 5-year-olds who must have at least one younger sibling, will tend to be smaller, and those which include 15-year-olds will tend to be larger. When, however, two-way interactions between countries and age-years are analysed no significant differences are evident (see Appendix A, Tables A.8 and A.9 for statistical details).

When the size of family is classified into small (2 children), medium (3 to 5 children) and large (6 children or more) in Table 3.4 the similarities and differences between the samples are clearer.

TABLE 3.4 *Size of family from which children were selected, in percentages, by country*

Family type	Australia	England	North America	Sweden
Small family (2 children)	31.7%	50.4%	44.9%	58.3%
Medium family (3–5 children)	61.7%	46.2%	52.8%	40.6%
Large family (6 or more children)	6.7%	3.3%	2.2%	1.1%

Family size may affect children's sexual thinking in that varied experiences of children within each family may be reflected. Yet the common factor in all families is that all respondents have at least one younger sibling, and that the family is a stable nuclear family with two parents living together.

As previously noted birth order of the children selected is an important variable. Table 3.5 indicates the differences between the four countries.

TABLE 3.5 *Mean birth order within family of children selected by country*

	Australia	England	North America	Sweden
Mean birth order	1.82	1.47	1.57	1.41
Standard deviation	1.38	0.89	0.86	0.93
Variance	1.90	0.79	0.74	0.86
N	240	240	178	180

Significant differences were found between the distribution of birth order in the family in the samples from the different countries, although these differences are not as high as in those seen in the size of family

77

analysis (with 3 d.f. F = 6.43 yielding < 0.001 significance). Since size of families differs one would expect the distribution of birth order to differ accordingly, since in larger families birth order will tend to be higher and in smaller families will tend to be lower, given the constant of a younger sibling. Examining the mean average birth order for each country reveals that these differences are again minimal and for the purpose of this research can be accepted as roughly comparable. When tested for differences by age-year the results are again significant (where d.f. = 5, F = 16.12 yielding < 0.001). But when two-way interactions between countries and age-years are analysed no significant differences are evident (see Appendix A, tables A.8 and A.9 for statistical details). The vast majority of children in each sample are first born with one younger sibling, the next largest group are second born with one older sibling. Only a small percentage have a higher birth order which can be seen in the detailed Table A.2 in Appendix A. The distribution of children with siblings of the same and opposite sex can be seen in Table 9.1.

To assess the socio-economic status of the families from which children were selected various measures were considered, based upon father's occupation. Although the mother's occupation had been noted in collecting family data, in searching for an international scale of occupations it was evident that the father's occupation yielded a more accurate comparative index of socio-economic status. It was essential to use an indicator which was comparable in all the countries from which the children were drawn. The final choice was the Standard International Occupational and Prestige Scale (Treiman, 1977) known as S.I.O.P.S. Separate prestige scales of occupations exist in the countries sampled, such as Goldthorpe and Hope (1964) in Britain, Congalton (1969) in Australia, and Duncan (1961) in the United States. The S.I.O.P.S. as devised by Treiman is based upon a large number of countries, including all those used in this study, and its validity is reasonably authenticated. The scale has a range of 90 points, with a score provided for each occupation. A gas meter reader, for example, was classified as 21, a customs inspector as 44, a primary schoolteacher as 57, and a physician as 78. The occupations listed in our study ranged from score 13 to score 78, with the objective of averaging a score of 46 for the sample from each country. The mean scores achieved can be seen in Table 3.6. It will be seen that the target of a mean score of 46 has been almost achieved, and while analysis of variance reveals significant differences (where d.f. = 3, F = 5.89 yielding < 0.001 significance) the mean scores in each country show these to be minimal, and are sufficiently comparable for the purpose of this study. In a three-way analysis of variance, by country the differences are significant (where d.f. = 3, F = 5.93 yielding < 0.001 significance),

TABLE 3.6 *Mean scores of father's occupation of children by country*

	Australia	England	North America	Sweden
Mean average score				
SIOPS	47.31	47.71	43.25	45.74
Standard deviation	11.97	11.49	10.44	12.85
Variance	143.19	131.96	109.07	165.04
N	240	240	178	180

(A more detailed analysis, by country, sex, age group and totals can be seen in Appendix A, Tables A.3 and A.4.)

but by age-year, and by two-way interaction between country and age-years, the differences are not significant. This would suggest that in terms of socio-economic status, as measured by father's occupation, the samples from the different countries are reasonably comparable.

Since ability and thinking levels are closely associated, estimates of the children's abilities as a five point scale ('well below average' to 'well above average') were requested from their teachers. Although standardised ability or intelligence tests are currently in use in many of the schools sampled, there were no tests yielding similar measures available for all of the age groups, and these certainly differed from country to country. Teachers' estimates of ability were therefore used, except in the case of Swedish five-year-olds who were not part of the compulsory school system. Swedish pre-school teachers generally felt unable to make such estimates.

TABLE 3.7 *Mean average ability of students as assessed by teacher's estimates by country*

	Australia	England	North America	Sweden
Mean estimated ability	3.31	3.32	3.40	2.76
Standard deviation	0.88	0.95	0.96	1.47
Variance	0.77	0.91	0.92	2.18
N	240	240	178	180

(A more detailed analysis of ability by sex and age year can be seen in Appendix A, Table A.7.)

Analysis of variance testing for main effects of country yielded significant differences (where d.f. = 3, F = 14.41, yielding < 0.001 significance). A three-way analysis of variance by country, age-year and

79

two-way interaction between them yielded similar differences. Even so, in terms of ability as measured by teachers' estimates, the samples of each country can be treated as roughly comparable with each other. This result is surprising since all teachers were using standardised categories as defined by themselves, within one country, by criteria assumed to be 'average', 'below-' and 'above average', and 'well below-' and 'well above average'. When separated from Sweden the results of the three countries combined on ability were not significant.

Overall then, controlling the samples for ability appeared to be most successful, and for socio-economic status was reasonably successful. Since mean size of families varied somewhat in each country and this also affects birth order, controlling for family size and birth order was less successful. However, a detailed examination of the results (see Appendix A, Tables A.1–A.6) reveal the differences to be minimal, making comparisons between countries and across age-years to be reasonably valid.

Scoring and evaluation procedures

Once the interviews were completed, all responses except a few which were qualitative were scored on previously constructed criteria based on a numerical hierarchy. Sometimes the categories forming the criteria had to be altered, extended or refined. Scoring ranged from a 0 to 3 point scale to as high as 0 to 14. All the Piagetian items were scored on a 5 or 6 point scale, depending on the nature of the subject discussed with the child. Details of the criteria are described as each series of items is presented, chapter by chapter.

The development of criteria for each item was a complex and time-consuming task, since most scales, apart from the Piagetian items, had to be constructed without reference to previous work. The item on origin of babies for example, was scored on a modified scale used by Anne Bernstein (1973), and one item on the wearing of clothes was scored on a modified combination of Kohlberg's and Piaget's criteria (Kohlberg, 1969). Even so, many Piagetian scales dealing with physical causality and other specific scientific topics were not suitable for adaptation to biological and sexual topics. Many items were scored on what we termed 'biological realism' scales, constructed by asking biologists to examine, and correct where necessary, statements of a factual non-technical descriptive type extracted and paraphrased from textbooks on human biology (see Appendix C). Yet other items scored in terms of social realism, 'Why do people get married?' for example, had no criteria of this kind upon which to construct a hierarchical scale.

The scoring was done by two independent scorers on the agreed criteria. Scores were then correlated and scorer reliability was found to be at satisfactory levels, only one or two as low as 0.75, most being at 0.80 and 0.90 levels. Examples of these correlations may be seen in Appendix A, Table A.7. To decide the final scores for a child, one scorer kept the allocated scores constant, but adjusted to a middle score where two or more points' discrepancy occurred. Scores of individual items were transferred to individual children's score sheets and then card-punched for analysis by an SPSS computer programme. Details regarding the statistical formulae and techniques used to evaluate the significance of the data can be read in Appendices A, B, and D.

Apart from problems of scoring children's responses from an interview situation two further problems have to be faced. One is how authentic the children's responses are, in that children may be supplying only answers calculated to please the adult, and particularly where sexual matters are concerned providing 'expected' answers. The question of deception was faced when constructing the interview content, as had been faced in earlier work, based upon a similar interview method, in the investigation of children's religious thinking. Children were assured at the beginning of their interview that it was not a test of any kind ('There are no right or wrong answers') and assurances given that the interviewers were genuinely interested in what the children thought. The probing follow-up questions also appeared to penetrate glib and deceptive answers, forcing the child to think further. When the layers of thought and reasoning are uncovered it is very difficult for a child to sustain an answer which is not genuinely his or her own. In an early publication Piaget (1926) described five types of answers children tend to give in a clinical interview situation. These are random answers, romancing answers, suggested conviction answers, liberated conviction answers and spontaneous conviction answers. The last two types are the aim of interviewers, to liberate ideas already thought through by the child, or to provoke spontaneous thought about a problem faced by a child for the first time. Unmotivated children or those who cannot comprehend the question tend to give random answers or answers quickly given as mere word association. The problem is to motivate such children or restate the question in terms they can understand. The romantic and suggested conviction answers are the deceptive ones, and the two factors mentioned above, the establishment of good rapport and follow-up probing discussion, appear to be adequate to overcome this problem.

Piaget (1929) pointed out in *The Child's Conception of the World* that 'if all the children of the same mental age arrive at the same conception of a given phenomenon, in defiance of the variations in their personal circumstances, their experience and the conversation they have overheard etc., this may be regarded as a prime guarantee of the originality of the conviction'. This statement needs modifying somewhat but its general meaning would appear to be valid in our experience. After so much work on cognition based upon clinical interviews few critics would dismiss the results on these grounds.

More cogent is the second problem, namely, how can we be sure what is scored is sexual thinking and not verbal ability or language facility? Ruth Beard, in discussing this problem in relation to Piaget-type interview methods, states (Beard, 1960),

> In recognising the existence of other conceptual schemas than verbal ones the importance of verbal concepts should not be under-estimated. The child's ultimate representation of the world is in the form, chiefly, of verbal concepts and these can be examined through social interaction . . . it *is through verbal concepts that the child builds an accurate picture of his environment* [our italics].

There does appear to be a growth of verbal ability, and the linguistic skill to express it, inter-relating intelligence and concept formation. Our assumption is, and appears to be verified by our analysis of children's sexual vocabulary (see chapter 16), that in the realm of sexual thinking, levels of understanding and the ability to verbalise them will tend to interpenetrate each other. We found that children often used inappropriate names, substituting pseudonyms for taboo words, but the meaning was invariably clear. It was this meaning that was scored, not the verbalism nor the fluency, and the criteria used were based upon this assumption.

Finally, the technical question of validity is an important one to examine in relation to our project, that is the degree to which our instrument, the interview schedule used, actually measures what it claims to measure. Most of the types of validity described in manuals of research such as content, predictive, concurrent and construct validity refer basically to testing instruments, such as intelligence and math-ematical tests. Two indicators of validity were evident in this study. The first was in several items in our interview where previous investi-gations had been made, for example, 'What is the origin of Babies' (Bernstein, 1973) in the USA, and 'Sources of Sex Information' (Farrell, 1978) in Britain indicated a similar range of responses, irrespective of different sampling frames. The second is a type of internal validity, when the six Piagetian scaled items, the six biological realism scaled items and the ten sexual vocabulary items were each combined, they yielded high reliability coefficients, as can be seen in Tables 3.8 to 3.10. The alpha coefficient used is a measure of that aspect of reliability known as 'internal consistency', indicating the extent to which the items making up the scale 'hang together'. A high coefficient of internal consistency means that different selections of items yield essentially similar scores.

TABLE 3.8 *Combined Piagetian scaled items, mean scores and alpha coefficients (six items)*

	Australia	England	North America	Sweden
Mean scores	10.73	10.51	11.15	10.93
Alpha coefficients	0.82	0.82	0.83	0.78

The six items in Table 3.8 included in the combined scales, reasons for choice of 'the best time to be alive', reasons for why people marry, the origin of babies, explaining gestation processes, reasons for wearing clothes and explanations of why people may be embarrassed at nakedness.

TABLE 3.9 *Combined biological realism scaled items, mean scores and alpha coefficients (six items)*

	Australia	England	North America	Sweden
Mean scores	18.81	18.60	18.31	20.03
Alpha coefficients	0.86	0.86	0.87	0.87

The six items in Table 3.9 were body differences during adolescence, body differences at birth, origin of babies, birth exit, reasons for birth and the gestation process.

TABLE 3.10 *Combined sexual vocabulary mean scores and alpha coefficients (ten items)*

	Australia	England	North America	Sweden
Mean score	23.38	23.34	22.69	25.93
Alpha coefficients	0.96	0.96	0.96	0.96

The ten items in Table 3.10 were explanations of the meanings of the words pregnancy, conception, stripping, rape, venereal disease, uterus, puberty, virgin, abortion and contraception. Further details regarding all the combined scales can be read in the first section of chapter 17.

The universally high alpha coefficients and their comparative similarity across all samples would argue for the internal consistency of items and for predictive and construct validity of a high order. These combined scales across all countries will be analysed later in terms of age cohort sequences. They would appear to support the instrument as a valid inventory for assessing children's sexual thinking. It should be recognised that one reason for the high coefficients is the extremely heterogeneous nature of the sample in terms of age span, 5 to 15 years, and that within a single age group the coefficients would inevitably be smaller.

In the following chapters details of respondents replies given are authentic, the responses quoted being taken verbatim from the written transcript of the interviews. No names of respondents will be used nor are schools identified.

A note on statistics used

Statistical analysis of the data yielded by the investigation has been kept as simple as possible. Because the number of subjects in various age cohorts in each country varies somewhat, the general results are reported in terms of percentage, so that valid comparisons may be made. Mean scores are also presented and, where suitable, their visual equivalent in the form of graphs. Chi-square and t-tests have been used to test for significant sex differences, and analyses of variance were applied to test the validity of the sample, and to certain 'global' combined scales reported in the final chapter. An example is the testing for the effects of the major independent variables (see Table 17.4). Two- and three-way analyses of variance were applied to most individual items. These are reported in various journal articles (see Bibliography) and also in tabular form in Appendix D.

Summary and discussion

The aims of the research were to measure the extent of children's sexual knowledge, to discover if there were detectable sequences and stages in their sexual thinking and what processes of thought they used to describe the biological functions of their bodies. Piagetian, Freudian, and Kohlberg's criteria were used to test their cognitive theories in various areas. Beginning in 1978 a series of trial discussions was held with Australian children as a basis for constructing an interview schedule suitable for children aged 5 to 15 years. A face-to-face individual clinical interview was then devised to apply to 5, 7, 9, 11, 13 and 15 year olds, refined and revised after several further trials.

The content of the interview schedule, administered in Australia, England and North America by the two authors, was designed to cover six clearly defined areas. The first was ageing and what was the best time to be alive in the human life sequence. The second concerned parents, their identity and roles as mothers and fathers, and as women and men. The third covered how children perceived sex differences in the newborn and during puberty, and surveyed children's sex preferences.

The fourth area explored was the origin of babies, the role of mothers and fathers in procreation, gestation, birth and related processes, including the area of 'not having babies'. The fifth examined children's ideas about sex education both at home and school, and the sixth area concerned clothes and nakedness. In addition children were asked to define the meaning of the words on a sexual vocabulary list.

Apart from the vocabulary. list towards the end of the interview, no sexual words were used by the interviewers, only the terms introduced by the children themselves. Sixty-three major questions were asked, about one-third of these contingent upon answers of a certain kind being received first.

The study may be described as a cross-national descriptive study of children's sexual thinking from 5 to 15 years, based upon regional clusters of schools, stratified for socio-economic status and other factors, and within schools systematic sampling from class lists of children who met the required criteria.

The English-speaking countries in addition to Australia – England and North America – were chosen as those providing educational models for Australian educators. Sweden was added as a contrast, being the only country having compulsory sex education for all children from the age of 8 years. All countries could be described as modern Western-type industrialised democratic societies, sharing similar education systems and assumptions. Interviews in Sweden were conducted in Swedish by man and woman teams, trained by the authors for the purpose. The interview schedule was translated into Swedish and back-translated for checking accuracy; all Swedish children's scripts were translated from Swedish into English. Scoring was done by two scorers working independently, using agreed criteria based upon Piaget's operational schema, Kohlberg's stages of moral cognition, and on biological realism scales devised with the assistance of several biologists and psychologists.

It is not claimed that national samples, in the strict sense of that term, are used, but rather descriptive samples of child populations not untypical of the countries involved. The geographical areas were urban-suburban of no less than 100,000 population in or bordering upon a large university town. The universities used as a base were La Trobe University, Melbourne, Australia; Reading University in Berkshire, England; The State University of New York at Buffalo, Upper New York State, USA; Brock University, Ontario, in Canada; and Stockholm University, in Sweden. Because of difficulties in gaining access to state schools in the USA some Canadian schools were used, the two being merged to form a North American sample. All children in every country came from co-educational state schools, except in the case of Swedish five-year-olds who were selected from co-educational kindergartens.

Each sample was controlled for socio-economic status, sex distribution, ability, birth order, a nuclear intact family and presence of at least one sibling younger than the respondent. This represented the best possible conditions for children to learn about their own bodies, the arrival of a new baby and the built-in psychosexual learning opportunities present in such a situation. Written parental permission was obtained for all children participating, a refusal rate of 20 per cent being average. Certain statistically significant differences were measured when samples were compared. A detailed examination of the results reveal such differences to be minimal, making comparisons between countries and across age years reasonably valid. The internal consistency of items and predictive and construct validity were of a high order, and appear to support the instrument as a valid inventory for assessing children's sexual thinking.

4 The ageing process

The first two sections of the interview schedule covered a series of questions on the ageing process, how children perceive and explain old age, and their choice of the best age to be alive, that is, how children perceive a particular stage of life as desirable or not. These sections were designed with two purposes in mind. One purpose was to use them to explore topics with the children to serve as a 'warming up' process. These areas were seen to be safer and would invoke less inhibitions than overt or even peripheral sexual areas. The second purpose was to explore the contents of the two opening sections as developmentally important in their own right. They do, in fact, cast some light on insights and lack of insights into sexuality at various stages of life. However, no overt questions about sexuality were asked about the ageing process since the children gave open-ended responses, in which sexuality was mentioned by them or ignored. This chapter outlines the first section on how children perceive, conceptualise and explain the ageing process.

Research into ageing is a comparatively new area, reflecting changing demographic trends in Western-type societies, where the aged are becoming a larger proportion of many populations, due to a declining birth-rate and increased longevity, the latter being a product of improved medical techniques, health services, dietary habits and other factors and the former due to the availability and increased reliability of contraceptives. In Australia, for example, the aged population has doubled since the turn of the century from 4 per cent to 8.5 per cent (Pollard, 1970) with much higher increases projected in the next decade to 12 per cent (Sax, 1979). Research into ageing generally covers medical, sociological, psychological and political aspects of the subject. For the purpose of this study our interest focussed upon how children regard the ageing process. Kahana and Kahana (1970) was one of the few studies to

87

explore how children's perceptions of grandparents changed as the children increased in age. The majority of studies have centred on the influence of children's literature in providing poor stereotypes of old people as living limited social lives (Barnum, 1977) as in 'the rocking chair syndrome' (Ansello, 1978) or as non-active beings (Storey, 1977).

Ahammer and Baltes's work (1972) was the first research in Australia to compare how adolescents, adults and older people view themselves and each other. This was followed up by a later study (Ahammer and Bennett, 1977). The first study revealed that on six of the ten dimensions used as indices, the aged were perceived in less desirable terms. The later study used more open-ended methods by asking university students and trainee nurses to list the five most typical characteristics of 'old people'. The results supported the first study. The majority of characteristics attributed to the aged were negative and most were related to a biologically-based decline model.

In our own study we adopted Ahammer's open-ended approach to determine what children at varying ages thought about old age. Bearing in mind that the youngest respondents were only 5 years old, the exploration of ageing was divided into three parts: What age has a person to be before you call them 'very old'? What happens to people when they get very old? What makes people get very old? In trial interviews it was found that 'very old' was better than simply 'old', since younger children often regarded teenagers as old, so the adverbial form was used to emphasise it was older adults they were to consider. Even so, a proportion of the younger children still gave low age estimates in answer to the first question. We have noted elsewhere research (Ames, 1946) on the difficulties children have in developing a sense of time, not only in 'telling the time' but in their perception of personal time, what age signifies, and how long a year, ten years or a century may be. The results of the three questions are set out in turn separately below.

'What age has a person to be before you call them "very old"?'

Respondents were asked to give a specific numerical age in answer to the question, and with few exceptions a specific age was given. Some of the younger children, perhaps because it was the first question and because they needed encouragement, had to be asked, 'Do you have a grandma (granny) or grandpa (grandpop)?' and, 'Are they very old?' and 'How old do you think your grandma (grandpa) is?' This was also a useful ploy in the next question about what happens to old people when they become old. Table 4.1 shows the percentages of children in Australia responding in terms of specific age groups. Since a definition of 'very old' in terms of longevity is relative it was decided to define 'very old' arbitrarily for evaluation purposes as 60+ years. This is the

TABLE 4.1 *Australian children's estimates of 'very old' in percentages (N = 240)*

Age-year	Up to 19	20–39	40–59	60–79	80–99+
5	28	25	15	15	17
7	0	12	35	38	15
9	0	15	30	30	25
11	3	5	25	47	20
13	3	7	27	43	20
15	3	3	7	72	15

age and shortly afterwards when most people retire, qualify for some kind of pension or 'senior citizen' status. Ages estimated up to 39 years were classified as 'unrealistic', from 40 to 59 years as 'semi-realistic' and 60 upwards as 'realistic'. These definitions are assumed in all subsequent discussions. It will be seen in Table 4.1 that Australian children develop from unrealistic estimates to more realistic estimates with increasing years, a high proportion at 5 years old being unrealistic. The younger the children the older any other person may appear relative to their limited experience and perception. It is not surprising therefore to find Australian children reflecting a growing realism in estimating old age. The percentage of 5-year-olds with 'realistic' estimates is slightly inflated by about 10 per cent of them talking in terms of 'hundreds of years old', Merlin-type stereotypes being as unrealistic as those at the opposite end of the scale.

TABLE 4.2 *English children's estimates of 'very old' in percentages (N = 240)*

Age-year	Up to 19	20–39	40–59	60–79	80–99+
5	30	33	13	10	14
7	0	15	25	27	33
9	0	3	17	45	35
11	0	0	10	65	25
13	0	0	10	55	35
15	0	0	3	67	30

The figures for England in Table 4.2 are similar in general age group trends to Australia although the 5-year-olds are more prone to be unrealistic in their estimates. At the same time from 9 years onwards estimates of the English children are likely to be more realistic. This may reflect the more widely publicised health and welfare services for older age groups to be found in England.

The same pattern is perceptible with the North American children in Table 4.3, the figures in the 80–99+ at 5 years again inflated by unrealistic estimates of well over the century figure. By 9 years of age a majority have gained a realistic view although 23 per cent still think of 80 years or more. In all, the Australia, English and North American children show very similar patterns in defining old age in specific ages.

TABLE 4.3 *North American children's estimates of 'very old' in percentages (N = 178)*

Age-year	Up to 19	20–39	40–59	60–79	80–99+
5	50	25	8	0	17
7	0	23	23	30	23
9	0	3	27	47	23
11	0	3	13	60	23
13	0	0	9	49	42
15	0	0	6	71	23

TABLE 4.4 *Swedish children's estimates of 'very old' in percentages (N = 180)*

Age-year	Up to 19	20–39	40–59	60–79	80–99+
5	26	23	10	3	37
7	0	0	13	40	47
9	0	0	7	50	43
11	3	0	33	17	47
13	0	0	3	33	64
15	3	0	7	33	57

The Swedish pattern as shown in Table 4.4 is a little different, it being noticeable that the 80-99+ group at 5 years is not as inflated with unrealistic Merlin-type suggestions as in the other countries. But the major difference is a slight number in the 60-79 column from 11 years compared with the other countries and the corresponding increase in the 80-99+ column. We would postulate that differing cultural factors in Swedish society may cause children and particularly teenagers to see the 60s as still young enough not to be regarded as 'very old'. Certainly the largest percentages are in the 'oldest' column after 11 years of age.

The Swedish disparity is still evident, when the mean age is calculated for each country as can be seen in Table 4.5. The Swedish children moving up to 75 as early as 7 years and maintaining that level from then onwards. The boys and girls in Sweden are relatively similar in their assessments but in some other countries there is a wide disparity between the sexes. For example, Australian 9-year-old boys assess old age on average at 48, whilst the girls of that age assess it at 71, and

TABLE 4.5 *Mean average age estimated as very old in all countries by age group (N = 838)*

Age-year	Australia	England	North America	Sweden
5	46	40	39	51
7	59	64	60	75
9	60	68	66	76
11	61	69	66	67
13	59	70	70	80
15	65	70	69	76

13-year-old Australian boys give a relatively low age of 55. Perhaps this is an illustration of girls' earlier social maturity and greater sensitivity in these matters.

The figures for Sweden are again earlier and higher when all percentages of children in the two categories of 60 to 99+ are added together (Table 4.6). The exception is the Swedish 11-year-olds largely due to a curious 33 per cent who assessed old age between 40 and 59. What, however, is most noticeable is that after 5 years the proportion of Australian children falls well below other countries, in most comparable age cohorts, largely but not entirely due to the lower percentage of boys perceiving old age realistically.

TABLE 4.6 *Percentage of children with realistic estimates of 'very old' as 60 years and upwards in all countries by age-year (N = 838)*

Age-year	Australia	England	North America	Sweden
5	33	25	17	40
7	53	61	54	87
9	55	80	71	93
11	68	90	84	64
13	63	98	91	97
15	88	98	94	90

It would appear to us that the older a person has to be before being viewed as 'very old' is an indicator of how realistically and maturely that society views old age. A recognition by a society of the retention of activity, interests and health by vast numbers of those well over 60 would be a pointer to the aged being accepted and respected, rather than rejected or seen as second class citizens. Unfortunately, the next section indicates the latter.

'What happens to people when they become very old?'

This second question is phrased in deliberately neutral terms to see if the children perceive old age in predominantly negative or positive ways. Since the trial interviews indicated an overwhelming biologically based decline model as the likely norm (Ahammer and Bennett, 1977), it was tempting to have added 'Are any things better in old age?', but this was rejected as too suggestive. Contingent questions were asked if positive responses about greater maturity, wisdom or experience were made. However, these positivisms were so few that the replies made no real difference to the final result.

Positive responses were calculated by noting every reply which indicated some kind of appreciation of the benefits or rewards to be enjoyed by old people, or those associating with them. Naturally, younger children spending perhaps more time with a grandparent see positive features in egocentric or hedonistic terms. 'They are nice and kind to me' (Australian girl, 5 years); 'They give me lollies and toys' (English boy, 5 years); 'They take me walks in the park' (English girl, 5 years); 'They are friendlier' (North American girl, 7 years); 'They're nicer and understand me more' (North American girl, 7 years); 'They've learned more, because they've been around a long time' (Australian boy, 7 years); 'They get smarter' (North American boy, 9 years); 'They know more' (English girl, 9 years); 'They are easier to talk to' (Australian girl, 9 years); 'They are more generous' (English girl, 11 years); 'They start giving things away because they're going to die' (English boy, 11 years); 'They're nicer to young people' (Australian girl, 11 years). Counted as positive, because it was usually voiced as of greater convenience, was the response 'Women stop their periods', a response made by both boys and girls at 13 years. The distribution of children revealing any kind of positive insight into old age can be seen in Table 4.7.

TABLE 4.7 *Percentage of children describing old age in positive terms all countries and by age-group (N = 838)*

Age-year	Australia	England	North America	Sweden
5	20	25	21	20
7	5	10	13	3
9	8	5	17	10
11	18	8	7	23
13	15	10	27	7
15	20	5	36	20

These percentages of children viewing old age positively are very small. The 5-year-olds, for reasons suggested above, view old age more positively in all countries. A decline appears then to take place until 9 years in

Australia, Sweden and America. In England positive comments continue
to decrease including 15-year-olds (a mere 5 per cent). In North America
it rises to 36 per cent of the 15-year-olds viewing old age positively,
having maintained more positive comments than other countries
except for a dip at 11 years (only 7 per cent). It is important to note
that interest in old age and provision for senior citizens is probably of
longer standing and achieves wider publicity in Canada and the USA
than in other countries over the last ten years or so. Most research into
gerontology is American-initiated and practically all specialised journals
devoted to this topic are American-based. Senior citizens in the USA in
certain areas appear to be politically active, often called 'Grey Power'
and therefore visible, on behalf of the aged. This may in part account
for a more positive, and possibly a more sympathetic view of old age
among the North American 15-year-olds.

Negative descriptions of old age, however, are universal. Only a tiny
proportion of children at the younger age of 5 years (3 per cent in
Australia, and 8 per cent in North America) did not cite at least one
negativism. The overall picture tends to be one of unrelieved gloom —
death, decay, disease, broken bones; increasing illness and accident
proneness; irritability, senility and loneliness are seen to be the major
characteristics. This can be observed quite dramatically in Table 4.8.

TABLE 4.8 *Percentage of children describing old age in negative terms
each using between three and nine negative descriptions
all countries and by age groups (N = 838)*

Age-year	Australia	England	North America	Sweden
5	45	48	48	77
7	75	85	60	57
9	90	93	60	83
11	95	95	93	90
13	93	88	91	83
15	98	100	90	93

There is a remarkable consistency across all countries. Negativisms
increasing sharply from 7 years upwards with the exception of Swedish
and North American children who do not reach 90 per cent or over
until 11 years of age. The figures do not convey the revulsion and often
disgust expressed about old age by many children of all ages. Descriptions
of wrinkled skin, sickness, feebleness and increasing fragility were often
accompanied by grimaces and emotional negativisms. One Swedish
boy (15 years) commented, 'My grandparents are only a little old, but
they look angry in their faces all the time'. Said a North American girl
(15 years), 'Slowly they get sicker, they slowly deteriorate. They lose

93

their memory, they lose their intelligence to a degree, they become nervous and worry about little things.' An Australian boy (15 years): 'They get less agile, and are not as fit or as strong as they used to be. Sometimes they go mentally ill like my grandma. She forgets.'

Children's views of physical characteristics of old age

The responses of the children were also classified in terms of their content, tabulations being made of physical, psychological, social-economic and sexual descriptions. In these tabulations all responses of a positive and negative type were included together. Physical descriptions, largely negative, included all forms of physical deterioration of skin, bones, posture, hearing and sight; all forms of sickness, mainly rheumatism, arthritis and heart trouble; difficulties in running, walking, crossing roads, poor eating habits, and death and burial. Upwards of 94 per cent of all children at all ages in all countries made at least one reference to these physical characteristics, overwhelmingly negative in their responses.

Children's views of psychological characteristics of old age

The psychological characteristics of old age included senility in all its forms of forgetfulness, poor concentration and deteriorating thinking powers. Increasing moodiness, bad temper, impatience, inability to cope with stress and failure 'to keep up with the times' were also voiced. For example, 'They are slower to understand. Their ability to react deteriorates', said a Swedish girl (15 years). The few positive descriptions tabulated under 'psychological' described increasing wisdom, confidence, patience and friendliness. 'They are wiser,' says one Australian boy (15 years), 'They try to help out the younger generation from their experience and try to put them on the right lines.' Kindness was the most frequent positive psychological characteristic noted by younger children of 5 and 7 years. The increasing perceptiveness of children with increasing age in this category can be seen in Table 4.9. Social development is a process of widening social experience and it can be expected that social judgment of other people, particularly older age groups, should become increasingly perceptive. Physical characteristics are relatively easy to identify, but psychological characteristics, as inferred from the observed behaviour of the old, are not. Curiously, the English children appear to be slower in these perceptions than their peers in the other countries, as well as describing old age in less positive terms (see Table 4.7).

TABLE 4.9 *Percentage of children describing psychological characteristics of old age in all countries by age year (N = 838)*

Age-year	Australia	England	North America	Sweden
5	0	5	0	13
7	8	5	3	10
9	10	5	20	10
11	25	15	20	27
13	28	25	46	30
15	55	33	55	50

Children's views of social and economic characteristics of old age

Social-economic characteristics were tabulated by including all responses which indicated increasing isolation, such as going to bed early, friends dying off, becoming more withdrawn, not going out as much; and increasing dependence on others such as having to live in special homes and an inability to live alone. Changed work and leisure patterns were noted, sometimes positively as releasing people for more time to read, to garden and to watch television. Generally, old age is seen as financially restrictive because of the need to live on a limited income. The younger children tend to make more positive social descriptions, such as grandparents having more time to play and go for walks in the park. Perceptions of social-economic characteristics do increase with age particularly at the 15-year-old level, as Table 4.10 indicates. Again in terms of social consequences children appear to be more perceptive earlier than of economic consequences simply because they would be more obvious, as observed social concomitants of old age at an earlier time. The economic descriptions are mainly those of older children from 13 years onwards. There are no clear patterns observable in the different countries in this category.

TABLE 4.10 *Percentage of children describing social-economic characteristics of old age in all countries by age-year (N = 838)*

Age-year	Australia	England	North America	Sweden
5	15	15	21	20
7	25	33	20	30
9	30	33	27	27
11	35	33	40	40
13	28	33	36	20
15	38	45	52	40

Children's views of sexual characteristics of old age

Sexual characteristics of old age were tabulated from responses which mentioned old women's increasing inability to have babies, to cease menstruation and for their breasts to sag or shrivel. Not surprisingly, most of these characteristics were voiced by girls. In both sexes an occasional reference was made to the diminishing sex urge or its extinction ('You don't have the sex urge any more', said an Australian boy, 15 years) and to the increasing role, occasionally described as enjoyable, of grandparenting. Over the whole sample only about 4 per cent of children in each country made sexual types of responses, the greatest number occurring amongst the teenagers. For this reason Table 4.11 tabulates only the percentages of sexual descriptions made by 13- and 15-year-olds. The recognition of sexual characteristics of the aged, although negative and misinformed, by such a small percentage would appear to indicate the association of sexual activity with mainly younger groups, children being reluctant to acknowledge it even in their parents, a much younger age group (SEICUS, 1970; Bell, 1966; Pocs and Godow, 1977). What is surprising in Sweden, with a universal sex education system, is that the figures are so low. Does the Swedish syllabus include the topic of the sexual activity of older people? Whatever the reasons, in most countries the combination of sexual taboos and ageing and death taboos (see discussion at the end of this chapter) would appear to inhibit any perception of the effect of ageing upon sexuality (Golde and Kogan, 1959). In addition it should be noted that sexuality is comparatively 'invisible' behaviourally in a way that psychological, social and economic characteristics and their effects are not.

TABLE 4.11 *Percentages of 13 and 15 year olds describing sexual characteristics of old age (N = 284)*

Age-year	Australia	England	North America	Sweden
13	8	10	0	0
15	13	8	7	3

The causes of ageing

To ascertain children's explanations of the ageing process the question was asked, 'What makes people very old?' and to make it explicit, illustrations from the child's previous responses were often used, such as 'Why is it old people get wrinkled skin, get ill more easily or have to stop work?' The question was put in this form rather than 'What are the causes of ageing?' since trial discussions revealed only older children from 11 or even 13 years upwards could comprehend the question in that form. Causation as a concept requires operational levels of intelligence, probably at the formal level, or at least transitional to formal operations (Piaget, 1951), and certainly the term 'cause' or 'causation' is not understood by young children.

As a guide to developing criteria for scoring the responses of the children, several university biologists were asked to comment on descriptions of the ageing process derived from two major authors. The descriptions were modified in the light of their comments and used as supplementary materials in determining a hierarchy of categories (see Appendix B) to which scores 0 to 6 were allocated. Thus a scale was devised which moved from simplistic answers to more complex responses based upon two categories, Piaget's operational thinking and biological accuracy or realism. Initially, two separate scales were devised but in the event they so closely approximated, with only minor discrepancies, only one was used. The Piagetian criteria formed the framework of the scale and the biological realism scale was placed alongside it as an illustrative hierarchy, as set out in Table 4.12.

It might be argued that the form of the question, 'What makes people very old?' invites a low scoring 'time causality' answer. However, the supplementary questions clarified the point of the exploration and children of all ages were pressed to explain the reasons for the overall deterioration they had previously illustrated. It is obvious from the results in Table 4.13 that children found the question extremely difficult, only a few (a total of 8) in the whole sample achieving the highest level of formal operations and full biological accuracy score of five. There appeared to be an almost universal retardation in relation to explaining the ageing process at the pre-operational level by the age of 13 years. Due to the only major translation error, which rendered the item invalid for the Swedish sample, Swedish responses and their scores are not included in the results.

In the three countries scored the results indicate a very poor understanding of senescence and its developmental place in the human life cycle. The lack of high scores might be explained by questioning the reliability of the item, since it does not scale in the expected manner and is atypical when compared with other Piaget-scored items. It does, however, scale in observable hierarchical stages indicating the diminishing frequency of score 1 ('time causality' thinking) with increasing age. There are two other possible explanations. The first is that the task is intrinsically difficult, in that no concrete or visual causative factors are seen to be at work in ageing, other than the external symptoms. If this were so, it would illustrate that regressive thinking has occurred where the task is too difficult. The second explanation would appear when joined to the first explanation, to support this viewpoint. The authors, when searching for definitive statements in biology textbooks to

TABLE 4.12 *Criteria for scoring 'causes of the ageing process' scale*

Piagetian level	Score	Piagetian description	Biological realism
Pre-operations	0	Nonsense replies, no response.	Don't know.
	1	*Time Causality* – no recognition of causality other than time.	Having birthdays; growing; getting older. Repeats proposition or symptoms of old age.
	2	*Artificialisms* – natural or theological artificialism. Includes finalisms.	Nature of God's will. It's always that way. It's automatic.
Transitional	3	*Transitional* – technically feasible explanations to child but inaccurate. Physical and psychological explanations not quite operational, nor co-ordinated.	Weather wrinkles the skin. Not eating enough food. Wearing out concepts; too much work. Death seen as near but not life-death sequence.
Concrete operational	4	*Physical and Psychological explanations* – physical causes are feasible. Explanations concrete and operational. Psychological causes are feasible but not peculiar to senescence. Explanations concrete and operational. Demographic explanations.	Internal organs deteriorate but no further causes given. The body deteriorates but no recognition of irreversibilities. Inherited defects. They think or feel older, only see older friends. Lack of exercise; worry and stress; smoking and alcohol. Necessary to avoid over-population.
Transitional	5	*Transitional Physicalisms* – incomplete formal propositions on physical causes. Life-death sequence co-ordinated. Reasonable descriptions of senescence.	Emphasis upon cells, hormones, blood, not upon essential organs. Irreversible body changes perceived.
Formal operational	6	*Physicalisms freed from limitations* – formal propositional thinking. Processes perceived accurately in terms of cause and effect.	At least one example of internal causes for irreversible change. Failure of cells or tissues to rebuild. Beginnings of an adequate scientific theory.

TABLE 4.13 *Percentages of children's scores on the 'causes of ageing' scale (1–6) by age-year, 3 countries only (N = 658)*

Age-year	Australia						England						North America					
	1	2	3	4	5	6	1	2	3	4	5	6	1	2	3	4	5	6
5	50	5	7	3	—	—	50	15	15	—	—	—	33	13	8	—	—	—
7	52	3	28	7	—	—	52	3	38	—	—	3	50	7	27	—	—	—
9	33	7	42	15	3	—	28	5	30	15	5	3	37	3	27	23	—	—
11	18	—	36	40	—	—	18	3	47	18	5	—	23	—	40	23	13	—
13	13	—	43	33	3	—	15	8	27	28	13	5	3	6	36	43	9	—
15	7	3	27	48	10	3	15	8	25	35	10	5	19	—	29	39	6	3

(Zero scores are not included.)

describe senescence and, in particular, to elucidate the causes of ageing, had great difficulty in discovering any teaching materials at all. In textbooks for children, high school and university students, which provide materials on the origins of life, and the conception, birth and development of living organisms, humans included, there was an almost universal absence of material concerning the deterioration of life. It occurred to us that this dearth of teaching material amounted almost to a taboo on the subjects of senescence and death, reflecting similar taboos in society at large. Indeed, we found it very hard to discover teachers in several universities who both specialised in human biology, and were also acquainted with current theories of ageing. If the paucity of materials, lack of coverage in school syllabuses, and social taboos on the topic are combined, it presents a powerful reason for the inability of children generally to explore or develop any knowledge about the ageing process. It would also account for widespread ignorance on the subject and poor cognitive skills in trying to provide theories and explanations.

Examples of the poor levels of thought applied to ageing can be seen in the following: 'Because when you're younger you're not old. When you're old you get older and start to get small. You evaporate' (North American boy, 7 years); 'Because they like wine and beer and smokes and that makes the body weak' (Australian boy, 9 years); 'It's just age. Sometimes it's from fighting with their husbands or wives' (Australian girl, 9 years); 'It's partly their attitude towards things. My grandfather joked around until his friends started to die, then he stopped joking' (North American girl, 13 years); 'God made it do that. If they didn't get old and die, the world would be too crowded. We'd still have gorillas here' (Australian girl, 11 years); 'They've spent their time, spent their use. Their body is now very old and worn out like a biro, when it comes to an end just throw it away' (English boy, 15 years); and another English boy the same age, 'Its what's in the body, the goodness has been used. It's tired like a bike needs new parts or needs repairing, but some can't be repaired. They get diseases easier of the heart and lung. Strokes are quite popular.' In this last response irreversible body changes are perceived (score 5) but the concrete analogy limits insight.

The low scores generally can be seen in Table 4.14 when mean scores are tabulated. The 'retardation' is clearly in evidence since a score of 3 does not quite achieve even concrete operational level (score 4). The mean score for the oldest group, 15 years, does not achieve the score of 4. A further breakdown of these scores reveals a considerable disparity between boys' and girls' scores. This can be seen clearly in graph form in Figures 4.1 and 4.2. Here the English and North American boys do climb to a mean score of 4 or above, but the girls achieve only a highest mean score of 3.20.

TABLE 4.14 *Mean scores of children's responses on the 'causes of ageing' scale (0–6) by country and age-year, 3 countries only (N = 658)*

Age-year	Australia	England	North America
5	0.93	1.25	0.82
7	1.70	1.85	1.40
9	2.48	2.28	2.17
11	2.83	2.60	3.03
13	2.83	3.15	3.41
15	3.50	3.25	3.10

The disparity between the sexes is very marked with significant differences in scoring (see Table B12, Appendix B), with boys scoring significantly higher in all the English age cohorts. four out of the six North American age cohorts and three out of the six Australian age cohorts. The scores, however, are so low for both sexes that little can be inferred about essential 'operational' differences. It tends to reinforce previous observations made about the dearth of knowledge, education and motivation in learning about ageing, senescence and its causes.

Summary and discussion

Three questions were put to the children about ageing. One was to see what children at varying ages defined chronologically as old age. It was found that young children are quite unrealistic about old age, most children arriving at the realistic age of 60 or beyond by the age 9 years, Swedish children appearing to achieve this level earlier by the age of 7 years, the other countries 'catching up' with Sweden by the teenage years. Australian boys in particular appear to be slower in achieving realistic estimates of old age.

The second question was 'What happens to people when they become very old?' Responses were coded in various ways, first in terms of favourable positive descriptions, then unfavourable or negative descriptions of old age. Few positive responses were found, the major group being the 5-year-olds, who probably had the most and warmest contacts with the old, through their grandparents. 13-year-olds showed some favourableness, especially in the North American group which retained it at 15, but in other countries positive descriptions tended to decline by 15 years. Negativisms were expressed by a majority in all groups painting an unalleviated gloomy picture of increasing weakness, senility, illness, decay and death. By 9 years in some countries more than 90 per cent of children produced this negative picture, illustrating a new word in the English language, 'gerontophobia'.

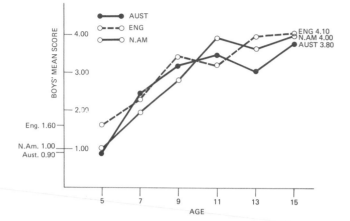

Figure 4.1   *Mean scores of boys' responses on 'causes of ageing' scale*
by country and age-year

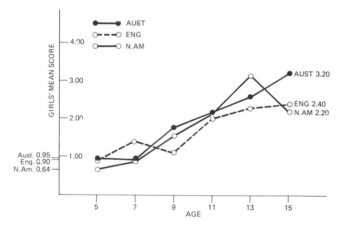

Figure 4.2   *Mean scores of girls' responses on 'causes of ageing' scale*
by country and age-year

The responses were categorised also as physical, over 94 per cent of all groups responding in this way; psychological, revealing growing perceptions of this characteristic of old age by the age of 15 years; social-economic, the social consequences of old age being perceived earlier than the economic. Finally, sexual characteristics of old age were categorised, the striking aspect of this being only 4 per cent responding in terms of sexuality. The largest cluster of sexual descriptions, again rather negative, were in the teenage years. Old age is seen essentially as a time of declining sexual powers, but for the majority it is a sexless period of life, a characteristic not mentioned, or mentionable, in connection with old age, confirming previous research at college student level (Golde and Kogan, 1959; Pocs and Godow, 1977).

The third question concerned the causes of ageing, and on a Piagetian and 'biological realism' it was found that most children barely achieved the beginnings of concrete operational thought in this area, providing technically feasible but inaccurate explanations of the causes of ageing. This retardation was particularly evident in girls, but both sexes came very low on the 'causes of ageing' scale.

Overall, the children show a quite realistic assessment of when old age occurs from 9 years on but reveal a disturbing negative ignorance about some of the pleasures, rewards and experiences of full maturity. Knowledge about and perceptions of the ageing process amount to widespread retardation of thinking. Negative aspects of old age dominate the children's responses and confirm the onset from a very early age of induction to a biologically based decline model, especially when the categories of physical, psychological, social-economic and sexual characteristics of old age are examined. These results tend to confirm Ahammer and Bennett's findings (1977) not only with Australian children, but in all the samples. With the increase in the incidence of the nuclear family and the distancing of old people in separate flats, homes and settlements, this confirms what may well be characteristic of Western-type industrial democracies. The early induction to this model may well be reinforced by stereotypes generated in children's publications as recent research indicates (Barnum, 1977; Storey, 1977; Ansello, 1978).

The failure of older children generally to mention sexual character-istics is of considerable interest since this is evident in Sweden also where compulsory sex education in schools is provided. Despite an advanced and broad syllabus which also covers masturbation and homosexuality, there appears to be no content recommended concerning the continuation of sex activity by older people.

Whatever the reasons, in most countries the combination of sexual taboos and ageing and death taboos would appear to inhibit any perception of the effect of ageing upon sexuality, as was shown by Golde and Kogan (1959) in the USA. It should be noted also that sexuality is comparatively invisible behaviourally in a way that physical, social and economic consequences of old age are not.

The low level thinking evident in children's perceptions of the causes of ageing may have several arguable explanations. The evidence appears to support the view that the question asked is intrinsically difficult and children regress in their thinking when examining the causes of ageing. Lack of teaching materials may well reinforce the difficulty and explain why even teenagers found it particularly difficult.

While gerontology studies are increasing it is our view that gerontology education needs to begin not with those about to retire, but with the very young who, denied an extended family educative environment, should be helped to see their own emergent development as part of the full sequence of life.

5 The best time to be alive

Little research has been done on how children regard various life stages. In Britain most of these have to do with adolescents (Eppel and Eppel, 1966), the closest to our study being that by Clautour and Moore (1969) who studied the attitudes of English 12-year-olds to present and future life roles. In the USA emphasis has tended to be upon coping behaviour, initiated by Lois Murphy's work in Topeka (Murphy, 1962; Murphy and Moriarty, 1976; Moriarty and Toussieng, 1976). Currently this tends to be focussed upon the topic of adolescent coping (Kelly, 1979; Prawat *et al.*, 1979; Konopka, 1976). The work of Vaillant (1977) looks at adult men and the tendency of some to remain 'perpetual boys' in their adaptive style and defences. These studies focus upon self-esteem, locus of control, future, present or past orientation and various typologies, and constitute a valuable contribution to how children, adolescents and later, adults, adapt to life's demands. The objective of the study reported here is to evaluate children's and early adolescents' choice of a particular life stage and their reasons for such choice; coping is involved in how the subjects see the problem. As Murphy and Moriarty observed: 'Each child struggles to find solutions and out of these struggles and these solutions develops an implicit or explicit view of life, as well as of self' (p. 13).

After discussing the characteristics of old age and the ageing process, each child was then shown a picture card. This consisted of a series of five human figures depicting in sequence from left to right, a baby, a primary school child, a teenager, an adult and an elderly adult. These were simple pen and ink sketches with minimal facial expressions, one with a male sequence of figures (Figure 5.1) and the other with a female sequence (Figure 5.2). The male series was used with the boy respondents and the female series with the girl respondents. Each human figure was identified in turn by the interviewer as 'This is a baby, this is

105

Figure 5.1

Figure 5.2

a boy (or girl) in primary (elementary) school, this is a teenager, this is a young man (or woman) and this is an old man (or woman)'. The respondents were then asked to point to the one they considered to be 'the best time to be alive'. All children, except about five in each country, made a specific choice without hesitation. Occasionally a child chose two adjoining figures such as the teenager and the young man, or pointed to the space between them. These children, when encouraged, invariably chose one or the other, or by their discussion justifying their choice indicated they favoured one 'age' in particular. No subject chose more than two figures, and only one (an 11-year-old Swedish girl) pointed out that there were good things about each stage of life depicted.

106

What the word 'best' meant was described by the children, the question being put deliberately in an open-ended manner, so that later discussion should not be too narrowly restrictive.

An exception was made with younger children, some of whom did not always immediately understand the question, and for them a variation was 'What do you think is the *happiest* time to be alive?' Admittedly, this may have introduced a slight bias towards hedonistic justification for the choice, but a review of answers given in the trial interviews revealed that there were no perceptible differences in the responses of the young children to 'best time' and 'happiest time'. The simple explanation of this may be that Kohlberg's (1969) pre-conventional level of 'naive hedonism' is a characteristic of 5- and 7-year-olds, and consequently is consistently reflected in their answers. It was also obvious from the replies that many children easily identified with their chosen figures in personal terms, often referring to them in the first person. In this way the figures were obviously 'a projective' picture device, the children using the figure in the illustration to talk about themselves, their own feelings and perceptions about the situation under discussion. Once the choice had been made they were then asked to give the reasons for their choice, 'Why did you choose that one?'. To encourage the child to elaborate, the supplementary question was also asked, 'What makes that one the best time to be alive?'

The two tasks, to choose and to justify the choice, impose a fairly complex cognitive exercise. Firstly, the child has to define what is meant by the question before making a choice. In choosing, the child has to compare one period of life with another, reflecting upon past and present experiences, both negative and positive, in contrast to what has been observed of the ages or stages still ahead, and what is perceived to be negative and positive aspects of those periods. In Piagetian terms this requires a series of accommodation and assimilation judgments, and making an evaluation based on 'better than' or 'not as good as'. Added to this is the complication of the child's limitations of experience and grasp of time and time sequences. Work on the psychology of time (Oakden and Sturt, 1922; Ames, 1946) over a long period indicates the difficulties younger children have in thinking in time sequences (Piaget, 1946; Coltham, 1960) and of 'mentally co-ordinating simultaneous transformations of two or more dimensions' (Cowan, 1978). The results of the two tasks, of choosing and justification for the choice, are set out and discussed separately below.

Children's choices of 'the best time to be alive'

In analysing responses to this choice, it was evident that 5, 7, 9- and 11-year-olds identified themselves with the second figure in the sequence, the 'primary school child', that is, 'childhood' and that 13- and 15-year-olds identified themselves with the third figure in the sequence, 'teenager'. It was obvious that although some of the 11-year-olds were beginning to identify with the teenage figure, these were only a very small proportion. For purposes of analysis and discussion therefore the two groups are treated in dichotomous terms. It also became clear that the choices could be grouped into three categories. There were those who looked back, nostalgically in many cases, to the past as the golden age, when life was simpler, less demanding and safe. There were those who found the present age or period currently being experienced as 'best' or the most satisfactory. Finally, there were those who found future periods of life as the 'best', finding the past and the present less attractive. These groups we have classified respectively as the Backward Choosers, the Contemporary Choosers and the Future Choosers. It should be noted that these terms are constructs concerned with temporality; no qualitative characteristic is intended by their usage. It may be that attempts could be made to define or classify these into personality types, such as optimists and pessimists, or psychological traits, such as regressive, conservative and adventurous. No such attempts are elaborated here since the intention is to present the choices only within a developmental sequence.

The 'backward choosers' – babyhood

Children who felt safe as babies and who feel under threat or pressure in some way currently may think nostalgically of the period in life in which they were protected, had no responsibilities and had few apparent worries. Babyhood is, of course, not necessarily perceived realistically and may, like many nostalgic views of past events, be seen in an aura of romantic wish-fulfilment. These babyhood 'backward choosers' are listed in Table 5.1. It will be noted that no age group has a predominance of 'backward choosers' preferring babyhood. The highest proportion is the English 5-year-olds almost 50 per cent of whom chose babyhood. Children in all countries were interviewed in the last term of their school year, with the exception of the North Americans, so that increasing awareness of 5-year-olds of the demands of schooling was probably common to at least three of the countries sampled. If schooling were a factor in these choices of English 5-year-olds, it would be surprising in view of the permissive play-way tradition of most English infant schools. It may, however, be explained by the fact that a greater proportion of 5-year-olds gave the answer, 'Babyhood is best because you have longer to live', which does not indicate a recidivist or regressive desire behind the choice, but rather a time calculation, longevity being the basis of the choice.

TABLE 5.1 *Percentages of children choosing babyhood as the best*
time to be alive by country and by age-year (N = 838)

Age-year	Australia	England	North America	Sweden
5	20	43	8	7
7	38	33	27	17
9	23	20	20	10
11	8	18	3	3
13	3	10	9	7
15	3	8	0	3

It will, however, be seen that the choice of babyhood persists and continues longer and more strongly in the English sample than the others, although the Australian 7- to 9-year-olds have a slightly greater proportion of babyhood choosers than the English at that age. An interesting result is to be seen in the Sweden sample, far fewer in percentage in choice of babyhood than all other countries.

While longevity is a frequent response most of the reasons advanced are of the nostalgic and unrealistic kind: 'Babies are good. They do good things. They do what Mummy says' (English girl, 5 years); 'I like sitting in prams. Its nice to be pushed around [sic]' (Australian boy, 5 years); 'He has more fun. He doesn't have to go to school. He plays with his rattle' (English boy, 9 years); 'You're cared for a lot. You've no grey hairs and there's more clothes for the baby than for the other children' (North American girl, 9 years). The few teenagers who choose babyhood do reveal insecurities such as 'You get a lot more attention. Everyone thinks a baby's cute. You get spoiled' (North American girl, 13 years).

The 'backward choosers' – childhood

These consist of only the 13- and 15-year-olds since the vast majority of 11-year-olds identify themselves as primary aged children. The frequency of this choice can be seen in Table 5.2.

TABLE 5.2 *Percentages of teenagers choosing childhood as the best*
time to be alive by country and age-year (N = 284)

Age-year	Australia	England	North America	Sweden
13	15	15	18	23
15	5	15	19	13

The percentages are fairly comparable for all countries, slightly higher in Sweden at 13 years, and dropping sharply in Australia at 15 years, only 5 out of 40 of the age group making this choice. The reasons for this backward choice of a younger age group are obvious reflections of pressures experienced both in school and at home which the respondents find rather wearing. 'You don't have to take so much responsibility for things. You don't have so many problems like smoking, family problems, children and so on' (Swedish girl, 13 years); 'You don't get so much homework, slaving away every night' (Australian boy, 13 years); 'You've more time to play with your friends. School's a happier place to be' (English girl, 13 years); 'Young kids are spoiled, they don't have as many responsibilities, and don't have to compete so much at sport' (Australian boy, 15 years); 'You haven't as many personal problems' (English girl, 15 years). It is interesting to compare these reasons with contemporary teenage choosers (see Table 5.4).

On the whole, 'backward choosers' of babyhood and childhood are few in proportion to the age years involved, and would tend to infer a reasonable adjustment to life's demands with increasing age. It illustrates Murphy's point (Murphy and Moriarty, 1976) about children's resilience. On the other hand, the figures may be some indication of the proportion of unhappy or disturbed children in the various populations, but such an inference must be accepted with caution, simply because of the fairly frequent reason for longevity ('You've got longer to live') advanced by younger children, which tends to inflate the proportion of backward choosers.

The 'contemporary choosers' — childhood

Approximately two-thirds of the total sample (554 out of 838) were attending primary, elementary, first school or, in the case of Sweden, kindergartens, and identified themselves with this age figure in the picture sequence. The choice of this figure, symbolising childhood, would appear to be indicative of satisfaction of contemporary experience, compared with the helpless condition of babyhood, and the pressures and anxieties foreseen in the future or conveyed by older brothers or sisters. For most who make this choice the present is safer, happier, less demanding and, in a curious way, freer. The answers, as we see later, indicate the carefree notion of childhood and the enjoyment of being protected, yet experiencing only a limited amount of independence. But first, the proportion of those who choose childhood should be noted in Table 5.3. In all countries, with the exception of North America, there is a gradual increase in the proportion of children choosing their contemporary age as the best time to be alive, until the age of 11 when, as Table 5.5 indicates, they tend to be forward looking, anticipating the pleasures and greater freedom of adolescence or adulthood. This trend appears to come slightly early at 9 years in the North

TABLE 5.3 *Percentages of children choosing childhood as the best*
time to be alive by country and by age-year (N = 554)

Age-year	Australia	England	North America	Sweden
5	25	33	33	48
7	28	33	57	53
9	43	45	40	57
11	30	38	33	40

American children, dropping from 57 per cent at 7 years to 40 per cent
at 9 years. This may indicate a greater social precocity induced by that
society or a reflection of what is termed its optimistic forward-looking
characteristics.

Only in two age cohorts are the 'backward choosers' larger in proportion to the 'contemporary choosers'. Forty-three per cent of English
5-year-olds choose babyhood compared with 33 per cent of 'contemporary choosers', and 38 per cent Australian 7-year-old children are
'backward choosers' compared with 28 per cent who choose contemporaneity. Conversely, three age cohorts reveal a clear majority choosing
contemporaneity, 57 per cent of North American 7-year-olds and over
50 per cent of Swedish 7- and 9-year-olds. Overall, when the two figures
of backward and contemporary choosers are combined the majority of
children from 5 to 9 years of age appear to conservatively opt for the
past or the present, rather than the future.

Reasons most frequently given which describe how children see their
contemporary experience can be judged from the following examples.
'You don't have to pay for many things; your parents do. They work
and you play more' (English 9-year-girl). 'You depend on your mum
and dad. You have clean clothes every day; your meals are always there.
There are no worries' (English, 9-year-boy). 'You're in the middle;
you're not a little girl, and not an old lady. It's just right' (North American 11-year-girl). 'You can muck around with friends. Older boys have
to compete harder at sport and school' (Australian 11-year-boy). Shades
of hardship can be seen, 'Things get harder as a teenager and you have
the hassle of getting through school and getting a job' (Australian, 11-
year-boy).

The 'contemporary choosers' — adolescence

Since adolescence has been characterised as a period of stress and turbu-
lence (Mussen, Conger and Kagan, 1979), rebelliousness (Goldman,
1969) and of sexual and social problems, one would expect teenagers to
opt for another period than their own as the best time to be alive. The
figures, however, to be seen in Table 5.4 would appear to suggest

TABLE 5.4 *Percentages of teenagers choosing adolescence as the best time to be alive by country and by year (N = 284)*

Age-year	Australia	England	North America	Sweden
13	55	50	52	43
15	69	67	49	61

considerable satisfaction by the 13- and 14-year-olds interviewed, with the contemporary age group in which they are living. 13-year-olds in Sweden are the exception but are a majority of contemporary choosers by the age of 15 years. Since the years 13 to 15 are suggested as the most unsettling ones of puberty and early adolescence, it is interesting to see the sharp rise in the percentage during this time. The exceptions to the rise are the North American teenagers who retain roughly the same proportion of contemporary choosers from 13 to 15 years. The figures do not argue for adolescence as a tranquil period, and may well be consistent with the generally accepted socio-psychological picture, but it could indicate that childhood may have presented just as many problems, possibly of a less noticeable or spectacular nature. One factor to be noted as implicit in some of the responses, although made quite explicit by a few, is the factor of the growing sexual awareness and growing enjoyment at contemplating or being involved in heterosexual encounters. 'If you are older you are trapped in a family. Teenagers are much more free' (Swedish girl, 15 years); 'You're more involved in sport. You think of sex more. Young boys hate girls, but when you're older you like them' (Australian boy, 13 years). The more typical response tends to be 'You're allowed to make some of your own decisions; you're not always told what to do' (English girl, 15 years). 'There's no-one to bossy you around. If you want some money you can take a part-time job weekends' (North American boy, 15 years); 'I like the period in which I am. I feel free and I don't have to take so much responsibility' (Swedish boy, 15 years).

The 'future choosers' — adolescence

For many children the best age is yet to come and in childhood adolescence is regarded by many as a more attractive prospect than the present. Yet the proportion of those contemplating adolescence as the best time to be alive is rather low, as Table 5.5 indicates. In Australia and England the proportions choosing adolescence increase as adolescence approaches. This is also roughly true of the North American children, with a dip at 7 years of age. The Swedish pattern is quite different, all the age cohorts finding adolescence moderately attractive throughout their development. The figures at 11 confirm the view that

TABLE 5.5   *Percentages of children choosing adolescence as the best
time to be alive by country and age-year (N = 554)*

Age-year	Australia	England	North America	Sweden
5	15	3	25	26
7	17	10	13	17
9	22	25	30	16
11	43	28	43	20

this age group still identifies with childhood. Some of the reasons
advanced for choosing adolescence are unrealistic such as, 'You get to
have a gun licence, and can drive a car and drink [sic]' (North American
boy, 11 years); and some realistic, 'They can go out more without
parents. At my age you can't go out on your own much' (English girl,
9 years). Sexual interest shows through in 'You look prettier, you're
more grown up and boys look at you' (English girl, 9 years). Comparisons
are made with other age groups, 'In secondary school you can do more
things than in primary school, like gym, football, tennis more often.
You're better off than him [points to young adult]. Anyway I'm not
anxious to get married quickly' (Australian boy, 9 years).

The 'future choosers' – young adulthood

A proportion of all ages are 'future choosers' of the fourth figure in the
picture sequence (Figures 5.1 and 5.2), the young adult. The frequency
of these choices can be seen in Table 5.6. A surprisingly high proportion
of 5-year-olds in Australia and North America make this choice. This
may reflect their identification with powerful parental figures such as
'I'll grow up to be big and strong like daddy, and I'll be bigger'n him'
(Australian boy, 5 years). Otherwise there is no clear pattern visible by
country or by age group. Increasingly, however, children perceive that
even with greater responsibilities there comes greater freedom and
adventure: 'It's more adventurous at that age, you can go mountain
climbing, racing cars and motor bikes, and travel to different countries'
(English boy, 13 years); 'I'd like to do more things my own way, without interference, and make all my own decisions. And just to be on my
own is important' (Australian girl, 13 years). Some do not see responsibilities as a burden or restriction, but rather as life's fulfilment: 'When
you're a teenager you aren't old enough to have children. At 20 you
can because you can get married. That's important so you can have
babies' (English girl, 11 years). A more balanced view is expressed by
a 15-year-old English boy: 'You've got your head together more then.
You know more about life than when you were younger. Your brain
works better and you know what to expect.'

TABLE 5.6 *Percentages of respondents choosing young adulthood as the best time to be alive by country and age-year (N = 838)*

Age-year	Australia	England	North America	Sweden
5	30	18	29	17
7	17	24	3	13
9	12	10	10	17
11	18	13	17	37
13	28	23	15	27
15	23	10	32	23

These responses illustrate Vaillant's (1977) mature persons who are characteristically anticipators, compared with 'perpetual boys', and Murphy and Moriarty's (1976) 'sensers' who seek out or welcome new experiences.

The 'future choosers' — old age

Not surprisingly, in view of the results on ageing described in chapter 4, those who choose old age are very few, 14 respondents out of 838 to be precise. There are five children making old age the choice from each of the Australian and English samples, most of these at 5 years of age for obvious reasons ('I like grandpa, he's fun to be with'), four from the North American sample and none from Sweden. The figures are so small as to have no significance but it is of interest to see that there is a cluster of half the number, seven respondents, in the 11 and 13 year age groups. There are some perceptive reasons advanced for such an untypical choice, representative of which is the statement by a North American 13-year-old boy, 'He [pointing to the old man] has been able to see as much life, to see what he's wanted to see. The younger ones are too limited'.

An overview of choices made

An overview of all the choices made by the respondents can be seen in Table 5.7 where the three categories of Backward Choosing, Contemporary Choosing and Future Choosing are set out so that comparisons can be made of each country by age-year. It may be useful to note certain tendencies year by year.

5 years: Australian and North American children tend to be more 'futuristic', English children tend to be 'backward' choosing and Swedish children tend to be mainly 'contemporary' choosers with a strong proportion 'futuristic'.

TABLE 5.7 *Percentages of choices made in the three categories of choice by country and age year (N = 838)*

Age-year	Choice made	Australia	England	North America	Sweden
5	Backward	20	43	8	7
	Contemporary	25	33	33	48
	Future	55	24	59	45
7	Backward	38	33	27	17
	Contemporary	28	33	57	53
	Future	34	34	16	30
9	Backward	23	20	20	10
	Contemporary	43	45	40	57
	Future	34	35	40	33
11	Backward	8	18	3	3
	Contemporary	30	38	33	40
	Future	62	44	64	57
13	Backward	18	25	27	30
	Contemporary	55	50	52	43
	Future	27	25	21	27
15	Backward	8	23	19	16
	Contemporary	69	67	49	61
	Future	23	10	32	23

7 years: North American and Swedish children tend to be 'contemporary' in choice, whereas Australian and English choices are fairly evenly distributed between all choices.

9 years: Swedish children tend to be dominantly 'contemporary' in choice whereas Australian, English and North American children are 'contemporary'–'futuristic' in tendency.

11 years: Australian, North American and Swedish children tend to be 'futuristic' in choice, with 'contemporary choice' a close-runner in Sweden. The English children appear to be about equally distributed between 'contemporary' and 'futuristic' choices.

13 years: All children of this age, in all countries, appear to favour 'contemporary' choice, with the spread of 'backward' and 'futuristic' choices approximately equal.

15 years: A tendency for 'contemporary' choice to be dominant in all countries, slightly less in North America (49 per cent) with 'futuristic' choice about a third of the choices.

This can be seen more clearly in Table 5.8 in the form of a matrix. By age cohorts the 5- and 7-year-olds show no clear tendencies, but

TABLE 5.8 *Matrix showing tendencies to make certain choices by country and age-year (N = 838)*

Country	Age-year					
	5	7	9	11	13	15
Australia	F	BCF	CF	F	C	C
England	B	BCF	CF	CF	C	C
North America	F	C	CF	F	C	C
Sweden	CF	C	C	CF	C	CF

(B = 'backward' choosers; C = 'contemporary' choosers; F = 'future' choosers. Larger capitals indicate major trends and smaller minor trends.)

accommodate most of the 'backward' choosers. The tendency, most clearly evident in all age groups, is for 13- and 15-year-olds to be 'contemporary' choosers. Interpretations may differ, but these tendencies would seem to be reassuring in terms of child development. Regressive choices, while not confined to younger age groups, would seem to argue for a healthy view of development in that decreasing numbers of children yearn for their previous stage of development or to return to babyhood. The dominant tendency for older children (we make a distinction here from teenagers) to be 'future' choosers again signals a healthy anticipation of the stages of life still to come. The 'contemporary' emphasis of the teenagers' choice is surprising but perhaps indicative of confidence to cope with the adjustments required in adolescence. The lack of any tendency for children or teenagers to choose old age simply underlines the need, as elaborated at the end of the last chapter, to educate the young into the realities of ageing, a process all will face, of whose compensations and positive aspects they appear to be almost totally ignorant.

By country, the matrix reveals two tendencies. The one shows consistency in choice in Sweden's 'contemporary' emphasis and North America with a fair consistency of 'contemporary' choice, with some 'futuristic' choosing. The other, revealed in Australian and English choices, shows inconsistent tendencies from age group to age group, achieving consistency only in the teenage years. Whether this would argue that Sweden is demonstrating a consistently cohesive tradition of helping children to accept and understand their own period of development, that North American culture is reflecting the cohesion of a forward-looking society, and that Australia and England display some confusion, is difficult to say.

Children's reasons for choosing the 'best time to be alive'

'What makes you choose that?' was the question put, once the child had pointed to one of the figures in the age sequence (Figures 5.1 and 5.2). The question was often supplemented by 'what makes that the best time to be alive?' Some examples of the reasons given have been presented in the previous section to illustrate how the children define and describe 'the best time'. Wherever possible, short monosyllabic answers were extended by further questions and probing, providing more of a reasoned discussion than a simple response.

It was therefore possible to assess the responses in terms of the level of reasoning used and to score answers on a Piagetian hierarchical scale. Set out in tabular form (Table 5.9) are the scoring criteria. While the major categories will be known to those familiar with Piaget's schemata of operational thinking, some of the categories are further described in sub-categories and illustrated with typical answers in the following text. Piaget's structures of developing thought, enabling us to identify the various processes of reasoning which children use in their problem solving, have been discussed earlier. The problem faced in this question requiring a justification for the age choice made is solved at varied levels at differing ages. The answers can be seen as increasing in complexity, but the quality of thinking can be categorised and scored in a hierarchical manner. It should be noted that the level of choice is not scored in this item, nor whether the child is a 'backward', 'contemporary' or 'future' chooser. It is only the level of thinking applied to that choice which is scored. It will be apparent that the lowest scores did tend to be associated with choice 1 (babyhood) and the highest scores did tend to be associated with choices 4 and 5 (young adulthood and old age). This seemed natural due to limitations of experience on the one hand, and widening social experience and more realistic judgment on the other. Many children, however, choosing figure 1 (baby) did score higher than scores 1 and 2, and many choosing figures 4 or 5 (young adult or old person) very often scored 3. Answers illustrative of the various levels are set out below.

Nonsense answers

'That one' [pointing to baby] — 'Why do you choose the baby?' — 'Cause he's a crybaby. He wets himself'; 'The old man. Because he's going to die.' These types of responses are obviously not answers to the question, made clearer by further probing, and therefore they are scored zero.

Pre-operational answers

'Babies are good and do good things. They do as Mummy says'; 'She's the one [pointing to figure 2], 'Cause she's smiling. She looks happy.' 'Why do you think she's happy?' — 'Cause she's smiling.'

TABLE 5.9 *Criteria for scoring reasons for choosing 'the best time to be alive' responses*

Piagetian level	Score	Elaboration of criteria
Non-classifiable	0	Don't know, no response, nonsense answers.
Pre-operations	1	Intuitive thinking, monocentric, transductive. Totally unrealistic.
Transitional	2	Pre-operational with some concrete operational features. Unrealistic attempts to generalise. Egocentric and hedonistic reasons. Ignores qualitative factors.
Concrete operations	3	Generalisations at concrete level successfully relating systems involving people, actions, objects and situations. Arguments reversible.
Transitional	4	Intermediate between concrete and formal operations. Attempts at propositions with concrete elements. Inductive and deductive logic attempted.
Formal operations	5	Full inductive and deductive logic applied in propositional form. Propositions may contain concretisms but the proposition dominates. Higher levels show balanced and comparative realism, i.e. advantages and dis-advantages.

Transitional: pre-operations to concrete operations

'It's more fun' [no elaboration after probing]; 'I like sitting in prams. It's nice being pushed around'; 'You've no worries'; 'You've more friends and you can play with dolls.' The frequent response, 'She's got longer to live' when choosing figures 1 or 2, is scored at this level because it is monocentric thinking, fixating upon longevity, but the answer is an attempt to generalise with egocentric and hedonistic elements.

Concrete operations

'Because you're big and strong'; 'You can wear dresses and look nice and pretty and have lots of parties'; 'You can go to X-certificate films'; 'You can muck around and no one gets angry if you dirty your clothes'; 'At 20 you can have babies, because you can get married then. That's important so you can have babies'; 'You can get a fast car and take girls out'; 'Not as many responsibilities. Young kids are spoiled. There aren't as many problems.'

Transitional: concrete to formal operations

'You're allowed to make some of your own decisions like staying out late. You're not always told what to do'; 'It's a more adventurous [age]. You can go mountain climbing and [drive] racing cars'; 'As a teenager you're at your physical peak. It's a crucial time which decides what happens [to you] later'; 'An important time to learn your sums and get a job when you grow up. But it's still fun to go out and play.'

Formal operations

'You've got your head together more. You know more about life than when you were younger. Your brain works better. You know what to expect'; 'I'd like to do things my own [way], make my own decisions. And I'd like to be on my own'; 'He's been able to see as much of life, to see what he's wanted to see. The younger ones are limited.'

The scores when collapsed into three categories (1 = 0, 1, 2; 2 = 3; and 3 = 4 and 5) roughly approximate to pre-operational, concrete operational and formal operational thinking and can be seen in Table 5.10. An examination of the figures reveals a consistent move from low scores (1) to high scores (3) with increasing age in every country, with the middle score (2) high from 7 to 11 years in three countries, with Sweden the exception. Nevertheless an identifiable sequence in each country from pre-operations through concrete operations to transitional-formal operations can be seen in Figure 5.3 by isolating percentages of highest scores (3) and plotting each country on the graph separately in terms of the highest score. Although there are slight falls in the percentages so scoring, accounting for the dips between Australian 9- and 11-year-olds, and between Swedish 11- and 13-year-olds, the upward trend with age is unmistakable. Taking the rough indicator of 50 per cent as the distribution signifying a move to another level, the following conclusions can be drawn.

Pre-operational thinking on this item is evident as the dominant level attained by 5-year-olds in all countries, continuing to include English and Swedish 7-year-olds. Two observations should be made. One is that the English 7-year-olds score 42.5 per cent at level 2 thus not quite

TABLE 5.10   *Percentages of scores on Piagetian criteria in reasons given for choice of 'best time' by country and age-year (N=838)*

Age-year	5	7	9	11	13	15
Australia						
P	87	23	8	10	0	0
C	13	77	80	77	45	18
TF	0	0	12	13	55	82
England						
P	90	57	25	5	0	0
C	10	43	62	58	40	38
TF	0	0	13	37	60	62
North America						
P	67	37	0	7	0	0
C	33	60	77	73	24	3
TF	0	3	23	20	76	97
Sweden						
P	57	50	20	0	10	3
C	33	30	40	27	33	17
TF	10	20	37	70	57	80

(P = pre-operational level; C = concrete operational level; TF = transitional to formal operations.)

attaining the 50 per cent indicator. The difference is only marginal. The other is that Swedish children do not normally begin school until 7 years of age, although most do attend sessional kindergartens at the ages of 5 and 6. As many writers indicate (Berry and Dasen, 1974), the factor of schooling does appear to be a vital one in attainment of operational levels, particularly the concrete level, in differing cultures.

Concrete operational thinking on this item is evident by 7 years of age in the Australian and North American sample, and quite clearly at 9 years of age in the English and Swedish sample. While in Sweden 40 per cent of the 9-year-olds have achieved concrete operations, a further 37 per cent have actually achieved transitional to formal operations (with the scores of 4 and 5 collapsed, most of these tend to be at the transitional level). By 11 years the Swedish results indicate that the majority achieve the highest score, arriving at transitional-formal operational levels earlier than the other three countries, where all the 13-year-olds pass the indicator of 50 per cent.

Since the age cohorts are at two year intervals it is reasonable to assume on this item that pre-operational thinking appears to be the major characteristic until 7 to 8 years, and that transitional to operational thinking tends to become the mode from 11 to 12 years of age.

This would appear to be consistent with other Piagetian research in Western-type industrialised countries. The significance of this will be examined when the total results are discussed in chapter 17.

When the mean scores for each age group were examined on the reasons for choice of 'best time to be alive', there were only three age cohorts – 7-year-olds in the North American sample, and 9- and 13-year-olds in Sweden – which revealed any significant sex differences in scoring (see Table B.13 Appendix B). Although all showed girls scoring significantly higher than boys in these cohorts, they are not sufficient to indicate general sex differences. This is also confirmed by ANOVA results (see Appendix D, Tables D1, D5 and D6). An interesting further result of analysis of variance is that this question is one of the four

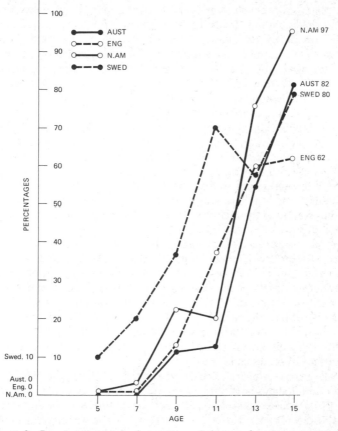

Figure 5.3   Percentages at each age line of those achieving transitional-formal operations on 'best time to be alive' scale

which indicates the main effects of socio-economic status (see Table D4) where the level of answers appears to be linked to father's occupation. In other words, the higher father's economic status, the higher the child's score tended to be.

Summary and discussion

The children were asked to complete two tasks. First, to identify from five figures representing a sequence from babyhood to old age (Figures 5.1 and 5.2) what they thought was the best time to be alive. They were then asked to give reasons for their choice. The results indicated that children could be classified in three groups, 'backward choosers', 'contemporary choosers' and 'future choosers'. Analysis by age indicated that 'backward choosers' tended to be among the younger children and that most 13- and 15-year-olds tended to be 'contemporary choosers'. North American and Swedish children were most consistent choosers, the Swedes predominantly opting for 'contemporary' choice at practically all ages, and the North Americans for 'future-contemporary' choices. While we would not infer national or cultural differences from such a limited sample, it would be valuable to test such a hypothesis with a larger and possibly longitudinal study.

Sexual reasons for choosing the best time are only occasionally overt, 'You can get a fast car and take girls out', or 'You can have sex legally, get married' or 'You can go to X-rated movies' when choosing the young adult in the picture sequence. There are, however, some implicit sexual references from the age of 9 upwards, girls looking forward to when they can wear make-up, nice clothes and stay out late at night; and boys reluctantly mentioning the teenage attraction of going out 'with the crowd'. Nevertheless, the vast majority never mention sexuality or sex as a factor in their thinking, even among teenagers justifying the choice of their own contemporary age as the best time to be alive. This widespread silence could be used to support the latency period concept, but other explanations may account for it. One thing is clear from the results, that diffidence at introducing sexual matters in discussion extends far beyond the so-called latency period into the time of pubertal and adolescent development. We postulate the cause to be simply the result of a long period of negative social training and the enforced observance of sexual taboos.

While cross-sectional studies may be criticised (Baltes and Nesselroade, 1972) and longitudinal studies may be deemed desirable, it is maintained that the cross-sectional study reported here adds useful dimensions to recent work on coping behaviour. If not directly then tangentially it supports the categories devised in the Topeka studies (Murphy and Moriarty, 1976), the follow-up Grant study (Vaillant, 1977) and

Kelly's (1979) work on high school boys. The various typologies suggested in these researches do appear in many of the responses of subjects reported here. It may also be inferred that children in all the countries reported appear to cope with their various life stages reasonably well. If 'backward choosers' can be identified with those fearful about coping with life's demands, it will be seen that most children do not fall within this category, the regressive choice to the safety of cosseted 'babyhood' declining in middle childhood, and few teenagers choosing 'childhood' as a less demanding period. Most children and adolescents are 'contemporary choosers', indicating in our view a healthy acceptance of current demands and stresses, reflecting an ability to cope. This evidence from the 13- and 15-year-olds is consistent, particularly with the findings of researchers on adolescent coping behaviour, arguing for considerable ego strength, self-esteem, achievement motivation and even feelings of competence to control events (Prawat et al., 1979).

In advancing reasons for their choice of a life stage, the levels of thinking scored indicate clear sequences in each country from pre-operational through to transitional-formal operations, although the cut-off points of change from one level to the next were not the same for every country. Generally, however, the age change from pre-operational to concrete operational thinking was 7-8 years and for transitional-formal operational thinking was 11-12 years. These results show a higher level of reasoning than in other questions put to the same subjects: why people marry, how do babies begin, what happens to babies inside their mothers, why people should wear clothes (Goldman and Goldman, 1980 and as can be seen in later chapters). We postulate that the higher level of performance on this item is due to greater familiarity with the subject area, its intrinsic interest to the subjects due to ego-involvement and lack of social taboos, evident in the other questions, in discussing such a topic. While the intention overall was to examine children's thinking about physical and sexual development, the 'best time to be alive' item has revealed other and equally provocative results.

6 Why people get married

For the purpose of this research we define marriage as an agreement between two adults of the opposite sex to live together. This agreement becomes legalised when authorised and certificated by the State, and solemnised when authorised and certificated by a religious institution. Many couples now prefer *de facto* rather than *de jure* marriage because of the wish to avoid a legally binding relationship and also because of changing perceptions of the nature of a sexual partnership (see Reiss, 1960 and 1970). Many *de facto* marriages lead to *de jure* marriages, particularly when a pregnancy occurs and the future parents may fear the label of illegitimacy for their children. A growing number of *de facto* marriages, however, continue if not for a lifetime then for periods long enough to be regarded as 'permanent', and certainly longer than the many *de jure* marriages which increasingly are terminating with divorce. Legal marriage, however, still remains the norm.

These distinctions and considerations apply to Australia, England and North America but they cannot be accepted without emendation for Sweden. In a society which has proclaimed the abolition of illegitimacy (Linner, 1977), where exnuptial births are beginning to approach the totals of births within wedlock (see Table 2.12), where *de jure* marriages are slowly decreasing, and the incidence of divorce also is in decline (see Table 2.15), the status of marriage is regarded differently. Swedish colleagues responsible for collecting data for this research have reported statisticians of repute forecasting that within twenty years half of the population of Swedish 8-year-olds will live with a single parent and most of the other half will be living with parents in a *de facto* marriage. Already it would appear the trend has begun in which legal marriage is ceasing to be the norm. These colleagues also report that many Swedish children interviewed for this study were well aware of this trend and therefore found the question 'Why do people get married?'

particularly difficult. They added that perhaps a more appropriate question for Swedish children would have been 'Why do a man and a woman want to live together?' The research was initially designed as a comparative study between Australian, North American and English children; the project had already begun when the authors first visited Sweden and the interviews in the original three countries completed before the involvement of Sweden was given official assent, consequently no items could be drastically changed for the Swedish interviews. This explains, in some measure, the fact that the Swedish results on this item are at variance with the other three countries.

Little research is known to us on how children regard marriage. The most relevant is that of Clautour and Moore's (1969) study of English 12-year-olds, who were asked if they hoped to get married when they grew up and what reasons they could give for their answers. They found that the majority of both sexes looked forward to marrying and having children, advancing a similar range of conventional reasons reported from our study in this chapter. The responses of the 1969 study were not, however, subjected to any scoring scale and covered only one year age cohort.

When asked the question 'Why do people get married?' the interviewers let the question stand as it was without any further elaboration or definition of what was meant by 'marriage'. It was felt that any attempt to explain the difference between living together and legal marriage would only lead to confusion, especially with the younger children. The replies from Australian, North American and English children indicate that they tended to accept the conventional view of legal marriage, although a few indicated, often indirectly hinting, that their parents were in a *de facto* relationship. On the other hand, it is apparent from Swedish responses that the reference to marriage, as such, caused some confusion in the children, particularly the older ones who were more aware than their younger siblings of the domestic arrangements of their parents. The implications of this will be examined when we discuss the results later in this chapter.

The answers were first coded into five categories named Sociobiological, Emotional-dependence, Sexual, Economic, and Legal-conventional reasons, so that the range of content could be seen more clearly. These categories were not placed in any hierarchical order, even though they were given a coded number of one to five. The categorisation was an essential preliminary to the later scoring criteria (see Table 6.5). Each category was examined separately in terms of age trends, particularly since many children gave more than one answer, but only the frequency of the categories used were first tabulated, not the quality or level of answer.

Socio-biological responses

All answers concerned with founding a family, having babies, perpetuating the family name or the nation or the human species were included in this category. The emphasis in most replies was predominantly 'to have children'; the continuance of the social unit largely being made in the responses of older children. When questioned further it was evident that the majority of children providing responses in this category saw marriage as a necessary preliminary to having babies, the possibility of having babies outside of marriage being rarely mentioned and then only by the older respondents. As can be seen from Table 6.1 there is some imbalance between the sexes in the choice of this socio-biological answer. Our expectation was that girls would tend to give this type of response more frequently than boys, since the bearing of children and the rearing of the family is still seen as a strongly entrenched social and biological role of women. This is evident in Sweden, for although there are considerably fewer responses in this category than any other country, many more Swedish girls at 7, 11 and 13 give socio-biological answers than Swedish boys. In the other three countries, however, more boys of practically all age groups respond in this category, with the exception of English 5- and 15-year-old girls, and Australian and North American 11-year-old girls. This male predominance may indicate a strong wish fulfilment to prove their masculinity by having children, especially among the 13-year-old boys. The Swedish boys in no group demonstrate this, the highest being 20 per cent with Swedish 5-year-old boys. In only two age cohorts, however, are any of the sex differences noted statistically significant when $p < .05$.

The total percentages, combining boys' and girls' responses, for each country provide a dramatic contrast between Sweden and the other three countries, especially when plotted in graph form in Figure 6.1. The distribution of percentages for Australia, England and North America vacillates up and down, but remains fairly high at all ages. The Swedish percentages are very low and can be explained partially in terms of the previous discussion of Swedish sexual partnerships. Marriage is no longer seen by many children as a necessary framework for producing and rearing children. The 'abolition' of illegitimacy and the increasing proportion of *de facto* relationships would account for fewer Swedish children's perceiving marriage as socio-biological in nature. The great majority opt for the next category of emotional-dependence.

Emotional-dependence responses

Answers which emphasise loving, liking, caring, sharing experiences, enjoying companionship and avoiding loneliness form this category,

TABLE 6.1 *Percentage of frequency of socio-biological responses to 'Why do people get married?' by country, sex and age-year (N = 838)*

Age-year	Sex	Australia	England	North America	Sweden
5	Boy	35	20	46	20
	Girl	35	30	36	20
7	Boy	45	45	63	7
	Girl	30	35	50	47*
9	Boy	45	50	53	7
	Girl	30	45	20	7
11	Boy	35	65	40	13
	Girl	50	50	73	33
13	Boy	75	70	75*	13
	Girl	50	60	23	27
15	Boy	50	45	69	0
	Girl	25	60	33	7

(* denotes significant sex differences in number giving this response)

including all responses with an emotive or dependency flavour. 'You have to have someone to talk to' (Australian girl, 11 years) and 'You are happier not living on your own' (North American girl, 13 years) are fairly simply statements of dependency, whereas 'Ladies can't fight on their own' (English boy, 5 years) expresses the dependency of women upon marriage partners for protection. 'Because they love (or like) each other' is the most common expression of emotional dependence, requiring supplementary probing to discover what the children meant by this statement and why marriage would then be necessary. These 'love' answers were not included in the category of sexual responses, unless they specifically referred to sex, kissing, smooching, sexual attraction and other sexual activities, such as 'sharing the same bed'. The results can be seen in Table 6.2. Although in several age groups girls predominate slightly, this is reversed at other ages when the boys slightly exceed the girls. The sex differences are not significant, with one exception of Swedish 5-year-olds where girls (67 per cent) greatly exceed the boys (27 per cent) in this category. The frequency is so universally high, a graph would reveal little difference in the general pattern.

Two interpretations could be deduced from these results. The first is that the 'romantic' view of marriage still persists strongly in the young with 'love' the word used most frequently to describe the basis of a marriage relationship. This is as true of the Swedish responses as of other countries, since in all countries about 70 per cent to 75 per cent

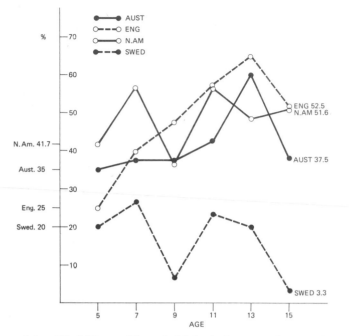

*Figure 6.1   All children with socio-biological answers by country
and age-year*

of all responses in the emotional-dependence category convey this romantic flavour. The second interpretation is that a fair proportion of these responses reflect dependence more in terms of friendship and companionship than romantic love. With hindsight we recognise that these two disparate types of responses might have been separated out in the analysis, but only a longitudinal study would reveal whether the friendship-companionship view rather than romantic love is increasingly perceived among children as the basis for marriage. Characterised as the difference between 'hot and cool' sex (Francoeur and Francoeur, 1974) it is obvious that further research is necessary before conclusions can be reached about the young's understanding of this distinction. Certainly, the 'hot' romantic view still dominates as mass publications for teenage girls and young women appear to indicate (see Horowitz and Gaier, 1976).

Sexual responses

In contrast to the previous category, overt sexual responses in answer to

128

TABLE 6.2 *Percentage of frequency of emotional-dependence responses to 'Why do people get married?' by country, sex and age-year (N = 838)*

Age-year	Sex	Australia	England	North America	Sweden
5	Boy	70	75	42	27
	Girl	55	60	55	67
7	Boy	80	60	88	80
	Girl	85	75	79	80
9	Boy	70	75	80	100
	Girl	95	75	93	100
11	Boy	100	80	100	93
	Girl	90	100	87	93
13	Boy	90	90	100	100
	Girl	100	100	100	100
15	Boy	90	85	100	100
	Girl	90	100	100	93

'why do people get married?' are very few in number. Anything which went beyond general romantic love statements to explicitly mention sexuality, sexual activity, kissing, necking, smooching, sexual intercourse ('sleeping together') and sexual attraction ('she thinks he's handsome and he thinks her pretty') were included in this category. In all only 5.6 per cent of the total sample (47 out of 838) made responses of this kind, 13 of them in the 5- to 9-year-old groups spread across the four countries. Apart from two responses at 11 years, the remaining distribution is in the 13 and 15 year age cohorts as set out in Table 6.3.

TABLE 6.3 *Percentages of teenagers responding with sexual answers to 'Why do people get married?' by country and age year (N = 284)*

Age-year	Australia	England	North America	Sweden
13	10	13	3	0
15	8	13	13	0

The figures are so small that no significant difference between the sexes can be calculated. The complete absence of such responses in the Swedish sample is interesting. Several reasons may be advanced to explain overall these small percentages. The first is that the interview schedule as used was not an adequate instrument to elicit this type of response. This may well be the case, but some sexual responses are in evidence revealing that some children found the interview situation an opportunity to express sexuality as a reason for marriage, however small a proportion of the total they were. When devised, the interview schedule was deliberately based upon an open-ended technique to elicit the greatest variety of answers possible. The second reason for the comparatively few sexual responses could be that 'love' is used as a synonym for sex, and that the category of emotional-dependence subsumes the sexual category. This is possibly true, but the overwhelming proportion of children using this expression after the age of five would tend to suggest a more generalised pre-sexual usage of the word 'love'.

The third reason for the limited response in sexual terms to explain why people marry could be the recognition by children of widespread and universal sexual taboos operating from a very early age, and a consequent inhibition of overtly expressing such ideas even in a confidential interview. The cumulative evidence of this probability is discussed in later chapters, not least the fact that any discussion of marriage involves some evaluation by the children of their own parents' reasons for marrying. To answer the question put to them in terms expressing sexuality would be to recognise and admit the sexuality of their parents, a fact which appears to meet with widespread resistance and which many children may find disturbing (Kulka and Weingarten, 1979; Pocs and Godow, 1977).

The authors conclude that all three reasons may combine to explain the sparsity of sexual responses to this item, but feel that it is the third one, the recognition of widespread sexual taboos which is the major contributing factor in creating verbal inhibition even in the teenage groups.

Economic responses

All answers which stated the need for a change in economic dependency ('You can't live with your parents forever': English girl, 13 years), the convenience of sharing resources ('Two people can buy a home more quickly': Australian boy, 15 years), the sharing of two incomes, or sheer greed ('Maybe the other person's rich': North American girl, 13 years) are included in this category. Only 41 children (out of 838) made such responses, slightly under 5 per cent of the total sample. Most of these tended to be in the 11- to 15-year age groups, with no real sex differences except for 15-year-old girls in Australia (25 per cent compared with boys at 5 per cent) and North America (20 per cent with no boys) giving this type of answer. Only six Swedish children made responses of an economic nature, including one 15-year-old boy.

It could be inferred that this response is limited in number because of social changes, of which children may be aware, which make economic factors relatively unimportant as a reason for marriage. These would include the higher status of women in society, their increasing economic independence and in some countries more generous welfare provision than had been known previously.

Legal-conventional responses

Any answers which emphasised that it was the custom or convention to get married ('It's the thing to do': North American girl, 15 years; 'People think you strange if you're single': Australian girl, 13 years); that marriage was a legal obligation if a pregnancy occurred ('You'd have to if you got a girl pregnant': Australian boy, 15 years); or enjoying a wedding, expressed naively by a few young children, were all coded as legal-conventional responses. These naive answers reflect the innocent perception of some 5-year-olds who associate marriage with church weddings, dressing up and enjoying lots of flowers as expressed by most of the 23 per cent of English 5-year-olds and 21 per cent of the North American 5-year-olds. Apart from these two age cohorts only a few single children scattered at various ages make these kind of responses. There is, however, some increase, not of naive answers, but in more sophisticated legal-conventional answers, by a proportion of teenagers, as Table 6.4 reveals. In all countries there is an increase in this type of response from 13 to 15 years, with the 15-year-olds the largest percentages of any age group. This would appear to reflect a growing awareness of social pressures, of what is expected and what is the conventional and legally binding thing to do in the man-woman relationship called 'marriage'. It is interesting to note that while about a third of the Australian and English 15-year-olds voice this as a reason for marriage, and about a quarter of the North American 15-year-olds, only a fifth of Swedish 15-year-olds do so. This is consistent with observations made earlier concerning the distinguishing features about marriage, illegitimacy and related matters to be seen in Sweden.

TABLE 6.4 *Percentages of teenagers responding with legal-conventional answers to 'Why do people get married?' by country and age-year (N = 284)*

Age-year	Australia	England	North America	Sweden
13	13	10	12	3
15	35	33	26	20

Scoring children's explanations of 'Why people get married'

Once the answers to this question were coded into the five categories described above, each response was scored on the criteria set out in

TABLE 6.5 *Criteria for scoring children's explanations of 'Why do people get married?'*

Piagetian level	Kohlberg level	Score	Elaboration of criteria
Not classifiable		0	Don't know, no response, nonsense answers.
Pre-operations	Verbalisms	1	Repetitive replies. No elaboration, 'just so' finalisms.
	Self maintenance	2	Naive egoism — prudential safety; exploitation by parents of their children or one partner of the other. Includes crude immediacy.
Concrete operations		3	Hedonistic egoism — gratification of needs.
Transitional	Social maintenance	4	Limited altruism — with hedonistic elements. Some obligations and mutuality implied but limited.
		5	Broader altruism with no hedonistic elements. Mutuality explicit but not full interdependence. Recognition of limits to mutuality.
Formal operations	Autonomy and interdependence	6	Interdependence including reciprocity, permanence and sexual exclusivity. Relationship expressed as friendship and mutual respect. Answers which go beyond or reject conventional marriage.

Table 6.5. These scoring criteria were devised by adaptation from Piaget's and Kohlberg's investigations, similar to the scoring criteria devised for several other items. The classifications listed in Table 6.5 are not as closely delineated as some Piagetian and Kohlberg scales. 'Self maintenance' and 'social maintenance' are adaptations made to fit the full range of explanations children gave in answering the question put to them.

Many children gave more than one explanation and in all cases each explanation was scored and noted. In some cases the scores were not identical for one child; perhaps a respondent scored 2 for a socio-biological response, 3 for an economic response and 4 for an emotional-dependence response. In such cases when assessing the level of thinking demonstrated by that child, the highest score (in the case cited, the score would be 4) was used in scaling the results across the age cohorts. As noted previously there were two widely used stock responses to the question 'Why do people get married?', both of which were used by children of all ages. One was, 'Because they want to have babies' and the other was, 'Because they love (or like) one another'. If these had been accepted at their face value there would have been little differentiation between the scores of the younger and the older children. Consequently a supplementary question was asked in each case about 'Why are babies important?' and 'Why does loving (or liking) mean people want to get married?' In these cases the total reply was assessed rather than the standard and almost predictable answer. Some samples from each level will indicate how the scale was used:

Non-classifiable nonsense answers

'Dads go to work and mums stay home' (English boy, 5 years); 'My dad's married. (Q) He's got a beard and curly hair' (English boy, 5 years).

Verbalisms and repetitive answers

'He likes to marry people' (Australian boy, 5 years); 'They love each other (Q) Because they like each other' (North American girl, 5 years); 'She goes to hospital to have babies' (English girl, 7 years); 'It's what happens, (Q) to get married' (English boy, 7 years).

Self maintenance—naive egoism

'They want children. (Q) They grow up to look after their parents' (English boy, 11 years); 'Kids help if parents are hurt' (Australian girl, 13 years); 'They have to have babies if they're married' (North American boy, 9 years); 'They want to go to church to marry' (English girl, 9 years); 'They want someone to talk to' (North American girl, 11 years); 'Girls and ladies need someone to protect them' (English boy, 9 years).

Self maintenance – hedonistic egoism

'Having kids is fun. You have birthday parties and give presents' (Australian girl, 9 years); 'It's no fun on your own' (Australian boy, 11 years); 'They like being with each other, they enjoy each

133

other's company' (English boy, 13 years); 'They're friends — each
morning they hug each other' (North American girl, 9 years);
'They buy each other pretty things' (North American girl, 11 years).

Social maintenance — limited altruism

'Children help continue the family name and tradition' (English
boy, 13 years); 'They can look after each other when they're sick'
(Australian girl, 11 years); 'Two people can look after children
better' (North American girl, 11 years); 'They like and care for
each other' (North American boy, 11 years); 'If you're married
you can have a wider experience, a large circle of friends' (North
American boy, 13 years); 'You want to share doing things, and it's
more normal to be in a family' (Australian boy, 11 years); 'A boy's
got to recognise his obligation if he's got a girl pregnant' (Australian
boy, 15 years); 'They think each other handsome and like to go out
together' (English boy, 13 years); 'Two incomes are better than one,
two people can buy a house more quickly' (Australian boy, 15 years).

Social maintenance — broader altruism

'The continuance of the human race depends on it [having
children]' (North American boy, 15 years); 'Society has to be kept
going, replacing the older generation' (Australian girl, 15 years);
'If you're legally married you don't break up so easily and that's
fairer on a baby' (Australian girl, 13 years); 'You marry to show
your love for the other person' (North American girl, 13 years);
'Someone to help as well as share your worries and your whole life
with' (Australian girl, 13 years); 'It's good to have someone to
depend on; you can't go on depending on your parents' (English
boy, 15 years); 'They're very close and good friends' (English boy,
13 years).

Autonomy and interdependence

'Are prepared to live their lives together. They want to share
responsibility' (Swedish girl, 15 years); 'To give your children what
you enjoyed as a child' (English boy, 13 years); 'Having babies
strengthens the bond between them [parents]' (North American
boy, 13 years); 'You don't have to marry, not today. If you have
babies, unmarried mothers are more acceptable' (Australian girl,
13 years); 'They like each other enough to stay all the time together
and not want another partner' (North American girl, 15 years);
'It's having the same interests and understanding each other'
(Australian boy, 15 years); 'They're good companions and fit in

with each other's personality' (English boy, 15 years); 'They have the same opinions. They think they suit each other well' (Swedish girl, 15 years); 'They're different from other loves, like loving your mother. You want to be together always' (North American girl, 13 years); 'They respect and admire each other' (Australian boy, 13 years).

The highest scores on the scale were then taken and the results for each country were tabulated separately. The first for Australian children is shown in Table 6.6.

TABLE 6.6 *Percentages of Australian children's scores on the Piagetian scale 'Why do people get married?' by age-year (N = 240)*

Piagetian stages	Scores	Age-year					
		5	7	9	11	13	15
Pre-operations	0	5	–	–	–	–	–
	1	25	5	–	–	–	–
	2	45	43	20	17	10	–
Concrete	3	20	37	48	28	10	12
Transitional	4	5	10	25	42	45	35
Formal	5	–	5	7	10	30	20
	6	–	–	–	3	5	33

It is noticeable that the scores generally, with the increase in age, show a hierarchical order from low to high scores in an almost symmetrical pattern. 5-year-olds were predominantly pre-operational, 7 to 9 years concrete-operational, and by 11 years transitional to formal operations appear to be the mode, very clearly established at 13 years of age, and beyond at 15 years they achieve clear formal operations at a 53 per cent level. In Kohlberg terms self maintenance is the norm up to 11 years where social maintenance is the dominant view (52 per cent), with a sizeable proportion (33 per cent) achieving autonomous thinking by 15 years. Table 6.7 reveals a similar hierarchical pattern for the English children both on the Piagetian and Kohlberg criteria. Indeed, the scores on both scales are almost identical, with a correlation of over 0.90.

The distribution of North American children seen in Table 6.8 is not quite as symmetrical, but the majority of children have moved to concrete operations a little earlier at 7 years. Transitional to formal operations are established at similar ages as the Australian and English children, with a 10 per cent increase on their scores at 15 years. On the Kohlberg scale the same trends are apparent as in the other two countries so far presented but with autonomous highest level (score 6) at a high of 45 per cent.

TABLE 6.7 *Percentages of English children's scores on the scale 'Why do people get married?' by age-year (N = 240)*

Piagetian stages	Scores	Age-year					
		5	7	9	11	13	15
Pre-operations	0	3	–	–	–	–	–
	1	15	10	–	3	–	–
	2	45	35	25	15	–	–
Concrete	3	30	33	30	20	25	12
Transitional	4	7	17	35	27	40	35
Formal	5	–	5	10	30	27	33
	6	–	–	–	5	8	20

TABLE 6.8 *Percentages of North American children's scores on the scale 'Why do people get married?' by age-year (N = 178)*

Piagetian stages	Scores	Age-year					
		5	7	9	11	13	15
Pre-operations	0	–	–	3	–	–	–
	1	17	3	3	–	–	–
	2	46	37	17	10	3	–
Concrete	3	33	53	50	20	18	7
Transitional	4	4	7	23	57	52	29
Formal	5	–	–	4	13	27	19
	6	–	–	–	–	–	45

The Swedish children present a quite different picture, the distribution being somewhat asymmetrical. On the Piagetian scale they barely get beyond pre-operations at 7 years (49 per cent) and they do not achieve transitional to formal operations until 15 years (56 per cent) on this item. On the Kohlberg scales the Swedish results are even more markedly dissimilar to the other countries. Self maintenance responses continue up to 13 years, with social maintenance responses and beyond dominating (56 per cent) only at 15 years.

This confirms observations made earlier at the beginning of this chapter, particularly those by our Swedish colleagues reporting that the question was 'too hard for many children' due to the different social assumptions made in Sweden about *de facto* and *de jure* marriages, about the status of illegitimacy and other rapidly changing social trends. Although this would appear to indicate that the Swedish children perform at a lower 'operational' level, other results indicate quite the contrary. What it does indicate is that where the question causes

TABLE 6.9 *Percentages of Swedish children's scores on the scale*
'Why do people get married?' by age-year (N = 180)

Piagetian stages	Scores	Age-year					
		5	7	9	11	13	15
Pre-operations	0	23	13	3	3	3	3
	1	3	3	–	–	–	–
	2	53	33	37	30	23	10
Concrete	3	17	40	40	27	30	30
Transitional	4	3	10	17	33	33	23
Formal	5	–	–	3	7	10	30
	6	–	–	–	–	–	3

some confusion or contradicts the child's social experience the ensuing answers will tend to be confused and possibly contradictory, resulting in consistently lower scores for the older respondents who with increasing social experience perceive the contradiction more clearly.

The contrast of the Swedish scores and those of the other countries can be seen more dramatically on the graph in Figure 6.2. The hierarchical progression of scores in almost linear form can be seen for the Australian, English and North American children, the latter starting higher at 5 years and finishing higher at 15 years. By contrast the Swedish progression is quite atypical, the mean average score for Swedish 5-year-olds being below that of all other 5-year-old cohorts and the Swedish 15 years mean average score well below that of 15-year-olds in the other three countries. Less confusion among the younger Swedish children is clearly portrayed, their responses scoring reasonably close to the other 5- to 9-year-olds in the other three countries. But with increasing social awareness, confusion about what 'marriage' and 'living together' is in Swedish society may cause teenage scores to fall behind the English-speaking teenage cohorts.

When the mean scores are examined for the question 'Why do people get married?', in the English-speaking countries only two age cohorts – Australian 7- and 15-year-olds – show any significant sex differences, the boys scoring higher than the girls (see Appendix B, Table B.14). In Sweden, however, from 7 years upwards all five cohorts show significant sex difference where $p < .05$, revealing Swedish girls scoring higher than Swedish boys. This is consistent enough to indicate that Swedish girls overall appear to reason at higher level than Swedish boys about marriage. This may well represent a cultural difference between Sweden and the other countries involved in this study. The main effects of age-year and country is confirmed in the ANOVA results in Appendix D (Tables D2 and D3), as is the interaction of sex and country, noted earlier.

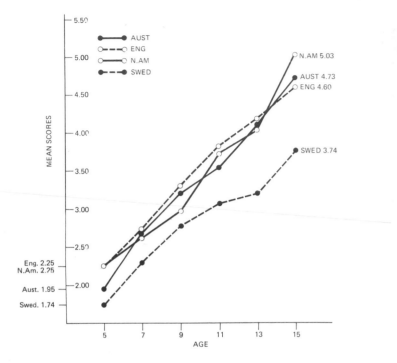

Figure 6.2 Mean scores on 'Why do people get married?' Piagetian and Kohlberg scales by age-year and country

Summary and discussion

Children were asked the question, 'Why do people get married?' The term marriage was undefined in view of possible confusion concerning *de facto* and *de jure* marriage. Considerable cultural and social differences were identified which might cause difficulties in this item for the Swedish children questioned. In all countries the responses were coded into five categories; these being socio-biological, emotional-dependence, sexual, economic and legal-conventional answers. It was found that the socio-biological category demonstrated idiosyncratic results for Sweden, particularly in responses which gave 'babies' as the reason for marriage, since Swedish children appeared not to see marriage as a necessary prerequisite for having children. The majority of responses were found to be in the emotional-dependence category with some slight sex differences in certain groups. Sexual responses were few, hypothesised as due to three factors, and economic responses were also rare. An increased number of legal-conventional answers were seen at 15 years of age due possibly to increasing awareness of social pressures.

Children were then scored on a 6-point scale based upon Piagetian and Kohlberg levels of thinking. Taking the highest score for each child it was found that the Australian, English and North American results scaled in a hierarchical order with increasing age, roughly comparable on the operational thinking scale and, with some slight discrepancies, on the Kohlberg scale. Sweden again demonstrated atypical results, attributed to the confusion and contradictions caused by the question, with older age groups becoming increasingly aware of Sweden's differential standards. Swedish girls, however, scored significantly higher than boys on this question.

Overall most children appear to retain a romantic view of marriage based upon love, although a sizeable proportion supported a friendship-companionship concept. Sexuality as a basis for marriage remains a silent area possibly due to considerable and continuing social taboos and a reluctance of children to recognise their own parents in active sexual roles. This point becomes very clear in the next chapter.

Three aspects in particular of these results reported have provocative implications. The first concerns the quite distinctive Swedish results both in several of the categories and on the Piagetian and Kohlberg scales. If the State abolishes 'illegitimacy' and if *de facto* relationships increase in a society this will obviously affect children's concepts of marriage and the reasons for their parents engaging in such a partnership. It is therefore not surprising that Swedish children do not advance socio-biological reasons for marriage to the same degree as the English-speaking children, but rather emphasise emotional-dependence as the major reason. In other words it is the quality of relationship between a man and a woman answering each other's needs which is seen by these children as the dominant reason for marriage, with children as a possible but not a necessary ingredient. This outcome is quite contrary to the teaching of certain religious groups. It is possible that the small proportion of Roman Catholics in Sweden, a predominantly Lutheran country, may account for these results. The authors postulate this to be unlikely in that the proportion of Roman Catholic children in the samples in other countries was not high, since all were taken from the state school system not normally patronised by committed Catholic families. Rather it is postulated that the English-speaking children reflect traditionally accepted ideas, rather than religious beliefs, in their views about marriage, but as Swedish trends become more general (in attitudes to illegitimacy and to *de facto* relationships) views about marriage in Australia and elsewhere will change accordingly.

The second implication is related, in the very small numbers (5.6 per cent) who mention sexuality as an important reason for marriage. As we observed earlier, this reason may be subsumed or sublimated under emotional-dependence answers, particularly 'love' responses. In this regard Swedish children's responses in the sexual category are zero. However, in another section asked only of those children who had volunteered information about human reproduction as being sexual in origin, reported elsewhere in full (Goldman and Goldman, 1980; see also chapter 12), Swedish children from 9 onwards overwhelmingly cite 'enjoyment' as the real reason for sex, not the begetting of children. Australian children from 9 onwards in comparison score low in this response. It appears to us that the respondents' failure to cite sexuality as one basis of marriage is not only an indicator of social inhibition, but also signals a need for education in human relations in schools to begin much earlier than is present practice and to be more realistic in content.

Finally, the evidence for 'love' as a major reason for marriage carries with it interesting implications, particularly as teenagers may be thinking increasingly in terms of friendship and companionship. This is a pattern recognisable in all the countries sampled including Sweden and may indicate a gradual move towards a more egalitarian view of marriage, and more equal status of men and women. This assumption, however, must be accepted with caution and needs more research to verify it. Overall the section of the research on 'Why People Get Married' highlights the importance of understanding children's perceptions of such matters, not only as developmental guides for parents and teachers, but also as possible indicators of social change.

7 Mothers and fathers: women and men

How children perceive their parents is a comparatively well researched area, particularly in the manner such perceptions may change with increasing age and social experience (Lamb, 1976; Johnson, 1975; and Santrock, 1970). If in terms of Freudian theories or other social learning theory, parents are children's models, then these perceptions and conceptualisations are of both theoretical and practical importance for child development. It may be argued that the quintessence of this perception is fundamentally sexual in the broad sense in which we have defined that term in chapter 1. Parents are sexual beings and as such may be delineated in basically three dimensions. The first dimension is the procreative role of parents in producing a child and its sibling(s). As we shall see, younger children do not always perceive this role, particularly that of the father, as being sexual in nature. Obviously step-parents, foster parents or adopted parents do not fulfil the procreative role in the case of a few children involved in this study. The second dimension in the sexuality of parents is in their roles as 'upbringers' related more to socially induced gender roles as Unger (1979a and b) has indicated. Even though these roles be socially determined stereotypes, nevertheless most children perceive them as relatively fixed roles appropriate to one sex or the other. The third dimension we identify as sexual modelling where children from birth to late adolescence perceive mothers and fathers (or their surrogates) as examples or exemplars of sexuality and sexual behaviour.

The procreative sexual role of parents is dealt with extensively in chapter 10, and sex-stereotyping of men and women, both as child upbringers and sexual models, has been touched upon in chapter 1 (Bee, 1974; Maccoby, 1967). The research literature is too voluminous to be extensively reviewed here, but it can be pointed out that only comparatively recently has the focus upon child-rearing been widened to include fathering as well as mothering (Johnson, 1975; Lamb, 1979). Occupational roles and how children view them in sex-role terms have been researched by Scheresky (1978), sex-stereotyping of aggression, constructive behaviour and rewards by Sternglanz and Serbin (1974), the dominant characteristics of the female role models by Horowitz and Gaier (1976), how children perceive future life-roles as adults by Clautour and Moore (1969) and a useful contribution of roles within the family by the Newsons *et al.* (1978). The most comprehensive survey on all these topics can be found in Ullian (1976), whose summary of six levels of sex-role conceptualisation clearly differentiates between biological, societal and psychological orientations. Parental power and identification with parents has been explored by McDonald (1979 and 1980).

In this study three areas were the focus of enquiry, using mothers and fathers as representative of females and males generally. Do children perceive differences between mothers and fathers, and if so what range of perceptions do they have? Are there any distinct roles attributed by children to one sex or the other? Do children have a favourite parent, are these the same sex or other sex choices, and what reasons are advanced to justify their choices? It has already been noted that the latter question cannot prove nor disprove Freudian theories of Oedipus or Electra situations in the family, but may provide more information and thus help to illuminate familial relationships during children's sexual development.

Differences between mothers and fathers

The interviewer introduced this section by saying, 'Here are a few questions about parents [mummies and daddies]. Now, mothers and fathers are different from each other in many ways. Tell me some of the ways in which they are different from each other.' Occasionally a child would misinterpret the question as meaning how one couple of parents differed from another couple, but a slight rephrasing overcame this confusion, such as 'In what way are mothers different from fathers?' The respondents were encouraged to give as many answers as occurred to them.

The responses were coded into five categories, most children responding in more than one category. Physical external differences of a nonsexual kind was the first category. These differences included height, colouring, hair, clothes, wearing spectacles, all of which were devoid of sexual significance. One 5-year-old English girl remarked about women wearing trousers; 'Scottish men can wear kilts'. The second category was physical, and included other differences which tended to be intrinsic and still non-sexual. These included personal mannerisms, comparative physical fitness, strength and agility, voices (but not perceived as sexually based), intelligence and abilities. Third came the category of overt sexual physical differences, for example, breasts, beards, capacity to bear children. The fourth described functional and social differences, including types of jobs, ways of spending leisure, responsibilities for driving the car, and child-rearing. Finally, attitudinal differences were categorised in terms of temperament such as more or less loving, permissive, disciplinary, and different personality and interests.

While the question was posed as a universal, that is, differences between mothers and fathers in general, it was clear that most children responded in terms of their own parents, often becoming anecdotal and slipping into the first person continually. Older children tended to widen their answers to differences between men and women generally. It should be noted that this was an open-ended question, not directed to role perception but rather differences of any kind between mothers and fathers which came to mind spontaneously. Specific role oriented questions were asked in the following section.

Non-sexual physical differences between parents

The results can be seen clearly in graphical form in Figure 7.1 where the vast majority of younger children give answers of this kind, decreasing with age as they perceive more subtle and less obvious differences. The decrease in these responses is reasonably linear until 11 years. While the proportion of the North American and Swedish children continue to decline, the English children have a sharp upward trend to 13 years followed by a decline and the Australians a slight upward trend arriving at roughly the same point at 15 years (37.5 per cent). When the overall results are examined later it will be seen that there may be similar sexual perceptions in these two country's samples which might explain these trends.

Non-sexual intrinsic differences between parents

These types of responses, as indicated, tended to refer not to physical characteristics but to differences which are less tangible such as comparative fitness, 'my dad's stronger than my mum' (English boy, 5 years), or particular aptitudes, 'Mum's quick with figures and helps me with my homework. Dad's hopeless' (Australian girl, 13 years). Many also mention that their parents come from differing social backgrounds, have had differing family traditions or been brought up differently: 'Dad left school at 13 and mum went on to graduate from High School' (North American girl, 13 years).

Intrinsic differences of this type are scattered throughout each age group and there is no clear pattern of distribution with age except in

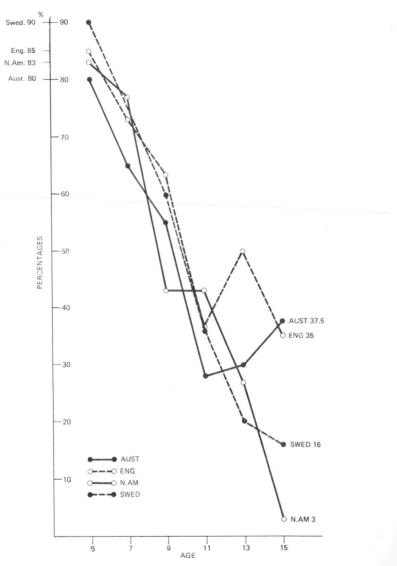

Figure 7.1   Children's descriptions of non-sexual physical differences between mothers and fathers by country and age-year

Australia and Sweden as can be seen in Table 7.1. These two countries do show some increase with age, Sweden in particular, but not so the English and North American children. With the exception of Australia

TABLE 7.1   *Percentages of children's descriptions of non-sexual intrinsic differences between mothers and fathers by country and age-year (N = 838)*

Age-year	Australia	England	North America	Sweden
5	8	5	17	3
7	10	22	17	7
9	10	10	–	13
11	10	33	33	30
13	13	15	6	23
15	15	25	–	33

the age with the greatest proportion of these intrinsic non-sexual responses is 11 years (about 30 per cent) mostly pre-pubertal.

Overt sexual differences between parents

All primary and secondary sex characteristics were included in this category, where parts of the body are named, and it is at least inferred that the parent of the other sex does not possess this characteristic, such as 'A mum's got bosoms and a man hasn't' (Australian boy, 11 years); 'Their voices are different because they're men and women' (North American girl, 5 years); 'The man's got hair on his chest' (Swedish boy, 5 years); 'A man can grow a beard' (English boy, 7 years) or 'Dad has to shave' (English girl, 13 years). The sex organ differences may be specified directly, 'Fathers have joeys and mothers don't' (Australian boy, 9 years); 'Mothers can have babies' (Swedish girl, 9 years) or indirectly, 'A man stands up when he goes to the toilet and a woman sits down' (North American boy, 9 years).

One might expect that recognition of overt sexual differences between parents would show incremental growth with increasing age. The scores to be seen in Table 7.2 do not, however, reveal such a clear-cut pattern. The Australian children do show an increasing awareness of sexual differences between mothers and fathers up to 9 years of age, an awareness that curiously levels off between 63 per cent and 70 per cent after 11. A less obvious increase to 7 years is observable in the English children but then a perceptible decline occurs only to peak (63 per cent) at 11 years then levels off in the high 40s. The North American pattern vacillates up and down with peaks at 7 and 11 years but plunges to a low level at 15 years (27 per cent). Sweden's pattern is again atypical, 40 per cent of 5-year-olds point out sexual differences, then comes a decline at 7 years with a slow increase to 13 years (50 per cent) with a small decline to 43 per cent at 15 years. It might be argued that this reveals a typical latency curve.

145

TABLE 7.2 *Percentages of children's descriptions of overt sexual differences between mothers and fathers by country and age-year (N = 838)*

Age-year	Australia	England	North America	Sweden
5	28	33	29	40
7	58	40	57	23
9	70	38	30	30
11	63	63	60	37
13	70	48	39	50
15	65	45	27	43

There are three age cohorts where there are significant differences between girls' and boys' responses in this category. 9-year-old Swedish girls more frequently identify their parents as sexually different than 9-year-old Swedish boys. At 15 years English and Swedish boys more frequently identify their parents as sexually different than the girls in those age cohorts. Although all these are statistically significant (see Table B1, Appendix B) they are not sufficient to merit any generalisation about sex differences in how children perceive their parents' differing sexuality.

Since the overt sexual differences would appear to be among the most obvious of all differences between fully developed men and women, it is evident to us that taboos in children about recognising and discussing the human body and nakedness, and their parents' sexuality, operate strongly in different countries at differing ages. This is particularly observable from 11 onwards in the case of the English, Swedish and North American children, the proportion of the latter dropping from 39 per cent to a low 27 per cent. It may, of course, be explained possibly by the position of this question being placed early in the interview sequence. Would the incidence of noting sexual differences have increased if the question had been asked later, such as after adolescent boy and girl differences, and differences between boy and girl newborn babies had been asked? The trial interviews did not indicate this to be the case.

The North American figures do roughly correspond with Pocs and Godow's (1977) findings, of inhibitions in college students in their descriptions of their parents' sexuality. They advanced four explanations, the myth of the non-sexuality of older age groups, incest taboos, expected parental socialisation roles to be sexually non-permissive and hesitancy of parents to discuss sexuality with their children.

Functional and social differences between parents

The responses in this category included all references to job differences, including housework and the maternal role of child-caring, social habits such as smoking, drinking and belonging to single sex clubs (golf or mothers' circle), driving the family car, having 'more' leisure than the other partner. The majority of responses in this category were mainly in the area of job stereotypes for males and females, the vast majority relegating mother to home duties not usually conceived of as 'work'. A common remark was 'Dad goes out to work and mum stays at home [*sic*]' (Australian girl, 5 years). Table 7.3 gives the percentages of responses made by the children.

TABLE 7.3   *Percentages of children's descriptions of the functional and social differences between mothers and fathers by country and age-year (N = 838)*

Age-year	Australia	England	North America	Sweden
5	20	20	29	7
7	33	38	27	30
9	40	53	67	20
11	38	45	40	47
13	28	38	42	43
15	38	43	68	40

Although in all countries the 15-year-olds have a higher frequency of this type of response, from the 5- and 7-year-olds there is no clear incremental gain with age.

The only observation to be made is that a considerable proportion of children do make sex distinctions in the way they view their parents' roles both in the home and at work, and that their viewpoint is strongly traditional and stereotyped. This will be illustrated more strongly in later items discussed in this chapter.

Attitudinal differences between parents

All responses revealing differences in personality and temperament were placed in this category, contrasts of behaviour, 'Dad yells at me, Mum is much calmer' (Australian boy, 13 years), and attitudes to the child, 'He's much sterner, and she's very easy going' (North American girl, 15 years), 'It's more fun to be with Dad; Mum worries too much' (English girl, 15 years). Father is frequently seen as the family disciplinarian, and mother as more loving and accommodating in attitude. There is a clear linear increase with age in this type of response, adolescents seeing attitudinal differences as more important, as Table 7.4 indicates. While attitudinal differences do not appear to be very important to the younger age groups there is a considerable acceleration

TABLE 7.4   *Percentages of children's descriptions of attitudinal differences between mothers and fathers by country and age-year (N = 838)*

Age-year	Australia	England	North America	Sweden
5	0	3	0	7
7	3	0	17	13
9	13	18	17	13
11	30	30	30	33
13	50	58	55	37
15	63	85	81	63

in the proportion noting these differences by the teenagers. This increasing concern is to be seen in all four countries, the graph (Figure 7.2) showing a close correspondence at most ages, with the English and North American 15-year-olds revealing a somewhat greater proportion than the Australian and Swedish 15-year-olds. It is interesting to note that the only significant sex differences in this item are to be found in 15-year-old Australian and Swedish girls (p < .05, see Table B.1, Appendix B).

Within the family it becomes increasingly important for children to be on-side psychologically with their parents. As pubertal characteristics develop they do discern, more sensitively, differences in attitudes between one parent and another.

The distinctive roles of mother and father

After asking in what ways mothers and fathers differed from each other, a statement was then made by the interviewer that 'There are some things a mother can do, that a father cannot do'. This was followed by the question 'What sort of things can a mother do that a father cannot do?' When this point had been clarified and the responses noted, the obverse point was put to the child about fathers. 'There are some things a father can do that a mother cannot do. What sort of things can a father do that a mother cannot do?'

These questions were designed to discover if there was any sex differentiation in the way children perceived the roles of mothers and fathers. Although it was asked of them as 'mothers' and 'fathers' it was evident that the responses included not only roles within the family, but roles of men and women generally in society. A criticism might be raised that the form of the question, especially when put separately for each sex, would encourage the children to sexually differentiate the roles of mothers and fathers. This section, however, did follow on naturally from the differences previously expressed by the children. The remarkable

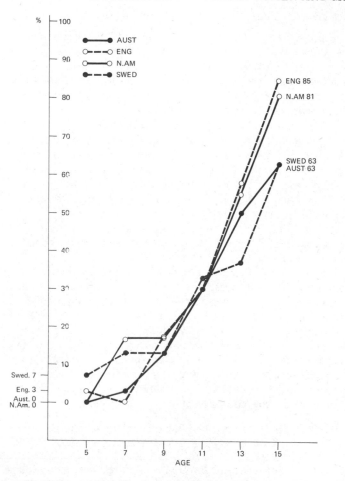

*Figure 7.2   Children's descriptions of attitudinal differences between
mothers and fathers by country and age-year*

volume of responses, some children making up to six replies to these role
oriented questions, indicates that their perceptions were certainly not
wholly determined by the questions themselves.

The answers were coded into six categories, then the number of
children and the percentage of each age cohort responding in the various
categories were tabulated. The six categories were roles involving domestic duties, roles involving production and care of children, leisure
time roles, conventional employment roles, authority-leadership roles
and roles shared with the marriage partner.

Roles involving domestic duties

All responses which involved work in or around the home and garden were allocated to this category. Included were activities such as shopping and gardening, but not roles directly involving children, this being identified as a separate category. A clear differentiation emerged of mother doing housework such as cleaning, washing, cooking, sewing, making beds, and occasionally gardening. Father on the other hand was seen as the conventional 'fixer' and repairman, looking after windows, roofs, garage, cleaning the car and frequently doing the garden, particularly heavy jobs such as mowing the lawn, cutting down tree branches or tasks involving the lifting of heavy objects. Much of this differential role allocation seemed to be biologically oriented, father's roles and skills in particular depending upon strength, as the younger children often indicated, confirming Ullian's observations (1976).

Set out in Table 7.5 is the proportion of children who see mother's role as domestic. While the respondents were not asked to identify the various roles or rank them in order of importance, the greatest proportion of responses in relation to mother were in this domestic category. In all countries the decrease of this response is apparent with increasing age; the younger children perceiving mother at home more, and doing domestic chores even if she has an outside job. Fathers are seen as occasionally 'helping' with the washing up, or cooking when mother is ill, but these were rare observations usually made by a handful of teenagers. There is a very close correspondence across all countries, the figures dropping more rapidly and consistently with the Swedish children, but unaccountably rising slightly at 15 years. When plotted in graph form this correspondence can be clearly seen (Figure 7.3).

TABLE 7.5 *Percentages of children attributing distinctive domestic roles to mothers by country and age-year (N = 838)*

Age-year	Australia	England	North America	Sweden
5	78	73	79	80
7	82	60	82	60
9	47	55	60	40
11	42	30	50	30
13	32	30	36	17
15	30	27	23	27

The decline does not mean a decline in mother's domestic duties, but probably a decline in those types of domestic roles perceived as distinctively the domain of mothers. This could be interpreted as an indicator of more egalitarian roles being undertaken domestically by both parents in the family, perceived by teenagers, but the figures for fathers do not

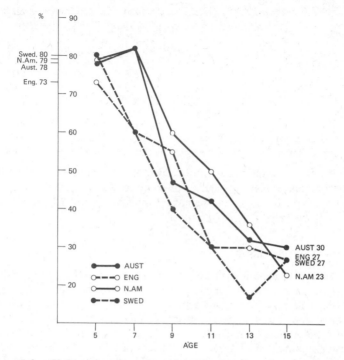

Figure 7.3   Children's perception of mother's role as involving
domestic duties by country and age-year

bear this out. More likely, it may be the children's widening conception
of a mother's roles to include duties or areas other than domestic, for
example sporting or leisure.

While there is a high incidence of domestic roles allocated to fathers
these are mainly in the role of domestic fixer and repairer and quite
distinct from mothers' domestic roles. The proportion of such responses
can be seen in Table 7.6. There is no apparent pattern to be seen in
these figures, but these roles which are distinctively the domain of
fathers on the domestic scene do not perceptibly decline with age as
do a mother's domestic roles. It does not necessarily indicate a sharing
of domestic roles with mother (this is included in the sixth category
and contains very few responses), but rather in domestic terms the roles
of mothers and fathers are seen as quite distinct yet complementary by
the children.

There are certain significant sex differences in the frequencies of
perceiving the parents to have distinctive domestic roles. Mother's
domestic role is seen by significantly more Australian 11 to 13-year-old

151

TABLE 7.6 *Percentages of children attributing distinctive domestic roles to fathers by country and age-year (N = 838)*

Age-year	Australia	England	North America	Sweden
5	55	60	38	50
7	28	50	40	47
9	43	43	47	23
11	30	20	30	13
13	47	45	45	20
15	20	30	19	40

boys, and by significantly more Swedish 15-year-old girls. Father's domestic role is seen by significantly more North American 15-year-old boys, and by significantly more Swedish 13- and 15-year-old girls (p < .05, see Table B.1, Appendix B).

Roles involving children

This category includes all responses mentioning the procreation of children, their care and feeding, including breast-feeding, talking to children and taking them to school. Discipline in relation to children is coded separately under authority–leadership roles. As one would expect these child-caring roles are seen as distinctively female by increasing numbers of children. The figures (Table 7.7) indicate that this view increases with increasing age in almost linear progression in all countries, reaching between 80 per cent and 95 per cent by the age of 15 years. Parenting, therefore, is seen by the children as a rather one-sided responsibility especially when the father's roles in this respect are tabulated (see Table 7.8). What is marked in Table 7.8 is that in three countries a third or more of the 15-year-olds see this as father's role also, perhaps illustrating Lamb's (1976) assertion that a change is occurring in male attitudes relating to roles previously thought of as distinctively female. What, however, is surprising by comparison, is the low 17 per cent of Swedish 15-year-olds who see father's role in these terms, since built into Swedish sex education programmes is the concept of the equality of the sexes, and other trends in egalitarian status of men and women are greater in Swedish society.

The contrast between the figures for mothers as distinct from those of fathers can be best seen in Figure 7.4 in graph form, the two sets of percentages showing no overlap whatsoever, with all scores for mothers being much higher than for fathers. There are no general sex differences on this item, although surprisingly in two age groups – the 15-year-old English and Swedish samples – boys more frequently allocate child-caring roles to father (see Table B.1, Appendix B).

TABLE 7.7 *Percentages of children attributing distinctive child-care roles to mothers by country and age-year (N = 838)*

Age-year	Australia	England	North America	Sweden
5	15	25	13	20
7	30	48	30	30
9	58	55	47	43
11	75	83	70	57
13	80	78	67	90
15	88	95	94	80

TABLE 7.8 *Percentages of children attributing distinctive child-care roles to fathers by country and age-year (N = 838)*

Age-year	Australia	England	North America	Sweden
5	3	3	4	10
7	0	5	0	10
9	8	15	3	3
11	20	13	13	13
13	5	20	12	17
15	38	33	39	17

Roles involving leisure

This third category was used initially to include all items not included in the first two, domestic and child-care duties, but in fact the residue of these responses tended to be leisure roles or activities, which were seen as distinctively gender oriented. These covered hobbies such as painting, dancing, 'messing about with the car' (Australian boy, 11 years), driving the car, smoking and drinking, making wine and, predominantly for men, sporting activities. The sports includes playing and watching football, hockey and baseball (ice hockey especially in North America), fishing, squash, swimming, cricket (Australia and England). The figures in Tables 7.9 and 7.10 show the reverse of the situation seen in the first two categories. Mothers are perceived in these leisure roles in some proportion up to 9 years, the tendency then decreasing to small or zero proportions. The exception is Sweden where the tendency may be explained simply by the ageing of the mothers, for as the children grow older so do the parents, and sport in particular tends to decrease. Yet hobbies or spare-time activities still continue with age. We are, however, examining what the child identifies distinctively as what one sex can do and the other cannot do, and it is this distinctiveness which declines as children perceive that perhaps they are not so distinctive after all.

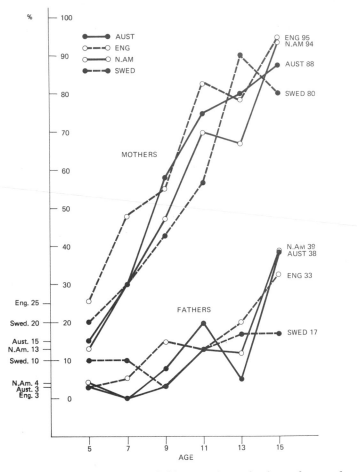

Figure 7.4   Children attributing child-care roles to both mothers and fathers by country and age-year

What is noticeable on an examination of Table 7.10 is that leisure roles are seen as more distinctively male, the majority of children in all countries perceiving this up to 9 years of age, continuing at a high level in the North American children until 11 years. Since sport composes a large proportion of these leisure roles identified as distinctively male, it is not surprising that there is a decline with the increasing age of the children, since as noted previously the age of the father is also increasing.

The difference in the numbers of children identifying leisure roles as distinctively male or female is most marked when seen in graph form in

154

TABLE 7.9   *Percentages of children attributing distinctive leisure roles to mothers by country and age-year (N = 838)*

Age-year	Australia	England	North America	Sweden
5	25	23	25	27
7	28	20	30	10
9	25	33	17	3
11	10	10	17	3
13	5	0	9	3
15	5	0	10	7

TABLE 7.10   *Percentages of children attributing distinctive leisure roles to fathers by country and by age-year (N = 838)*

Age-year	Australia	England	North America	Sweden
5	55	45	50	77
7	83	50	60	60
9	58	60	63	50
11	33	38	67	40
13	40	33	30	23
15	20	15	29	23

Figure 7.5. The distribution lines do not overlap between the sexes at any age, with mothers very low on the percentage scale. Significant sex differences in perceiving the father having distinctive leisure roles are seen in the Australian and English 15-year-old groups; boys more frequently than girls allocating these roles to father (p < .05, see Table B.1, Appendix B).

Stereotyped employment roles

The same imbalanced picture is evident in children defining jobs which can be done solely by women and not by men, and vice versa. Housework was specifically excluded from this classification, but all other mention of employment was coded into this category. Most mothers if they are employed are seen exclusively as typists, receptionists, hairdressers or shop assistants. 'Who ever heard of a male typist?' asked one incredulous 13-year-old English boy! The figures for mothers are so low as to be considered not worth tabulating since the highest proportion in any age cohort is only 5 children (17 per cent), with five cohorts having no responses in this category. As reported, what few responses there were in relation to mothers were decidedly sex stereotypes. Typical was the 11-year-old Australian girl who said 'Men can be doctors, but a girl can't'.

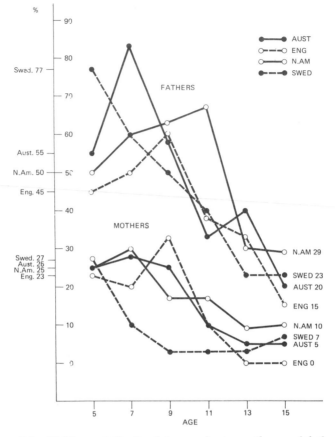

Figure 7.5   *Children attributing leisure roles to mothers and fathers by country and age-year*

In contrast, the figures for fathers, identifying distinctive jobs they can do which mothers can't do, were fairly high as Table 7.11 indicates. The statements were usually about building, digging or work with machines, which had a distinct biological orientation since strength and muscles were cited as the reason for their being the prerogative of males. In Ullian's terms (1976, p. 34) there was some societal orientation as in the previous quotation about 'Men can be doctors but a girl can't' and these did tend to come from the older children (10- and 11-year-olds). Psychological orientation, however, was not discernible possibly because our sampling ceased at 15 years.

156

TABLE 7.11 *Percentages of children attributing distinctive employment roles to fathers by country and age-year (N = 838)*

Age-year	Australia	England	North America	Sweden
5	28	33	46	20
7	38	43	50	27
9	35	25	27	13
11	38	45	43	13
13	20	30	31	20
15	45	45	39	23

Authority-leadership roles

This category included all references to being 'boss' of the family, the dominant parent, handling the finances, and being the disciplinarian. Occasional references to being 'the defender if a robber broke in' (English boy, 11 years) and 'My dad can do everything' (Australian boy, 11 years) were also included.

As was to be expected the mother is rarely identified as either the authority or the leader in the family, and this is expressed by one or two children in various age groups almost as quirks of a particular family. 'Dad's hopeless with money, so mum looks after that side very well' (English boy, 13 years), and 'Ma organises the holidays and outings. We never see much of Dad, he's always down at the boozer' (North American boy, 13 years). The only sizeable number of responses referring to mothers in any age group are the English and North American 13-year-olds (20 per cent each) whose comments reflect what they regard as an atypical situation.

The figures for fathers identified in authority or leadership roles are also sparse up to 13 years of age, suddenly appearing at that age and increasing at 15 years, as Table 7.12 shows. The exception is Sweden, perhaps a reflection of more egalitarian social attitudes, but plainly in the other countries there is an appreciable proportion who see the father's role distinctive in this respect. At 13 years girls slightly outnumber boys, but at 15 years 40 per cent of North American girls (compared with boys' 13 per cent) and 55 per cent of the English girls (compared with the boys' 30 per cent) see fathers in this distinctive role. In Australia 15-year-olds are slightly weighted towards the boys (40 per cent) compared with the girls (30 per cent) in this category. Clearly the English and North American teenage girls see or expect to see their fathers in this dominant role of authority. Since it is often asserted that teenage girls see their fathers as 'models' for their first

157

TABLE 7.12 *Percentages of teenagers attributing distinctive authority-leadership roles to father by country and age-year (N = 284)*

Age-year	Australia			England		
	Boys	Girls	Totals	Boys	Girls	Totals
13	10	15	13	10	20	15
15	40	30	35	30	55	43
	North America			Sweden		
13	19	22	21	–	–	–
15	13	40	26	3	–	3

heterosexual relationship, it is of interest to see these large percentages of teenage girls responding in this category.

Shared roles

There was little indication of awareness of roles in the family which could be shared by mothers and fathers, except where father takes over the cooking or washing or other domestic chores in an emergency, when the mother is sick or 'it's her evening at bingo' (English girl, 13 years). Since included in this category was the shared role of procreation of children (it was included in category 2 also) one would expect to find a reasonably large proportion identifying some roles as 'shared', especially as more egalitarian views are current, and marriage is seen by about a third of the children in terms of partnership. Johnson (1963) emphasised the centrality of fathers in reporting that both girls and boys need to identify not only with mother's role but with father's role in order to internalise appropriate sex-role orientation. In her later study (1975) she develops the theory that while mother through attachment is the basic socialising agent, father's role (later) is dominant in sex-typing for both sexes. By differentiating his paternal role toward opposite sexed children more than the mother, father reinforces 'femininity' in the girl and 'masculinity' in the boy.

There were, however, only 32 children with responses of this shared role kind representing only 3.8 per cent of the whole sample. These responses are distributed sparsely over many age cohorts, the only country revealing any sizeable groups in this category being North America. The distribution for that country is set out in Table 7.13. Other countries had mainly one or two children per age-year including Sweden. Shared roles are therefore seen more readily by the North American children than other groups especially from 9 years onwards.

To end this section on a lighter note one Swedish 11-year-old girl

TABLE 7.13 *Percentages of North American children in terms of shared roles for both sexes by age-year (N = 178)*

Age-year	5	7	9	11	13	15
Percentages	4	3	17	10	12	19

replied that both mother and father do the same thing, 'They both wash their hair, but she washes it in the sink and he washes it in the bath.'

Choice of the favourite parent

After the role oriented question about parents, the children were then asked, 'Do you have a favourite parent?' If the answer was 'yes', they were then asked to say which parent was the favourite and to give reasons for their choice. If the reply was 'No', and the indication was that both parents were well regarded by the children, the follow-up questions were 'What do you like best about your mother?' and 'What do you like best about your father?' It was brought to our attention by our Swedish colleagues that this question about a favourite parent posed difficulties for the Swedish children since there is considerable emphasis upon equality of the sexes in Swedish education and upon liking both parents equally. Consequently Swedish children have a very high proportion of 'both parents' answers and often tend to state nothing more specific than 'they are both equally nice'. Consequently, Swedish responses are not included in this analysis, although they are included in the 'reasons' section.

The children's choices in each country are best examined separately, first the choices by the boys, then the choices made by the girls. We will look first at the Australian children's choices set out in Table 7.14.

TABLE 7.14 *Percentages of Australian boys' choice of favourite parent by age-year (N = 120)*

| Choice | Age-year | | | | | |
	5	7	9	11	13	15
Mother	25	20	25	20	10	20
Father	50	30	20	10	5	30
Both parents	25	50	55	70	85	50

The pattern of Australian boys' choice of mother is fairly constant at each age with a dip at 13 years to 10 per cent. Apart from this age group about 20–25 per cent firmly chose their mothers.

Choice of fathers by Australian boys declines with increasing age to 13 years (5 per cent) and rises to 30 per cent at 15 years. The choice of both parents rises with increasing age, while there is some decline to 50 per cent at 15 years.

Australian girls' choices reveal a somewhat different pattern (see Table 7.15), choice of mother declining with increasing age to 15 per cent at 13 years and an increase to 35 per cent at 15 years. Choice of father tends to be low throughout the age range. Choice of both parents, however, has a very similar pattern to the boys, increasing with age and a decline to 50 per cent at 15 years.

TABLE 7.15 *Percentages of Australian girls' choice of favourite parent by age-year (N = 120)*

| Choice | Age-year | | | | | |
	5	*7*	*9*	*11*	*13*	*15*
Mother	60	55	35	45	15	35
Father	20	10	20	0	10	15
Both parents	20	35	45	55	75	50

The English boys' choices shown in Table 7.16 show mother choice to be fairly constant from 5 to 9 years, and then to decline to 15 years. The mother choice pattern is not too dissimilar to the Australian boys'. Father choices vacillate at differing age groups tending to decline at 11 and 13 years and rise again at 15 years.

TABLE 7.16 *Percentages of English boys' choice of favourite parent by age-year (N = 120)*

| Choice | Age-year | | | | | |
	5	*7*	*9*	*11*	*13*	*15*
Mother	25	30	25	10	20	10
Father	25	45	25	10	15	45
Both parents	50	25	50	80	65	45

The English girls' choice of mother shown in Table 7.17 is reasonably constant until 11 years, increasing to a high of 70 per cent at 13 years (just above the average menstrual age), then drops to 50 per cent at 15 years. Choice of father by the English girls show a higher choice from 5 to 9 years than Australian girls, dropping to a constant 20 per cent from 11 to 15 years. Choice of 'both parents' by the English girls is low throughout the age range, unlike the Australian girls, reaching only 30 per cent by 15 years.

The North American boys' choice of mother vacillates in no discernible pattern with very low percentages at 5 and 11 years, as seen in Table 7.18. Choice of father tends to decline with age, whereas choice

TABLE 7.17   *Percentages of English girls' choice of favourite parent by age-year (N = 20)*

Choice	Age-year					
	5	7	9	11	13	15
Mother	55	50	50	60	70	50
Father	35	45	35	20	20	20
Both parents	10	5	15	20	10	30

TABLE 7.18   *Percentages of North American boys' choice of favourite parent by age-year (N = 89)*

Choice	Age-year					
	5	7	9	11	13	15
Mother	8	38	33	7	31	31
Father	54	25	27	33	19	19
Both parents	38	37	40	60	50	50

of both parents tends to increase with age levelling off at 50–60 per cent at 11 to 15 years.

The American girls' choice of mother seen in Table 7.19 shows the dominance of this choice at all ages. Choice of father is made by less than one-third of the girls, dropping to 13 per cent at 9 and 15 years. Choice of both parents is low but a slight rise to 27 per cent is indicated at 15 years.

TABLE 7.19   *Percentage of North American girls' choice of favourite parent by age-year (N = 89)*

Choice	Age-year					
	5	7	9	11	13	15
Mother	64	79	67	73	65	60
Father	27	21	13	27	23	13
Both parents	9	0	20	0	12	27

Sex differences in choice of mother

For the choice of mother by boys, the most striking feature is the low percentages generally, the highest being 38 per cent of North American 7-year-old boys and 31 per cent of North American 13- and 15-year-old boys. Australian and English boys' choices generally decline with age, the highest percentage being 30 per cent. The expected maternal choice by younger boys, declining with age, is not in evidence.

A quite different picture for girls in the choice of mother is apparent. Here the percentages are quite high for younger age groups, beginning between 55 per cent and 64 per cent at 5 years. The North American girls remain high throughout as do the English girls. In these two countries the figures are high at 13 years, just above the average menarcheal age. In Australia, however, there is a perceptible decline with age to a low of 10 per cent at 13 years and with a rise to 35 per cent at 15 years. The picture of maternal choice by girls is as one might expect for North America and England, but atypical for Australia. Girls more frequently choose mother, in significantly greater numbers than boys, in the following age groups — Australian 7 years, North American 5, 7 and 11 years, and English 11, 13 and 15 years (see Table B.1, Appendix B).

Sex differences in choice of father

North American and Australian boys show a similar pattern for about 50 per cent choices of father at 5 years and a gradual decline to 11 years. There is a perceptible increase at 15 years in choice of father by the Australian boys, but not for the North American. The English boys choices are high at 7 and 15 years. By contrast choice of father as favourite parent remains very low for Australian and North American girls. It is highest of all three countries with 7-year-old English girls (45 per cent) but then levels off at 11 years to only 20 per cent. Only clear choices of one parent or the other are presented here. Their significance will be discussed later.

Reasons for choosing a favourite parent

The reasons given by the children for their choice of a favourite parent, or when choosing 'both' explanations of what they liked best about each parent, were coded into seven categories or roles set out in Table 7.20. These were reduced to three 'trends' indicating materialistic, emotional-social, and personalised relationship reasons, either for preferring one parent or what they liked best about each parent.

In the gift-providing role the parent provides or buys presents or 'good' things, or 'she gives me spending money and buys me pasties' (English girl, 7 years). Father 'buys me a bike and toys' (Australian boy, 5 years), and 'At the fairground he lets me go on the Merry-Go-Round' (English girl, 7 years). These replies tend to be from the younger age groups. Similarly appreciated is the basic sustenance provided by a parent, advanced by many: 'Mum makes good food, cakes and that' (English boy, 7 years); 'She really looks after you a lot' (Australian girl, 9 years). Father's role in this category tends to be the money earner,

TABLE 7.20   *Categories of reasons given for choice of favourite parent*

Trend	Category and description
Materialistic	*Gift provider* treats, sweets, Christmas gifts, pocket money. *Basic sustenance* meals, clothes, basic home requirements, bringing in the money. *Personal services* parent drives, arranges, conducts visits, holidays, sports events, fixes or repairs, available to help.
Emotional-social	*Succurant* loving, comforting, nursing when sick, assurance giving. *Teaching and induction* activities which allow child to participate in adult duties, shopping, helping with car, game playing with parent.
Personalised relationship	*Psychological support* sympathy, empathy, concern, tolerance, being 'on my side', lenient and permissive. *Companion-friend* confidante, adviser, relationship as more equal and not dependent, a good friend or companion to be with.

which indirectly provides the basic sustenance. Personal services covers a very wide range of parental activity, seen and appreciated by many children in being driven to parties, to school, to after-school activities, to football or other sporting activities: 'Dad takes me swimming' (Australian boy, 9 years); 'Dad helps me fix my Meccano' (English boy, 11 years); 'Mum's always there to help and spends more time with us' (English girl, 11 years); 'She takes us to the zoo, the park, the museum' (English girl, 13 years). The considerations voiced are mainly materialistic, the child receiving objects or services from the parent.

The next category, emotional-social, covers any succurant activities (giving succour) to the children who see themselves as emotionally dependent. To be loved, comforted, nursed when sick, 'to be cosseted', as one child put it, 'that's why I like Mum so much' (English girl, 11 years); included also are all teaching or induction roles of parents. Parents are liked when they admit children to adult activities, which include both teaching activities and induction to a wider social world. 'My mother teaches me how to make dresses and how to use the sewing machine' (Australian girl, 11 years); 'Dad plays tennis with me and shows me how to improve my game' (English boy, 13 years); 'I spend most time with him doing technical things' (English boy, 13 years); 'Mum lets me help with the ironing, and going out shopping' (North

American girl, 13 years). All these reasons for liking a parent are emotional-social in nature and represent an advance upon materialistic provision.

The last two categories are grouped together as personalised-relationship reasons, where the child is appreciative of being treated more as an equal, and is 'on the same wavelength' (Australian girl, 15 years) with a parent. Sympathy, empathy and psychological support are all part of this perception and are obviously regarded as of growing importance by teenagers.

The seven categories listed in Table 7.20 appear to form an hierarchical order, but scoring from 1 to 7 proved to be not only difficult but unrewarding in trying to discern trends. When the categories were collapsed into three, as the column 'Trend' indicates, and modal tendencies were tabulated, the results set out in the form of a series of matrices become more relevant. Four groups of reasons are examined: boys' reasons for choice of mother, girls' reasons for choice of mother, boys' reasons for choice of father, and girls' reasons for choice of father.

Reasons for choice of mother

Table 7.21 shows that Australian boys show emotional-social trends at 5 years (mostly succurant roles preference). It also shows materialistic trends up to 11 years, and personalised-relationship trends as teenagers. The English boys reflect materialistic trends up to 9 years, then prefer personalised-relationships from 11 onwards. The North American boys reveal mixed trends and the Swedish boys have a clear run of emotion-social preferences for mother until 15 years when personalised-relationship becomes the mode. Across the age cohorts 5- and 7-year-old boys are dominantly materialistic and 15-year-old boys universally prefer personalised-relationship with their mother.

TABLE 7.21 *Trends in boys' reasons for choosing mother by country and age-year (N = 419)*

| Age-year | Trends in | | | |
	Australia	England	North America	Sweden
5	E	M	M	E
7	M	M	M	E
9	M	M	E	E
11	M	P	P	E
13	P	P	E	E
15	P	P	P	P

(M = materialistic; E = emotional-social; P = personalised-relationship trends.)

Where the girls' reasons for choosing mother are concerned (see Table 7.22) the personalised-relationship trend with mother dominates as one would expect from 11 years onwards, and with Australian and Swedish girls from 9 years onwards. This need of girls for psychological support and a higher level of relationship with the parent of the same sex is very noticeable and may be related to earlier maturing trends. The 7-year-old girls' dominant trend appears to be materialistic. It is interesting that the only significant sex differences in choice of mother show Swedish girls responding more frequently than Swedish boys at 9 years in the 'personal services' category, and at 9 and 13 years in the 'psychological support' category (see Table B.1, Appendix B).

TABLE 7.22   Trends in girls' reasons for choosing mother by country and age-year (N = 419)

| Age-year | Trends in | | | |
	Australia	England	North America	Sweden
5	M	M	E	E
7	M	M	M	E
9	P	E	E	P
11	P	P	P	P
13	P	P	P	P
15	P	P	P	P

(M = materialistic; E = emotional-social; P = personalised-relationship trends.)

Reasons for choice of father

Australian boys' choice of father (see Table 7.23) reveals emotional-social trends, mainly succurant at the earlier ages of 5 and 7 years and teacher-induction trends at 11 and 13 years. The 'comradeship' concept of a boy with his father is not apparent, and then only tenuously with Australian, North American and Swedish boys at 15 years. Certainly, the teacher-induction trends are dominantly evident in all countries except North America, where materialistic preferences give way to the other two trends alternately at 9 and 13 years (emotional-social) and 11 and 15 years (personalised-relationships). Apart from North America the teacher and perhaps male modelling role are more important to boys than the companion-comrade idea. The most interesting sex difference which is statistically significant (see Table B.1, Appendix B), is to be seen in Australian boys of 7, 11 and 15 years who choose father for 'personal services' reasons significantly more than girls, and Australian 5, 7 and 15-year-olds together with English 13- and 15-year-olds, who choose father for 'teacher-induction' reasons significantly more than girls.

TABLE 7.23   *Trends in boys' reasons for choosing father by country and age-year (N = 419)*

Age-year	Trends in			
	Australia	England	North America	Sweden
5	E	E	M	E
7	E	M	M	E
9	M	E	E	E
11	E	E	P	E
13	E	E	E	E
15	P	E	P	P

(M = materialistic; E = emotional-social; P = personalised-relationship trends.)

TABLE 7.24   *Trends in girls' reasons for choosing father by country and age-year (N = 419)*

Age-year	Trends in			
	Australia	England	North America	Sweden
5	E	E	E	E
7	M	E	M	M
9	E	E	E	P
11	E	E	P	P
13	P	E	P	E
15	P	P	P	P

(M = materialistic; E = emotional-social trends; P = personalised-relationship trends.)

Girls, in choosing fathers (see Table 7.24), advance somewhat mixed reasons, the emotional-social trends appearing very strongly with Australian 5, 9 and 11 year girls and very dominantly throughout the English girls until the age of 15 years. Perhaps as Lamb observes (1976), the role of father during later childhood is as crucial for girls as it is for boys. The trends, however, in North America show personalised-relationships dominant from 11 years onwards. In Sweden trends are not easy to discern but 9, 11- and 15-year-old girls prefer personalised-relationships. In terms of age groups only 7-year-old girls evince dominant materialistic trends with their fathers, emotional-social (mainly succurant) dominates the 5-year-old girls, and emotional-social (mainly teacher-induction) dominates the 9-year-old girls' choices.

Summary and discussion

This chapter examines how children perceive the differences between

166

their mothers and fathers as representatives of females and males generally. It examines the questions – What are these differences and the
range of perceptions of differences by the children? Do children have
a favourite parent? Are their favourites the same sex or other sex
choices? and What are the reasons advanced to justify their choices?
Five categories of differences between mothers and fathers were
found. Children's perception of physical external non-sexual differences
declined with age in all four countries. The intrinsic non-sexual differences show no clear pattern except for the Australian pre-pubertal 11-
year-olds revealing the greatest proportion. There was no observable
pattern of incremental growth with increasing age in the perception of
overt sexual differences, as might have been expected, similarly in the
functional and social differences. Attitudinal differences did positively
correlate with age, that is the older the child in all countries, the higher
the percentage who recognised such characteristics differentiating
mothers from fathers. This differentiation dominates all other perceived
differences in importance by the teenage years, even including the overt
sexual differences which are the more visually obvious. This may be
accounted for by a psycho-social approach whereby adolescents aim to
establish some form of independence and consequently their views
often clash with that of their parents (Bettelheim, 1965).

The question concerning the roles of parents contained five response
categories. In domestic duties there is a decreasing recognition with
increasing age, yet the roles for mothers and fathers, even though seen
as quite distinct, are also seen as complementary. Mother is essentially
concerned with the internal house activities and father's activities are
concerned with the external house.

In the production and care of children role, sex distinctions are
quite clear. All children see roles involving children as uniquely female.
Younger children are more likely to see father overwhelmingly in a
leisure role than mother. Employment provides another disjunction,
mothers are seen as low status occupiers, while fathers may occupy
higher status jobs, sometimes seen as due to the biological fact of greater
strength.

The authority-leadership roles in the family show the father's dominance emphasised, especially by teenagers. Rarely was the mother seen
in such a role so that it is not surprising that there was little indication
of awareness of role-sharing by mother and father. In view of the fact
that more than one-third of the children did identify marriage in terms
of partnership this is interesting. Yet it may be that the nexus is indicative
of intergenerational change.

Overall, children view adults in terms of traditional sex-roles which
is directly related to their perceptual differences of men and women.
In light of the fact that this study was cross-national and included

children from Sweden which has had compulsory sex and human education in schools for some thirty years, the similarity of responses in the four countries, including three without compulsory sex education, does not augur well for enlightened approaches to sex-roles and human relationships in their various forms. It appears that present societal sex-roles are of stronger import than the content of educational courses aimed at lessening such distinctions. Even so, the influence of such human relationships courses cannot be dismissed since there can be hope only through the oncoming generations, due to the almost entrenched sexual stereotyping by older living generations.

Society needs to accept an increased leisure role for women, an increased parenting role for men, a more egalitarian attitude to employment, and overall increase in shared roles of women and men. That is, society needs to reject the sex-typed individual and promote androgynous persons; as Silvern and Ryan (1979) note, 'Androgynous persons should be maximally flexible, free to respond appropriately to situations regardless of whether they call for traditionally masculine or feminine traits of behaviour' (p. 740). The prognosis for such an acceptance seems to lie with the younger generation, with continued sex education, continued government programmes, and a concerted effort on the part of adults to promote communities of androgynous persons.

The question asking for a choice of favourite parent showed a fluctuating tendency in responses. Overall, boys in all ages were less likely to choose their mother as favourite in contrast to the girls who regularly prefer their mother. With fathers the reverse pattern is so, with boys generally preferring their fathers. These results do accord with the way children perceive their mothers and fathers in sex stereotypical roles. Their sex stereotyped activities, which are most relevant to and part of the child's world, are consequently perceived by the child as inherent and belonging to that particular sex.

In giving reasons for choice of a favourite parent, both boys and girls generally progress with age from materialistic through emotional-social to personalised-relationship categories. The exceptions to this are the Swedish children who rarely mention materialistic reasons and generally progress from emotional-social at 5 years of age to personalised-relationships. This earlier tendency of Australian, English and North American children to perceive materialistic reasons accords with the role of mother and father, as mentioned earlier, seen in terms of domestic duties. The teenage tendency in all countries to a personalised-relationship trend concurs with their recognition that attitudinal differences in mothers and fathers are of paramount importance.

8 Children's sex preferences

There is little dissent from the view that, while sexuality is biologically determined, sexual behaviour is strongly influenced by cultural and social expectations. As was pointed out in chapter 1, Unger (1979a) refers to 'gender' as the social label used to distinguish the two groups of people called male and female. Maccoby (1967) and her contributory authors in reviewing research on sex differences all emphasise the social learning of gender identity and its acquisition. In this sense, as Brown (1957) pointed out in developing his *It Scale for Children*, a girl adopts the feminine role and learns how to be a woman, and a boy adopts the masculine role and learns how to be a man.

Cognitive developmental research has established (Kohlberg and Zigler, 1967) that children have to identify their own gender (I am a boy or a girl), to recognise its stability (I will remain a boy or a girl) and to accept its constancy (I have always been a boy or a girl, and will continue to be so). These three, gender identity, gender stability and gender constancy, were investigated by Slaby and Frey (1975) on the assumption that this awareness is finalised in the years 4 to 8. As Kohlberg and Zigler had already indicated, gender identity appears to be mediated by the rate of general intellectual development. The years of 4 to 8 appear to be crucial for establishing gender identity and gender constancy, and in this the achieving of concrete operational thinking is of some importance.

The questions covered in this chapter were designed to see how children looked at gender identity, whether gender stability and constancy had been achieved, their sex preference in terms of personal identity and choice of friends, and the reasons for these preferences. Consequently the first question put was, 'If you could have chosen, would you have chosen to be a boy or a girl?' The children were then asked to give reasons for their preference. The second question was,

169

'Who makes a better friend, a boy or a girl?' Again, they were asked to say why they preferred a boy or a girl as a friend. Many studies have shown that sex differences are evident in friendship; these will be reviewed later in this chapter.

The first question on gender identity was seen as an interesting hypothetical question by most children. However, some of the older respondents, particularly Swedish teenagers, regarded it as 'silly' because it was unrealistic. Nevertheless, replies were received and evaluated. The second question on sex preferences in choice of friends again interestingly caused some problems to some of the older Swedish children. Educational emphasis upon sexual equality in Sweden and other factors have possibly led most of the older ones to say 'both' or 'it depends', giving more qualified answers than was evident in the other three samples.

Choice of gender identity

The question did not provide a direct opportunity to test gender constancy but in the 5-year-olds references were often made such as 'I was a girl when I was a baby, and the doctor changed me into a boy. (Q) With some medicine' (Australian boy, aged 5). So much for castration theory! Or, 'My mum picked me for a girl, and that's what I became' (North American girl, aged 5). These kinds of references, however, were not made after year 5.

As was to be expected most children chose their own sex, but a greater proportion of girls 'changed sex', that is, evinced a preference for being a boy. There were naturally highly significant differences (p < .001, see Tables B.2 and B.3, Appendix B) in boys choosing to be boys, and girls choosing to be girls, although not quite so significant in certain teenage groups. Those contrasting figures can be seen in Tables 8.1 and 8.2. The only age groups with any sizeable number of boys so choosing are the Australian 13-year-olds and the North American 15-year-old boys. This total number of boys in all samples was 23 (out of 419 boys): Australia 8, England 3, North America 10 and Sweden 2. The contrast with girls is obvious and confirms Brown's (1957) findings. The total number of girls choosing to be a boy was 55 (out of 419 girls); Australia 12, England 21, North America 14 and Sweden 8. This is 13 per cent compared with boys' reversals at 5.5 per cent. Brown's findings were that boys' choices were predominantly masculine and that girls' choices were predominantly feminine. Girls were significantly more variable than boys in their preferences. However, since Brown was investigating sex-role choices in a different context, the age variations of the girls are somewhat different.

We would postulate that these figures indicate that girls become increasingly aware of the restrictions of being a girl, and the relative

TABLE 8.1 *Percentages of boys choosing to be a girl by country and age-year (N = 419)*

Age-year	Australia	England	North America	Sweden
5	–	–	8	7
7	10	5	13	–
9	–	–	7	7
10	10	5	13	–
13	20	–	7	–
15	–	5	19	–

TABLE 8.2 *Percentages of girls choosing to be a boy by country and age-year (N = 419)*

Age-year	Australia	England	North America	Sweden
5	15	–	–	7
7	–	10	14	7
9	10	10	27	7
11	10	20	13	–
13	15	50	18	21
15	10	15	20	7

greater freedom of being a boy. The higher incidence of 'reversals' is for most countries the 13 year age group, with menstruation already experienced or at least imminent. The exceptions are the 9 year North American girls (27 per cent) and the very small distribution of 'reversals' among the Swedish girls, although there are 21 per cent who so choose at 13 years.

Most boys who choose to be a girl cite the reason 'curiosity' since they say it's a side of life they just do not know. One English 11-year-old boy had reservations: 'As long as I could change back if I didn't like it. I'd like to try something new. (Q) You are much more polite. Boys can hit girls, but girls can't hit boys'. Not one of the girls' answers, choosing to be a boy, is of this kind. Girls' reasons are that boys have a more exciting life and have many more choices of activity and employment open to them. Social restrictions on girls are often expressed by girls such as, 'I'd be a boy, because I'd like to be a doctor' (North American girl, 13 years), or 'A boy, because then I could go fishing and to football matches with my Dad' (Australian girl, 11 years). On the other hand one boy states he'd like to be a girl, because 'It's easier. Girls get away with more things' (Australian boy, 11 years), or 'It's nice to be at home all day' (English boy, 9 years). The reasons for their choices of the same sex are to be seen in the next sections.

Reasons for gender choice

The responses were coded into five categories: Recreational, Vocational, Behavioural/Temperamental, Sexual, and Independence/Dominance reasons. Recreational included all references to sports, hobbies, games and play, with frequent sex bias expressed. Vocational indicated preferences because of building or trade possibilities for boys, including being a soldier, a fireman, a professional sportsman, or positive desire by the girl 'to be a housewife'. The few girls who stated vocational reasons other than home duties tended to choose to be a boy. Behavioural/ temperamental covered all responses where the same sex were seen as compatible and easier to get on with or, by inference, girls suggesting boys were rough, noisy, aggressive and dirty and boys suggesting girls were soft, silly, unfair or plain bad-tempered. Sexual reasons covered responses where boys liked taking initiative in dating, or girls enjoyed being passive or pursued: 'If you want to go out with a girl, you can ask her to go out. If I were a girl I couldn't say "No" to a boy and hurt his feelings' (North American boy, 11 years); 'Boys do all the talking. They ask you to go out, you don't have to say anything' (Australian girl, 15 years). Independence/dominance reasons are those where one sex, usually male, is seen as freer, more independent or dominant; girls' reasons in this category included those which stated they got preferential treatment because they were girls, and assertions of sexual equality.

Recreational reasons for gender choice

Boys show a predominance in this type of reason at all ages, as can be seen in Table 8.3 and put typically by an English boy of 11 years, 'I like being a boy, mucking around. I like jogging, climbing, rugby, soccer, games not normally played by girls. I'm not being a chauvinist pig but I think boys are the stronger sex'. Younger boys see this as important for informal play such as climbing trees, making dens, and older ones almost overwhelmingly in terms of organised sports. Most frequently voiced by boys is the opinion that a wider choice of sports is open to them as boys. The exceptions are Swedish boys, who at 15 years have only 27 per cent making recreation their major reason for being a boy.

Girls, as the figures (Table 8.4) indicate, have a much lower response in this category than boys. The younger girls like to play with dolls, wear pretty dresses, play at mothers and fathers, whereas the older girls think knitting and sewing and other 'domestic'-based hobbies are attractive. Swedish girls reveal least interest in this category of all the countries from 11 onwards, although all girls show a decreasing interest from 9 onwards. Occasionally, sex-role stereotypes are evident: 'I do

TABLE 8.3 *Percentages of boys giving recreational reasons for choosing to be a boy by country and by age-year (N = 419)*

Age-year	Australia	England	North America	Sweden
5	70	85	69	73
7	60	75	75	73
9	65	90	73	56
11	85	80	73	53
13	85	85	69	67
15	70	65	69	27

TABLE 8.4 *Percentages of girls giving recreational reasons for choosing to be a girl by country and age-year (N = 419)*

Age-year	Australia	England	North America	Sweden
5	25	40	55	53
7	30	50	64	20
9	40	65	80	36
11	35	55	60	7
13	35	45	29	7
15	20	40	20	7

recorder lessons and boys really can't do that. (Q) They'd think it cissy' (English girl, 7 years); 'Boys have more exciting things to do than girls, like ride motor bikes and camping or mountain climbing. Girls can (do that) but you wouldn't think too much of her' (Australian boy, 11 years); 'Camping (is) O.K. but not the other things. They'd be tomboy' (American boy, 15 years). Significant sex differences can be seen in Table B.4, Appendix B.

Vocational reasons for gender choice

This is not as dominant a category as the recreational reasons, and it is noticeable (Table 8.5) that there is an increase among 15 year boys in all countries as they become more aware of vocational choices. A high percentage (47 per cent) is to be seen among the North American 11-year-old boys. Younger boys see hobbies as vocational preparation, as the Australian 7 year boy remarked, 'You can grow up and be a soldier . . . and boys can fix billy carts and help their Dads'. Older boys see it in work terms: 'There's nothing a boy can't be if you've got ability, like the professions or learning a trade, being a schoolteacher or a politician. But if you're a girl all kinds of jobs are closed to you' (English boy, 15 years).

173

TABLE 8.5 *Percentages of boys giving vocational reasons for choosing to be a boy, by country and age-year (N = 419)*

Age-year	Australia	England	North America	Sweden
5	25	10	23	7
7	20	20	31	7
9	20	20	27	7
11	25	25	47	13
13	20	30	25	–
15	40	35	38	20

TABLE 8.6 *Percentages of girls giving vocational reasons for choosing to be a girl by country and age-year (N = 419)*

Age-year	Australia	England	North America	Sweden
5	15	10	27	–
7	25	15	21	27
9	20	25	40	13
11	15	20	20	53
13	20	10	24	7
15	10	15	13	20

The frequency of vocational reasons given by girls is curiously similar to the boys (Table 8.6) with the difference of less emphasis at 15 years, whereas the boys have increased their interest. Young North American girls appear more interested (9 years at 40 per cent) and also 11-year-olds in Sweden (53 per cent). Many girls opt for self interest or the easier life: 'I don't want to do the military service. I like long hair and plaits' (Swedish girl, 7 years); 'Men go to work and all they do all day is work. Women stay home and do the ironing and washing and making beds. It stops them from getting bored' (English girl, 9 years); 'I'd stay at home and have kids. It's not so complicated as being a man' (North American, 15 year girl).

Behavioural/temperamental reasons for gender choice

What is a virtue with one sex is often a vice with the other. Boys take pride in their toughness, their fearlessness, their aggressiveness whereas girls find this behaviour rough, foolish and naughty. Girls on the other hand express preference for cleanness, pretty things, patient and sensible behaviour. Characteristics such as 'good, sweet, nice and sensitive' are claimed by girls to be desirable feminine traits. Up to 13 years of age boys tend to dismiss these characteristics contemptuously as 'cissy' and 'soft': 'Girls have silly squeaky voices. They're afraid of snakes and they won't play rough' (North American boy, 11 years). Plainly each sex has acquired behavioural and temperamental stereotypes of their own and the opposite sex.

TABLE 8.7 *Percentages of boys giving behavioural/temperamental reasons for choosing to be a boy by country and by age-year (N=419)*

Age-year	Australia	England	North America	Sweden
5	5	15	8	13
7	10	30	6	27
9	20	20	33	40
11	20	30	33	60
13	20	20	13	13
15	15	10	25	40

TABLE 8.8 *Percentages of girls giving behavioural/temperamental reasons for choosing to be a girl by country and by age-year (N=419)*

Age-year	Australia	England	North America	Sweden
5	20	35	–	7
7	25	30	29	60
9	45	55	33	60
11	40	40	40	40
13	30	40	26	40
15	20	25	20	53

These are not so evident with 5-year-old boys, but tend to increase with age until 13 and 15 years, presumably with the growth of sexual attraction to girls. This category is interestingly strong in Swedish boys with a high 60 per cent at 11 years and a still high 40 per cent at 15 years. The same emphasis is seen younger and generally stronger in Swedish girls also, perhaps Swedish culture reinforcing sex-roles of this type.

Girls across all countries give this reason more strongly than boys, feeling temperament and acceptable sex-role behaviour to be important, particularly up to 11 years of age. Apart from Sweden this tends to decline at 15 years. As we shall elaborate later, expressions of hostility or aversion are very common of one sex for the other and most of these negativisms appear to be in the behavioural/temperamental category.

Sexual reasons for gender choice

Boys are not as motivated in this category as are the girls (see Tables

8.9 and 8.10) but it must be remembered that the term 'sexual' is used in a very broad sense. For the boys sexual reasons are of two main types; they like being boys because they enjoy taking the initiative in dating or because they like wearing boy-type clothes. An English boy (7 years) put this latter point: 'Boys wear trousers everyday and girls usually wear dresses. (Q) People can pull them (dresses) up and see their pants'. Occasionally older boys express relief that they don't menstruate or have the pain of having to bear a baby.

TABLE 8.9 *Percentages of boys giving sexual reasons for choosing to be a boy by country and by age-year (N = 419)*

Age-year	Australia	England	North America	Sweden
5	5	15	15	7
7	30	15	6	–
9	10	5	33	–
11	20	5	13	7
13	10	15	6	–
15	10	15	31	–

TABLE 8.10 *Percentages of girls giving sexual reasons for choosing to be a girl by country and by age-year (N = 419)*

Age-year	Australia	England	North America	Sweden
5	40	55	55	47
7	50	50	50	27
9	60	30	60	47
11	45	45	53	53
13	40	40	24	27
15	55	85	67	33

The girls generally appear to find this a dominating reason for wanting to be a girl, reflecting the need to be attractive, to wear make-up and lipstick, to wear pretty dresses and jewellery, and to fulfil their feminine role by producing babies. This can be seen (Table 8.10) as a strong tendency from 5 years of age in all countries, not as dominant with Swedish girls at 13 and 15 years, although North American girls have a low 24 per cent at 13 years increasing to 67 per cent at 15. In practically all age groups significantly more girls gave 'sexual' reasons in the choice of their own sex than did boys in choosing theirs (see Table B.4, Appendix B).

Reasons of independence/dominance for gender choice

Presumably it takes considerable social experience to recognise that one sex may be treated as more independent or dominant than the other. If this is so it is not surprising that these types of answers occur only from 11 years onwards. There are no significant differences between boys and girls in giving this type of response, although with the boys it is a slightly higher frequency (Tables 8.11 and 8.12). Boys see it as better to get preferential treatment, status or being 'boss': 'If you're a boy, you get perks, the best of everything, the best food. It's natural selection, I suppose' (English boy, 15 years); 'I can stay out late at night and go into the city. If I were a girl I wouldn't have so much freedom' (North American boy, 13 years); 'I'm looking forward to being head of a family, that's a man's rightful place, to be looked up to', this pedestal type posture being seen by an Australian 15-year-old-boy.

TABLE 8.11   *Percentages of boys from 11 years giving independence/ dominance reason for choosing to be a boy by country and age year (N = 211)*

Age-year	Australia	England	North America	Sweden
11	5	10	20	—
13	20	25	13	47
15	50	35	38	47

TABLE 8.12   *Percentages of girls 11 years giving independence/ dominance reasons for choosing to be a girl by country and age-year (N = 203)*

Age-year	Australia	England	North America	Sweden
11	5	—	—	—
13	—	15	12	47
15	25	25	33	47

This category may be misleading for included in it are assertions of equality, the most frequent response made by older girls as 'independent'. These are most frequent at 15 years of age. It also explains the high figures, the same for both Swedish boy and girl teenagers (47 per cent). Here, assertions of equality of the sexes are made. It is seen as good to be a boy or a girl because each has freedom and growing independence, the dominance concept not usually expressed. One would postulate that this may be the product of egalitarian emphases in Swedish education over the last few decades.

An overview of reasons given for gender choice

Looking at the five categories of reasons for gender choice separately obscures the trends that may be discerned at certain ages. By taking the modal scores in each age group certain trends do stand out, as the separate matrices for boys and girls indicate in Tables 8.13 and 8.14. The boys in all countries up to 9 years are dominated by recreational reasons for choosing to be a boy. This trend continues in the Australian and English boys, with dominating roles stressed by 15-year-old Australian boys and some of the same tendency for English 13-year-old boys. At 11 and 15 years North American boys have mixed tendencies, the 15-year-olds being the only male age category where sexual reasons occur in any proportion (31 per cent for each category). Swedish boys show a tendency towards behavioural reasons at 11 years and independence reasons as teenagers.

TABLE 8.13 *Trends in boys' reasons for gender choice by country and age-year*

Age-year	Australia	England	North America	Sweden
5	Recreational	Recreational	Recreational	Recreational
7	Recreational	Recreational	Recreational	Recreational
9	Recreational	Recreational	Recreational	Recreational
11	Recreational	Recreational	Behavioural Vocational	Behavioural
13	Recreational	Recreational Dominance	Recreational	Independence
15	Dominance	Recreational	Dominance Sexual	Independence

TABLE 8.14 *Trends in girls' reasons for gender choice by country and age-year*

Age-year	Australia	England	North America	Sweden
5	Sexual	Sexual	Sexual	Sexual
7	Sexual	Sexual	Sexual	Behavioural
9	Sexual	Behavioural	Sexual	Sexual
11	Sexual	Sexual	Sexual	Sexual
13	Sexual	Sexual	Behavioural Sexual	Behavioural
15	Sexual	Sexual	Sexual	Sexual Independence

For the girls the trends are overwhelmingly sexual in all countries, perhaps reflecting the prevailing emphasis in these countries of the sex-role of girls and women. English 9-year-old girls and North American 13-year-old girls have a tendency to put 'behavioural' first, as do Swedish 7-year-old girls. There are some different emphases by Swedish teenage girls, perhaps reflecting more egalitarian attitudes, but the trends are not strong ones.

The major overall distinction is that boys prefer being boys because of greater play and sports opportunities, to develop skills of strength and speed, and later their masculine dominance or independence. Girls prefer being girls overwhelmingly because of their feminine roles of developing domestic skills and hobbies, playing the sexually attractive role of being women and fulfilling their biological role by having babies.

Sex preferences for friends

While the literature on children's friendships based upon diverse theoretical and research frameworks is evident, it is still a comparatively new and unresearched field (Mannarino, 1980). Comprehensive surveys of this literature, such as those by Hartup (1970 and 1978), focus upon peer norms in friendship choice, peer interaction, friendship dyadic structures, the role of friendship in socialisation processes, social maturing and future life relationships, children's expectations of friendship, and developmental values attached to friendship. While all studies indicate sex differences and early preference for own sex friendships, there is little research on the reasons for such preferences. The second question in this section of the interview was put to explore this particular area.

Sex preferences in choice of friends can be seen operating in all schools and community groups, in childhood (5 to 11 years) the pattern being dominated by choice of same sex, and in later years becoming more heterosexual, as dating and mating becomes more evident. Hence the question, 'Who makes a better friend for you? A boy or a girl?', and the follow-up question asking for reasons for that choice. As noted before, most children opted for one sex or the other, but in Sweden there was a strong tendency particularly among the boys to choose 'both', possibly the product of long-term educational emphasis. For the purposes of analysis the figures for the choices made by boys (Table 8.15) are treated separately from those made by girls (Table 8.16).

Although Australian boys from 5 to 11 years strongly prefer a boy as a friend, 5- and 7-year-olds show a moderate proportion of 'girl' or 'both' preferences, this decreasing sharply at 9 and rising again at 11, the teenage tendencies of attraction for the other sex being obvious

179

from 13 onwards. A similar trend up to 9 years is observable in English boys, but by contrast the lowest choice of 'girls' is at 11 years, and is slow at increasing (only 25 per cent at 15 years). North American boys tend to follow a trend almost identical to Australian boys, while Swedish boys after 7 years manifest the 'both' responses, with these predominating gradually from 11 years onwards.

TABLE 8.15   *Percentages of boys' choice of friend by country and age-year (N = 419)*

Age-year	Sex choice	Australia	England	North America	Sweden
5	Boy	75	80	69	80
	Girl	20	10	23	7
	Both	5	10	8	13
7	Boy	60	80	62	33
	Girl	15	10	32	7
	Both	25	10	6	60
9	Boy	90	85	80	60
	Girl	5	10	7	–
	Both	5	5	13	40
11	Boy	75	95	73	13
	Girl	5	–	27	–
	Both	20	5	–	67
13	Boy	30	80	44	–
	Girl	35	15	31	–
	Both	35	5	25	100
15	Boy	45	60	63	20
	Girl	20	25	25	–
	Both	35	3	13	80

Whether the English teenage boys' low figures can be seen as in any way symptomatic of heterosexual retardation is dubious until other factors are considered. A great deal depends upon what interpretation the term 'a better friend' is given, perhaps seen differently in different societies. We come back as in chapter 6 to the dominance of 'romantic love' as the basis of sexual relationships, with a growing minority tendency to see companionship and friendship as more important.

Overall the girls similarly choose their own sex, the English girls from 7 to 13 showing marked lack of heterosexual choice. The comments above about English boys' heterosexual retardation apply to the girls also. These heterosexual choices are also very limited with the North American girls until 15 years of age. Australian girls show some interest in the other sex throughout the age range (signified by choice of 'boy' and 'both') with heterosexual choice increasing at 13 years.

TABLE 8.16 *Percentages of girls' choice of friend by country and age-year (N = 419)*

Age-year	Sex choice	Australia	England	North America	Sweden
5	Boy	15	10	27	27
	Girl	75	80	73	47
	Both	10	10	–	27
7	Boy	20	10	14	20
	Girl	75	90	86	47
	Both	–	–	–	33
9	Boy	15	–	13	20
	Girl	75	100	80	47
	Both	10	–	7	33
11	Boy	15	5	7	13
	Girl	70	95	93	47
	Both	15	–	–	40
13	Boy	25	10	23	33
	Girl	55	80	71	27
	Both	20	10	6	40
15	Boy	10	25	40	7
	Girl	70	70	53	33
	Both	20	5	7	60

The Swedish girls are the most atypical of this pattern after 7 years of age, the move to choice of 'boy' and 'both' being marked but becoming very evident from 11 to 15 years.

Overall the patterns of choice are as expected for both sexes, being that of their own sex up to the end of childhood, as Hartup (1978) noted. The nature of social activity also varies by sex according to Edelman and Omark (1973). Hartup suggests that divisions between the sexes in early childhood are based on shared interests of the same sex rather than avoidance of the opposite sex. This can be seen clearly in the results of the next section. However, there would appear to be some cultural differences. Some national groups, such as the English and to a lesser extent the North Americans, appear to be slower in heterosexual friendship interests. The Swedish children appear to be atypical compared with the Australian, English and North American children.

Reasons for choice of friends

Having chosen the one who makes a better friend by indicating 'boy', 'girl' or 'both', the children were asked to give their reasons for choosing one sex or the other. If they had answered 'both', then they were asked 'What is it that makes a boy a good friend?' followed by 'What is it that makes a girl a good friend?' The responses were coded into four categories: identity of activities and interests, identity of feelings, social pressures, and sexual attraction or activities. Many more categories could have been used such as Bigelow's (Bigelow and La Guipa, 1975) or the four selected could have been broken into many sub-categories, but it was found that all responses could be coded satisfactorily into the four selected categories. Bigelow's work in Canada and later (Bigelow, 1977) in Scotland found Grades 1 to 8 thought of best friend as the same sex and were asked to write an essay on what they expect of their friends compared with acquaintances. In our study there was a subtle difference, since the question was directed to reasons for choice of one sex rather than the other as a friend. The results are therefore not strictly comparable, although expectations of a friendship do provide some commonality. Some reasons for sex choice of friends have been studied by Eder and Hallinan (1978). In all these studies, including the one reported here, the children tend to assume dyadic friendships, although occasional references are made to triadic friendships.

The two categories containing the most responses were identity of activities and interests, and identity of feeling. Under activities and interests boys tended to prefer boys because they asserted they could muck about together, play the same sports, ride bikes, go camping, or simply that there was a greater range of activities to choose from with a boyfriend. Girls tended to choose girls to share the same activities or interests in playing with dolls, dressing up, going shopping and simply because they like the same things. 'Girls are more likely to stick together. (I) prefer a boy; you think the same things, like sport or riding a bike' (Australian boy, 15 years); 'You can play rough games and have more variety than with girls. Girls also get ahead of you at school' (English boy, 9 years). While the first part of this 13-year-old English boy's reply reflects social pressure, 'I'm not old enough to have a girlfriend', the next contains a more important reason, 'I want to do completely different things, like football. Unless she's one of these tomboys, and if she were you might as well have a boyfriend'. A very typical Swedish response is 'Both': (Q) 'It's easier to talk to a girl, and with boys we can do things together as boys' (Swedish boy, 15 years). The girl shares feelings and the boy shares activities. The overwhelming choice of boys in giving 'identity of activities' as the prime reason for choosing a friend can be seen in Table B.5, Appendix B.

Identity of feeling responses were placed in this category where feeling at ease, mutual trust, and very importantly 'keeping a secret' were mentioned. As also being able to confide in, talk to, share troubles with or simply 'be on the same wavelength'. 'It depends', says an

Australian girl, aged 11, 'on their attitudes, whether they're snobbish or friendly. It doesn't matter if it's a boy or a girl, if you can trust them.' Nevertheless most boys felt they could trust another boy, and most girls felt they could trust another girl, more than the other sex. Frequently both boys and girls referred to the other sex as 'gossipy' or 'they tell their friends and laugh at you' or 'they can't keep a secret'. A Swedish boy of 15 says, 'Both, if you can trust them and they're friendly and are fair and honest'. A Swedish girl of 15 spans several categories, 'A girl. She must stand up for me. Be able to talk about everything and not give me away, and have the same interests as I have.'

Social pressures as a category includes all reference to the same sex being more accessible. Some had experienced outright social rejection. 'Girls run away from you' (Australian boy, 9 years). An American boy of 11 says, 'You've more common interests with boys, and round my age the two groups keep separate, and if you cross over its difficult'; 'People think you're getting into mischief with a boy (Q) like kissing' (English girl, 9 years). Mourning the loss of earlier childhood girl-friends, an Australian boy (15 years) says rather sadly, 'When you're very young you can play together. After 12 you can't do that. It's how society works.'

Sexual attraction and activities relating to sex naturally includes someone to date, kiss, take to the movies or to be taken out by. For many boys to have a boy as friend helps you with girls; 'It helps you when you're chasing, or dating them, because you can pair off' (Australian boy, 13 years). Also in this category is the reason that girls have a girlfriend to share pretty things, 'making yourself more beautiful'. It also includes where a same sex choice is made, 'because I'm not attractive to girls (for boys)' although heterosexual longings are plainly in evidence. Not surprisingly, in view of the social taboos discussed elsewhere, there are few overt sexual responses given in choosing a member of the other sex as a friend, even in the teenage years. Only the occasional teenage girl and about 25 per cent of teenage boys make overt references to sex. These responses appear to be sublimated under the cover of feelings and expressed under the second category.

Tabulating the modal scores of boys and girls each in turn it is possible to identify quite differing trends between the sexes. In Table 8.17 the trend of boys choosing their own sex is justified up to 11 years in terms of identity of activities and interests. This corresponds closely with boys' reasons for choice of their own sex identity as a boy, since play and sport in a wide variety of choices are open to boys. The 'feelings' trend comes in late at 13 years with English boys and not until 15 years with the Australian and the North American boys. Indeed, the longer lasting outdoor sporting preoccupation of Australian boys may account for 'the feeling' reason only sharing the modal trend at 15 years. The

TABLE 8.17 *Modal trends of boys' reasons for choice of a boy as 'better friend' by country and age-year*

Age-year	Australia	England	North America	Sweden
5	Activities	Activities	Activities	Activities
7	Activities	Activities	Activities	Activities
9	Activities	Activities	Activities	Feelings
11	Activities	Activities	Activities	Feelings
13	Activities	Feelings	Activities	Feelings
15	Activities Feelings	Feelings	Feelings	Social Pressure

major exception is again the Swedish boys, who share a preoccupation with identity of activities only up to 7 years. From 9 to 13 the 'feelings' quality of friendship with another boy is dominant and then, curiously, gives way to 'social pressure'. This latter category may, however, be confused by the constant choice of both sexes and the justification for this by the Swedish boys.

The preoccupation by boys with activity, seen in reasons given earlier for choice of own sex, and now evident in reasons for friendship with own sex, can be explained in terms of both nature and nurture. Hutt (1978a) has documented evidence that from birth males are better equipped physiologically for a physically active life, quoting further research to verify that activity levels of boys at birth and during early childhood are greater than in girls (Korner, 1969; Goggin, 1975). There is also evidence to suggest that pre-school boys engage in physical activities more frequently than girls (Clark *et al.*, 1969; Brindley *et al.*, 1973). Even indoors there are indications that boys are allowed physical activities by parents (Hutt, 1978b). Adults, Hutt suggests, are more tolerant towards boys' physical and athletic activities, more accepting of their restlessness, and related untidiness and messiness. The earlier emphasis upon 'feelings' in Swedish boys may reflect changes in nurturing practice in that country, that is, a differing cultural emphasis.

Where girls are concerned there is expectedly a different pattern of trends, as can be seen in Table 8.18, the 'feelings' justification appearing much earlier at 9 years of age in all countries, with Swedish girls showing a preponderance of this at 7 years. Although identity of activities and interests tend to continue alongside 'feelings' as the major reason for choosing a girl as a friend, the feeling element supplants it between 9 and 11 years. The 'feelings' reason is clearly dominant with the Swedish girls from 7 years of age. The more mixed nature of the reasons for choice of a girlfriend given by girls can be seen in Table B.5, Appendix B.

TABLE 8.18   *Modal trends of girls' reasons for choice of a girl as 'better friend' by country and age-year*

Age-year	Australia	England	North America	Sweden
5	Activities	Activities	Feelings	Activities
7	Activities	Activities	Activities	Feelings
9	Activities Feelings	Activities Feelings	Feelings	Feelings
11	Feelings	Activities Feelings	Feelings	Feelings
13	Feelings	Feelings	Feelings	Feelings
15	Feelings	Feelings	Feelings	Feelings

The results for girls lends further emphasis to the evidence from Hutt (1978a) that parents of first-born infants rated girls as softer, more fine-featured and smaller than boys. Actual differences and parental expectations, stemming from sex stereotypes, become confused as Rubin's (Rubin *et al.*, 1974) study reveals. Girls tend to show greater dependency upon mother than do boys, especially in stressful situations and mothers appear to be more protective towards daughters; and there is less of a tendency to encourage independence or autonomy as with their sons (Baumrind and Black, 1967; Hoffman, 1972). This process would certainly assist in encouraging the feeling elements in relationships by girls. The early interest by girls in dyadic friendships (Brindley *et al.*, 1973), as opposed to the groupings by boys, would also tend to strengthen the 'feeling' as opposed to the 'activities' element in friendship.

It may also be that the difference between boys and girls in friendship expectations is due to earlier social maturing of girls and accompanying perceptions of what makes for a good relationship. Perhaps the earlier incidence of 'feelings' as a reason for friendship by both boys and girls in Sweden reflects the human relations work seen in Swedish schools from the age of 8 years, and the influence of nurture.

Reasons for choice of other sex friends

An examination of the incidence of various reasons for boys choosing a girl, and girls choosing a boy, are of interest. Where the reason given is 'identity of activities or interests' the girls choosing a boy are very few, the highest proportion being 20 per cent of 7-year-olds and 25 per cent of 9-year-old Australian girls. It is slightly higher with Swedish 5- and 7-year-old girls but this is inflated by a high proportion of 'both' answers. The boys choosing girls in this category are somewhat higher

185

in some countries, as can be seen in Table 8.19. After 11 years only one or two children so choose, but the popularity of this choice is evident at 7 years before the social conventions, so accurately observed by the children, inhibit heterosexual friendships.

TABLE 8.19 *Percentages of boys choosing a girl for 'identity of activities and interests' reasons by country and age-year (N = 277)*

Age-year	Australia	England	North America	Sweden
5	15	15	31	—
7	35	20	38	20
9	10	5	7	7
11	20	5	7	20

TABLE 8.20 *Percentages of boys choosing a girl as 'better friend' for 'identity of feelings' reasons by country and age-year (N = 211)*

Age-year	Australia	England	North America	Sweden
11	10	—	7	73
13	50	5	38	60
15	65	35	38	60

TABLE 8.21 *Percentages of girls choosing a boy as 'better friend' for 'identity of feelings' reasons by country and age-year (N = 213)*

Age-year	Australia	England	North America	Sweden
11	40	30	7	40
13	20	45	31	60
15	45	45	56	30

Perhaps the most interesting analysis is to see choices of the other sex as friend, under the category of 'feelings'. Earlier we pointed out that this category could well act as a concealed answer for sexual reasons. The results tabulated for each sex separately can be seen in Tables 8.20 and 8.21 from the age of 11 upwards. The previous ages are excluded since they contained only a few children with such heterosexual choices. The progression of boys' percentages can be seen with increasing age and sexual maturity, except in the case of Swedish boys where again choice of 'both' sexes tends to confuse and inflate the the results. Where girls are concerned the progression is not so apparent, but the proportions are fairly high. There is a clear progression with age in the North American girls and partly so with the English girls. From this it would be safe to assume that sexual feelings are probably concealed within the more general expression of feelings involving trust, patience, warmth and understanding.

Expressions of aversion to the other sex

In scoring and coding responses of the items covered in this chapter, the authors noticed the many unsolicited negative responses to the other sex by both boys and girls. Accordingly all these negativisms were tabulated and all respondents expressing such aversions were calculated. The incidence for boys can be seen in Table 8.22. These percentages are very high, increasing with age in most countries between 9 and 11, and then decreasing in the teenage years, except with the English boys where it still remains high (50 per cent) at 15 years. The Swedish pattern is again different with fewer negativisms expressed by fewer boys and ceasing at an earlier age. The incidence can be seen for girls in Table 8.23. In all countries more girls express negativisms about the other sex than do the boys, with the exception of North America where the incidence is about the same for both sexes. A decrease occurs in the teenage years. The English 15-year-olds of both sexes have the highest aversion rates to the other sex, but Swedish teenage girls have a significantly higher aversion rate than Swedish teenage boys (see Table B.6, Appendix B).

TABLE 8.22 *Percentages of boys expressing aversion to the other sex by country and age-year (N = 419)*

Age-year	Australia	England	North America	Sweden
5	10	35	23	13
7	35	50	50	–
9	55	55	54	13
11	45	50	40	27
13	25	30	13	–
15	15	50	25	–

The negative comments range from mildly disparaging remarks such as 'Boys are a bit rough' (English girl, 11 years) and 'Girls are a bit silly' (American boy, 11 years), to downright hostility: 'I can't stand the way girls yell and carry on. They're a pain in the neck' (Australian boy, 15 years) and 'Boys are dirty, messy, noisy creatures. I just don't like them' (English girl, 13 years). These comments were often made in a querulous tone of voice.

TABLE 8.23 *Percentages of girls expressing aversion to the other sex by country and age-year (N = 419)*

Age-year	Australia	England	North America	Sweden
5	40	65	27	47
7	75	80	50	73
9	65	70	47	20
11	45	50	33	47
13	30	25	35	27
15	10	25	7	13

Two points stand out. One is that the highest incidence of aversions for both boys and girls approximates to childhood, beginning with relatively fewer negativisms, the aversions growing with increasing separateness of the sexes, and only receding as greater social maturity and biological needs begin to appear. The English figures indicate aversions to be particularly high for girls and longer lasting for boys, which might explain the delayed heterosexual interests of the English teenagers noted elsewhere (Schofield, 1968). The other point is that educational systems may well appear to strengthen rather than diminish aversions to the other sex by attitudes of teachers and the expectations of schools and society. The Swedish data is relevant here since the numbers of children expressing negativisms are considerably less, particularly in boys, where school programmes and society in general stress the equal worth and equal status of both sexes. The high figure of 73 per cent revealing negativisms by Swedish 7-year-old girls may be explained by the fact that formal schooling has only just begun at that age.

Aversions to own sex

There were a small number of children, 21 boys and 40 girls, who expressed an aversion to their own sex, in all 5 per cent of the boys and 9.5 per cent of the girls. The greatest number of boys in any one age-year were 30 per cent of Australian and 20 per cent of North American 13-year-olds. The girls, outnumbering the boys by two to one, tend to have a wider age distribution of aversion to their own sex, but the major concentration is in the teenager years as Table 8.24 shows. Various explanations or sources can be offered as to why these sexual aversions are expressed; from parents who wanted the child to be the other sex, through unsatisfactory experience of friendship with their own sex, to the beginnings of homosexuality. The high proportion of girls in this category may be explained by their perception of the lower status of women in society and the growing awareness of this by some girls, except noticeably in Sweden. It is difficult enough to cope with

TABLE 8.24 *Percentages of teenage girls stating aversion to their own sex by country and age-year (N = 142)*

Age-year	Australia	England	North America	Sweden
13	20	35	6	–
15	15	20	20	–

negativisms about the other sex, which hopefully they will outgrow, but much more difficult to live with negativisms about one's own sex, which form an essential part of one's own sexual identity.

Summary and discussion

The questions covered in this chapter were designed to explore how children perceive gender identity, whether gender stability had been achieved, and their sex preferences in terms of personal identity and choice of friends. The first question was, 'If you could have chosen, would you have chosen to be a boy or a girl?', followed by asking the reasons for their choice. The second question was, 'Who makes a better friend, a boy or a girl?', and again the children were asked to give reasons for their choice.

In choosing a gender for themselves the majority chose their own sex, but boys were more likely to choose their own sex than girls, their greater number of sex 'reversals' being at 13 years, the age around which menstruation had occurred or was likely to occur. The reasons given were coded into five categories – recreational, vocational, behaviour-temperamental, sexual, and independence-dominance. In the English-speaking countries the boys gave recreational reasons for choosing to be boys until 13 years, this continuing with English boys to 15 years. At 15 years Australian boys favoured dominance as a reason, and the North American boys were divided in choosing sexual reasons and dominance reasons at that age. In the Swedish sample boys left recreational reasons behind at 11, giving greater freedom of behaviour, then choosing independence as their reasons for wishing to be boys at 13 and 15 years. In contrast girls at all ages gave sexual reasons for wishing to remain girls.

In choosing a friend in terms of sex identity most similarly choose their own sex, but heterosexual choice begins to develop in the teenage years. There is a much slower move to heterosexual preferences in North America, and almost a retardation factor evident in the English sample.

Reasons given for preferences for their own sex as friends fell into mainly two categories, identity of interests or activities and identity of feelings. The English-speaking groups at all ages tended to give

189

identity of activities for choosing a friend, linking up with their recreational reasons for wanting to be a boy. In Sweden the categories were more mixed giving 'feeling' reasons, that is, needing to be on the same wavelength as a friend, from 9 years. Feelings become important to boys in the English-speaking teenage groups, presumably as heterosexual interests develop. Again the girls provide a contrasting picture, with activities an early choice, but this giving way to identity-of-feeling reasons for wanting to be a girl by the age of 9 years, and in Sweden earlier at 7 years. Feelings as a basis for friendship then dominated the girls' choices up to and including the 15-year-olds, whether homosexual or heterosexual friendships are chosen.

Considerable aversion to the other sex was voiced by children of both sexes in very high proportions. Such negative expressions were tabulated into 'aversion scores'. High aversion scores were particularly noticeable among the English-speaking boys, reaching the high proportion of those voicing negativisms (on average about 55 per cent of them) at 9 years of age then slowly declining as heterosexual interest began to develop. But the aversion rate remained high (50 per cent) among English 15-year-old boys in particular; perhaps accounting in part for the heterosexual retardation factor noticeable in this group. In contrast Swedish boys were low on aversion-to-other-sex scores.

Greater and longer hostility towards the other sex was, however, evident among girls in all countries from the age of 7 years, and still substantial at 11 years. In the teenage years it begins to subside somewhat, although 25 per cent of English 15-year-old girls still express negativisms, again contributing perhaps to the English heterosexual retardation phenomenon noted earlier.

There were some respondents of both sexes who expressed strong aversions to their own sex, about 5 per cent of boys and 10 per cent of girls. This appeared to peak at 13 years, and was almost non-existent in Sweden. Various suggestions were made to explain this own-sex negativism. Girls expressed own-sex aversion in greater proportion than boys, the highest being 25 per cent of English 13-year-old girls. This own-sex negativism may stem from a growing awareness of the disadvantages involved in being female in a male-dominated society.

What stands out from the findings elaborated in this chapter are the relatively fixed sex-typing and gender role concepts children develop very soon in their social life, that is, by 7 years. This is also the time when the same-sex friendships develop and hostilities to the other sex increase, leading to segregated activities in the playground and out of school. It would appear to us that early education is needed in home, school and society stressing the commonality of the sexes, and appreciating and accepting sex differences. The deficit in female status evident among girls may not, of course, be changed or alleviated until society at large ceases to derogate feminity and the 'harder' aspects of 'masculinity' are softened. Can the malaise of sex hostility, so evident in the adult world, and reflected in these children's responses, be moderated by the school or are teachers themselves carriers of the infection? Sweden is relevant here, since an educational drive is evident in Swedish schools to stress the equality of the sexes. It is noticeable that hostility to the other sex is less evident among the Swedish children in this study, the boys especially. Commenting on the Swedish school programmes to minimise gender differences, Yorburg (1974) concludes that 'despite deliberate efforts to break down sex typing in the home and on the job, and despite the opportunities and advantages of the welfare state, which tend to equalise the resources of men and women ... the lag [between reality and what is thought to be desirable] is less extreme in Sweden than in most other countries (p. 98)'.

Such a view is, however, somewhat optimistic. Since the cumulative evidence from Hutt and Hartup (*op. cit.*) indicates the early genesis of differing gender and sex expectations through parental and other early experiences (as opposed to schooling), later educational programmes become remedial, seeking to rectify already established attitudes and expectations. While such remedial programmes, as seen in Sweden, may have some effect, the task is far too extensive and complex to be left to schools, but might best begin with parents, parent preparation programmes and parent-as-teacher emphases.

9 Children's perception of sex differences in babies and adolescents

An essential ingredient in understanding children's sexual thinking is how soon children begin to recognise sex differences, not only in parents but in terms of their own sexuality. The term 'sex differences' is used here to distinguish it from 'gender differences', the labels applied by society to behaviour, roles and other related matters of the two sexes (Unger, 1979b). Sex differences are used here as the biological and anatomical differences to be observed in the sex organs, and include both primary and secondary sex characteristics. Research has been conducted in this area, such as Kreitler and Kreitler (1966) and Moore and Kendall (1971), but frequently the age range has been limited to young children, or related to other areas such as the origin of babies (Bernstein, 1973). An interesting report by Mehl, Brendsel and Peterson (1977) of the effect on children ranging from 2 to 14 years of being present at the birth of a sibling indicates the small but increasing numbers of children who have the opportunity of observing sex differences in the newborn.

In our current research two questions were asked, 'How can anyone know that a newborn baby is a boy or a girl?' and 'Do the bodies of boys and girls grow differently as they grow older?' If the answer to the second question was positive they were then asked to describe such differences. It must be borne in mind that all the respondents were selected on the basis of having at least one younger sibling. Those who had more than one often had one or more older siblings as well. On average, each age cohort had 70 per cent who were first-born, and about 30 per cent who were later in the birth order of the family. These children, in our view, therefore experienced the best possible conditions for observing sex differences, particularly in babies, having been witness to the arrival, bathing, dressing and undressing of a newborn baby, possibly sharing a bath and other family experiences where the naked condition could be observed. Growing up, they would have the opportunity to observe growing differences in themselves and their younger and possibly older siblings.

This experience would, however generally, be limited by the sex range of children in the family; a boy limited to brothers, and a girl limited to sisters, would within the family have opportunity to observe only the same sex characteristics. An analysis of the sample by same sex siblings and other sex siblings can be seen in Table 9.1. It will be noted overall that 65 per cent had other or both sex siblings and only 35 per cent of the total sample had only same sex siblings. Even so, with or without opportunity to observe other sex characteristics in family situations, the range of 5 to 15 years provides many opportunities to observe the other sex particularly in the ages 5 to 7 years before children are segregated for bathing, changing clothes and other physical purposes. Unless there was a very thorough sex segregation from babyhood onwards both in the family and school it would be extraordinarily difficult to provide no opportunity, even by accident, for observations of the sexual parts. The widespread incidence of children's body play with themselves and each other in the early years illustrates this.

TABLE 9.1 *Children showing distribution and percentages of those with siblings of the same and other sex*

Relationships	Distribution	Total	Percentages
Boys with sister(s) only	136		
Boys with brother(s) and sister(s)	137		
		273	65% of boys
Girls with brother(s) only	140		
Girls with brother(s) and sisters	135		
		275	65% of girls
Boys with brothers only	148		36% of boys
Girls with sisters only	142		34% of girls
		290	
Totals N =		838	100% of total

The two questions put to the children about differences between male and female newborn babies and male and female pubertal and post-pubertal differences are important items. Between them they test physiological knowledge and contribute significantly to an analysis of levels of biological realism in each child and group of children. They also throw light on theories concerning the latency period. If the

Freudian hypothesis of the oral, anal and genital stages, followed by a latency period, is true one would expect many 5-year-olds to be aware of sexual differences and to show relatively little embarrassment when asked the question about newborn babies, and for inhibitions to occur strongly at 7 years with recognition of differences being repressed until about 10 or 11 years of age. A similar observation might be made about castration fears, but there is little evidence for these in the responses of the sample. Only four children, all boys, two at 5 years of age and one at 9 made remarks relating to castration, such as, 'We began as girls and a penis grew later' (quite the opposite to castration). The third, an Australian boy, aged 11 replied, 'If it's a boy it'll have a penis. Girls will have a vagina. (Q) It's not sticking out, it's cut, it's right in'. This is the only overt reference to 'cutting' or castration. There is one further reference, in the answer to pubertal differences about girls, 'when they're little they have a dinkle [penis] and when they're older they don't: (Q Why?) Because it changes. It goes away' (English boy, 5 years). The strongest evidence expected would be from the responses of girls but no observations of this kind are made by girls in the entire population sampled.

No direct nor suggestive questions, in these two areas of latency or castration fantasy, were asked. Indeed, in the order of questioning the query about pubertal differences preceded the newborn baby question so that the question about newborn babies would not suggest answers to the pubertal one. However, the results are presented in chronological order — sexual differences between newborn babies first, and pubertal differences second. A third section, dealt with later in this chapter, concerns children's language used to describe the sex organs, which provides some insight into inhibitions at certain ages.

'How can anyone know a newborn baby is a boy or a girl?'

As discussed elsewhere, the question was deliberately open-ended with no suggestive phrasing used. If the child, however, provided a non-sexual answer such as 'the doctor (or nurse or mother) tells you' this was followed up by, 'How does the doctor (or nurse or mother) know?' The only other encouragement is where references were made to the baby's clothes being pink or blue, or boys' or girls' clothes, and then the point was put, 'Supposing the baby wasn't wearing any clothes, how would you know?'

Scoring of this item was firstly attempted on a Piagetian scale, using well-established criteria, but it soon became clear that these were appropriate only with the younger age groups, particularly at the pre-operational level. A biological realism scale was therefore devised which incorporated some Piagetian criteria but also included some general

TABLE 9.2 *Criteria for scoring 'How can anyone know a newborn baby is a boy or a girl?'*

Score	Category and descriptions
0	*Non answers* Don't know. No response. No comprehension. Nonsense 'I like boy babies better, you can see their faces'.
1	*Irrelevant physical factors* Hair, colour of eyes, voice and clothes, size of baby. Answers tend to be monocentric and egocentric.
2	*Authoritarian and artificialisms* Doctor, mother, nurse tells you or 'a book tells you' or 'The vicar knows because the baby was born in a church'. Official colour tags, clothes or bedclothes (blue or pink). 'It's always a girl; change to a boy later by medicine'. 'You have to wait until they're grown up before you know'. 'It's a boy or girl name' (provided by Authority).
3	*Semi-recognised physicalisms* Correctly based perception but content vague. 'They have different bottoms'. 'Girls don't have same kind of bum'. 'Boys stand up going to the bathroom and girls don't'.
4	*Physicalisms recognised by pseudonyms* Physical location is correct 'between the legs', 'where they go wee-wees' but only named by crude pseudonyms.
5	*Physicalisms understood and named partially* At least one sex organ is named correctly.
6	*Physicalisms understood and named correctly* Correct names for sex organs of both sexes.

pre-physiological distinctions. The criteria are set out in Table 9.2. Apart from naming the sex organs, some difficulty was experienced in interpreting what younger children meant when they referred to 'bottom' or 'bottoms'. In context these were often seen to mean the rear or buttocks, but also they clearly meant in some contexts 'the bottom part of the body', that is, the genital area. This was an important distinction which had to be made in allocating an appropriate score. Roughly speaking the scores 0-2 were seen as pre-operational, scores 3 and 4 as concrete operational, and scores 5 and 6 as formal operational but because of criteria difficulties with older groups we have not nominated this as a strictly Piagetian item. Some specific examples of the various levels are given below with fuller details.

Score 1 *Irrelevant physical factors*

'Because mum dressed her in a dress. There's no other way to tell' (Australian girl, 7 years); 'The face probably looks like a boy or

195

a girl, and the hair's longer for a girl' (Australian boy, 7 years);
'You can see it by the face, and if it cries a lot it's a boy' (Swedish
boy, 7 years); 'If the baby's bigger it's a boy' (English girl, 5 years).

Score 2 *Authoritarian and artificialisms*

'Because they would've told the nurse if it was a boy. (Q) The nurse
looks on the name tag around its wrist. (Q) The doctor put the
name tag on the wrist' (Australian girl, 5 years); 'The doctor tells
you. He operates on your stomach to see if it's a boy or a girl.
(Q) Is it different stuff? Boys and girls are born different. Boys
come out a different place [points to navel] and girls here [points
to chest]' (North American boy, 7 years). Some answers reveal
mixed answers at levels 1 and 2, such as: 'My mum told me. (Q)
The doctor told mum. Mum looked at the baby. If the baby is
littler or bigger in the tummy. (Q) A boy is the biggest' (Australian
girl, 5 years); and 'By hair. (Q) My mum told me it was a boy.
(Q) The doctor tells her. (Q) He looks through a magnifying glass
at their eyes, and he can tell by the eyebrows' (North American
boy, 7 years).

Score 3 *Semi-recognised physicalisms*

'Boys stand up to go to the wee-wee, and girls don't. (Q) They
just do it. (Q) Don't know' (English girl, 7 years); 'They're
different down there. (Q) Well, some kind of different bottom.
(Q) Shapes are different, dunno really' (Australian boy, 9 years).

Score 4 *Physicalisms recognised by pseudonyms*

'The tooty. The boy's got only one bum and the girls have two.
And boy's got something sticking out like a hose', (Australian boy,
7 years); 'Girls don't have dicky birds' (English girl, 7 years); 'A boy
has those things [he laughs]. It's very rude. We call them Wallies.
And a girl hasn't. She has those chest things' (Australian boy,
9 years); 'Girls have an exit and boys have a little willie' (Australian
girl, 11 years). There are many mixed levels such as: 'I do, when
my sister was little I knew, as she had girl's hair all curly. (Q) Well,
girls have got privates. What women have on their bums, like boys
have willies' (English boy, 5 years).

Score 5 and 6 *Physicalisms with named parts*

'You can tell by its penis, it's a boy. (Q) She's got something,
don't know what its called. I call it a hamburger' (Australian boy,

196

7 years); 'If it's got a penis or not. If it has it's a boy. Girls have a virginia' (English boy, 11 years); 'Down between your legs, where they go to the locker room. (Q) It's embarrassing, but the boy doesn't have a slit down the middle but has a round tube. (Q) A penis' (North American boy, 13 years); 'You can see if the baby has a penis or not, the girl has a vagina' (Swedish girl, 15 years).

The age, sex and country attached to these quotations should not be taken as indicative of trends in those groups. They are presented solely as illustrations of the scoring. Not all replies were as clearly expressed, and mixed and confused answers had sometimes to be interpreted for scoring purposes.

To assess the distribution of scores the scale was collapsed from 6 points to 3 points (by combining 0, 1 and 2; 3 and 4; 5 and 6). The results may be seen in Table 9.3. Roughly speaking score 1 indicates unrealistic, incorrect and non-perceptive answers; score 2 indicates partially correct answers with some imprecise notions and terminology; score 3 indicates physicalisms realistically understood and the sex organ(s) correctly named. For various reasons the Swedish results will be looked at separately after the other three countries have been examined.

TABLE 9.3 *Percentages of children's scores on sex differences of newborn babies by country and age-year (N = 838)*

Age-year	Scores	Australia	England	North America	Sweden
5	1	80	74	88	43
	2	8	23	12	50
	3	12	3	–	7
7	1	65	57	70	26
	2	15	28	27	67
	3	20	15	3	7
9	1	20	37	54	7
	2	20	28	23	53
	3	60	35	23	40
11	1	3	5	5	–
	2	23	38	36	50
	3	74	57	57	50
13	1	–	3	–	–
	2	17	3	12	43
	3	83	94	88	57
15	1	–	–	–	–
	2	7	3	16	43
	3	93	97	84	57

The results for the Australian, English and North American children indicate that 5 and 7 years are strongly unrealistic, the English making the most advance at 7 years. By the age of 9 a growing number, the majority in the Australian sample, have achieved a realistic view of sexual differences in the newborn, and by 11 years the other two countries have caught up. In the teenage years the great majority indicate they have achieved realistic ideas and vocabulary. The middle score of 2 nowhere has more than 38 per cent (English 11-year-olds) in these three countries, but reveals a sizeable middle group at all ages up to and including 11 years with confused and imprecise notions.

The Swedish results indicate a somewhat different picture. At 5 to 9 years the children are noticeably more advanced, the figures for unrealistic levels dropping quickly towards zero after 7 years. This could be explained by first home, then school, consistently teaching physiological facts about basic sex differences. The figures from 11 years on, however, are somewhat puzzling, for with the minimal amount of sex education the other three countries appear to have caught up with Sweden, increasing their realistic scores while only 57 per cent of Swedish teenagers score at this level. The reason would appear not to be lack of knowledge but some complexity in scoring words used in English and Swedish and some difficulties in attributing words as being 'realistic', or classified as 'pseudonyms' in each language. It is noticeable that Swedish children use fewer pseudonyms than do the other children, and the 'correct' views may be masked by this verbal complexity. Thus, if the scores are collapsed in a different way to include the use of pseudonyms in the highest score (those locating differences but only with pseudonyms for both sex organs), the distribution of score 3 seen in Table 9.4 is somewhat different. With this collapsing of scores, the proportion of Swedish children achieving a realistic grasp of sex differences shows a clear symmetrical progression with age well ahead of all other countries until 13 years (with Australian children almost catching up at 11 years).

TABLE 9.4 *Percentages of highest scores on 'sex differences of newborn babies' by country and age-year (N = 838)*

Age-year	Australia	England	North America	Sweden
5	20	23	4	57
7	32	40	30	71
9	77	60	46	86
11	90	83	85	93
13	100	97	88	100
15	94	100	84	93

On both sets of figures in Tables 9.3 and 9.4 there is no evidence for a latency period. On the contrary there are not even slightly higher realism scores at 5 years leading to a decline at 7, but simply a marked increase with age, of increasing realistic awareness of sex differences and a decreasing inhibition in describing and explaining them. There is also no evidence to support widespread castration fantasies or fears, only one child referring overtly to castration as an explanation of a girl's lack of a penis, and the remaining few referring to the boys beginning as girls and 'growing' their penis later. Freudians may well rejoin that these fears are concealed or distorted by the process of repression. All that the authors are stating, however, is that these results produce no supportive evidence for castration theory but do appear to throw doubts upon the existence of a latency period.

Sex differences in perceiving sex differences

It is interesting to examine whether one sex or the other scores better on this item, namely whether either sex scores higher or lower in perceiving sexual differences in newborn babies. To analyse this the mean scores were computed for each year, by sex, as Table 9.5 reveals. Despite the fact that there are some discrepancies between mean scores of boys and girls, there are only four age cohorts which reveal significant sex differences in the scoring (see Table B.15, Appendix B). These are the North American and Swedish 5-year-olds and Swedish 9-year-olds, where the girls score significantly higher than the boys. The remaining age group is the English 5s, where boys become significantly higher than the girls. No inferences about general sex differences in perceiving how a newborn baby can be identified as a boy or a girl can be made from this, even though analysis of variance indicates main effects of sex at the .05 level. A similar result of main effects of socio-economic status can be seen (see Appendix D, Tables D1 and D4).

The overall mean scores, combining boys and girls, can be seen in Figure 9.1 showing the considerable similarity of all countries in increasing scores with age, Swedish children revealing higher scores initially but levelling off in the teenage years to below the other countries. This difference, discussed previously, can be explained partially by difficulties in identifying what are and what are not sex pseudonyms, thus possibly distorting scores at the higher level. The graph generally would appear to illustrate the myth of the latency period.

Physical differences in puberty

The authors initially had some difficulty in phrasing this question to achieve responses of the kind required, without providing cues or

TABLE 9.5 *Mean scores on 'sex differences of newborn babies' by country, sex and age-year (N = 838)*

Age-year	Sex	Australia	England	North America	Sweden
5	Boys	2.05	2.03*	1.54	1.93
	Girls	2.00	1.35	1.91*	3.53*
	Totals	2.03	1.83	1.53	2.73
7	Boys	3.10	2.85	2.38	3.27
	Girls	2.15	2.00	1.50	3.13
	Totals	2.63	2.43	1.94	3.20
9	Boys	4.30	3.95	3.00	3.67
	Girls	4.40	2.60	2.13	4.93*
	Totals	4.35	3.28	2.57	4.30
11	Boys	5.20	4.80	4.67	4.73
	Girls	5.15	4.40	4.20	4.40
	Totals	5.18	4.60	4.43	4.57
13	Boys	5.50	5.55	5.19	4.40
	Girls	4.95	5.65	5.29	4.73
	Totals	5.23	5.60	5.24	4.57
15	Boys	5.80	5.65	5.69	4.73
	Girls	5.75	5.90	5.47	4.67
	Totals	5.78	5.78	5.58	4.70

(* Indicates significantly higher scores by one sex.)

suggested answers. In fact, to prevent this, the question on pubertal body differences was placed in the interview order *before* the newborn baby question, for obvious reasons. The final wording of the question, after much trial and error, was, 'Do the bodies of boys and girls grow differently as they grow older?' Even so, some children confused the question but supplementary clarifications provided the appropriate focus. If they answered 'Yes' then they were asked to describe the differences. The term 'pubertal differences' is used as shorthand to describe sex differences with growth and is not used in any strictly technical sense.

The cut-off age for children recognising any substantial sex differences at all with physical growth appeared to be 9 years. By that time only one or two children evinced 'don't know' answers, and after 9 years 100 per cent of each sample answered in the affirmative. The results for the earlier years can be seen in Tables 9.6 and 9.7 showing boys and girls separately. There are no striking sex differences in these responses save that 5-year-old girls had more difficulties than boys of that age, except in Sweden, where the picture is reversed. The time lag

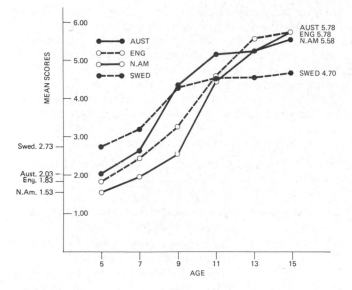

Figure 9.1 Mean scores on 'sex differences of newborn babies' by country and by age-year

TABLE 9.6 *Percentages of boys with 'Don't know' or 'No' answers to pubertal differences by country and age-year (N = 274)*

Age-year	Australia	England	North America	Sweden
5	15	5	8	27
7	25	5	6	20

TABLE 9.7 *Percentages of girls with 'Don't know' or 'No' answers to pubertal differences by country and age-year (N = 274)*

Age-year	Australia	England	North America	Sweden
5	20	25	46	13
7	5	10	–	7

to 9 years may be explained by some children being slow to perceive differences in age groups older than themselves, natural egocentricity perhaps preventing the growth of awareness in this area. The descriptions, however, of such differences show a considerable range of differentiations when perceived.

Scoring of this item followed closely the criteria used in assessing responses to sex differences in newborn babies, except that a score for authoritarian and artificialist answers was inappropriate. No doctor or nurse is required to assert that there are differences between girls and boys as they develop! As a result the scores are not exactly equivalent, as perusal of the Table 9.8 will indicate, although when compared with Table 9.2 some close similarity is observable. The scoring on pubertal differences tends to be strictly biological with a few Piagetian parallels. This is why it is included in the biological realism scales later and not in the Piagetian scales, although three levels are categorised as pre-sexual, transitional sexual and fully sexual stages. Some specific examples of the various levels are listed below, with fuller details.

TABLE 9.8 *Criteria for scoring descriptions of pubertal differences*

Score	Category	Descriptions
0	Non-answers	Don't know; no response; no differences; nonsense answers, 'I like girls better'.
1	Pre-sexual	Differences are *non-sexual*: head hair, faces, skin, eyes (may wear spectacles), shoes, clothes. Bigger, fatter, stronger, quicker.
2		*Vague physical differences*: no sexual association; girls round, boys flat; girls become ladies, both become mothers and fathers — no elaboration. Clothes different, bathing suits different, no elaboration.
3	Transitional sexual	*Secondary sex characteristics*: one or more perceived in one or both sexes, hairiness in particular. Voice change in boys. Blushing. 'Girls mature faster than boys', no elaboration.
4		*Primary sex characteristics — one sex only*: 'Girls have these big things', breasts, chest, boobs. Boys can produce sperm/tadpoles. Girls menstruate. Vague descriptions.
5	Fully sexual	*Primary sex characteristics — both sexes*: boy's penis grows and girls get breasts. Girls menstruate and lose blood; boys have wet dreams. Both can have coitus.
6		*Both primary and secondary sex characteristics — both sexes*: girls' and boys' sex organs grow, pubertal hair recognised as sexual. Coitus and child production possible.

Score 1 *Non-sexual*

'They're both the same. (Q) No, not exactly the same. Girls have got hearts, boys haven't. [Their] heart's in the stomach. And boys have different bones from girls, to the legs and arms' (Australian boy, 5 years); 'Boys are stronger than girls, and can run faster, like in the Olympics' (North American girl, 7 years); 'Yes, they've got different coloured hair, and their body gets a different colour' (Swedish boy, 5 years).

Score 2 *Vague physical differences*

An Australian girl, 9 years, provides an answer and gives a bodily description using her hands: 'Ladies grow sideways like this

←○→ and men grow wide like this ←○→'; 'My mum's chest gets fat, and men are just low like you [points to male interviewer]. You know, a low chest' (English boy, 5 years); 'They wear different clothes, like on the beach, girls have bikinis and boys wear shorts. (Q) Don't know why, they just do' (North American boy, 7 years).

Score 3 *Secondary sex characteristics only*

'When people are smaller like me they don't have hairs on their chest. If you have hairs on your chest you're a big strong man. (Q) Girls don't they get it under their arms' (English boy, 9 years); 'Boys get deeper voices, deeper somewhere and lots of hair. They have to shave. Girls don't' (Swedish boy, 9 years); 'Girls grow faster than boys, grow taller though not as strong' (North American girl, 11 years).

Score 4 *Primary sex characteristics – one sex only*

'Girls have tiny boobs then get bigger and bigger and bigger and bigger and when they stop growing she knows she's a lady' (Australian girl, 9 years); 'Ladies have milk when their breasts grow so they can feed babies. Men can't do that. They have different smells' (North American boy, 11 years). An interesting mixed level example comes from an English 5-year-old boy: 'Yes a boy's different. My ears will get bigger. I can play football then. I'll get bigger all over. Girls – their hair gets longer. When they're little they have a dinkle [penis]. When they're older they don't. (Q) Because it changes. It goes away'.

Score 5 and 6 *Primary and secondary sex characteristics – both sexes*

'My build will expand, be more sturdy. I'll have hair on my face, chest and groin. My wee-wee erection will start getting bigger.

203

Girls have no hair on their face or chest. Hips expand and they grow breasts. Bodies will take a different shape. Menstruation happens to girls but I don't know what it means' (English boy, 11 years); 'Girls mature earlier and get breasts. Boys mature later and their penis gets bigger and they're generally stronger. They get hairy too' (Swedish girl, 15 years).

Again it should be noted that the countries, ages or sexes cited in these examples are not necessarily indications of trends, but are merely intended as illustrations of scoring criteria used.

As in the previous item on newborn babies, the scales were collapsed (from 1 to 6), to 3 points signifying pre-sexual, transitional sexual and fully sexual answers (see Table 9.8). The results can be seen in Table 9.9. The Swedish figures will be looked at separately after the results of the other three countries have been examined.

TABLE 9.9 *Percentages of children's scores on pubertal sex differences by country and age-year (N = 838)*

Age-year	Scores*	Australia	England	North America	Sweden
5	1	63	55	67	27
	2	15	23	8	33
	3	5	–	4	3
7	1	58	55	53	30
	2	25	25	33	43
	3	5	–	3	3
9	1	30	33	67	30
	2	45	53	23	43
	3	23	5	7	10
11	1	18	8	13	10
	2	48	55	40	50
	3	30	37	43	33
13	1	5	5	9	13
	2	50	42	55	80
	3	42	53	33	7
15	1	8	8	10	–
	2	30	43	29	73
	3	60	48	58	27

(* Zero scores are not included in the figures shown.)

The results for Australia, England and North America show a clear age progression from low score to middle thence to the highest score.

In other words there appears to be a reasonably symmetrical move through pre-sexual to transitional sexual, to fully sexual answers attained by the majority at 15 years of age. The Australian and North American children score in a similar pattern; although at 9 years the North Americans are somewhat behind, by 11 years they have caught up. The English pattern is much slower, almost retarded by comparison, achieving generally all three stages later than most other groups. The exception is the higher pre-sexual score of the North American children at 9 years. In very general terms in these three countries pre-sexual answers tend to be left behind between 8 and 9 years, and fully sexual responses achieved by 15 years. The continued existence of a large proportion of middle scores (transitional sexual answers) at 13 years points to considerable vagueness both in awareness and ability to vocalise on the subject.

The Swedish results reflect a similar pattern to those found in the newborn babies item, the figures for pre-sexual answers starting much lower in Swedish children at 5 years, the transitional sexual answers dominating and increasing up to 11 years. There then appears to be no progress by the majority from transitional to fully sexual responses in the teenage years. The reason appears to be not due to lack of knowledge, but as in the previous item appears to be the result of difficulties caused in translation and determining what is realistic sexual terminology and what is not. If, as in the previous item where the same difficulty was encountered, the scores are collapsed differently to allow for language problems, on highest scores, the Swedish results begin to compare similarly at 13 and 15 years with those of the other three countries.

Again, on the figures presented there appears to be no support whatever for viewing the years from 7 onwards as a latency period. It is, on the contrary, a period of progressive increase in sexual awareness and of increasing ability to verbalise and discuss sexual matters.

Sex differences in perceiving pubertal differences

The differences between the sexes in mean scores can be seen in Table 9.10. Only five age cohorts, however, when subjected to a t-test show any significant difference (see Table B.16, Appendix B). These are the English 5- and 7-year-olds, and the Australian and North American 15-year-olds, where the boys score significantly higher than the girls. The remaining age cohort is the Swedish 5-year-olds, where the girls score significantly higher than the boys. These are so scattered that no general inferences can be made about sex differences on this item. The ANOVA results (see Appendix D) confirm this, although indicating some interaction between sex and age-year in Table D.5.

The overall mean scores, combining boys and girls, on pubertal

TABLE 9.10 *Mean scores on pubertal differences by country, sex and age-year (N = 838)*

Age-year	Sex	Australia	English	North America	Sweden
5	Boys	1.40	2.00*	1.39	1.20
	Girls	1.90	1.00	1.18	3.27*
	Totals	1.65	1.50	1.28	2.23
7	Boys	1.80	2.15*	1.81	2.00
	Girls	1.85	1.35	1.86	2.33
	Totals	1.83	1.75	1.83	2.17
9	Boys	3.05	3.05	1.80	2.20
	Girls	3.55	2.35	2.40	3.07
	Totals	3.30	2.70	2.10	2.67
11	Boys	3.50	4.15	4.00	3.67
	Girls	4.05	4.35	4.00	3.07
	Totals	3.78	4.25	4.00	3.37
13	Boys	4.60	5.00	4.25	3.40
	Girls	4.05	4.55	3.82	3.67
	Totals	4.33	4.78	4.04	3.53
15	Boys	5.20*	4.90	5.63*	4.20
	Girls	4.25	4.25	3.73	3.87
	Totals	4.73	4.58	4.68	4.04

(* Denotes significant sex differences.)

differences can be seen in Figure 9.2, again revealing considerable similarities between all three non-Swedish countries, but even with Swedish children scoring higher initially the 15-year-olds' mean scores in all countries arrive at a similar level. Certainly the graph shows, as does Figure 9.1, that in discerning growing sexual differences the latency period developmentally does not exist.

Correlations between the two scales

Since the two scales described in this chapter cover similar ground in scoring awareness of the sex differences of newborn babies and sex differences as children develop to puberty, one would expect some correspondence in the scores. The results, showing the various Pearson's product moment correlations, are set out in Table 9.11.

These correlations appear to be rather low, but they are relatively high when it is realised that after the lower scores there is not a one-to-one correspondence in the level of awareness attributed to each score

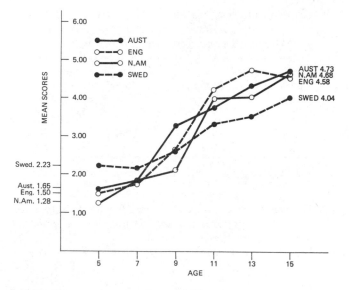

Figure 9.2   Mean scores on pubertal differences by country and age-year

TABLE 9.11   *Correlations between scores on 'sex differences of newborn babies' and 'pubertal differences' by country and sex*

	Within sex	Total
Within Australian sample	0.64	0.52
Within English sample	0.62	0.60
Within North American sample	0.67	0.51
Within Swedish sample	0.66	0.54

in each scale. Because of the wide differences in the scoring of boys and girls, in some age groups the correlations are higher when taken within sex than within each country.

The other sex factor in the family

Taking the combined highest scores of 5 and 6 in each of the scales as indicators, Tables 9.12 and 9.13 set out the comparisons between those boys and girls with experience of living with a sibling of the other sex in the family, and those boys and girls without that experience. In all four sets of figures, a considerable percentage more of those children with other sex siblings achieve higher scores than those without. In all four a Chi-square test yields significant differences. These differentiated

TABLE 9.12 *Percentages of highest scores of children, with and without opposite sex siblings in family, on 'sex differences of newborn babies' scale by sex*

| | Boys | | Girls | |
Score	With sisters (N = 273)	Without sisters (N = 148)	With brothers (N = 275)	Without brothers (N = 142)
5+	52.0	39.8	54.5	35.2
< 5	48.0	60.2	45.5	64.8

(Chi-square = 5.72, p < .05.)   (Chi-square = 14.03, p < .01.)

TABLE 9.13 *Percentages of highest scores of children, with and without opposite sex siblings in family, on 'pubertal differences' scale by sex*

| | Boys | | Girls | |
Score	With sisters (N = 273)	Without sisters (N = 148)	With brothers (N = 275)	Without brothers (N = 142)
5+	25.7	16.9	31.3	16.9
< 5	75.3	83.1	68.7	83.1

(Chi-square = 4.93, p < .05.)   (Chi-square = 9.96, p < .01.)

scores are more marked in the 'newborn babies' than in the 'pubertal differences' results, but are consistent throughout all countries and age cohorts. This confirms that children exposed to family living with one or more siblings of the other sex have a built-in sex education process within their family life, at least where knowledge of sex differences is concerned.

Children's terminology for sex organs

During the discussion of the questions on newborn babies and of pubertal differences, most children discussed the presence of, or absence of the sex organs. In describing them, names were used which differed from the technically correct terms of penis and vagina. Where the children did not use other technical terms, such as testes or vulva, we termed the substitute words as sexual pseudonyms. They could have been called colloquialisms, or nicknames, but the term pseudonym, meaning 'fictitious name', seemed more literally appropriate.

Children also demonstrated the use of pseudonyms in describing breasts, nipples, buttocks, contraceptives, sperm, and coitus. Sometimes these words were comically mispronounced such as condems (condoms), constructions (contractions), do intersections (have intercourse), Phillipian tubes (fallopian tubes). We confine our discussion and reporting to the major male and female sex organs, the penis and the vagina. By our definition, more than 60 pseudonyms were used to describe the penis and more than 40 to describe the vagina. Their widespread use is indicative of a considerable number of taboos at work in the psychosexuality of children. Several children confided that they could not use the 'correct' term because that was 'rude', 'dirty' or 'naughty'. The use of pseudonyms, on the other hand, obviously helped them to avoid embarrassment. While some knew the correct terms and found relief in the use of pseudonyms, others clearly did not know the correct terms for the sexual organs or if they had known them had repressed them.

As we have noted previously the difficulties of translation into Swedish and back-translation into English made this rather too complex to analyse from the Swedish results. As a consequence we regretfully had to exclude the Swedish sexual pseudonyms from this analysis. In all, we were able to identify in Swedish only 7 pseudonyms for penis, and 18 for the vagina. The following comments are therefore confined to the three English-speaking countries. However, as previously reported in this chapter, in the Swedish sample more 15-year-old girls than boys know the correct terms for the sex organs (see Table B.7, Appendix B).

The terms used were so numerous and varied (see Table 9.14) that we did not attempt to classify responses other than in the crude manner of identifying those children who used only pseudonyms to describe the sex organs, those who used a mixture of one correct term and one pseudonym, and those who used both correct terms for penis and vagina without the aid of any pseudonyms. The proportions of each group can be seen in Tables 9.15, 9.16 and 9.17.

In any examination of these tables it should be recognised that in the younger age groups a fairly high percentage of children throughout the interview saw no reason to discuss the sexual organs, or identify them in any way, either because their explanations were non-physical and not biologically realistic or, the more remote possibility in our view, because they skilfully avoided all mention of them deliberately by systematic, evasive and misleading answers. The comparative figures seen in Table 9.15 indicate a major trend and one major difference between countries. The first is that the use of pseudonyms seems to increase with age until about 11 years as children become more aware of sexuality and of the taboos surrounding it. It decreases perhaps as children attain or approach puberty and begin to question taboos and the need to disguise verbal references to the sex organs. This trend is visible in all three countries.

TABLE 9.14 *Pseudonyms used for sex organs*

Categories	Penis	Vagina
1 Associations with urination or excreta	Pee pee	pee pee
	Peesin	
	Wee wee	wee wee
	Tinkle	Bottom: the little
	Tinkler	thing the wee
	Sprinkler	comes out of
	Tickle	
	Tossle	Tooty
	Dink	Dinky
	Ding	Ding
	Dingle	
	Winky	
	Winkle	
	Wiggly	
	Diddly	
	Diddly-do	Doody
	Doo-doo	Doo-doo
	Jobby	Jobby-wee
	Kiki	
	A waterwork	The exit
		Bladder
		Tube with a hole in it
Total	20	12
2 Analogies	Hose	Hole
	Hot dog	Hamburger
	Weiner	Pancake
	Sausage	Muffin(s)
	Cobbler	Box
	Cobblers	Crack
	Nuts	A flat one
	Balls	A short one
	Duals	Notch
	Sac(k)	Split
	Tossle	Slit-down the middle
	Rooty	Slit
	Fiddle	Scooter
	Prick	Birth Canal
	Cucumber	
Total	15	14

(cont'd)...

PERCEPTION OF DIFFERENCES IN BABIES AND ADOLESCENTS

Categories	Penis	Vagina
3 Names of people	Dick	Fanny
	Dicky	Lilly
	Fred	Mary
	Joey	Regina
	John	Virginia
	John Willy	Venus
	Jimmy	
	Percy	
	Peter	
	Tommy	
	Thomas	
	Willy	
	Wally	
Total	13	6
4 Anatomical or sexual	A one bum	two bums
	A long one	Privates on their bums
	Father's One	Mother's One
	An erection	A clit
	A long bit	Something inside
	Dildo	Pinky
	Groin	Groin
		Crotch
		Crutch
		Cunt
Total	7	10
5 Animal or bird association	Bird	
	Dicky bird	
	Tail	Pussy
	Dog	Beaver
	Cock	
	Top cat	
	Pecker	
Total	7	2
6 Miscellaneous	Boy toppy	Girl toppy
	Privates	Privates
	Thing-a-me-bob	Thing-a-me-jig
	Gentiles	Genentiles
	A thing	A kind of nothing
	Bike	'Gina
Total	6	6

TABLE 9.15   *Percentages of children using pseudonyms only by country and age-year (N = 658)*

Age-year	Australia	England	North America
5	10	25	21
7	10	23	27
9	20	25	20
11	15	30	36
13	10	5	12
15	3	–	13

The major difference is between Australia on the one hand and the two remaining countries on the other. If these figures are indicators of cultural inhibition, then Australian children would appear to be far less inhibited in the verbal expression of words describing the sex organs than the English and the North American, the latter appearing to be the most inhibited.

Table 9.16 seems to confirm the same patterns, the trend of using mixed pseudonyms and correct terms until about 11 years and then a diminution, with less numbers of Australian children compared with the other two, the North American children appearing the most verbally inhibited. Table 9.17 provides the complementary side of the picture, showing a clear trend in all countries to increase usage of correct sexual terms when discussing the sex organs. The progression is symmetrical, the same inhibitory verbal difference between Australia and the other two in evidence, with North American children slowest to adapt and use correct sexual terminology. It may be of interest to compare these results with those in chapter 16, when children's understanding of sexual vocabulary is presented.

TABLE 9.16   *Percentages of children using pseudonyms and 'correct' terminology by country and age-year (N = 658)*

Age-year	Australia	England	North America
5	15	28	25
7	23	26	30
9	30	20	23
11	30	43	56
13	15	20	40
15	5	15	23

Summary and discussion

This chapter covers the topic of how children perceive and identify sex differences in newborn babies, and in those growing up to puberty.

TABLE 9.17 *Percentages of children using no pseudonyms but only correct sexual terms by country and age-year (N = 658)*

Age-year	Australia	England	North America
5	13	–	4
7	20	8	–
9	50	33	20
11	68	55	37
13	83	80	60
15	93	85	77

These were explored by asking 'How can anyone know a newborn baby is a boy or a girl?' and 'Do the bodies of girls and boys grow differently as they grow older?' Criteria used for scoring responses on the newborn babies question were on a biological realism scale with some Piagetian criteria used in the early stages, but it cannot be claimed as a strictly Piagetian item. A progression from unrealistic to realistic recognition of sexual differences was seen with increasing age, in all countries, with younger children in Sweden being much more realistic at an earlier age than in other countries, but these other countries 'catching up' in the teenage years. A sizeable middle group, however, in all countries remain vague and inhibited concerning identifying the sex organs of babies. Certain differences between boys' and girls' perceptions were noted.

On what is termed 'pubertal differences', covered by the second question, the same trends are evident. Scoring was identified in three stages, being pre-sexual, transitional sexual and fully sexual answers, depending on the biological realism expressed in the responses. Children tended to move up from pre-sexual between 9 and 11 years and to have achieved fully sexual answers between 13 and 15 years. However, there remained a sizeable middle group who remained (as transitional-sexual answers) vague and confused up to 13 years. Sweden demonstrated the same trend as in the newborn babies item.

Some interesting correlations were seen between these two items, although the scoring did not completely correspond. However, on examining the scores of children who had grown up with siblings of the other sex compared with those with sibling(s) of only the same sex, it was found that those who had siblings of the other sex in the family achieved higher scores in significantly higher proportions than those without such. It appears that where observing sex differences of children is concerned, such children in a mixed sex family have a 'built in' sex education process provided for them.

Finally, since a wide range of children's vocabulary used to describe the sex organs involved the use of pseudonyms, examples were given of more than sixty pseudonyms for 'penis' and more than forty pseudonyms for 'vagina'. These were taken as inhibition indicators of a society in which Australia proved the least inhibited and North America the most inhibited of the countries examined. Sweden was not included in this analysis because of translation difficulties.

What emerges as the most important finding of this chapter is the exposure of the latency period as a myth. If the Freudian hypothesis of the oral, anal and genital stages followed by a latency period is accurate one would expect many 5-year-olds to be aware of sexual differences and to show relatively little embarrassment when asked the question about newborn babies, and for inhibitions to occur strongly at 7 years with recognition of differences being repressed until about 11 years of age. Neither the experience of the interviewers in observing the children in the sample, nor their responses, substantiate such a phenomenon. On the contrary 4-year-olds score low in terms of realistic answers, and the evidence indicates an increasing awareness with increasing age and decreasing inhibition in discussing the sexual parts of the body. Other evidence from this study, discussed elsewhere, supports the view that the latency period is an inadequate theory to explain children's sexual thinking.

It is the view of the authors that the concept of latency has contributed to some current views of child-rearing that sex education can be delayed until the pubertal period of development. In its popularised version the alleged latency period may well have strengthened the view of children as non-sexual beings, inhibiting the giving of sex information and explanations at a period of development when children appear to be actively engaged in seeking to understand sexual matters.

Related to the latency period, postulated as a causal factor for its onset, is the alleged universal incidence of castration fears. There appears to be little evidence of this in the responses evaluated in the sample, although no direct or suggestive questions were asked on this topic.

Freudians may well rejoin that these fears are concealed or distorted by the process of repression. All that the authors are stating, however, is that these results produce no supportive evidence for castration theory but do appear to throw serious doubts upon the existence of a latency period.

Developmentally, the earlier insights of the Swedish children on both questions regarding babies and later development are of interest. The English-speaking samples are remarkably similar, with Australian children scoring slightly higher throughout the age range and the North American children somewhat low. Whether these are indicators of social inhibition, in relation to each culture, is debatable. But in overall results on sexual thinking, the grouping was found to be similar — the English-speaking groups fairly identical, with the North Americans lowest, and

Swedish children particularly in the early years scoring much higher by comparison. In these particular questions the lower scores by Swedish teenagers appear to be due to translation problems in deciding whether terms used to describe the sex organs are sexual pseudonyms or not. The Swedish earlier 'precocity' may, in the authors' view, be due to two factors. One is the broader social tolerance of sexuality evidenced in Swedish legislation relating to illegitimacy, marriage, divorce and *de facto* relationships, signifying a less inhibited or repressive approach to human relationships in that country. Children may absorb such ideas from parents, the media and other sources and may as a result be more knowledgeable and less inhibited in exploring sex differences. The other is the Swedish official policy of compulsory sex education for all children from 8 years of age. While this does not directly affect the responses of Swedish 5- and 7-year-olds, there is supportive evidence to show that this policy is disseminated downwards and affects the content of teaching in the kindergartens, where sex education particularly in discussing the arrival of new babies in the family is fairly widespread. In this Swedish sample all the 5-year-olds were in kindergartens.

The indications are that where children's questions are answered directly and sex organs described with correct uninhibited vocabulary there is no difficulty in young children identifying sex differences, even though the origins of such differences may remain a mystery throughout their schooling. There appear to be no cognitive or developmental factors which would prevent children perceiving sex differences realistically from an early age.

10   The origin of babies

The period of pregnancy and the arrival of a new baby in a family is potentially the most educative situation for children to develop biological understanding and to progress in their sexual thinking. Indeed, many modern parents actively use this time to help a child already established in the family to prepare psychologically for the new arrival. The entire sample of children interviewed for this study had experienced the event of a new baby in the family, a small handful in fact having witnessed the baby being born in hospital.

Later chapters will cover gestation, the birth process, determination of the baby's sex and other related matters. The topics covered by this chapter focus upon 'origins' of babies, namely how babies are begun, and what role, if the child perceives any such role, mothers and fathers play in this process. The emphasis here is upon how children perceive and explain human reproduction and, if they provide no biological or sexual explanations, what myths they develop in order to explain the phenomenon of pregnancy. There is evidence to show that pregnancy myths have changed somewhat over the last few decades; the stork, the mulberry bush and even God as explanations almost disappearing. It is of interest therefore to see what new myths, if any, have taken their place and whether or not children have become more realistic, as more parents have made the arrival of a new baby less of a mystery. More than thirty years ago Conn (1947) was the first to follow up Piaget's (1951) assertion that children's ideas about the origin of babies should follow the same sequence of cognitive developmental stages as their ideas of physical causality. Conn came to a curious conclusion: 'It is inconceivable [sic] to the child of pre-school age that the baby may be in the mother'. He also asserted that sex information is beyond the grasp of intelligent children of 7 to 8 years. It was not, he reports, until the ages of 9 and 10 that children first notice and discuss the mother's bulging appearance during pregnancy.

Kreitler and Kreitler (1966) and a replication study in Israel by Moore and Kendall (1971) sought to test out both Freudian cloacal theory of childbirth and Piaget's cognitive theories applied to pregnancy. These were useful suggestive studies but had limited samples and rather diffused and unconvincing results. The most important work in this area to date has been Bernstein (1973), who wrote in her introduction (p. 4), 'The dearth of empirical studies about children's thinking about human reproduction reflects the cultural discomfort that lingers over the topic of sexuality, especially as it appertains to children.' This point is reflected in the sample of 3 to 4, 7 to 8 and 11 to 12-year-old children she used for her investigation in California which were 'selected largely on the basis of availability', reflecting the same problem we experienced in the USA, but also producing an upper socio-economic bias to her sample. She adds, 'Given the hesitance of many parents to have their children questioned about sexual matters random sampling was beyond the scope of this study' (p. 16).

Nevertheless, her work was the first thoroughly researched approach to the origin of babies to produce results which cast light upon children's thinking about human reproduction. The authors acknowledge their dependence upon her work in the first section of this chapter and her generosity in making material available to us. While her questions and focus were in detail rather different, this study covers essentially the same area as Bernstein, extending the sample in age upwards to 15 years, in greater number in North America (178 compared with 60), more randomly by gaining access to the public schools, and comparatively (with 838 children from four countries). Dr Bernstein's work and an important article (Bernstein and Cowan, 1975) will be referred to in this section, and the results compared at the end of this chapter.

It followed naturally, in our investigation, from the question, 'How can anyone know a newborn baby is a boy or a girl?' to ask 'How are babies made?' This was varied to include, 'How do you think babies are begun?' Contingent questions, depending upon the first response, were 'Where is a baby made?' or 'Where do babies come from in the first place?' Bernstein's major question was 'How does the baby happen to be inside the mother's body?' Trial interviews revealed that in Australia initially our first question, with the range of contingency questions, produced the most comprehensive responses.

Whatever the replies to 'How are babies made?' two further questions were put, even though their content may have been partially covered in the previous answer: 'Does mother do anything to start a baby?' and 'Does father do anything to start a baby?' If the answer was positive, the child was then asked to describe what mother/father respectively does. If their descriptions had previously covered the roles of mother

217

and father, responses to these 'role' questions still helped to clarify any vague reference made earlier. Where mother's or father's role had not been mentioned in answering the first question, this gave a further opportunity to the children to be as specific as they could be. To avoid suggestive answers, the approach was deliberately open-ended, the question not being as pointed as 'What does the mother/father do to start a baby?' since with many younger children one parent or both were not seen as playing any direct or necessary role.

'How are babies made?'

In assessing the value in terms of a score of a child's level of thinking, the total responses which included the answer to this first question and all further contingency questions were taken into account; mother's and father's roles, as the child described them, were also considered. The answers, therefore, when taken as a whole were often quite extensive. The criteria for scoring were based upon Piagetian cognitive levels; pre-operational, concrete operational and formal operational thinking, with transitional stages in between. How these were translated into human reproductive levels were by adaptations from Bernstein's categories. The six levels she outlines (Bernstein and Cowan, 1975) with few exceptions and some minor adjustments proved satisfactory in scoring our much larger and more varied sample. The criteria are set out in Table 10.1.

Several points should be noted in this criteria. First it might be seen as critical that when children were asked 'How are babies *made*?' this might appear to suggest an artificialistic response (score 2). Trial interviews and later analysis does not indicate this to be so, the incidence of artificialist answers not extending noticeably beyond 7 years, as would be expected. Second, it was difficult to distinguish at the upper end of the scale between scores 4 and 5, since many answers were vaguely expressed in relation to the significance of ovum and sperm. Similarly it was difficult to score accurately (and consistently) when determining whether a score of 5 or 6 should be given, due to the many factors involved in an answer. The scorer reliability on this item was very high ($r = 0.95$) so that a reasonable level of consistency seemed assured. This factor did, however, raise a third point in scoring the Swedish results which contained responses not as fully expressed as in the English-speaking samples, due to differences of interviewer techniques. For this reason an undue proportion of Swedish responses appear to be scored 'down' at the upper end of the scale, since adequate means of assessing a high score could not be deduced from the limited data available. This point will be discussed later when the results are examined. Examples of the various levels of responses are set out below.

TABLE 10.1 *Criteria for scoring 'How are babies made?'*

Score	Piagetian level	Category and descriptions
0	Non answer	*Lack of comprehension* No answer, don't know and nonsense answers 'I've got a baby brother'.
1	Pre-operations	*Spatial causality* Perceived only a 'where' not 'how'. Babies have always pre-existed.
2		*Artificialisms* Sent by Jesus, God, doctor or father, 'manufacturers' from materials. The digestive fallacy: babies formed by food. Father's role manual and mechanical, not biological.
3	Transitional	*Technically feasible but unrealistic* Semi-physical, semi-psychological, semi-artificial. Includes the agricultural fallacy: 'seed planting'. Animistic distortions, zooisms where organs decide. Several factors voiced but no co-ordinated system.
4	Concrete operations	*Physical explanations, technically realistic* Reveals awareness of biological process, but cannot explain why they occur. Co-ordinates variables with system but not genetic transmission. Eggs and sperm recognised but not fertilisation.
5	Transitional	*Miniaturisms* Babies are pre-formed in miniature either as ovists (egg activated by sperm) or animalculists (sperm uses ovum as incubator). Fertilisation not seen as fusion. Genetic transmission is additive not interactive. Original substance invariable except in size.
6	Formal operations	*Physicalisms freed from pre-causality* Physiological process understood. Fertilisation involves exchange and fusion of genetic substances. Origin of new being from both parents. Provision of a reasonably sophisticated and coordinated scientific theory.

1 *Spatial causality*

'The mother always had it there. (Q) In the tummy. (Q) Ever since she was a little girl. (Q) All little girls have them, lots of tiny seeds. Then they grow: [What starts them to grow?] Dunno' (Australian girl, 5 years); 'It was just there. (Q) It never was anywhere else. It's there and the doctor gets it out' (North American boy, 5 years).

An intermediate response including some artificialism but denoting spatial casuality is, 'God made babies before woman and puts them in girls before they get down to earth' (North American girl, 7 years).

2 Artificialisms

'It was made out of bones, then some skin, and a bit of hair. (Q) God done it. My mother told me that when other people die he makes them [babies] out of skin' (Australian girl, 7 years); 'I don't know, I never saw. Jesus makes them in a factory' (North American girl, 5 years); 'In mother's tummy. I've been there. A seed in mother's tummy where she has an apple. No, it's something white, maybe mashed potatoes' (Swedish girl, 5 years); 'By eating good food. (Q) She swallows it and it grows into a baby, if it's good food' (English boy, 7 years); 'The father does it. (Q) He buys the seed from the seed shop and puts it into the mummy. (Q) He pushes it up her bum with his hand' (Australian boy, 7 years).

3 Technically feasible but unrealistic

'They are seeds, put in there. They're cultivated somehow and grow. (Q) The father waters it and grows like a plant' (Australian boy, 9 years); 'The doctor gives an injection that starts it to grow. (Q) From the seed, it's a kind of tube that grows and grows until it becomes a baby' (English girl, 9 years); 'It's because they're married. (Q) That's when you have children. (Q) People have children if they get married. (Q) They sleep together and cuddle. (Q) The baby just grows from the food mother eats. (Q) Father warms her tummy in bed and it grows' (North American boy, 11 years); 'By the woman. When the lady likes a man they get an egg in their stomach, and then it goes into a baby. (Q) He has to be by her side to help her' (North American boy, 9 years).

4 Physical explanations, technically realistic

'Father has a little dot, when they start to mate he pushes the dot onto her. (Q) He lies on top. The fluid goes inside her. She has a tube connected to the navel. As the baby's coming off, the tube comes out of the navel and the baby is formed' (Australian boy, aged 11 years); 'Yes well they can lay down together and he puts something up her. I can't say what they are doing. It is a pretty ugly word — sexual intercourse' (Swedish boy, 5 years); 'The mother's stomach looks like elephant's ears inside. Father has things he pokes up with his cock, like tadpoles and one gets up the mother's tube.

It turns into a tiny baby' (North American boy, 7 years); 'By an egg of the man. It turns into a baby inside the mother's stomach. (Q) It's in his winkle. He puts it in the lady's vagina and it [the egg] goes up into the mother's stomach' (English girl, 11 years); 'A man and a woman. He gets on her and sticks his penis up her slit and the baby starts. (Q) The goo, the wet stuff does it. (Q) Don't know how' (North American girl, 11 years).

5 Miniaturisms and pre-formations

'The man and the woman things down there come together and the man's little bodies come out. Sperms meet in the mother's tummy and fertilise the egg in the mother's womb. (Q) Down here [points to stomach] but towards the back. (Q) Sperm hits the egg and sets it off. The baby's in the egg' (English boy, 7 years); 'A man and a woman go to sperm. The man's cock goes into the woman and it (Q) the sperm, forms the egg. The lady's period makes blood for the baby' (North American girl, aged 11); 'The man's penis goes into the girl's vagina and he pushes the seed in the girl and the girl gets pregnant. [Q How does pushing do it?] It sort of removes seed from its spot in a little corner, pushes it out and the spot grows into a baby' (North American boy, 13 years).

6 Physicalisms freed from pre-causality

'A man and a woman have sexual intercourse without contraceptives. There sprouts out sperm from the penis into the vagina. The sperm cell that first reaches the egg fertilises it and then a baby is started. It's either a girl or a boy depending on if it is an X or Y chromosome sperm cell that comes first into the egg' (Swedish boy, 15 years); 'When the man and woman have sex, the sperm from his penis goes into the vagina and fertilises the egg (Q) it gets inside and joins it. It forms a cell which then goes into two, then four, then eight and so on and forms a body. (Q) It's a kind of black spot with a white ring round it and tiny particles moving inside. It doesn't look like a baby at first' (English girl, 13 years).

Some of the difficulties previously discussed concerning accuracies of scoring at the higher levels can be seen from some of these examples. A number in each cohort, particularly with the older respondents, could well be scored 5 rather than 6, or 4 rather than 5. This, however, is a problem common to all tasks where qualitative assessment is largely an estimating rather than a measuring process.

The distribution of scores on the 6 point scale is presented in Table 10.2. The scale produces a symmetrical distribution of scores, showing

TABLE 10.2 Percentages of children's scores (1–6) on the 'origin of babies' scale by country and age-year (N = 838)

Age-year	Australia						England						North America						Sweden					
	1	2	3	4	5	6	1	2	3	4	5	6	1	2	3	4	5	6	1	2	3	4	5	6
5	25	65	10	—	—	—	37	45	18	—	—	—	17	67	17	—	—	—	37	17	23	23	—	—
7	15	60	18	7	—	—	35	30	33	2	—	—	27	60	13	—	—	—	13	3	20	40	13	3
9	13	20	27	40	—	—	18	13	15	37	15	—	33	20	30	17	—	—	3	—	10	43	40	—
11	—	5	8	72	15	—	10	—	17	42	28	3	7	—	13	63	17	—	—	—	3	50	37	10
13	3	—	—	57	30	10	—	—	3	47	30	20	—	—	—	36	39	24	—	—	3	43	50	3
15	—	—	—	30	32	38	—	—	—	7	58	35	—	—	—	13	26	61	—	—	—	27	67	7

(Scores 1 and 2 = pre-operations; 4 = concrete operations; 6 = formal operations.)

increasing scores with increasing age, the higher scores moving towards the right as the table indicates higher age in a typical scale distribution, with only one aberration in the slightly lower scores of the North American children. It will be noted that the pre-operational level continues for a considerable time until the majority cross over (to score 4) at the concrete operational level (9 years in England, 11 years in Australia and North America). Again the exception is Sweden where 23 per cent of 5 years have already achieved indications of concrete operational thinking, and 7 years where 56 per cent are concrete operational or above. At the other end of the scale (score 6), the North American children at 15 years show the largest proportion in achieving a formal operational level with the Australian and the English children achieving nearly 40 per cent. The Swedish children, however, only minimally achieve the highest level (7 per cent) but interviewer discrepancies may account for this result. The results can be seen more clearly in graph form in Figure 10.1.

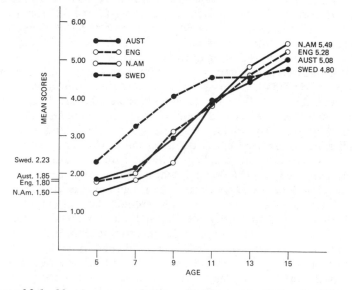

Figure 10.1   Mean scores on 'origin of babies' scale (1-6 points) by country and age-year

When the 6-point scale is collapsed, however, (1 = 0, 1, 2 and 3; 2 = 4; 3 = 5 and 6) to make it into a three-point scale depicting the level of pre-operational, concrete operational and formal operational, as can be seen in Table 10.3, these discrepancies are not as evident.

TABLE 10.3 *Percentages of scores (collapsed 1-3) on 'origin of babies' scale by country and age-year (N = 838)*

Age-year	Australia			England			North America			Sweden		
	1	2	3	1	2	3	1	2	3	1	2	3
5	100	–	–	100	–	–	100	–	–	77	23	–
7	93	7	–	97	3	–	100	–	–	43	40	17
9	60	40	–	47	38	15	83	17	–	17	43	40
11	13	72	15	27	43	30	20	63	17	3	50	47
13	3	57	40	3	47	50	–	37	63	3	43	54
15	–	30	70	–	7	93	–	13	87	–	26	74

(Score 1 = pre-operations; 2 = concrete operations; 3 = formal operations.)

The Swedish children still exhibit an earlier maturing of thought up to 11 years of age, with the other children 'catching up' at 13 and 15 years. This 'catching up' phenomenon is very marked in the North American children who are comparatively retarded until 11 years of age, then in a short period of one intervening step only (11 to 13 years) move ahead of all the rest, by achieving 63 per cent of highest scores. The slowest to move through the scale are the Australian children who also achieve the lowest proportion of formal operational scores.

It is of interest to compare at least the North American results with Bernstein's (1973). The scores from that study can be seen on the 6-point scale in Table 10.4. By comparison with Table 10.2 the 7-year-olds in our sample were well behind the Bernstein sample, and also the sample applied to the 11-year-olds. The scaled sequence is evident in both studies, but accelerated in the Bernstein study. This is due without any doubt to the different sampling of the two studies, since this present study drew upon a public school sample representing the normal range of ability and socio-economic status. Bernstein's sample by contrast was a self-selected group from the area around the university campus (Berkeley Campus, University of California) and the fathers' occupations, as the Appendix on Demographic information (pp. 142-4) on her sample indicates, were upper middle-class. Practically all the fathers of 7- to 8-year-olds were graduates, half of them holding a higher degree at master's or doctorate level, many of these being university teachers or physicians. The same is true of Bernstein's 11 to 12 year sample. There was also an age discrepancy in both age groups; Bernstein's study was composed of 7 *and* 8 year olds, and of 11 *and* 12 year olds, thus making half these samples on average one year older than those in this present study who at most were 7 years 11 months, and 11 years 11 months, in their respective age groups. One would then expect higher scores from higher ability, higher S.E.S. and older children whose

TABLE 10.4 *Bernstein's percentage of scores (0–6) on 'origin of babies' scale by year (N = 60)*

Age-year	Percentages of scores							
	0	1	2	3	4	5	6	N
3–4	5	60	30	–	5	–	–	20
7–8	–	30	–	40	20	5	5	20
11–12	–	–	–	–	10	50	40	20

(Adapted from Bernstein, 1973, p. 44.)

parents were enlightened enough to volunteer them for interview in their own homes.

Nevertheless, the two studies do not provide contradictory results, but on the contrary confirm the presence of a discernible scale based upon pre-operational, concrete operational and formal operational levels. Illustrations from the two samples could well be interchangeable to illustrate the various levels. Furthermore, the six levels of thinking about the origin of babies described in a later publication (Bernstein, 1978) in non-Piagetian terms is also confirmed in this present work, as is illustrated in the final section of this chapter.

Sex differences in scoring on 'origin of babies' scale

One difference in the results of the two studies Bernstein reports is that among her 7-year-old boys the results were much lower than with the girls of that age due, she hypotheses, to possible embarrassment of the boys talking to a female interviewer. This sex discrepancy of scores is not to be seen in the North American 7-year-olds in the present study, possibly due to boys and girls being interviewed by same sex interviewers.

T-tests revealed significant sex differences in scoring on the 'Origin of babies' scale in four age cohorts (see Table B.17, Appendix B). Boys scored significantly higher than the girls in the English 5- and 9-year-olds, and in the Australian 13-year-olds. Girls scored significantly higher than boys in the Swedish 9-year-old cohort. These in themselves, however, are insufficient to merit firm generalisations about sex differences in this item (see also Appendix D, Table D.1).

The roles of mothers and fathers in the origin of babies

Although the responses to the questions 'Does a mother do anything to start a baby?' and 'Does a father do anything to start a baby?' were used to help assess the level of thought arrived at in the 'origin of babies' scale, it is of interest to examine the responses to these queries separately.

Do children see one parent or the other as vital to the process, excluding the other? Does one parent play an active role, and the other a passive role, in the child's perception of what occurs in procreation? Large numbers of children depict mother as doing nothing, except waiting for the 'seed' to grow, not even being involved in its 'planting'. Many see the father as more active not biologically, but as a manufacturer. Other children seem to leave it entirely to the medical profession!

An analysis of the responses was made on a 5-point scale, identified at three levels which we have labelled asexual, non-sexual and overtly sexual. The criteria are set out in Table 10.5. The first section needs no further elaboration but examples of scores 3, 4 and 5 are set out below.

TABLE 10.5 *Criteria for scoring 'roles of mother and father' in procreation*

Level of response	Score	Mother	Father
Asexual	0	Don't know and no response.	
	1	He/she does 'nothing'.	
	2	Does something but unspecified.	
Non-sexual	3	*Post-conceptual activity*	
		Rests, diets, exercise, special food or drink; stops smoking, drinking; visits doctor, hospital.	Drives car, looks after children, housework, pays bills, takes mum to hospital.
	4	*Pre-conceptual activity*	
		Eats food to conceive; stops taking birth-control pills; receives seed non-coitally by operation, through mouth, kissing or navel; gets married.	Buys special food or seed; puts seed in food or drink; inserts seed manually; conveys seed by kissing or navel join; gets married.
Overtly sexual	5	*Sexual intercourse*	
		Making love, coupling, explicit physical joining; perceived coital activity by sex organs	
		Producing egg.	Producing sperm.

Post-conceptual activity (score 3)

This is placed low in the scale since there is little awareness of causation. While some answers, particularly for father, appear to be irrelevant, in a causative sense some of the mother's actions are seen as essentially pre-conditions for a healthy pregnancy, but the pregnancy is already there.

'Mother doesn't smoke. She stops eating some foods and eats others which make it grow' (Australian girl, 9 years); 'Only doctors start the baby. If the baby isn't made they shut the stomach back up. (Q) Like a zip' (English boy, 7 years); 'Dad drives her there, (Q) to the hospital in the car. Mum then sees the doctor and arranges a time for the baby to be cut out' (North American boy, 5 years).

Pre-conceptual activity (score 4)

This section is essentially a repeating of artificialist means of starting a baby or setting in train the non-biological antecedents. It also includes the 'digestive fallacy'.

'Dad makes it by skin and bone in the jungle. (Q) Mummy? She got her gloves on and then puts the skin over her and puts in the bones' (English boy, 5 years); 'Yes, mother's asleep, her mouth open. The star comes slowly and quietly down. The doctors make it come down into the right mouth and it goes into a big hole' (Australian girl, 7 years); 'As soon as she eats a bit more, the food goes down into her tummy and makes a baby' (North American girl, 7 years); 'Mother and father get married, but fathers don't have babies' (Swedish boy, 5 years); 'Yes, she finds the man, gets better acquainted and then they'll get married. (Q) She rests and the mother gets the egg stuck on the navel and it grows' (North American boy, 9 years); 'The father mixes the seed in the cocoa one night and she swallows it' (Australian girl, 7 years).

Sexual intercourse (score 5)

This section includes direct reference to both parents involved in coitus or specific physical joining of the sex organs.

'It's the mother starts it after the willy goes in. (Q) It's been in the mum all the time but putting the willy in starts it to grow, like water on a plant, the liquid goes in' (English boy, 9 years). Some answers reflect the all-powerful medicos helping or authorising the sex act. 'Yes, I'm not sure, but they go to hospital and ask can they put their things together and start off a baby' (English boy, 7 years). 'Yes. They get put to sleep by an injection. The doctor puts them together and get the sperm started' (English girl, 7 years). Even at this level the answer may be selective: 'No, the mother doesn't do anything. It's the father who has to pass the sperm' (Australian girl, 11 years).

TABLE 10.6 Percentages of children's scores* on the 'mother's role in procreation' scale by country and age-year (N=838)

Age-year	Australia					England					North America					Sweden				
	1	2	3	4	5	1	2	3	4	5	1	2	3	4	5	1	2	3	4	5
5	43	3	33	15	—	43	—	20	30	—	38	—	33	25	—	27	—	17	30	20
7	25	3	40	28	3	18	5	35	33	5	13	—	57	27	—	20	3	10	33	20
9	23	5	13	20	25	18	3	18	22	35	13	7	33	30	10	7	3	3	23	60
11	10	8	5	10	60	13	5	3	10	50	17	—	13	17	40	—	—	—	10	87
13	13	—	8	—	73	10	—	8	3	78	6	—	9	6	70	—	—	—	3	93
15	—	—	—	—	98	5	—	3	—	92	7	—	—	—	93	—	—	—	3	97

(*Zero scores are not included in the calculations. Scores 1 and 2 = asexual; 3 and 4 = non-sexual; 5 = overtly sexual.)

It should be noted that there are two separate scores, one for awareness of mother's role, and the other for awareness of father's role. In the last example, the mother's role score is 1 and the father's role score is 5, indicating passivity in one and activity by the other parent.

How mother's role is perceived

The scoring of the responses to the mother's role were made on the criteria shown in Table 10.5 and the results are presented in Table 10.6. The results are symmetrical and in an increasing age hierarchy, the lowest scores diminishing and the highest scores increasing as children grow older. Taking the criterion of 50 per cent of responses in an age group signifying a move upwards in score, it will be seen that asexual responses are fairly well confined to the 5-year-olds and that by 7 years the majority have moved up to non-sexual thinking about mother's role in procreation. Overtly sexual answers come earliest in the Swedish children at 9 years, and latest with the North American children at 13 years. The Australian and English children achieve this at 11 years although in the years preceding an obviously increasing number of children are approaching this stage. These results are roughly consistent with the scores on the 'origin of babies' scale.

When the mean scores for each age are calculated a similar hierarchical trend is evident in Table 10.7 and visually apparent in Figure 10.2. The Swedish higher scores at an earlier age, leading to a sudden increase at 9 years of age, with a sustained high level of overtly sexual scores until the other countries 'catch up', is a phenomenon previously noted and discussed. This picture of earlier Swedish insights and higher scores is beginning to take a consistent and predictable shape, due in part no doubt to the introduction of compulsory sex education at 8 years of age.

TABLE 10.7 *Mean scores on the 'mother's role in procreation' scale by country and age-year (N = 838)*

Age-year	Australia	England	North America	Sweden
5	2.05	2.23	2.35	2.97
7	2.73	2.88	2.90	2.90
9	2.75	3.40	2.97	4.21
11	3.80	3.20	3.24	4.73
13	3.98	4.30	4.08	4.80
15	4.88	4.75	4.74	4.97

How father's role is perceived

The results are set out in Table 10.8 showing the distribution of scores on the 'father's role in procreation' scale, based on identical criteria to

TABLE 10.8 Percentages of children's scores* on the 'father's role in procreation' scale by country and by age-year (N=838)

Age-year	Australia					England					North America					Sweden				
	1	2	3	4	5	1	2	3	4	5	1	2	3	4	5	1	2	3	4	5
5	60	—	23	15	—	58	—	18	18	—	50	—	29	17	—	37	3	7	20	23
7	53	5	13	18	5	33	8	13	25	5	50	—	30	13	—	13	—	10	27	30
9	20	3	8	33	33	23	5	8	15	48	33	3	23	13	13	—	7	—	20	86
11	5	3	—	10	83	8	5	—	15	60	10	3	3	23	53	—	—	—	10	90
13	5	3	—	—	93	10	—	—	—	88	9	3	—	13	73	—	—	—	7	93
15	—	—	—	—	98	—	—	—	—	100	—	—	—	—	100	—	—	—	3	97

(*Zero scores are not included in the table. Scores 1 and 2 = asexual; 3 and 4 = non-sexual; 5 = overtly sexual.)

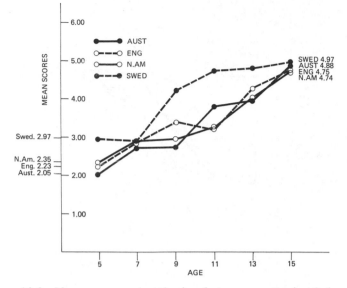

Figure 10.2 Mean scores on 'mother's role in procreation' scale by country and age-year

that for the mother's role as set out in Table 10.5. The pattern is again symmetrical showing a hierarchy of scoring with increasing age and is almost identical with the scores of 'mother's role in procreation' scale. The Swedish forwardness and the North American backwardness are the same for perceptions for father's role as was evident for mother's role. There is, however, one marked difference. At the lower end of the scale children in all countries are slower to leave asexual responses, seeing no clear role at all for the father up to 7 years of age, with the exception of the Swedish children who see the father having an active if non-sexual role, comparatively earlier.

This may well be that the mother's role is highly visible in terms of increased girth during pregnancy. As the carrier or walking incubator of the baby, the mother is probably seen earlier by the young children in an active role, albeit non-sexual, more than the father.

The difference can be seen when mean scores on the 'father's role in procreation' scale are set out in Table 10.9 and visually in Figure 10.3. The lower starting point is marked on the graph when Figure 10.3 is compared with Figure 10.2, particularly the discrepancy to be seen between 7-year-olds perceiving mother's and father's roles. The overall view, when comparing how children perceive mother's and father's roles in procreation, is that father's tend to be seen in passive or inactive asexual or non-sexual roles, while when overtly sexual roles are described

231

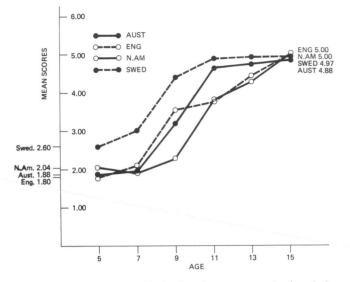

Figure 10.3 Mean scores on 'father's role in procreation' scale by country and age-year

TABLE 10.9 *Mean scores on the 'father's role in procreation' scale by country and age-year (N = 838)*

Age-year	Australia	England	North America	Sweden
5	1.88	1.80	2.04	2.60
7	1.95	2.10	1.90	3.00
9	3.20	3.53	2.30	4.40
11	4.68	3.78	3.80	4.90
13	4.75	4.48	4.30	4.93
15	4.88	5.00	5.00	4.97

the father is seen as the more active and the mother more passive by a sizeable proportion of the children. This may be explained in terms of 'receiving' a seed or sperm being more passive than 'giving' it as a more active process, since the coital act is only partially understood.

Sex differences in perceiving the procreative role of parents

In view of the child-bearing role of women, it is interesting to examine whether girls score higher than boys, or whether there is any same-sex alignment in scores, girls perceiving mother's roles more realistically, and boys perceiving father's roles more realistically.

232

Using t-tests as indicators of significant differences, the following results can be seen in tabular form in Tables 10.10 and 10.11. It should be reiterated that in all countries children were seen only by same sex interviewers (boys by a man and girls by a woman interviewer) so that the factor of embarrassment on the part of children or sex bias on the part of interviewers may be minimised. Differences in the reliability of interviewers may be a factor in these discrepancies but are unlikely in view of the random differences among the age groups. We are inclined to postulate real sex differences in perception of the mother's role, the boys being more aware and informed. This fits with the more aggressive and questioning roles of boys evident in Western-type societies (Torrance, 1962 and 1963) and with the more egalitarian education practised in Sweden. Boys' dominance is also evident, but not as strongly, in the perception of father's role in procreation. The most marked differences, with almost complete male higher scoring in all but the 15-year-old group, is to be seen in the English sample. There is evidence elsewhere to indicate that sex differences in a more 'closed' society may be culturally induced, and the work cited for Britain may well illuminate these results (Lloyd and Archer, 1976). Too much must not be made of this, however, since these discrepancies are not as evident in the 'origin of babies' scale. It should be noted that the main effects of sex in an analysis of variance were not significant in 'the origin of babies' scale, $F(1,790) = 2.41$, but were significant for both mother's $F(1,790) = 50.27$, and father's role in procreation, $F(1,790) = 15.06$ (see Appendix D). A more detailed examination of the figures reveals that the discrepancies between the two items ('origin of babies' and 'parents' role') are not inconsistent with each other.

TABLE 10.10 *Sex differences in perceiving mother's role in procreation by country and age-year*

Age-year	Australia	England	North America	Sweden
5	—	Boys +	—	Girls +
7	—	Boys +	—	—
9	—	Boys +	—	Girls +
11	—	Boys +	Boys +	—
13	Boys +	Boys +	Boys +	—
15	—	—	—	—

(Boys + or Girls + indicates significantly higher scores: see Table B.17, Appendix B.)

Summary and discussion

Previous work on the origins of babies as perceived by children was

TABLE 10.11 *Sex differences in perceiving father's role in procreation by country and age-year*

Age-year	Australia	England	North America	Sweden
5	–	–	–	–
7	–	Boys +	–	–
9	–	Boys +	–	Girls +
11	–	Boys +	Boys +	–
13	–	Boys +	Boys +	–
15	–	–	–	–

(Boys + or Girls + indicates significantly higher scores: see Table B.17, Appendix B.)

reviewed and Bernstein's work (1973) was noted as the major contributor in this field. Although questions in Bernstein's investigation were framed somewhat differently and sampling differences were considerable, comparisons are possible between Bernstein's and this present study. On the 'origin of babies' scale, based upon Piagetian criteria, it was found that operational levels could be discerned with increasing age. Bernstein's higher scores were explained by marked differences in age groupings and the high SES composition of the sample. Nevertheless, both studies confirm the identification of an hierarchical scale. In this present study Swedish children were seen to be much higher scorers at a perceptively earlier age, and the North American the lowest. Concrete operational thinking, approximately equivalent to knowing and describing the physiological basis of procreation without being able to understand or explain it, was not, apart from Sweden, arrived at until about 11 years. The Swedish initial high level was matched at higher age groups in the other countries, a 'catching up' phenomenon noted previously as occurring.

The second part of the chapter was devoted to outlining the results of the roles of mothers and fathers in procreation, consisting of two sets of responses, for mother and father analysed separately. Three levels of asexual, non-sexual and overtly sexual answers were identified, the asexual largely confined to the youngest age groups, but only non-sexual roles were perceived up to quite a late stage (11 years) with Swedish children well ahead and North American comparatively backward. The results were almost parallel between children's perceptions of the role of father in procreation and their perception of the role of mother, except that father's role was not perceived as active as the mother's in the non-sexual stage of answers. Mothers, however, tended at a later age to be less active in the sex act, being rather passive recipients compared with father actively providing sperm.

Already sex stereotypes appear to be forming in late childhood, that in coitus mother passively receives and it is the father who is the initiating and aggressive sex partner. If this is so, it implies that much more is needed in sex and human relations education to emphasise the mutuality of a sexual relationship and the complementary roles of both sexes in contributing to procreation.

The results reported also indicate that in some of the English-speaking countries boys appear to be significantly more perceptive generally about the procreative process than do girls. This is more evident where the perceived roles of parents are concerned than in the 'origin of babies' item, and more evident regarding mother's role than father's role. The Swedish results are reversed in that girls in some age-years appear to be more perceptive than their male peers. Differences in the reliability of interviewers may be a factor in these discrepancies but are unlikely in view of the random differences among the age groups. We are inclined to postulate real sex differences in perception of the mother's role, the boys being more aware and informed.

Three considerations emerge from these findings. The first is that the results from the Swedish sample displaying much earlier insights into the origin of babies and the contributory roles of parents would appear to indicate that* children, given an early sex education pro-gramme and a less inhibited social climate, are able much earlier than is assumed in the English-speaking countries to understand the physical facts of the origin of babies without intellectual confusion.* In contrast, North American children show a much slower rate of cognitive develop-ment in the area of birth and procreation in the pre-teenage years but catch up in the later teenage years.* It is our assessment of the four samples involved in this study that sex education in schools is much more controversial and inhibited due to political and religious pressures in North America than in the other areas.* This may well account for the earlier low levels of sexual thinking in the North American sample.* The catching up of the North American teenagers may be accounted for by possibly more intense social interest and activity, and earlier boy/girl relationships and dating habits of teenagers in Canada and the United States.* It may also be that because information is received later and sexual motivation is greater with the onset of puberty that North American teenagers achieve a spurt of learning about procreation between 13 and 14 years of age.* Within the English-speaking countries the English sample reflects the earliest development in understanding the procreative process at years 9 and 11 scoring higher on both scales 'origin of babies' and 'parents' roles'. This may be explained by the fact that within these countries, the English system tends to encourage some sex education at the top end of the elementary schools. This earlier differential over their Australian and North American peers, however, is not continued in the teenage years. There is some evidence from other sections of this research that the English teenagers are not as advanced socially in terms of heterosexual friendships as their North American and Australian peers, which may be an important factor. Early cognitive stimulation in terms of sexual knowledge combined with teenage inhibitive behaviour and attitudes in the British sample may well 'equalise' the delayed cognitive stimulation in terms of sexual knowledge and earlier teenage sexual interests in the North American sample.

The Australian sample reveals certain differences with the other English-speaking samples, closely following the English sample's trends in the 'origin of babies' item, and the North American sample at certain age levels in the parental roles item. Little sex education occurs before the beginning of secondary schooling in Australia and may well explain this mid-way position between England (earlier sex education programmes) and North American (delayed sex education programmes). While sharing closely many cultural and educational traditions with England Australian teenagers tend to reflect the socio-sexual attitudes and behaviours of North American teenagers.

◆The second consideration from the results is that where children are deprived of honest answers and explanations, they will construct their own explanations and myths.◆ Sexual thinking shares this inventive myth-making in common with children's thinking about religion (Goldman, 1964), politics (Connell, 1971) and other areas of knowledge. Where babies are concerned new myths have replaced the old, becoming medical in nature, reflecting the power and mystique associated with doctors, nurses, operations, hospitals and the secrecy surrounding them. How educators can utilise these myths in helping the child's cognitive development is an important question.

The third consideration, noted by Bernstein, is the children's capacity to be misled and confused by analogies. As a teaching device in some areas, analogies have a useful function to perform, but practically all the biological analogies in explaining the process of birth and procreation are taken too literally. Eggs are seen as brittle encased objects produced by hens, geese and ducks. Seed is seen as the beginnings of plants growing in soil attached to the wall of the mother's stomach, watered occasionally by the father's semen. It would appear to us that sex educators, if they promote analogies to explain sexual matters, should select carefully those which can be used and extended towards a realistic understanding rather than those which lead children into a cognitive cul de sac.

Finally, we concur with Dr Bernstein's latest work (1978) in identifying six levels of explanations of children's thinking about the origin of babies. We would, however, change the labels somewhat, as in the light of our research more accurate descriptions of children's explanations appear to be possible. Bernstein's labels are placed in brackets below:

1 The geographers
2 The manufacturers
3 The agriculturalists (The in-betweens)
4 The reporters
5 The miniaturists (The theoreticians)
6 The realists (Putting it all together)

11   Gestation and birth

Having examined how children perceive and explain the origin of babies, it is important to evaluate how they perceive the processes which follow, particularly the gestation period and the actual birth event. These are difficult processes for children to understand because they are internal and invisible, apart from the external symptom of the swollen 'stomach' of the mother. Some concrete experience is possible if children are encouraged to feel the foetus moving or listen to its internal activities. Even so, they are dependent for knowledge and insight upon information conveyed by the adult world, either through verbal or pictorial descriptions. The verbal descriptions may be vague and ambiguously worded. The pictorial, usually two-dimensional, illustrations can also be confusing since maps or representations of this kind are something of a cognitive puzzle not really approximating to reality in the child's mind until experience and maturing ability help the translation. Alternatively, given no information, children will surmise or invent explanations of their own as they do with the procreative process.

In order to explore this the children were asked questions in four areas. 'How long does it take to grow before the baby is born?' covering the length of gestation; 'What happens to the baby when it's inside the mother?' covering the gestation as a developmental process; 'Where does the baby come out of the mother's body (at birth)?' which covers questions about the birth exit; and 'Why does the baby have to get out?' namely, the developmental necessity for the birth process to occur at a particular time. These four areas, length of gestation, the gestation and foetal developmental process, the birth exit and developmental necessity for birth are presented each in turn in this chapter.

Length of gestation

The form of the question resulted from several trial versions. Even so, the occasional young child gave a firmly literal answer to 'How long does it take to grow before the baby is born?' as 'Ten inches'! No children were asked this question unless they had indicated that the baby was somehow produced inside the mother. The almost universal assurance that this was so, ensured that this question was put in almost every case.

Answers were classified as unrealistic, semi-realistic and realistic, depending upon the relative accuracy of the estimate given by the child. The unrealistic category answers ranged from 'a few minutes' (after doctors had unzipped the stomach and placed the baby inside for quick maturing, rather like a micro-wave oven) to 'a hundred years'. These were all in the 5-year-old group or occasionally at year 7. 'It's 25 years till it gets out' (North American girl, 5 years) and 'It's a very long time. I'd say 9 years' (Australian boy, 7 years). The latter respondent had the right digit but his unit of time was wrong. Wherever time units were given, minutes, hours, days, weeks, months or years they were coded to the nearest month, for example 'One year' becoming '12 months'. The results may be seen in Table 11.2.

TABLE 11.1   *Criteria for scoring 'length of gestation' scale*

Score	Criteria	Category
3	Between 8–10 months	Realistic
2	Between 6–8 months and 10–12 months	Semi-realistic
1	Any other time estimate	Unrealistic
0	Don't know, No response, Nonsense answers	Unscoreable

Taking all countries together it is clear that there is a symmetrical pattern of increased scores from unrealistic to realistic estimates with increasing age. The unrealistic figures in the early years coincide with children's lack of development in 'the psychology of time'. The breakthrough age to realism in the English-speaking countries is fairly uniform at 11 years, if 50 per cent or more achieving score 3 is used as the indicator, all three countries developing at a similar rate of increase. The Swedish children reveal considerably higher realistic estimates at an earlier age, a majority at 9 years but a sizeable 33 per cent at 7 years. The other countries do 'catch up' but not until 13 years. When only realistic scores are plotted on a graph (see Figure 11.1) the Swedish advance pattern is obvious, as is the similarity of the other three countries.

TABLE 11.2 *Percentage of childrens' scores* on 'length of gestation' scale by country and age-year (N = 838)*

Age-year		Scores	Australia	England	North America	Sweden
					Country	
5	1	Unrealistic	80	88	83	60
	2	Semi-realistic	8	5	8	7
	3	Realistic	–	3	–	10
7	1	Unrealistic	78	55	72	40
	2	Semi-realistic	13	28	21	23
	3	Realistic	8	13	7	33
9	1	Unrealistic	40	38	43	10
	2	Semi-realistic	25	30	23	23
	3	Realistic	35	32	30	67
11	1	Unrealistic	15	18	7	–
	2	Semi-realistic	23	17	13	3
	3	Realistic	62	65	80	97
13	1	Unrealistic	–	7	3	–
	2	Semi-realistic	10	10	–	–
	3	Realistic	88	83	97	100
15	1	Unrealistic	–	–	–	–
	2	Semi-realistic	–	5	–	–
	3	Realistic	100	95	100	100

(* Zero scores are not included.)

Sex differences in length of gestation estimates

When the realistic scores are broken down by sex, as Table 11.3 shows, it is evident that there are perceptible sex differences in most age groups in the early years, a greater proportion of girls than boys in all countries scoring 'realistically' at 7 and 9 years (English 9-year-olds the exception) and 11-year-old Australian girls also. The widest discrepancy of scores is at 9 years in Sweden (girls 80 per cent compared with boys 53 per cent). It is possible that girls are more motivated to learn in this area than boys, due to either biological self-interest or closeness to mother and identification with her, particularly in the early years (see chapter 7).

The gestation process

The question 'What happens to a baby while it is inside the mother?' invited the children to provide descriptions of what they think happened during the gestation period. Frequently simplistic responses, such as 'It kicks' or 'It grows' were given, and follow-up questions were

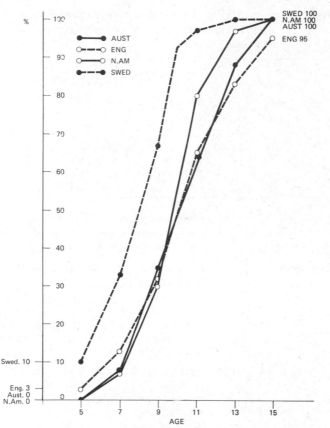

Figure 11.1 Children scoring realistic levels on 'length of gestation'
scale by country and age-year

needed to get the children to elaborate and explain what the gestation process was. An analysis of the type and range of answers indicated that the item could be scaled, both in Piagetian terms of cognitive levels and in terms of biological realism. The criteria for scoring are set out in Table 11.4 with the Piagetian levels identified and the descriptions illustrating the levels of biological realism achieved.

The gestation period and what happens to the 'baby' can be seen in several ways. It can be seen as a series of random events, as a purposive period of preparation for birth, as a foetal developmental process and as a nurturing-feeding process in which food and the means of receiving it become the major focus of interest. In this last identified area considerable confusion was evident, the umbilical cord often confused with

241

TABLE 11.3 *Percentage of children achieving realistic level on the 'length of gestation' scale by country, age-year and sex (N = 838)*

Age-year	Australia Boy	Australia Girl	England Boy	England Girl	North America Boy	North America Girl	Sweden Boy	Sweden Girl
5	—	—	—	5	—	—	7	13
7	5	10	5	20	—	14	27	40
9	25	45	35	30	20	40	53	80
11	50	75	70	60	80	80	100	93
13	90	85	75	90	100	94	100	100
15	100	100	95	95	100	100	100	100

TABLE 11.4 *Criteria for scoring the 'gestation process' scale*

Piagetian levels	Score	Category and description
Pre-operations	0	No response, don't know, 'Nothing' or nonsense.
	1	*Monocentric* — one aspect only. 'It just grows'; end purpose only seen 'It has to get born'; single activities 'It turns round on its back', 'It kicks, crawls, cries, tries to breathe'.
	2	*Artificialisms* Digestive artificialism, focus on receiving food to make baby grow; eating and receiving food; God cares for it, God makes it grow.
Transitional	3	*Semi-physical explanations* — some developmental process grasped. Change occurs of its own momentum — Anthropocentric. Two or three factors but not co-ordinated in system.
Concrete operations	4	*Physical explanations* tinged with egocentricisms. More sophisticated 'gradualism'. Awareness of a physical process but description is explanation. Need for separate food-digestive systems seen.
Transitional and formal operations	5	*Propositional thinking* — moving towards a less naive and logically operational statement. Grasps the diffusion process of feeding in the womb. Gradual growth in cellular division, skeletal growth, embryo to foetus.

the windpipe, the spinal cord and the fallopian tube. Since the storing of 0 and 1 are self-evident, our examples of responses below start at score 2.

Score 2 *Artificialisms*

'It gets made and they put all the different parts on it, the arms and legs' (Australian girl, 7 years); 'God makes it grow (Q) by feeding it, by giving Mum food. The baby eats it through the mouth' (North American boy, 5 years); 'It eats and kicks. It looks at TV there inside. I was looking at Speedway when I was in mother's tummy' (Swedish boy, 5 years). An English girl, aged 7, who estimated that the gestation process took only seven weeks, states a developmental view but artificialist causes, 'I just think God makes it grow. It gets a nose, fingers and fingernails'.

Score 3 *Semi-physical explanations*

'It grows with food, milk shakes and sandwiches and spaghetti. It starts to crawl through the tunnel' (Australian girl, 7 years); 'It grows and gets bigger. It talks, kicks, eats its mother's food. I have heard that through mother's navel. It's the same thing as for the cow mother' (Swedish boy, 5 years); 'The baby grows. I've seen disgusting pictures where the feet and hands are like buns' (Swedish girl, 7 years). An English boy, estimating gestation to take 4 years says, 'It grows with mother's energy, or God's, I don't know. First they're little round balls then their legs and bodies grow, and their heads'.

Score 4 *Physical explanations*

'It gets more prepared to go into the outside world. It gets a head, a face, then legs, arms, body and its insides. It gets hair and teeth and eyes' (Australian girl, 9 years); 'It grows a tail like a fish and feeds through the mother's fallopian tube. The tail disappears as it grows' (English boy, 9 years); 'It grows into a human baby. It sucks in the mother's blood and uses it to stay in the mother's tummy' (North American girl, 11 years); 'The placenta grows to feed it, to give it blood so it can live. The umbilical cord feeds the baby. It gradually turns to face the other way' (Australian boy, 11 years); 'It starts growing and feeds on the mother's milk. (Q) It's produced in the mother's breasts and he sucks it from the inside' (English boy, 13 years).

243

Score 5 *Propositional thinking*

There is no higher score, so that transitional and formal operational answers are scored together, due to the difficulties in scoring with any reliability at this level. Many biological inaccuracies are evident but the beginnings of a systematic theory are there. 'The cells join and make an embryo, a big cell or lots of cells. These produce more and some eggs and grows head and brain and eyes. It gets nerves, which grows. It just goes on like that because of the cells' (Australian boy, 11 years); 'It starts forming and growing, producing cells and shaping arms, getting a brain. Hearts and lungs form and go into action. (Q) Its caused by certain chemicals' (North American girl, 13 years); 'It develops by cells dividing, gradually growing into a human. It's the nutrients it gets from the mother's blood . . .' (English boy, 15 years); 'It's connected to the mother by the placenta, which protects it and gives it oxygen and makes it grow. It develops its own characteristics. It all happens in the womb by meiosis. It takes three months before it looks like a baby' (Australian girl, 15 years).

The difficulty of this item is seen in the results in Table 11.5, only one country, Sweden, achieving 50 per cent of its 15-year-olds at the highest score. There is a clear scale, the characteristic move from low to high scores to be seen from left to right in each country. The distribution of percentages is reasonably symmetrical, showing increasing understanding with increasing age. The majority, however, except in the Swedish results, fail to achieve transitional to formal operations (score 5) remaining at the concrete operational level. This illustrates our comments made earlier about the 'invisible' nature of gestation and how children must find it hard to understand even when it is explained in detail. We suspect, however, that few children do get an explanation in detail or in sequential descriptions. The low scores even at secondary school level would indicate that biology when taught may not cover human biology at all adequately. We shall refer to this matter at a later time.

The mean scores for each age groups are set out in Table 11.6 and in graph form in Figure 11.2. The higher scores of the Swedish children were at once evident with the familiar 'catching up' process occurring, as in many other items. Overall, the majority of children appear to achieve concrete operations on this item by the age of 11 (the English do so marginally but not clearly until 13 years) but the English-speaking countries do not get much higher. This is seen clearly in Table 11.5.

Sex differences on the 'gestation process' scale

T-tests were used to determine if there were significant boys' and girls'

TABLE 11.5 Percentages of children's scores on the 'gestation process' scale by country and age-year (N = 838)

Age-year	Australia					England					North America					Sweden				
	1	2	3	4	5	1	2	3	4	5	1	2	3	4	5	1	2	3	4	5
5	58	23	5	–	–	48	35	3	10	–	67	13	8	–	–	37	40	17	3	–
7	45	23	18	14	–	45	23	13	13	3	40	37	13	10	–	17	7	57	20	–
9	34	10	28	28	–	23	5	23	40	5	33	7	37	17	3	7	3	67	20	3
11	10	–	38	42	10	18	7	30	40	5	10	10	16	37	27	7	–	30	57	7
13	17	3	23	44	13	13	13	24	35	15	6	6	24	39	24	3	–	10	77	10
15	–	5	15	62	18	3	15	13	43	28	3	3	26	29	39	7	–	7	33	50

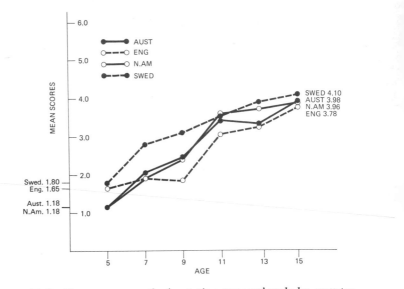

Figure 11.2 Mean scores on the 'gestation process' scale by country and age-year

TABLE 11.6 *Mean scores of children on the 'gestation process' scale by country and age-year (N = 838)*

Age-year	Australia	England	North America	Sweden
5	1.18	1.65	1.18	1.80
7	2.03	1.90	1.90	2.80
9	2.48	1.85	2.40	3.10
11	3.43	3.08	3.60	3.57
13	3.33	3.28	3.71	3.90
15	3.98	3.78	3.96	4.10

scores. The results showed that sex differences were apparent in ten of the eighteen age cohorts within the English-speaking samples, boys scoring consistently higher on this scale. In contrast, the Swedish sample yields only one age cohort at 7 years where there is a significant sex difference in scoring, the girls scoring higher than the boys (see Table B.19, Appendix B). This is confirmed by analyses of variance (see Appendix D, Tables D.1 and D.9 especially).

While these results may reflect genuine differences between boys' and girls' thinking on this item, we conclude that the differences are more satisfactorily explained by less reliable interviewer returns with the English-speaking samples. Scorer reliabilities on this item are high

(0.91) but in collecting the data, that is the responses in the interview, there were considerable differences in length of answer received, affecting the quality of response. This is reflected in the lower scores achieved by girls. The Swedish exception would support this view, particularly in view of other results reported in this chapter.

'Where does the baby exit at birth?'

There is no obvious orifice by which a baby may leave the mother's 'tummy', certainly not in children's ideas about childbirth until a comparatively late stage in development. When children were asked 'Where does the baby get out of the mother's body?', the replies revealed a wide variety of possibilities. All apertures in the human body were suggested — mouth, ears, nose, eyes and anus — as well as what must appear as a semi-closed opening, the navel, popularly referred to as 'the belly button'. A large group of children scoring no obvious exit hole, or listening to adult conversations, came to the conclusion that cutting the mother open is the only explanation. There were some difficulties in clarifying what children meant when they referred to 'the bottom' as the exit for the baby, as in a previous item (see chapter 9), since it could refer to anus, urethra or vagina, and the phrase 'from between her legs' was often used. Despite this it was possible to arrange the exits (or caesarean method) in a hierarchical scale and score the responses accordingly. The scoring criteria are set out in Table 11.7. In allocating scores, correct or incorrect terminology did not influence the result, only a clarification was sought about what was precisely meant by 'bottom' or 'between the legs' or 'the penis part of the lady'. Examples of the various responses are given below.

TABLE 11.7 *Criteria for scoring the 'birth exit' scale*

Score	Descriptions
0	No response, don't know, nonsense answers.
1	Mouth, ears, nose, or other unexplained apertures.
2	Anus or navel.
3	Caesarean always, usually from 'stomach' occasionally from 'chest'.
4	Vagina, including Caesarean only in an emergency.

Score 1

'It comes out of the mouth. They operate by a special machine' (Australian boy, 9 years).

247

TABLE 11.8 Percentages of scores on the 'birth exit' scale by country and age-year (N = 838)

Age-year	Australia				England				North America				Sweden			
	1	2	3	4	1	2	3	4	1	2	3	4	1	2	3	4
5	13	23	22	13	3	53	17	13	5	21	42	13	—	43	7	37
7	5	22	35	28	8	40	23	23	3	21	47	20	—	47	—	40
9	13	43	8	35	3	33	8	43	—	27	27	23	—	17	—	73
11	—	10	—	90	3	22	3	72	13	20	3	50	—	23	—	77
13	—	14	3	83	5	7	3	85	3	9	6	79	—	3	—	97
15	—	5	—	95	—	—	3	97	—	3	—	97	—	3	—	97

Score 2

'The belly button. It's the birthday button where you was born'
(English girl, 7 years); 'A special part of the bum. (Q) Where you
get rid of poo' (Australian boy, 7 years).

Score 3

'They cut the stomach open. They've got tools to get the baby out'
(North American boy, 11 years); 'Doctor cuts Mum's stomach open
and put a long Band-Aid on. It's where they put it in. (Q) The baby
when it was tiny' (English girl, 5 years).

Score 4

'The opening just behind the vagina. (Q) Some tubes that go into
the vagina' (English boy, 11 years); 'The vagina. Sometimes it's
too small a pelvis and has to be cut open. Its a vasectomy' (English
girl, 13 years). Most older children said the one word 'vagina'.

The scores, set out in Table 11.8, show a typical scaling sequence,
low scores predominating in the earliest ages and highest scores in the
oldest age cohorts. The hierarchical order is reasonably symmetrical.
In the English-speaking countries the realistic explanation (score 4)
occurs in the majority of children by 11 years, the Australian children
having the greater proportion (90 per cent) and the North American
the least (50 per cent). In Sweden the realistic level is achieved by 9
years, although 40 per cent of children do so as early as 7 years. Even
more striking is that 37 per cent of Swedish 5-year-olds give a realistic
answer. There is a marked lack of varied response in the Swedish children, only two children mentioning Caesarean and these are aged 5 years,
all other age groups responding by 'anus' (score 2) or 'vagina' (score 4).
The highest scores are set out in graph form in Figure 11.3.

Several observations can be made about these. First the anus response
is very evident among 5- and 7-year-olds, particularly strong in the
English and Swedish children. It is also surprisingly high (43 per cent)
in Australian 9-year-olds, although this figure may be slightly inflated
by translation of the term 'bottom' or 'bum' into what was actually
meant. These results would appear to support Freud's cloacal theory
of how children explain the 'birth exit' (see chapter 1). It is also consistent with the 'digestive fallacy', very strongly held by the younger
children, that the origin of babies can be explained by mother eating
food. Mother eats food and she becomes fat. The food is the baby and
it comes out where food normally comes out, through the anus. The
syllogism is complete.

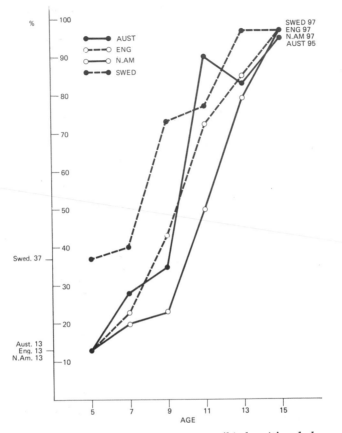

Figure 11.3 Percentages of highest score on 'birth exit' scale by country and age-year

The second observation about the 'birth exit' results is that the Caesarean operation as the normal process of delivery is seen as a popular explanation particularly in the North American responses, among 5- and 7-year-olds. It is consistent with artificialist explanations by many children of this age and represents a second operation. The baby was put in by the doctor, incubated and then taken out, each stage requiring an operation. This appears to be a fairly recently developed medical myth, 'conception and birth by Caesarean'.

Sex differences on the 'birth exit' scale

In most age cohorts there were few discrepancies between boys' and

250

girls' scores, but in separating out the highest score by sex, some differences were evident. Some differences, with more girls scoring at the realistic level than boys, were present in Swedish 5-year-olds (54 per cent to 20 per cent), Swedish 7-year-olds (47 per cent to 33 per cent) and Swedish 9-year-olds (87 per cent to 60 per cent). They could also be seen in Australian 5-year-old girls (20 per cent to 5 per cent) and Australian 9-year-old girls (45 per cent to 25 per cent). The North American children showed a dominance in the other direction, more American boys than girls having a highest score at 5 years (15 per cent to 10 per cent), 7 years (32 per cent to 7 per cent) and 9 years (33 per cent to 13 per cent). The only other marked difference is at 11 years where 87 per cent of Swedish boys have the highest score compared with the girls' 67 per cent. However, only four age cohorts reveal statistically significant differences between the sexes (see Appendix B, Table B.18). The main effects of sex, as the ANOVA results indicate (see Appendix D.1), are not significant.

Explanations of birth necessity

'Why would the baby have to come out (of the mother)?' was the question asked after children had made an estimate of the length of gestation. Although a few estimates of the gestation period seemed to be endless ('Over a hundred years'), children recognised that the process had to end. It was recognised as 'necessary' for the child to be born and to leave the mother's body. The various reasons for this necessity, however, differed considerably from mere physical discomfort or inconvenience to 'completion of time' and 'developmental necessity'. The criteria for scoring were devised in terms of biological realism, the details of which are set out in Table 11.9. Examples of scores at each level are set out below.

Score 0 *Nonsense answers*

'So it will grow up to be good' (Australian, boy, 5 years).

Score 1 *Physical inconvenience or discomfort*

'I didn't want to come out, because I thought it was nice in mother's tummy' (Swedish girl, 5 years); 'The baby would get tired of being in there, and people would get tired of waiting' (English boy, 5 years); 'Mums couldn't walk, she'd be too fat and heavy' (North American girl, 7 years); 'The nurse and the mother want it out. (Q) They want to have a baby to nurse' (Australian girl, 5 years).

251

TABLE 11.9 *Criteria for scoring the 'birth necessity' scale*

Score	Criteria and descriptions
0	Don't know, no response. Non-comprehension, nonsense answers or repetition. 'To see its mummy'.
1	*Physical inconvenience or discomfort* For mother, baby, also nurse or friends. Mother: heavy, kicks, hurts, tiring, too fat, 'She wants a child'. Baby: cramped, hot, bored, squashed.
2	*Physical impossibility* For mother or baby, can't stay forever, can't grow more, too big to stay or get out. Can't breathe or eat enough to survive. To get air or food.
3	*Survival explanations* Death danger to mother or baby by suffocation, starvation, burst stomach. Danger of deformity. May have to operate. Or *Social extension argument* Danger to civilisation. To experience wider social experience. To learn to live, to live its own life, wants mummy or friends. Must come out to grow. Wants to learn to talk.
4	*Completion of time* Full term, fully developed. Bursting of sac or bubble. Ready to come out, it's due, natural, destined. It knows when, instinct. It's finished growing. Can exist now outside. Trying to move, push or kick its way out.
5	*Developmental necessity* Foetus development finished. Labour pains, birth pangs, baby forced out. Mother's muscular contractions. Message to brain, 'It's programmed'.

Score 2 *Physical impossibility*

'It wants some milk to drink, more food' (Australian boy, 7 years); 'He gets too big in there. He can't stay there forever. He can't breathe in there. It stops growing in there. There's no room to grow' (North American girl, 9 years); 'The body can't take it any more, it can't stretch further' (English girl, 11 years).

Score 3 *Survival and social extension explanations*

'Mother would die. Her stomach isn't big, it'd get too big and she'd burst' (Swedish girl, 9 years); 'To see the world, to see his mother and family. (Q) So it can learn to live. So it can learn to write and learn how not to spill things over the carpet' (Australian boy, 7 years).

Score 4 *Completion of time*

'It's the way life goes. It comes out to start a new life. (Q) So it can be fully grown. It forces its way down, its ready to come out'

(Australian boy, 13 years); 'It's in a big bubble and it might break. It's fully formed, it's ready to live on its own away from mother' (English girl, 15 years); 'It's finished. It's ready to come out. It's functions are prepared for life outside the mother' (Swedish girl, 15 years).

Score 5 *Developmental necessity*

'It's able to survive on its own. It needs no internal nutrition. It's developed its own nervous system, to breathe, eat, digest, everything is ready' (North American boy, 13 years); 'It's pushed by the cervix, down the vagina and out by contractions. They're called labour pains' (English girl, 15 years); 'A message is sent somewhere and it's activated. (Q) The muscles are activated and the baby comes out. The body is ready and can't wait. The water in the sac breaks' (Australian boy, 15 years).

The results may be seen in Table 11.10. Some characteristics of a scale are visible but not as symmetrically as in some previous scores. Nevertheless there is a perceptible move to higher scores with increasing age. The difficulty of the question is indicated by the sparseness of the highest level (score 5). However, when scores 4 and 5 are combined, and the completion of time and developmental necessity categories do overlap to some extent, the increased proportion of higher scores with age is much more in evidence, as Table 11.11 indicates. It is apparent that the Australian children score earlier and in greater proportion later than the children in other countries, with a curious dip at 9 and 11 years. The American children after no highest scores in the early stages develop high scores at 15 years, with the English children scoring rather high at 11 and 13 years. Curiously, the Swedish children on this item are the lowest scorers, revealing an earlier start but not the highest scores at 15 years. The general increasing nature of the mean scores can be seen in Table 11.12 and in graph form in Figure 11.4. All the countries follow each other closely, the Swedish score higher at 5 years but finishing just below all other countries at 15 years.

Sex differences on the 'birth necessity' scale

On mean scores, when separated by sex, t-tests reveal some significant differences between boys' and girls' scores in several age cohorts, 7-year-old Australian and English boys scoring higher than the girls of that age, North American boys scoring higher at 11, 13 and 15 years, and Australian boys at 13 and 15 years. There is one marked sex difference in the Swedish sample at 7 years, the girls scoring significantly higher than the boys (see Table B.20, Appendix B). These do appear to

253

TABLE 11.10 Percentages* of scores on the 'birth necessity' scale by country and age-year (N=838)

Age-year	Australia					England					North America					Sweden				
	1	2	3	4	5	1	2	3	4	5	1	2	3	4	5	1	2	3	4	5
5	—	18	43	18	—	33	35	23	3	—	38	29	21	—	—	20	27	53	—	—
7	—	23	40	28	5	15	28	30	20	—	23	30	43	—	—	30	23	40	3	—
9	5	32	55	5	3	—	50	23	25	3	17	30	40	10	3	3	30	47	10	—
11	3	23	45	28	—	—	8	35	28	30	—	23	23	43	10	3	30	27	37	3
13	3	13	23	38	23	—	30	20	50	—	—	18	33	49	—	—	20	30	37	10
15	—	5	13	73	10	—	10	30	53	8	—	13	10	65	13	—	10	47	40	3

(* Zero scores are not included.)

TABLE 11.11 *Percentages of highest scores (4 and 5) on the 'birth necessity' scale by country and age-year (N = 838)*

Age-year	Australia	England	North America	Sweden
5	18	3	–	–
7	33	20	–	3
9	8	28	13	10
11	28	58	53	40
13	61	50	49	47
15	83	61	78	43

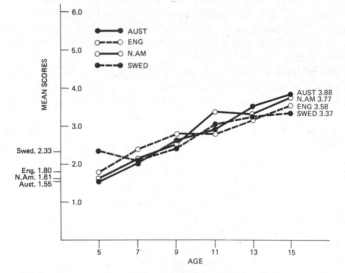

Figure 11.4 Mean scores on the 'birth necessity' scale by country and age-year

indicate overall some genuine sex differences on this item and are confirmed by ANOVA results as listed in Appendix D. Three-way interactions between sex, age-year and country are also significant.

Summary and discussion

Children were asked questions covering four areas, the length of gestation, the birth exit of a baby from its mother's body and the reasons for birth occurring at a particular time.

Estimations of the gestation period were scored on unrealistic, semi-realistic and realistic answers, the last named being any period

255

TABLE 11.12 *Mean scores of the 'birth necessity' scale by country and age-year (N = 838)*

Age-year	Australia	England	North America	Sweden
5	1.55	1.80	1.61	2.33
7	2.05	2.40	2.13	2.10
9	2.68	2.80	2.53	2.43
11	2.93	2.80	3.40	3.07
13	3.58	3.20	3.32	3.27
15	3.88	3.58	3.77	3.37

from 8 to 10 months. The Swedish children proved the earlier realistic scorers at 9 years, the English-speaking countries generally achieving realistic responses by 11 years. Girls were found in most groups to score realistically at an earlier age, possibly due to greater concern and interest in this area.

The gestation process was scored on Piagetian criteria with equivalent biological realism levels, the Swedish children again scoring higher on the scale at 5 years and finishing higher at 15 years. Overall, the majority of children found the item difficult, since it describes an 'invisible' experience not open to first-hand exploration; the scores of transitional – formal operational thinking were rarely achieved. Concrete operations were evident at year 11 but children did not progress much higher than this area in the 15-year-old groups. Considerable sex discrepancies were found in scores, the boys tending to score significantly higher than the girls in the English-speaking samples.

In trying to determine the birth exit of the baby from its mother's body, children chose every orifice possible, and large numbers at 5 and 7 chose Caesarean, by cutting the child out of 'the stomach', as the normal means of childbirth. Larger numbers, however, identified the anus as the normal exit, appearing to support Freud's cloacal theory and the 'digestive fallacy' of food as the causative origin of babies in the early years. At 9, Swedish children tend to achieve realistic ideas of the vagina as the birth exit whereas in English-speaking countries it was 11 years. Girls appear to be better informed earlier than boys.

In reviewing children's explanations of why birth becomes necessary after a certain period of gestation, these begin with younger children in terms of physical inconvenience and discomfort and proceed in middle to late childhood in terms of mother's or baby's survival. Few older children saw developmental necessity in sophisticated or realistic terms, being satisfied with the idea of 'readiness' or completion of time as a sufficient explanation. More sophisticated and realistic explanations, attempting to identify and describe the biological process, did not really appear until 15 years of age, the majority at that age still preferring simplistic explanations. This does not in our view argue for a level of difficulty in posing this question to children but the probable dearth of instruction in human biology and human procreation in schools, even among the adolescent population. Animal analogies and two-dimensional illustrations may appear to present the facts, but we suspect that instruction in such complex biological processes is either not attempted or is too vaguely presented.

As we have commented earlier, unless mothers during that period of gestation have helped their children to understand what is happening inside them by using pregnancy as an educative period, children will have little concrete experience upon which to base their understanding. It should be noted that the potential for the best conditions of educating children did exist in the samples chosen, since every subject had a younger brother or sister, thus providing experience of the gestation period and advent of a new baby in the family. From the results reported we would postulate that few parents utilised the arrival of a new baby to educate their children in these matters. We would also suggest that the children received little in their sex education or human relations courses (if they had received any such instruction at school by the time they were interviewed) to help them develop an understanding of birth processes, except in the case of children in the Swedish sample.

The fact that most Swedish children had attained realistic perceptions of the gestation period and the birth exit by 9 years of age is probably an indicator of the advantage they experienced in a compulsory sex education programme from the age of 8 years (Linner, 1978). Evidence taken in all the areas from which the English-speaking samples were chosen indicated that sex education was a contentious matter, and school authorities tended to limit most of this instruction to the secondary or high school age groups; and then often when parental permission had been secured. It is clear, therefore, that Swedish children had an advantage in addition to a wider societal tolerance of sexual matters and less inhibition in discussing such matters with children. The effectivism of Swedish school policy in introducing such courses in the pre-pubertal period is well illustrated in most of the results reported in this chapter.

On the 'birth necessity' scale, however, the Swedish results are lower than the English-speaking samples and no such early advantage appears. The best indicator is that of mean scores in each age cohort (Table 11.12) and shows the Swedish children only a little behind their English-speaking peers. We would posit two possible reasons to explain this difference. The first is that the answers in the English-speaking cohorts were much fuller, the interviewers having acquired more experience through the pilot interviews and in formulating the final interview schedule. In providing explanations for why babies are born after a certain period of gestation, fuller answers tend to be scored slightly higher, since ambiguities or nuances can be used to determine scores more accurately. The Swedish interviewers, trained by the authors, did not generally elicit responses as full as those for the other countries, and therefore poorer interviewer reliability intervened to obscure the real results. A second reason may have been in the translation of responses, a common difficulty in cross-cultural studies, which would limit accurate scoring of the item. The two reasons together compound the problem.

Such difficulties did not appear to affect the first two items, the length of gestation and identifying the birth exit, since terse, mono-syllabic, one-word factual answers were more easily and more accurately scored. From this it can be inferred not that the Swedish teenagers in particular were backward in 'birth necessity' explanations, but that their advantage on this item of an earlier systematic sex education pro-gramme cannot be demonstrated.

On the 'birth exit' item the results provoke two observations. The first is that the comparative frequency of younger children's identifi-cation of 'birth exit' as the anus tends to support Freud's theory that young children generalise in this way (Freud, 1963), known as the cloacal theory. It is also consistent with the 'digestive fallacy', very strongly held by the younger children, that the origin of babies can be explained by mother eating food. Mother eats food and she becomes fat. The food is the baby and it comes out where food normally comes out, through the anus. The syllogism is complete (Bernstein, 1973; Bernstein and Cowan, 1975).

The second observation about the 'birth exit' results is that the Caesarean operation as the normal process of delivery is also seen as a popular explanation among 5- and 7-year-olds. It is consistent with artificialist explanations (Piaget, 1930) by many children of this age and represents a second operation. The baby was put in by the doctor, incubated and then taken out, each stage requiring an operation. This appears to be a fairly recently developed medical myth, 'conception and birth by Caesarean'.

Overall, the impression is reinforced that children not instructed in this topic of gestation and birth find its 'invisible' nature difficult to comprehend. They frequently resort to explanations by mythology, as they do so in explaining the origin of babies, the medical myths of hospitals, operations — particularly the cutting open of mother to insert and withdraw a baby, which is strongly held in the early years. The doubt remains whether this topic is covered adequately in biology or human relations courses in the countries from which these samples are drawn.

12 Coitus and the sex determination of babies

Two areas are closely linked with the previous biologically based questions, namely the function of coitus in human life, and how a baby's sex is determined. Both areas appear to be difficult for children to grasp, not only because of strong taboos on these subjects but also because they are by their nature intrinsically obscure. Coitus is a private activity, especially where children are concerned, parents usually taking carefully thought-out measures to prevent children witnessing it, even by accident. It is not normally a matter to be discussed when the family is together and reference has already been made to the reluctance of children to recognise parents as sexually active adults. Nevertheless, the majority of children between the ages of 9 and 11 years are beginning to be aware of coitus as a causative factor in the making of babies, however confused and unsophisticated their perceptions are. The authors were interested and intrigued to find out if children perceived any function beyond the progenitive one for coitus.

If coitus and its purposes or functions are a mystery, the determination of the sex of a baby appears to be an even greater one for children. How it is determined or 'decided' that a particular baby is to be a boy or a girl, and who or what decides it, are questions rarely asked by children themselves, and when faced with the problem they reveal considerable cognitive difficulties. If the antecedents of making a baby, coitus itself, is only partially comprehended, the connecting of this with the sex determination of babies at conception is viewed and explained only in the crudest and confused terms well into the teenage years. This chapter is concerned with two basic questions. First, do children having identified coitus as a necessary process in making a baby, see sexual intercourse as having other purposes or functions? Second, what do children perceive to be the cause or determining factor in the sex identity of a baby?

259

The purposes and functions of coitus

In the trial interviews it became apparent that children are well aware of some activity going on between men and women of an intimate nature. Referring to sexual intercourse by various names in addition to the correct ones, such pseudonyms as screwing, humping, rooting, having contraceptions, having it off, or even more vaguely as 'doing it', children revealed this awareness increasingly with age. Consequently, towards the end of the interview a question was added asking those who had already made reference to coitus, 'Apart from wanting a baby, why do people want to make love (have sex, sexual intercourse, screw, hump)?' Two points should be emphasised about this question. First, it was put to only those children who were aware of coitus and had made a direct reference to it already in the course of the interview. It came under the heading of a 'contingent' question and was asked subject only to certain prior responses. The second point to note is that the question was framed in the child's actual terminology, the interviewer using such words as 'sexual intercourse' only if the child had used them. For example, one child was asked, 'Apart from wanting a baby, why is it *a mum and dad will have a you-know-what together in bed?*' – the exact form of words previously used by the boy himself.

The number of children asked this question in these circumstances can be seen in Table 12.1 in terms of the percentages of each age cohort. In practically all cases the reference to coitus was made in the origin of babies discussion, with an occasional reference when sexual differences between men and women, and between newborn babies were discussed. From the age of 7 years those children who made this reference had done so in the origin of babies context. Nevertheless, when the question was put to them, practically all the English-speaking 5- and 7-year-olds responded with 'I don't know' type of responses or were plainly too perplexed to formulate a reply. A few at this age level replied in a repetitive view 'just to have babies' or 'They wouldn't want to do it unless they wanted a baby'. Those responding in this way are presented in Table 12.2. It will be seen in the previous table (12.1) that the younger age cohorts in Sweden had a much higher incidence since many more of the Swedish 5- and 7-year-olds (50 per cent each) had made previous reference to sexual intercourse.

A consequence of the limited replies at 5 and 7 years, pointing out the purposes or functions of coitus in addition to begetting children, is that we shall present the results only from 9 onwards, except that some later discussion of the Swedish younger age years will provide some further details.

The majority of children who replied with an additional purpose or function of coitus (see Table 12.3) gave only one reply, sometimes a

TABLE 12.1 *Percentages of respondents asked the coitus question by country and age-year (N = 838)*

Age-year	Australia	England	North America	Sweden
5	10	3	4	50
7	22	3	7	50
9	40	48	17	100
11	95	80	50	100
13	100	97	94	100
15	100	100	100	100

TABLE 12.2 *Percentages responding 'To have babies' to coitus question by country and age-year (N = 838)*

Age-year	Australia	England	North America	Sweden
5	—	3	3	7
7	—	—	6	7
9	18	20	6	7
11	18	10	18	—
13	8	3	18	—
15	5	9	—	—

TABLE 12.3 *Percentages of children providing additional purpose for coitus other than begetting children by country*

Australia	England	North America	Sweden
54	42	52	87

single word or phrase. About a quarter gave two additional purposes, and a handful of children mentioned three. Since all were legitimate or correct 'alternatives' to the progenitive purpose, no attempt was made to score or scale the responses on a hierarchy. Instead the responses were classified into seven groups and examined in terms of their distribution. The order in which they are set out below indicates the frequency or 'popularity' of the type of response, beginning with the category most frequently used down to the category least frequently used. The quotations are in the children's words.

1 *Enjoyment* The most frequent response was in terms of coitus as enjoyment, pleasure or fun. 'It makes you feel good, happy, excited'; 'It's nice'; 'They may like having sex. They may not want a child, and they may not want to be married'.

2 *Expression of love* The most frequent category asserted coitus

261

to be an expression of love, or the proof of love, it stems from liking, loving or being warm to a person. It is a symbol 'of complete trust', 'something special between two people'; 'It helps people to come closer emotionally.'

3 *It's natural* Much lower in frequency is the view that coitus is instinctive: 'it's based upon sexual attraction'; 'It's natural if you're married'; 'it's natural if you're in love' and 'for men and women'.

4 *Experiment* The remainder of responses are much fewer in frequency, including this suggestion that people engage in coitus 'to see what it's like'; 'a new experience they've never had before'; or 'you've got to try it out sometime'. Several stated 'they'd like to know they're capable'.

5 *It's binding* A few children see coitus as an act which strengthens a bond between people. 'It consolidates a marriage' or, as one 13-year-old put it, 'it's a bondage in marriage'.

6 *Necessity* A very few saw coitus as necessary not because of instinct, desire or passion but 'being forced to do it for money'.

7 *Peer pressure* Only three, all boys, gave this as a purpose of coitus, 'so they can brag about it' and 'so they can seem [to be] like everyone else'.

One unclassifiable response is worth quoting: 'They wouldn't want to unless they're sex mad like The Sex Pistols. At 25 you start going off it' (English boy, 11 years).

Coitus as enjoyment

Apart from two 5-year-olds and five 7-year-olds in Sweden, no children earlier than 9 years responded in this category. At 9 years it is the most frequent of all responses, as indicated by Table 12.4. In the light of books such as Masters and Johnson (1975), *The Pleasure Bond* and more popular publications such as Alex Comfort's (1972) *The Joy of Sex* the results under this category are interesting. There is a clear progression with age of those who see the function of coitus to be enjoyment. More Swedish children express this earlier at 9 years, compared with the majority of English-speaking 13-year-olds who do not achieve this view until that age. It is noticeable in most age groups (in ten out of the sixteen cohorts) that considerably more boys express this function of coitus than do girls. It is understandable that girls, who may face more serious consequences if a pregnancy should occur, are more reluctant to see it in this way. Nevertheless, a sizeable and increasing proportion of teenagers of both sexes see enjoyment as the major purpose of sex apart from the procreation of children.

TABLE 12.4 *Percentages of 'enjoyment' responses to coitus question by country and sex from 9–15 years (N = 564)*

Age-year	Sex	Australia	England	North America	Sweden
9	Boys	6	20	8	73
	Girls	6	–	–	47
	Totals	6	10	4	60
11	Boys	36	25	33	73
	Girls	24	35	–	80
	Totals	30	30	17	77
13	Boys	80	60	75	100
	Girls	30	30	41	47
	Totals	55	45	58	73
15	Boys	65	90	81	100
	Girls	60	60	47	100
	Totals	63	75	67	100

Coitus as an expression of love

Not as frequent as pleasure is the response that coitus is part of a love relationship, and a physical expression of love. The total figures in Table 12.5 show an increase with age of this response, but also reverses the emphasis seen in 'the enjoyment' responses in terms of sex differences. In the great majority of age groups (in thirteen out of the sixteen cohorts) considerably more girls respond in terms of 'love' than boys. This romantic emphasis is most marked, particularly in the teenage years, with the curious exception of 15-year-old Australian boys. The sex bias of boys in terms of pleasure, and girls in terms of love, when discussing the purpose of sexual intercourse, is we believe of considerable social significance. It is interesting to see this in all countries, including Sweden. The cohorts showing significant sex differences in frequency of responses of 'enjoyment' and 'love' reveal this very clearly (see Table B.8, Appendix B).

Other purposes of coitus

The remaining categories of responses are so infrequent as not to merit further analysis. 'It's natural' purpose is given by only 4 per cent of the whole sample and is expressed mainly at 15 years; 'experimental' purpose forms only 3 per cent of responses and again is mainly at 15 years; 'it's binding' is expressed by 1 per cent and 'necessity' by less than 1 per cent of the whole sample.

TABLE 12.5 *Percentages of 'love' responses to coitus question by country and sex from 9–15 years (N = 564)*

Age-year	Sex	Australia	England	North America	Sweden
9	Boys	30	6	8	20
	Girls	15	10	–	47
	Totals	23	8	4	33
11	Boys	30	6	8	20
	Girls	25	20	27	47
	Totals	28	13	17	33
13	Boys	10	10	19	7
	Girls	50	35	41	53
	Totals	30	28	30	30
15	Boys	60	5	31	33
	Girls	35	50	73	60
	Totals	48	28	52	47

The sex determination of babies

Despite the previous section, most children still regard coition's main purpose to be procreative. They do not, however, necessarily see it as the context for sex determination. How that foetal being becomes a boy or a girl, at what stage its sex identity is determined, at conception or later, must be related to the vagueness with which children view gender stability and gender constancy (Slaby and Frey, 1975). As some younger children assert, all babies are born the same sex and only later it is decided what sex they will be. Change of sex appears possible in the early years, everyone born as girls, some then being 'changed by medicine' to boys, or on the Freudian hypothesis all are born as boys and some have their penis removed to become girls. Assuming, however, that many of the 5- and 7-year-olds interviewed had achieved gender stability and constancy, at what point sex identity is 'fixed' or 'determined' is almost an unanswerable question for them, as is also who or what determines it. Add to this the 'invisible' nature of the process and the fact that it is not taught in schools until the later years, there is no doubt that this topic posed the most difficult question of the whole interview.

'What decides whether a baby is going to be a boy or a girl?' was the first wording of the question. The word 'determines' was used only with older respondents. A variant was, 'How is it decided whether a baby is going to be a boy or a girl?' Another was, 'When a baby is started, how does it become a boy or a girl?' The word 'who' was never

264

asked lest it suggested authoritarian or artificialist answers. Even so, many children changed the 'what' to a 'who' signifying God, Jesus, doctors and parents as the deciders. Occasionally it was the child itself in the womb exerting a will.

It is not surprising in the light, or rather dark, of this confusion that the responses contain a high proportion of 'don't know', 'can't say' and 'I haven't the faintest idea' type of answers, which could be scored only as zero. In the English-speaking countries these zero scores were in particularly high proportions among the girl respondents, the implications of which will be discussed later under 'sex differences'.

The criteria for scoring what we call the 'genetic determination of sex' scale are set out in Table 12.6. It will be seen that some Piagetian categories are included but these are used only descriptively. There is no attempt to justify these as Piagetian criteria, although it was originally planned that way. Examination of the results led to a biological realism scale, with seven scores seen at three levels, non-sexual, sexual transmission and genetic transmission type answers. Examples of these scores and levels are given below.

Score 1 *No causality*

'It's just so. It's one or the other. (Q) They can tell by taking photos' (English boy, 5 years); 'You can't tell till it comes out. (Q) No one knows, till it comes out' (Australian girl, 7 years).

Score 2 *Artificialisms*

'God decides what is best for the mother and father' (North American boy, 5 years); 'The clergyman decides at the baptism or perhaps the father decides, probably father' (Swedish boy, 7 years); 'It's the nurse or the doctor' (Australian girl, 7 years); 'Its own body, the body asks to be a boy or a girl' (Australian boy, 9 years).

Score 3 *Semi-physical, semi-psychological, zooisms*

'All the seeds have a little boy or girl in them' (Australian girl, 7 years); 'Only the doctor knows. (Q) It's what you think it is. I thought it was a boy, and so did my Dad, and it was' (Australian boy, 5 years); 'If you eat a little it will be a boy. If you eat a lot it will be a girl' (Swedish boy, 7 years); 'It's decided by the egg, if it's a boy egg it will be a boy, and if it's a girl egg it will be a girl' (English girl, 9 years); 'It's like those minnows. If it's a girl minnow within the shell it's a girl. If it's a boy minnow, it's a boy' (English boy, 9 years); 'Dad decides it's going to have boys; Mum decides it's going to have girls' (North American girl, 11 years).

265

TABLE 12.6 *Criteria for scoring the 'genetic determination of sex' scale*

	Score	Category and description
Non-sexual	0	*Unscoreable* Don't know, no response, lack of comprehension. Nonsense answers.
	1	*No causality* Confusion of prediction with causality. Finalism: 'It's just so', 'They can X-ray', 'Tell by the hair'.
	2	*Artificialisms* The manufacturer decides; medicine, chemists decide, seed makers; baby itself decides.
	3	*Semi-physical, semi-psychological, zooisms* There are boy or girl seeds, sperm, eggs. The internal organs decide — womb, stomach, tubes. Parents wish, desire, will it.
Sexual transmission	4	*Concretely physical and psychological* Quantifiable judgment. Previous analogies used as fact; size and shape of sperm or egg; the one with most cells; longest tailed, stronger, bigger, faster 'seed'; angle of impact of sperm on egg, speed or impact; position in womb — higher (girl) or lower (boy). Accuracy of terms used not considered.
	5	*Nature of sexual intercourse* Sex decided by sex joining; egg and sperm, one or other dominant i.e. the stronger (as opposed to one sperm being stronger than another, or one egg than another).
Genetic transmission	6	*Miniaturism or preformation* Ovist — male or female latent in mother's egg. Animalculist — male or female latent in sperm. Sex is invariable, fixed in either and non-interactive.
	7	*Physiological interfusion* Interactivism — perception of chromosomes, genetic contribution of both parents at conception; XX and XY combination; DNA. Accuracy of terms used not considered.

Score 4 *Concretely physical and psychological-quantifiable*

'I don't know. The way the cells join. They might join in different places. That's just a guess' (Australian boy, 9 years); 'It depends on the side of the egg it gets in. If on the right it might be a boy, and so on' (North American boy, 13 years).

Score 5 *The nature of sexual intercourse*

'It's the sperm, the one that gets there fastest, the one with the largest tail 'cos it can swim faster. (Q) Because when it meets the egg it depends which is strongest' (English boy, 13 years); 'The egg and the squirm when they meet, kind of fight it out. The bossier one wins. If the egg wins, it's a girl. If the squirm wins, it's a boy' (Australian girl, 11 years).

Score 6 *Miniaturism or preformation*

'If it's a boy egg or a girl egg, a girl sperm or a boy sperm. (Q) It's got a chance of two out of four what it's to be' (North American boy, 15 years); 'Sperm and egg. When they meet one is dominant and becomes the baby. (Q) Don't know how' (Australian girl, 13 years); 'I think it's the amount of hormones, if it's 51 per cent male hormones then it's going to be a male. (Q) Like a sperm; hormones make up the sperm' (Australian boy, 15 years).

Score 7 *Physiological interfusion*

'There are XY boy chromosomes and XX girl chromosomes and depending on which meets which it is a boy or a girl' (English boy, 15 years); 'It's D.N.A. and that stuff. (Q) When an egg with an X thing is fertilised by a sperm with a Y, the baby is male, X and X make a female' (Swedish boy, 15 years); 'Both parents decide. (Q) Through their genes. Their chromosomes mix. It's really chance, depending on the dominant chromosomes' (Australian girl, 15 years).

Table 12.7 shows the distribution of scores on the 7 point scale. It is immediately obvious that while the scores are reasonably symmetrical, increasing gradually with increasing age, and move from left to right in a scaling hierarchy, the lower scores dominate and continue for a considerable period, indicating the difficulty of the question. No majority of children in any age group achieve the highest score of 7, except the Swedish (50 per cent) and North American (almost, at 48 per cent) 15-year-olds. Since scores 6 and 7 are the only types of realistic answers, the sparsity of higher scores can be seen in Table 12.8, where scores 6 and 7 are combined to make a 'highest score'. This 'highest' scoring becomes apparent in any real percentage terms at 11 years in Sweden only, and 13 years generally. The Swedish pattern of scoring higher and earlier is obvious, although the familiar catching up at 15 years is evident, with the Australians having the greatest proportion. What this means is that while non-sexual explanations have given way to sexual

267

TABLE 12.7 Percentages* of scores on the 'genetic determination of sex' scale by country and age-year (N = 838)

Age-year	Australia							England						
	1	2	3	4	5	6	7	1	2	3	4	5	6	7
5	20	30	20	—	—	—	—	10	28	15	—	—	—	—
7	10	40	20	3	—	—	—	5	20	8	13	—	—	—
9	10	3	40	15	3	—	—	—	8	23	20	5	5	—
11	5	8	18	20	5	—	—	—	—	20	23	13	8	—
13	5	5	18	20	—	20	5	3	—	10	25	—	20	10
15	—	—	3	18	5	48	23	—	—	3	18	3	40	15

Age-year	North America							Sweden						
	1	2	3	4	5	6	7	1	2	3	4	5	6	7
5	8	21	17	—	—	—	—	50	13	33	—	—	—	—
7	3	20	23	10	—	—	—	33	10	20	3	—	—	—
9	10	7	30	10	—	—	—	50	3	17	3	3	—	—
11	7	7	30	27	—	7	—	10	—	20	10	17	7	3
13	—	12	—	33	—	21	6	—	—	3	17	3	23	47
15	—	—	3	16	7	19	48	—	—	10	17	13	10	50

(* Zero scores are not included. Scores 1–3 = non-sexual; 4–5 = sexual transmission; 6–7 = genetic transmission.)

TABLE 12.8 *Percentages of highest scores (6 and 7) on the 'genetic determination of sex' scale by country and age-year (N = 838)*

Age-year	Australia	England	North America	Sweden
5	–	–	–	–
7	–	–	–	–
9	–	5	–	10
11	–	8	7	34
13	25	30	27	70
15	71	55	67	60

TABLE 12.9 *Mean scores on the 'genetic determination of sex' scale by country and age-year (N = 838)*

Age-year	Australia	England	North America	Sweden
5	1.40	1.10	0.97	1.77
7	1.60	1.18	1.47	1.27
9	2.07	2.17	1.54	2.00
11	1.87	2.07	2.07	4.10
13	3.02	3.23	3.35	5.60
15	5.45	4.35	5.60	5.73

transmission answers, genetic transmission of sex identity is not really grasped until 15 years, Sweden being earlier at 13 years.

The mean scores shown in Table 12.9 indicate the depression of scores generally until 13 years in the case of the English-speaking countries and 11 years in the case of Sweden. When one considers that score 2 is only at the artificialist stage of thought, one can realise how depressed these scores are. The mean scores can be seen graphically in Figure 12.1 with the Swedish sudden increase at 11 years and the 13-year 'spurt' in the other countries very visible.

Sex differences on the 'genetic determination of sex' scale

A factor which grossly depresses scores on this scale is the very high proportion of zero scores, signifying 'I don't know', 'I can't say' and 'I haven't a clue' responses. These were very marked in the girls' responses, the result being that in almost every age cohort of the English-speaking samples the boys score significantly higher (see Table B.21, Appendix B). The size of this discrepancy can be seen in Table 12.10 where the percentages of zero scores are presented and confirmed as highly significant in terms of main effects of sex (see Table D.1). Several reasons may be advanced to explain these marked discrepancies.

269

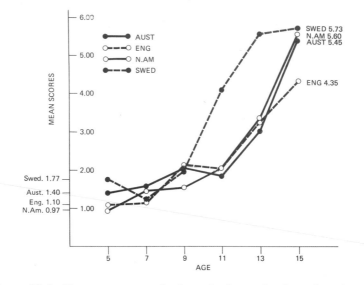

Figure 12.1 Mean scores on the 'genetic determination of sex' scale by country and age-year

TABLE 12.10 *Percentages of zero scores on the 'genetic determination of sex' scale by country, age-year and sex (N = 838)*

Age-year	Australia		England		North America		Sweden	
	Boys	Girls	Boys	Girls	Boys	Girls	Boys	Girls
5	10	50	10	85	39	73	7	—
7	10	45	20	90	13	79	33	33
9	15	45	5	75	20	67	13	13
11	25	65	—	75	—	47	20	—
13	5	50	10	55	—	53	7	7
15	5	5	5	40	—	13	—	—

The first is that girls do score lower perhaps because they are less motivated and less knowledgeable in this area. In other words boys are more scientifically orientated particularly in the teenage years. The Swedish returns would not support this explanation up to 13 years but may well do so at 15 years. The second is that girls were less willing to guess at an answer or explore the question, preferring to be more honest than attempt a speculative reply. While this is a possibility, the Swedish scores do not indicate this to be the case unless Swedish girls are different from their female peers in other countries. On the other hand, the English results may well indicate a culturally different response level, less prone to guess at answers and more inhibited in answering. The third explanation is that it could be due to interviewer discrepancies on this particular item solely in the English-speaking countries, one interviewer not pursuing the respondents to make some kind of positive response after an initial zero response. We postulate that the second and third reasons together, a mixture of cultural differences and interviewer unreliability on this item combine as major factors to depress the scores.

Should this be the case we can hypothesise that if the scores of the girls had been equal to the higher levels achieved by the boys, the results would resemble, at the highest levels, the figures in Table 12.11. When these hypothetical results are compared with the actual results on Table 12.8 there is some increase in the proportion of those scoring higher, but the differences between 'hypothetical' and 'actual' are not markedly higher. The increases are only marginal at the 15-year level in the Australian and North American samples, and the only marked increases are seen in the English sample. Since the same calculation was done with the Swedish sample, the percentage of 15-year-olds scoring high is greater, because it was the only Swedish age group in which the proportion of high scoring boys (80 per cent) exceeded the girls considerably (40 per cent). The hypothetical figures are, of course, those for boys.

TABLE 12.11   *Hypothetical percentages of highest scores (6-7) on the 'genetic determination of sex' given equal scoring of boys and girls*

Age-year	Australia	England	North America	Sweden
5	–	–	–	–
7	–	–	–	–
9	–	5	–	13
11	–	5	13	26
13	40	40	38	74
15	75	75	69	80

The first reason, genuine sex differences in that boys are more scientifically orientated than girls at the age of 15 years, may well explain the discrepancies at that age.

Overall, the results appear to indicate that up to 15 years the area of genetic determination of sex at the time of fertilisation is intrinsically difficult in cognitive terms, requiring a high level of formal operational thinking in addition to formal scientific instruction in that particular area.

Summary and discussion

Two areas were explored in this section, how do children perceive coitus in terms of its purpose and function apart from procreation, and how do children explain the origins of their sex identity? In the first section, the question was asked only of children who had indicated earlier in the interview that they knew of coitus as a sexual joining of woman and man. Children who had revealed no awareness of this were not asked the question. Fifty-four per cent of the Australian children, 42 per cent of the English, 52 per cent of the North American and 87 per cent of the Swedish children revealed awareness of other purposes than procreation in sexual intercourse. These were seen in order of importance as enjoyment, an expression of love, a natural activity, an experiment, a bond, a necessity or to satisfy peer pressures. The two dominant responses were coitus as an enjoyable fulfilling activity and coitus as an expression of love. Both responses increased from 9 to 15 years but the most interesting feature is the bias of boys towards sexual intercourse as pleasure, and the bias of girls towards it as a romantic expression of love. This dichotomy between the sexes was marked in all countries including Sweden. Only in Sweden did the younger children respond in any number, the 5- and 7-year-olds providing answers of enjoyment and love, whereas they were absent at these ages in the English-speaking countries.

How children understand or perceive the origin of sex identity in a baby was then explored, by asking the question, 'What decides whether a baby is going to be a boy or a girl?' The responses to this question were scored on a 'genetic determination of sex' scale, three levels being identified as non-sexual, sexual transmission and genetic transmission answers. Non-sexual responses were dominant up to 9 years, and sexual transmission answers were dominant up to 13 years in all countries except Sweden where higher scores tended to be seen earlier. Genetic transmission answers, revealing some kind of integrated realistic system for explaining sex determination, were evident only at 15 years generally, and at 13 years in Sweden.

Considerable sex differences were seen in the contrasting higher scores of boys in the English-speaking countries, and reasons were explored for these discrepancies. These were not thought to reflect genuine sex differences except in the year 15, where it was felt boys may be demonstrating a greater scientific interest and orientation than the girls.

The total picture is one of very slow development on the topic of sex determination, due possibly to several factors. It would appear that the task of providing explanations in this are intrinsically difficult since it requires also a higher level of formal operational thinking in order to hypothesise. Children appear to require also sequential lessons in human biology to be equipped to develop scientific realism. Few of them would appear to have experienced such teaching before the age of 15 years.

This underscores the dominance of mathematics and the physical sciences taught in secondary schools to the detriment of the biological sciences. If children and adolescents are to understand their own growth and development, including their own biological origins and sexuality, some corrective in the balance of biological science teaching would seem to be indicated.

13 Not having babies

Research has indicated the awareness, knowledge and usage of contraceptives by young people often based upon samples of students in their last years at school. Examples are Schofield (1968) in England, Venner (1972) in the USA, Collins (1974) in Australia, and Sundström (1976) in Sweden. There is little research, however, about this area in the earlier years and a sparsity of information about the whole area of children's perceptions of what we call 'not having babies'. 'Not having babies', as we define it, involves ideas of preventing which children may have before contraceptive devices and even coitus are known to them. This includes also birth-control practices of various kinds, post-conceptual means available to people who do not wish to have babies, and post-natal means of disposing of unwanted babies.

Events stemming from these happenings in the adult world are widely publicised in the media and children are daily exposed to reports such as, 'Dead baby found in dustbin', 'Attendance at abortion clinic rises', 'Schools fight for contraceptive machines' and 'Family adopts Vietnam baby', events often described in sensational terms. Even though many children may not know what they mean, the words abortion, contraception, birth-control, the pill, adoption, fostering, orphanages are in common usage and overheard from adults' conversations, referring to outcomes of sexuality as practised by 'grown ups'.

The authors decided in planning the interviews to follow through questions about the origin of babies (conception), what happens inside the mother (length of gestation and the gestation process), the birth process (birth exit and the birth necessity) and related questions, with enquiries about children's understanding of the 'not having babies' area. Two questions were asked. 'What do people do if they don't want to have a baby?'; often this was answered in post-conceptual terms such as abortion methods, or in post-natal terms such as adoption or other

274

disposal methods. In these cases a contingency question was asked, 'What do people do if they don't want to start a baby?' The two questions, with supplementary probing, provided through most children's responses the 'not having babies' universe of thought.

To retain the open-ended non-suggestive approach, the words contraception and abortion were not used, the children leading the interviewers, the children's vocabulary being used in follow-up discussion. Only after this exploration was finished were two questions on vocabulary asked, 'Have you heard the word "abortion"?' and 'Have you heard the word "contraception"?' If the answers were affirmative the children were then asked to describe what they thought the word meant. An analysis and presentation of the vocabulary results are made in chapter 16. In this chapter three sections are covered, knowledge of and insights into birth-control, abortion, and post-natal disposal of unwanted babies.

Children's perceptions of birth-control

The majority of children responded to the questions 'What do people do if they don't want to have a baby?' and 'What do people do if they don't want to start a baby?' with indications of some kind of awareness of methods, however crudely or partially expressed, by which humans try to control the situation. If they had not reached the stage of being aware of sexual intercourse as the cause or origin of babies, then some attempt to control the cause was made by reversing or avoiding artificialist origins, such as 'tell the Doctor or Jesus not to do it'.

Criteria for scoring the responses are set out in Table 13.1 and the categories arranged in an hierarchy. The hierarchy is not intended to place the responses in a value judgment order, showing progress from 'good' to 'bad' methods of birth-control but on what we perceive to be a natural and widening awareness of knowledge. While it may be argued that the 'knowledge of contraception' scale, which results from this ordering of categories, reflects a value judgment order, it is difficult to imagine a hierarchy very different from the one devised.

The categories and descriptions given in Table 13.1 are self-explanatory and require little further illustration. A few responses often of mixed levels may be of interest. 'The pill goes down the stomach and dissolves the baby and it goes out in the bowels. You should take three pills a day'; a confusion of contraception and abortion by a North American boy, aged 7 years. 'They ask the doctor and he tells them how to do it', says an English 7-year-old girl; 'If you don't want to start one you don't get married. There's no other way'. 'They don't take the pregnant pills', says a North American 7-year-old girl. 'The tubes are tied, the vocal cords', says a 15-year-old Australian girl, 'And you go on the pill. I don't know how it works'. 'You have vasectomies', says an

TABLE 13.1 *Criteria for scoring 'knowledge of contraception' scale*

Score	Levels	Categories and descriptions
0	Nothing	*Unscorable* Don't know, no answer, nonsense answers.
1		*Nothing can be done* Except the reverse of artificialisms, 'God, Jesus, Doctor don't do it' Causal agent takes no action.
2	Natural	*Abstention methods* Avoidance of abstention of causal act, 'Don't get married, don't swallow seed, don't get too close in bed, don't eat special food, kiss, have intercourse'. Get divorced.
3		*No interference with nature methods* Withdrawal or 'safe periods' (even if factually incorrect, 'it's O.K. just after menstruation'). Masturbation or oral sex.
4	Surgical	*Surgical methods – one partner only* Hysterectomy or vasectomy, castration; use of sterilisation, neutering – ignore terminology.
5		*Surgical methods – both partners* Both do not have to, but either may!
6	Devices	*Use of device(s) – one sex only* Include any chemical, pill, tablet, spermicide, IUD (coil), condom, cap.
7		*Use of device(s) – both sexes* At least two must be named, one for each sex. Both do not have to, but either may.

English 13-year-old, 'cut the fallopian tubes. Or use male or female condoms. Some people are naturally sterile'. A comprehensive answer comes from a North American 15-year-old girl, 'Use contraceptives. These are methods to make sure the sperm won't enter the woman. Jellies kill it. Or you have oral sex called something beginning with C..., you use the tongue or mouth on the genital area. Or masturbating, self induced when you have an orgasm. Someone could do it to you or you do it to yourself'. Compare this with the simplistic statement by a Swedish 7-year-old girl, 'They get divorced', or another by an Australian 13-year-old girl, 'They just can't fuck each other. No other way'.

'Nothing can be done' responses (Score 1)

The heading is slightly misleading since it includes not only 'nothing can be done' responses, but also those which refer to non-sexual causal agents, that is not taking any action, or a reversal or abstention by artificialist agents. However, the general impact of all these responses is one of inevitability, it happens or it doesn't, and the decision is fundamentally out of the hands of the parents.

As one would expect this category of answer is largely the province of the youngest age groups as Table 13.2 indicates. There are no responses in this category after year 11. What is surprising is its continuance quite strongly up to 9 years of age in the English-speaking countries. It is interesting to note this response is hardly in evidence in the Swedish sample. In practically every age group within the English-speaking countries boys outnumber the girls in this category by 2 to 1; for example, 7-year-old Australian boys 30 per cent to 15 per cent girls, and 9-year-old North American boys 30 per cent to no girls responding. Plainly, girls are somewhat more aware of alternatives to 'Nothing can be done' than are the boys.

TABLE 13.2 *Percentages of children responding 'Nothing can be done' on the 'knowledge of contraception' scale (N = 554)*

Age-year	Australia	England	North America	Sweden
5	23	28	24	7
7	23	13	28	7
9	20	15	20	—
11	8	3	4	—

Abstention methods (Score 2)

These responses include non-sexual assumptions, as when the causative agent is actively avoided or abstention from the causative 'special food' is suggested. The distinction with the previous category, in this respect, is that something can be done and parents are not passive recipients of the inevitable. The category also includes answers based upon sexual or partial sexual assumptions, and it is the sexual (or transitional sexual) behaviour which has to be abstained from. With increasing age and awareness this type of response predominates within this category. By 9 years abstinence is seen in sexual or near sexual terms. In viewing the results in Table 13.3, these should be compared with Tables 10.6 and 10.8 on the mother's and father's role in the origin of babies. Sexual type answers here are appearing in some magnitude by the age of 9, earlier in the case of Swedish children, and by 11 years the majority in each country have arrived at sexually causative factors in the origin of babies.

In the English-speaking countries absention appears to reach its peak

277

TABLE 13.3 *Percentages of children responding with abstention methods on the 'knowledge of contraception' scale (N = 838)*

Age-year	Australia	England	North America	Sweden
5	10	25	35	17
7	28	33	14	37
9	38	38	17	23
11	53	38	30	20
13	33	20	33	–
15	20	18	7	–

as a response at 9 and 11 years, then declining in the teenage years. The decreasing number at 13 years, and particularly in the Australian (20 per cent) and the English (18 per cent) samples at 15 years reflecting a corresponding ignorance of alternatives. The high percentage of Swedish children at 7 years (37 per cent) reveals an earlier awareness of coitus as the cause of babies, with a correspondingly earlier decline in abstention methods from coitus, as Swedish children become aware of birth control alternatives. While, in this category, one may see the 20 per cent of Swedish 11-year-olds compared with the 20 per cent of Australian children as indicative of a four year retardation, the gap is somewhat narrower than this, as later evidence reveals.

There are some sex differences concealed within the total results of those who see abstention as the only method of birth-control. Taking the sexual based answers from 9 years, Australian girls at 9, 13 and 15 give more frequent 'abstention' responses, as do 13-year-old North American girls (47 per cent to 17 per cent). In the English sample 9-year-old boys (50 per cent to 25 per cent) and 11-year-old boys (60 per cent to 15 per cent) are more frequent 'abstention responses'. There are no discrepancies visible in the Swedish sample between the boys and girls. From this no sex differences of a universal nature can be deduced on abstention methods, but it may be that there are differing cultural factors operating between the English speaking countries; 'self-control', for example, taught as a means of 'keeping out of trouble', may be more forcibly impressed upon English boys than upon English girls, while the reverse may be so in Australia. The evidence, however, is too slight to lead to any firm conclusions.

No interference with nature methods (Score 3)

The withdrawal method, the 'safe period' and rhythm methods were included in this section, as distinct from abstention. So also were masturbation and oral sex, whether defined as being done solo or in sexual partnership. These were included in view of evidence such as Schofield's (1968) that genital apposition may be a fairly widespread practice among adolescents who are sexually active. One Australian 7-year-old boy said, 'That mother sleeps with her husband, but keeps her legs straight so the seed can't get in'.

The results to be seen in Table 13.4 present the figures for teenagers, since only 3 individual children scattered through 3 different countries gave this response before 13 years. The sparse responses at all ages may be due to the fact that all the respondents were drawn from public school systems and therefore will tend to be predominantly non-Catholic. Our assumption is that any Roman Catholic children interviewed may have parents who do not feel sufficiently committed to send them to a Roman Catholic school, and therefore these children may not be aware of 'natural' methods taught by certain religious groups. The figures may be low also because genital apposition may not be thought of by teenagers as a form of coitus interruptus or withdrawal and so may be voiced as 'Don't do it', that is, don't penetrate. Their responses would then be classified under the abstention category and the two sets of scores may therefore have a slight overlap.

TABLE 13.4 *Percentages of teenagers giving 'No interference methods' on the 'knowledge of contraception' scale (N = 284)*

Age-year	Australia	England	North America	Sweden
13	–	3	3	–
15	5	20*	13	10

(* The distribution is 5 per cent of boys and 35 per cent of girls.)

The only group showing any magnitude in 'no interference' response is the English 15-year-old cohort. The 20 per cent response in this group consists of 35 per cent of the girls and only 5 per cent of the boys, the difference being statistically significant ($p < .05$) as Table B.23 in Appendix B indicates. It is just possible that this imbalance is idiosyncratic of this particular group due to a higher proportion of girls from committed Roman Catholic families or some other social factor. The overall result under this category is that these particular aspects of natural birth control appear to be little known.

Surgical methods of birth control (Scores 4 and 5)

Responses included under 'surgical' ranged from outright castration to the more accurately described hysterectomy and vasectomy operations.

279

There was some confusion evident about abortion operations, but only pre-conception operations were included here. There was also some confusion about what sterilisation surgery involved, being sometimes seen as the tying or cutting of vocal cords, umbilical cords and sundry named internal tubes.

Originally the analysis tabulated those who responded in terms of one sex having the operation separately from those who saw it as applicable to both sexes, principally to see if children were aware only of 'own sex' operations, rather than both sexes being surgical candidates. No such distinctions were found, except that boys seemed to be aware of mother sterilisation rather than father sterilisation. Scores 4 and 5 are combined and are set out in Table 13.5. They reveal a generally increasing awareness with age of surgical methods of birth control, the greatest awareness being evident among North American 15-year-olds (55 per cent) and the least among the Swedish children. It may be that in Sweden the awareness and availability of contraceptive devices, certainly included in the educational syllabus in Swedish schools, overwhelms the possibility of surgical methods in their thinking. It is curious that so few Swedish children (4 out of 180) list this in their responses.

TABLE 13.5 *Percentages of children responding with surgical methods on the 'knowledge of contraception' scale (N = 838)*

Age-year	Australia	England	North America	Sweden
5	3	–	–	–
7	5	3	7	–
9	13	10	13	–
11	23	18	23	3
13	35	30	34	–
15	28	28	55	10

The use of contraceptive devices (scores 6 and 7)

Birth-control devices were defined as all 'artificial' objects, constructions or chemical substances used for preventing conception during sexual intercourse, as distinct from all the other methods previously listed. In scoring these incorrect terms were disregarded, provided the devices described could be identified. The word 'artificial' is not used in any pejorative sense. The scoring was divided into two categories, those responses where only one sexual partner was seen as the preventive agent and those responses where both sexes were seen as potential preventive agents. The second category did not mean both sexes had to

280

use devices together, but that each sex had one or more devices available from which to choose. As the criteria list notes, 'Both do not have to, but either may'.

In the English-speaking samples the pattern to be seen in Table 13.6 is very similar, awareness of a one-sex device increasing with age to 13 years then decreasing at 15 years, presumably as knowledge of both-sex contraceptive devices increases (see Table 13.7). The earlier awareness of the Swedish children is seen in this trend occurring sooner, peaking at 11 years, decreasing at 13 and with an increase again at 15 years.

TABLE 13.6 *Percentages of children responding by 'use of one-sex-only devices' on the 'knowledge of contraception' scale (N = 838)*

Age-year	Australia		England		North America		Sweden	
	Boys	Girls	Boys	Girls	Boys	Girls	Boys	Girls
5	—	—	—	5	—	—	—	7
7	10	25	10	25	6	—	40	7
9	20	10	10	45	33	33	40	27
11	35	25	25	40	33	27	27	47
13	35	60	30	40	44	53	—	7
15	15	45	10	—	25	40	—	33

There is no 'own-sex device' which dominates, but the pill is seen by both boys and girls as the dominant one-sex device. Boys' second most frequent choice is the condom, rubber, wetcheck or other name used, obviously an 'own-sex' device. Girls in this response category (score 6) rarely mentioned the condom, since it tends to be included by girls in both-sex devices (score 7) when listed at all. In fact, in the only three age cohorts showing statistically significant differences, English 9-year-olds, Australian and Swedish 15-year-olds, it is the girls who score highest on 'one-sex' devices (see Table B.23, Appendix B).

Some marked sex differences are apparent in the Australian 13 and 15 years, in the English 9 and 11 years, in the North American 15 years and the Swedish 11 and 15 years; where girls have a greater proportion of scores. Only two age cohorts show marked sex differences the other way, the Swedish 7 and 9 years, where boys are the more numerous. This weighting, at least in the English-speaking countries, may reflect the 'leave it to the woman' attitude alleged to be a male characteristic in some cultures' approach to birth-control, an attitude accepted or rejected by females. Too much, however, should not be read into these results because of the small numbers involved.

Table 13.7 indicates the percentages of respondents aware of both-sex devices on the criterion 'Both do not have to, but either may'. The overall totals are very low until the age of 15 and even at that age the figures for boys and girls combined are only 63 per cent and 64 per cent respectively for the Australian and North American 15-year cohorts. The English 15-year-olds achieve 93 per cent and the Swedish 98 per cent, the English girls and the Swedish boys scoring significantly higher in these age groups.

TABLE 13.7 *Percentages of children responding by 'uses of both-sex devices' on the 'knowledge of contraception' scale (N = 838)*

Age- year	Australia		England		North America		Sweden	
	Boys	Girls	Boys	Girls	Boys	Girls	Boys	Girls
5	—	—	—	—	—	—	7	—
7	—	—	—	—	—	—	7	7
9	—	—	—	5	—	—	20	33
11	5	5	—	10	7	7	73	40
13	40	5	45	40	31	24	100	93
15	75	50	90	95	75	53	100	97

When separated by sex, the picture shows girls in the Australian and North American samples markedly fewer in number than the boys at all ages. While there are discrepancies between the sexes in Swedish 9- and 11-year-olds, the girls being more numerous, the results are more equal at 13 and 15 years. In terms of awareness and knowledge of both-sex devices, Swedish and English 15-year-olds are the most numerous with the North American and Australian the least, the 15-year-old girls in both countries in particular having less knowledge at this level. This finding does not necessarily conflict with the 'leave it to the woman' stereotype, since this is only expressive within a one-sex device response. Indeed, almost all girls in the 13- and 15-year cohorts listed 'the pill' as the first and obviously prime method of control.

It sheds more light on the details to analyse the 15-year cohorts by number of contraceptive devices named, since nearly all revealed not only knowledge of the pill and condom, but quite a range of devices. These details are shown in Table 13.8. The range of knowledge is greater among both sexes in Sweden compared with the English-speaking countries, since the vast majority of Swedish 15-year-olds are able to name and describe 4 or more contraceptive devices. The majority in the other countries tend to know a much narrower range, particularly the Australian and North American 15-year-olds. Of these countries, the English 15 years appear the most knowledgeable.

TABLE 13.8 *Percentages of 15-year-olds with knowledge of contraceptive for both-sex devices by sex and number named (N = 838)*

Country	Number of devices known, at least one for other-sex use					
	2	3	4	5	Sex totals	All totals
Australia						
Boys	16	20	20	19	75	
Girls	14	26	–	10	50	63
England						
Boys	46	20	20	4	90	
Girls	14	46	25	10	95	93
North America						
Boys	56	14	5	–	75	
Girls	20	14	6	13	53	64
Sweden						
Boys	–	12	42	42	100	
Girls	6	21	44	26	97	98

Overall trends in contraceptive knowledge

The mean scores on the 'knowledge of contraception' scale were calculated and the results are seen in graphic form in Figure 13.1. The advanced scores of the Swedish children are evident from 9 years onwards, and the similarities between the English-speaking countries are very close. The 'catching up' of Sweden process is again observable but the levelling off of Swedish scores at 13 years is misleading. If the scale had been extended to 8 or 9 points, on more sophisticated and discriminating criteria, it is our estimate that the 'catching up' process may not have occurred.

Trends may be observed in different countries when the highest score for each respondent was taken and the modal characteristic calculated by identifying in each age cohort the largest number grouped in any one score. The results are set out in a matrix (Table 13.9) indicating the characteristic level at each year separately for boys and girls.

Taking Australia first the trend is to say initially 'Nothing can be done', then with 'Abstention' added, 'Devices' not being dominant until 13 years. Devices for both sexes are not identified by both boys and girls until 15 years. From 7 to 11 the girls' trend is solely 'Abstention', showing earlier awareness of coition as the origin of babies.

The English children show an earlier awareness than the Australians, the girls at 7 years revealing a knowledge of one-sex devices, the boys

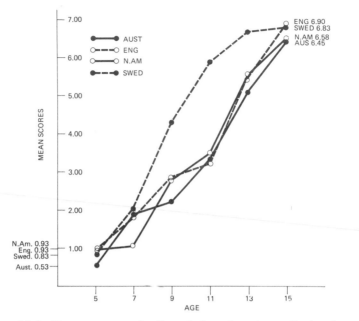

*Figure 13.1   Mean scores on the 'knowledge of contraception' scale
by country and age-year*

however from 7 to 11 years still voicing 'Abstention'. Devices for both sexes are the trend for the English children at 13 years.

The North American trend is 'Nothing can be done' and 'Abstention' until 9 years, when one-sex devices predominate, giving way to both-sex devices at 13 years. There is a close similarity between boys and girls in the North American sample.

The Swedish trend shows a similar pattern to the North American, with boys naming one-sex devices earlier at 7 years and two-sex devices showing the earliest appearance of all country age cohorts with 9-year-old girls. From 11 years onwards the trend is for both boys and girls to know both-sex devices.

Concerning knowledge of both-sex devices, the comparative trend appears to be that the Swedish girls (9 years) are earliest; then the Swedish boys (11 years); the Australian boys and English boys and girls (13 years); and the Australian girls (15 years). Significant sex differences overall (see Appendix B, Table B.23) are so scattered through various ages and countries, they do not appear to indicate a general pattern of sex differences.

284

TABLE 13.9   *Trends in the 'knowledge of contraception' scale*

Age-year	Sex	Australia	England	North America	Sweden
5	Boy	Nothing	Nothing	Nothing	Nothing)=
	Girl		Abstain	Abstain	Abstain
7	Boy	Nothing	Abstain	Nothing	Devices (1)
	Girl	Abstain	Devices (1)	Abstain	Abstain
9	Boy	Nothing	Abstain	Devices (1)	Devices (1)
	Girl	Abstain	Devices (1)		Devices (2)
11	Boy	Abstain	Abstain	Devices (1)	Devices (2)
	Girl		Devices (1)		
13	Boy	Devices (2)	Devices (2)	Devices (2)	Devices (2)
	Girl	Devices (1)			
15	Boy	Devices (2)	Devices (2)	Devices (2)	Devices (2)
	Girl				

(The terms used are defined in Table 13.1 more fully. Devices (1) is where only a one-sex aid is identified (score 6) and Devices (2) is where both-sex aids are identified (score 7).)

Children's perceptions of abortion

During the often extensive discussions with the children which followed from the question 'What do people do if they don't want to have a baby?' practically all children, directly or indirectly, referred to disposal of a child after birth if unwanted. Most older children make a clear distinction between pre-conceptual prevention, and pre-natal and post-natal disposals, although not in these sophisticated terms. The younger children did not see the differences so clearly between birth-control, abortion and adoption, but all three were explored in the interview by contingency questions. Some children showed confusion between the words 'abortion' and 'adoption', saying the one word and by the context clearly meaning the other. A few, such as the 13-year-old English boy, confuse desertion with abortion, as 'When the man has it off, the woman has a baby and the man runs off and leaves her'.

The criteria for scoring what we have called the 'knowledge of abortion' scale is set out in Table 13.10. The scores were arranged similarly to the 'knowledge of contraception' scale in what we perceive to be an orderly progression from limited to wider knowledge, and are not intended to be seen on a scale of moral values. Where the respondent gives more than one answer with different scores, the highest score is recorded. Examples of scores 2, 3 and 4 are given below.

285

TABLE 13.10 *Criteria for scoring the 'knowledge of abortion' scale*

Score	Category and descriptions
0	*Unscoreable* Don't know, no response, nonsense.
1	*Unspecified methods of abortion* 'Stop the baby growing'; 'Don't go to hospital'; 'Doctor don't do nothing'.
2	*Abortion by non-medical means* By exercise, by smoking or drinking a lot: 'She diets'; 'She plays lots of tennis'; 'Drinks wine every night'; 'Falls down the stairs'.
3	*Abortion by medical means* By tablet, pill, medicine, drug injection — often used 'to make baby come out in the toilet'.
4	*Abortion by surgical means* Operation, cutting, scraping, vacuuming: 'Doctor cuts her open and kills it'; 'Nurse cuts the cord'; 'They kill it with a knife'; 'They vacuum it away'.

Abortion by non-medical means (score 2)

'They get rid of it. (How?) By mother doing a lot of running and jumping up and down. (What does that do?) It loosens the baby and it falls out' (North American boy, 9 years); 'My mum drinks wine every night and goes and sits in a hot bath' (Australian girl, 11 years).

Abortion by medical, non-surgical means (score 3)

'She takes a tablet. It puts the baby to sleep in the mother. (Q) It probably disintegrates' (Australian girl, 13 years); 'Yes one can kill the baby before the 12th week. (Q) One can use a saline solution' (Swedish boy, 15 years).

Abortion by surgical means (score 4)

'They operate away the foetus at a hospital, when it's very little. I think its disgusting to throw small babies in the paperbaskets' (Swedish girl, 11 years); 'These people who say they are nurses and doctors, they cut the eggs out' (English boy, 13 years); 'You more or less kill the baby. You take it out of the body. (Q) The doctor puts up a hook into the vagina and pulls it out' (North American girl, 15 years); 'In an abortion, the baby is taken out. The doctor puts his hand into the womb and disconnects the baby. There's an injection then to cause the baby to come out' (Australian boy, 15 years).

The results can be seen in Table 13.11. Although in the English-speaking countries knowledge is very sparse at 5 and 7 years, the results

TABLE 13.11   *Percentages of scores on the 'knowledge of abortion'*
scale by country and age-year (N = 838)

Age-year	Score	Australia		England		North America		Sweden	
5	1	3		3		4		10	
	2	–		3		4		7	
	3	3		3		–		–	
	4	3	(9)	–	(9)	–	(8)	–	(17)
7	1	5		5		3		20	
	2	3		–		–		3	
	3	5		8		10		13	
	4	–	(13)	8	(21)	–	(13)	7	(43)
9	1	5		8		7		40	
	2	3		3		3		–	
	3	8		10		17		10	
	4	20	(36)	15	(36)	3	(40)	17	(67)
11	1	20		13		23		43	
	2	–		5		–		–	
	3	20		13		20		20	
	4	20	(60)	35	(66)	10	(53)	33	(96)
13	1	38		35		55		37	
	2	–		–		–		–	
	3	5		20		15		–	
	4	45	(88)	25	(80)	18	(88)	63	(100)
15	1	55		43		36		50	
	2	3		–		–		–	
	3	15		20		29		3	
	4	27	(100)	35	(98)	29	(94)	47	(100)

(1 = Abortion unspecified; 2 = by non-medical means; 3 = medical non-surgical means; 4 = surgical means. The figures in brackets are the total percentages of respondents with some knowledge of abortion in each age cohort.)

for these age groups are included since Swedish 7-year-olds are becoming aware of abortion at that age. In the English-speaking countries the results are very comparable, the total percentages signifying some awareness of each age cohort being very similar. Apart from knowledge of non-medical means of abortion (score 2) which is limited, most children seem aware of abortion as a possibility, however vague, by 11 years in these countries. The Australian and English children are roughly comparable in becoming aware of medical methods of abortion, both surgical and non-surgical, with the North American children appearing to be aware of these methods much later, catching up by the age of 13. By contrast the Swedish figures show a greater general aware-ness of abortion even in the youngest age group, the majority being aware by 9 years. More Swedish children also are knowledgeable about medical, surgical and non-surgical methods, earlier than the English-speaking children.

One interesting feature of Table 13.11 is the sudden increase in 'unspecified means of abortion' (score 1) at 13 and 15 years. One would expect these figures to diminish with age, as more specific methods of abortion become known. This apparent regression, however, can be explained by an examination of the percentage scores of boys and girls separately, as set out in Table 13.12. Since they reveal a regular pattern and the score discrepancies between the sexes are common across all countries, we would suggest that these reflect genuine sex differences in responses, and are not due to interviewer differences. By examining the verbatim responses of girls, we postulate that not only are these genuine sex differences but may be due to feelings of revulsion on the part of girls about abortion. Their unwillingness to specify the methods, we interpret as demonstration of inhibitions, induced by revulsion or at least by moral disapproval. It is natural that girls, being the future child-bearers, may feel this revulsion or disapproval more than boys and for it to be reflected in the scores.

TABLE 13.12 *Percentages of teenage 'unspecified methods of abortion' responses by country, age-year and sex (N = 284)*

Age-year	Sex	Australia	England	North America	Sweden
13	Boys	20	15	50	7
	Girls	55	55	59	67
15	Boys	5	35	31	20
	Girls	70	50	40	80

It is a consequence of these sex differences that when the mean scores are set out (see Table 13.13), from 9 years onwards the mean scores of the girls tend to depress the overall results. In the Swedish and Australian samples the girls' scores actually decline, from 13 to 15 years, leading to the drop on the graph, as can be seen clearly in Figure 13.2. Teenagers are probably well aware of the controversies centred on abortion and their responses are therefore explicable in these terms.

Children's perceptions of other baby disposal methods

No direct questions were asked about institutionalising, fostering or

288

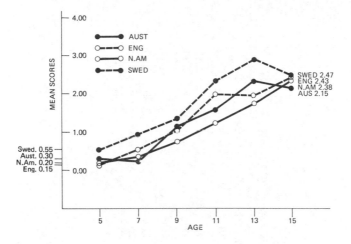

Figure 13.2   Mean scores on the 'knowledge of abortion' scale by country and age-year

adopting unwanted babies, but many children volunteered information on these means of disposing of unwanted babies. We report here the 30 per cent of the total sample, about equal percentages in each country, who made such responses. The large majority of these scored also on the two other scales on contraception and abortion. In some age groups the percentages ranged from zero to 53 per cent. They are too small in number to make anything more than a descriptive presentation, but they do provide suggestive material for further research.

Scoring was tabulated on the criteria set out in Table 13.14 which we have termed the 'post-natal disposal' scale. The range of examples is seen in the table itself. It is obvious from these that many children are aware of other solutions to unwanted babies than pre-conception prevention and post-conception disposal. The scores on this post-natal disposal scale, set out in Table 13.15, indicate overall that a reasonably large proportion of 5-year-olds see giving the baby away rather like an unwanted parcel. Says an Australian 5-year-old boy, 'They ring up and say they don't want it and they take it next door and if they don't want it they send it back'; an Australian girl of 7 years says, 'When it's born they give it away to somebody. I had a friend in England like that. She has brown skin and her family had white skin'. There are some who, rather than give the baby away, see its commercial value and would sell it. These crude disposal methods decline after 5 years, although it is of interest the 50 per cent of Swedish children who mention this kind of disposal as a possibility. The small figures for

TABLE 13.13 Mean scores on the 'knowledge of abortion' scale by country, age-year and sex (N = 838)

Age-year	Australia			England			North America			Sweden		
	Boys	Girls	Total	Boys	Girls	Total	Boys	Girls	Total	Boys	Girls	Total
5	0.25	0.15	0.30	0.30	0.00	0.15	0.31	0.09	0.20	0.40	0.07	0.55
7	0.30	0.20	0.25	0.80	0.35	0.58	0.38	0.29	0.36	1.00	0.87	0.94
9	0.70	1.55	1.18	1.65*	0.40	1.03	1.27*	0.27	0.77	1.47	1.27	1.37
11	1.55	1.65	1.60	2.40	1.60	2.00	1.73	0.73	1.23	2.20	2.53	2.37
13	2.70	1.95	2.33	2.30	1.60	1.95	2.06	1.41	1.74	3.80*	2.00	2.90
15	2.50	1.80	2.15	2.60	2.25	2.43	2.56	2.20	2.38	3.33*	1.60	2.47

(* Statistically significant differences, with boys scoring higher, see Table B.24, Appendix B.)

TABLE 13.14   *Criteria for scoring 'post-natal disposal' scale*

Score	Criteria and descriptions
1	*Simple methods of disposal* 'Give it away'; 'Sell it, it's worth at least $1,000'; 'Send it back to the hospital'; 'Kill it and hide it away'.
2	*Institutional methods* 'Send to an orphanage or children's home'; 'Give to the nuns'.
3	*Adoption or fostering methods* 'Give it to people who've been wanting a baby and can't'; 'Pay for it to be looked after'. Adoption (abortion often confused but context makes clear the meaning); fostering.

TABLE 13.15   *Percentage of scores on the 'post-natal disposal' scale by country and age-year (N = 838)*

Age-year	Australia			England			North America			Sweden		
	1	*2*	*3*	*1*	*2*	*3*	*1*	*2*	*3*	*1*	*2*	*3*
5	33	–	5	18	–	5	17	4	8	50	–	17
7	28	3	5	20	13	10	20	3	7	20	–	10
9	13	15	8	3	20	15	3	13	10	3	7	7
11	–	10	8	3	13	23	3	27	17	3	3	13
13	3	5	8	3	10	8	6	–	18	–	3	10
15	–	–	10	–	–	30	–	3	16	–	–	33

(1 = Giving or selling; 2 = Institutionalising; 3 = Adopting or Fostering.)

institutionalising (the highest is 27 per cent in North American 11-year-olds) perhaps reflect the decline in orphanages and other institutions. Adoption outnumbering fostering by 5 to 1 is obviously known about with increasing age. The curious sudden increase at 15 years in the Swedish and English samples (33 per cent and 30 per cent respectively) is interesting.

Overall the figures cannot be used as indicators of any kind, except to illustrate that about a third of the total sample demonstrate awareness of the full range of solutions to an unwanted baby problem, however limited and confused their perception of the original cause of the problem may be.

Summary and discussion

'Not having babies', an area comparatively unresearched, covers what are children's perceptions of birth-control, abortion and other disposal methods of unwanted babies. The problem of unwanted babies is known to children from an early age through watching programmes on television and overhearing adult conversations. Two questions were asked, 'What do people do if they don't want to have a baby?' and 'What do people do if they don't want to start a baby?' From this ensuing discussion three scales were devised: the 'knowledge of contraception' scale, the 'knowledge of abortion' scale and the 'post-natal disposal' scale.

Children's perceptions of birth-control as a fact of life and the methods used were scaled at 7 levels, with four major categories: 'Nothing can be done', natural, surgical, and devices-type methods of contraception. 'Nothing can be done' responses tended to be non-sexual and dominant in the years 5 to 9 but with little evidence of it by Swedish children. Natural methods of birth-control were analysed at two levels, abstention from the causative act and what we classified as non-interference methods, such as withdrawal or rhythm methods. The latter type of response was almost entirely absent, the former dominant through the years 7 to 11 as children became increasingly aware of coitus as the major causative factor of pregnancy. Similar to other Swedish results, Swedish children arrive at this stage earlier and leave it behind earlier than the English-speaking children.

Surgical methods of birth-control were scored at two levels, one where children saw an operation on one sex as the prevention process, and the other where both sexes could have an operation. Mother sterilisation seemed to be known more by boys, but generally awareness of surgical methods increased with age, the greatest among North American children and the least in Swedish children. It was postulated that contraceptive education in Swedish schools and easier availability of birth-control devices accounted for this.

The category of contraceptive devices was also scored at two levels, where children listed one-sex-only devices and where they listed both-sex devices. Older boys generally were more aware of both-sex devices, particularly the condom and the pill, than the older girls, except in the case of Swedish children with both sexes tending to know a greater number of devices much earlier for use by both sexes. The range of devices known by 15-year-olds varies by country, the earlier and wider knowledge shown by boys and girls in Sweden, the later and more restricted knowledge shown by Australian and North American 15-year-old girls.

Overall trends in the varying countries were compared revealing abstention method dominant with Australian and English boys until 11 years, with devices known earlier in other countries. In knowledge of both-sex devices the trend appears to be Swedish girls at 9 years, Swedish boys at 11 years, Australian boys and English boys and girls at 13, and Australian girls at 15 years. North American 15-year-olds of both sexes develop their contraceptive knowledge late, the girls particularly. Curiously this is one of the few items in the study which indicate socio-economic status apparently influencing the results. As is seen in the ANOVA results (in Appendix D) the main effects on contraceptive knowledge scores of father's occupation is significant (at the .05 level). That is to say the higher father's socio-economic status the more contraceptive knowledge his child will tend to have.

Children's perceptions of abortion were classified at four levels: unspecified, non-medical, medical, medical non-surgical and medical surgical. Descriptions overall increased with age almost uniformly in the English-speaking countries with the majority at 11 years of age, contrasting with much larger proportions of Swedish children at 7 and 9 years. A major sex difference was identified in the teenage years, more girls giving 'unspecified' abortion methods than boys, revealing increasing awareness but reluctance to voice the methods or describe them. It was postulated that this reflected revulsion or at least moral disapproval of abortion as they perceived their approaching role as child-bearers.

Although only 30 per cent of the total sample provided solutions for the unwanted baby problem in terms of post-natal disposal methods, it was evident that children were increasingly aware of child disposal by selling, institutionalising, adopting and fostering.

The most significant evidence in this chapter emerges from the analysis of scores on the 'knowledge of contraception' scale. Whether the age at which children are aware of various methods is soon enough for them to face their earlier maturing is a matter to be discussed in the final chapter.

14 Children's perceptions of sex education

Sex education, alongside religious education, is among the most contentious issues facing public school systems in the English-speaking world. There is evidence that this is a world-wide phenomenon (Fraser, 1972) and that even in Sweden, despite a widely accepted thorough-going sex education programme in schools, there is still some opposition voiced by certain community groups. The major controversies centre round three issues: whether schools should be educating in this area rather than parents, at what age should formal sex education begin, and what should be the content of any programme, whether taught by parents or teachers.

There is no shortage of polemical writings on all these matters but little hard evidence as the outcome of research. In the USA Spanier (1977) has investigated the influence of parents, Gebhard (1977) the effectiveness of school programmes, Monge, Dusek and Lawless (1977) particular groups of 9th graders, 15 to 16 years, and Dickinson (1978) adolescent sex information sources. In Britain Schofield (1968) indicated the number of teenagers who had not received any sex education, and Farrell (1978) reports on the sources of sex education for 1,556 16 to 19-year-olds. Since television has produced several sex education programmes for children in Britain, some evaluation of these has been attempted (Rogers, 1974) and in Sweden a current evaluation of their programmes is being conducted and assessments by outside observers have been attempted (McConaghy, 1979). In Australia there is no comparable evaluative research, nor even basic surveys of children's accessibility to sex information.

This study did not set out to fill these gaps but sought to look at three questions: at what age and by whom do the children themselves think sex education should be conducted?; whom would they trust to ask questions about sex, and what have been their major sources of information?; what do they consider the most important aspects of sex they need to know, and how does that compare with what they actually did learn? This chapter reports on these three questions under the sections headed, 'Children's views on sex education', 'Sources of sex education', and 'What children want to know'.

Children's views on sex education

The purpose of this section of the interview was to discover in sequence whether children 'should be taught about their own bodies, and babies, and things like that?' (other children who knew the vocabulary and had used it were asked if they 'should be taught about sex?'), and about 'what age they should be taught?' Since this was a general question and did not raise the identity of who should teach such matters, parents or school teachers, questions focussed more upon school lessons were asked a little later in the interview — 'Should there be lessons at school (relating to sex)?' and 'What age did you have such lessons (if any)?' It is of interest in comparing these two approaches, the broader and the narrower, also to compare what the children thought to be an appropriate agency and age, and what they actually got.

Some caution should be exercised in accepting reports of children in this and later sections in the chapter, as to what actually happened in schools, since the young are notoriously vague in recollecting what happened and when. Their reports are often partial and distorted by various factors. Nevertheless, if children have reported that they have received no sex education, even if they have done so at various times in school or at home, it is an indicator that such experience may have made negligible impact.

'Should children be taught about sex?'

Allowing for a looser phrasing of this question with younger children, so they could understand it in their own terminology, the results are set out in Table 14.1. The overwhelming majority of children are positive in their response, increasing with age to almost universal approval by 9 years. It is interesting to note the reasons of those who were negative. Many of the younger ones show limited understanding of the question. 'No. (Q) Because children hurt babies' (N. American boy, 5 years); 'No. (Q) Because children don't have babies, only Mummies do' (English girl, 5 years); 'No. (Q) Because they might be frightened in case anyone steals the baby' (Australian girl, 5 years). Other answers at this age were, 'It's too hard for kids'; 'They'll get to know when they're bigger'; 'They might already know, they can see their own body' and the perceptive child who reports, 'No. Because they

TABLE 14.1 *Percentages* of responses in Yes/No categories to 'should children be taught about sex?' by country and age-year (N = 838)*

Age-year	Australia		England		North America		Sweden	
	Yes	No	Yes	No	Yes	No	Yes	No
5	80	15	78	22	67	33	73	23
7	85	15	95	3	87	13	77	20
9	97	3	90	10	97	3	97	3
11	97	3	100	–	97	3	100	–
13	100	–	100	–	97	3	97	3
15	100	–	100	–	100	–	100	–

(*The very small number of 'Don't know' responses are not included.)

might forget what they are taught and if they learn themselves they might remember' (English girl, 5 years).

While some 7-year-olds give similar responses, others reveal an awareness of sex taboos beginning: 'The mother may not want the child to know' (English boy, 7 years); 'If you look at pictures, you might kiss it' (English boy, 7 years); 'No, because if they do they'd tell others' (Swedish girl, 7 years). Another Swedish girl of this age says, 'No, because boys think it dirty, but I think it's fun'. At 9 years this is more in evidence, although fewer children voice a negative reason: 'No, because I think it's rude' (English boy, 9 years); 'No, my mother wouldn't let me know about babies. And I've never known and not yet found out' (North American boy, 9 years); 'It seems ridiculous' (Swedish boy, 9 years).

Among those who had responded positively there appeared to be no sex differences; the overwhelming number agreeing that children should be taught. When, however, the question was asked 'should there be lessons at school (about sex)?' not only does there appear to be a little more reluctance earlier, but some sex differences begin to emerge. In Table 14.2 the number of negatives are much greater, although the majority in any age cohort support school lessons in this subject. The negativisms continue quite strongly until 9 years and even as high as 30 per cent among Australian 11-year-olds. Negativisms about school lessons are evident between 35 per cent and 40 per cent in all 5-year-olds, the number diminishing with age. Sweden still has 27 per cent negativisms at 9 years but these have practically disappeared by 11 years.

The greater negativisms to school lessons in sex is to be seen among 5-year-old boys (Australia 45 per cent to 25 per cent, North America 46 per cent to 27 per cent and Sweden, 53 per cent to 27 per cent of

TABLE 14.2 *Percentages* of responses in Yes/No categories to 'Should there be lessons about sex at school?' by country and age-year (N = 838)*

Age-year	Australia		England		North America		Sweden	
	Yes	No	Yes	No	Yes	No	Yes	No
5	60	35	60	40	56	36	57	40
7	70	28	87	13	84	16	60	27
9	75	25	65	33	73	20	70	27
11	70	30	90	10	87	13	97	3
13	90	10	97	3	94	6	100	–
15	100	–	90	10	97	–	100	–

(**'Don't know' responses are not included.*)

girls) and 7-year-old girls (Australia, 40 per cent to 15 per cent boys and 20 per cent to 5 per cent boys). 9-year-old North American girls (33 per cent) and 11-year-old Australian girls (45 per cent) also show a greater proportion of negative responses to sex education at school than do boys in these cohorts.

Overall we interpret these results, when comparing Tables 14.1 and 14.2, as indicating overwhelming support by children for a broad concept of sex education, negativism almost non-existent by 9 years, but when asked to narrow the agency down to the school there are more negativisms to be seen. These continue longer but are largely dispersed by 11 years, with the exception of the Australian children. The pattern of negativisms about school lessons is no different, interestingly, for Sweden, although a greater proportion of 9-year-olds in Sweden will have had such lessons. Comments made by Swedish children, given later in the next section, may explain this result. We infer that more children would be happier to receive sex education from parents, but that nevertheless reluctance to accept it at school is not marked after 9 years of age. Some children around this age commented that it was all right at school if the parents were agreeable.

'At what age should sex be taught?'

Immediately after the broader question of, should children be taught about their bodies, about babies, about sex (the terminology used to help the child understand what was involved), they were asked at what age children should be taught, or at what age should they learn about such matters. The results can be seen in Table 14.3. The children with few exceptions understood the question to mean, when should it begin,

TABLE 14.3 *Percentages of estimated ages at which sex should be taught by country and age-year*
(N = 838)

Age-year	Australia				England				North America				Sweden			
	1	2	3	4	1	2	3	4	1	2	3	4	1	2	3	4
5	23	28	13	3	18	43	8	8	33	25	4	4	17	50	3	—
7	3	30	35	13	3	48	33	13	7	50	20	10	3	70	3	—
9	—	55	30	13	—	73	15	3	—	40	37	20	3	67	17	3
11	—	53	43	3	3	65	27	5	—	57	40	—	83	10	—	—
13	—	53	45	—	—	40	60	—	—	55	42	—	87	3	—	—
15	—	53	45	3	—	50	50	—	—	39	61	—	13	77	7	—

(1 = 1–4 years; 2 = 5–11 years; 3 = 12–16 years; 4 = 17 plus.)

or the range of age in which such information should be taught or be available. If they gave only a beginning age it was taken to mean that from that age onwards sex information should be given. A careful examination of the scripts made this clear. The estimated ages reported, are the beginning ages for being taught about sex, as the children see it. For the purpose of categorising we have roughly categorised the choices as pre-school, primary school, secondary and post-secondary.

Firstly, it should be noted that there is almost no support for this to be left until after 17 years (post-secondary) except for 20 per cent of North American children at 9 years. This is an age group who would have experienced no sex education in school at that age. At the other end of the age estimates 1 to 4 years is seen as appropriate by a number of 5-year-olds, possibly reflecting egocentric considerations. The support among older children for starting early comes solely from the Swedish 11- and 13-year-olds, who comment, 'At 4 years when they are wondering. It's important not to lie about anything'; 'When they start asking questions'; 'Very early on. Afterwards it's so embarrassing'. A Swedish 15-year-old says, 'They are all ready at 2 years, when they ask "What has father got there?"'

The Swedish results generally differ from the English-speaking results since from 5 years onwards a majority voice the 5- to 11-year-olds as needing to know about sex. Many had experienced some teaching in Swedish pre-school (which includes the equivalent of early primary school in other countries) or earlier than the age of 8, cited as the compulsory age for sex education in schools. Taking the 11- and 13-year-olds as expressing 1 to 4 years as the initial age for sex teaching, the Swedish children see the primary years as the appropriate time. Few wish to see it delayed until the secondary years, that is after 11. There is considerable variety among those who support a 5 to 11 years beginning: 'Yes, a little older than now, 11 years; now they're just silly' (Swedish girl, 9 years); '7 years, when you can understand it' (Swedish boy, 11 years); 'Yes, 9 years not sooner, you must know a little first' (Swedish girl, 11 years); 'Yes at 10. Otherwise you know nothing when you menstruate. You need to go carefully in 2nd grade (8 years)' (Swedish girl, 11 years); 'You should start at 5 years old. Then give them the facts at about 10 years' (Swedish boy, 13 years); 'At 10 in school, but mother and father must certainly tell about it earlier at about 7 or 8 years' (Swedish girl, 11 years); '7 or 8 or when they start asking questions, about 4 to 5 years of age' (Swedish girl, 15 years); 'At 5 to 6 years. It varies with the child's maturity'. This Swedish 15-year-old girl's reply was frequent among the 15-year-olds in all four countries.

The English-speaking children also tend to support teaching in the primary school years (5–11), but in some age cohorts the percentages

299

are evenly divided between primary and secondary, and in a few the secondary years get the major emphasis. Table 14.4 indicates these trends, where 50 per cent or more support one age span rather than another (pre-school and primary year are merged if together they form 50 per cent or more). It should be made clear that the children have not stated that they should be taught about sex in these institutions named, but within the years roughly covered by these institutions. It is the North American and English teenagers who opt for the secondary school, either dominantly or marginally, as the appropriate age. The Australian 7-year-olds and North American 9-year-olds share this view. Overwhelmingly, children generally see the need for some information, answers to questions, teaching by parents or teachers, some time during the years 5 to 11. The vast majority, as is reported in the previous section, wish to see something available in school lessons.

TABLE 14.4 *An interpretation of Table 14.3 in terms of trends chosen by age cohorts in four countries*

Age-year	Australia	England	North America	Sweden
5	Primary	Primary	Primary	Primary
7	Primary Secondary	Primary	Primary	Primary
9	Primary	Primary	Primary Secondary	Primary
11	Primary	Primary	Primary	Pre-school
13	Primary	Secondary	Primary	Pre-school
15	Primary	Primary Secondary	Secondary	Primary

At what age is sex education taught in schools?

The children report a quite different picture in how they perceive the ages at which they first received any instruction at school. The figures can be seen in Table 14.5. Those who reported such lessons in the primary schools frequently described them in different terms to formal sex education: 'We did a project on babies just four of us, and made a picture book for the class (English boy, 7 years); 'We were doing families, and we were shown a film about mothers and fathers, and how they have children' (Australian girl, 11 years).

In Table 14.5 the age groups have been categorised a little differently, where to use the British and Australian terminology the 5 to 7 years are roughly 'infants' (pre-school in Sweden), the 8 to 11 years are roughly 'primary' and the 12 to 15 years are roughly secondary.

TABLE 14.5 *Percentage of estimated age at which sex education was first given at school by country and age-year (N=838)*

Age-year	Australia			England			North America			Sweden		
	5-7	8-11	12-15	5-7	8-11	12-15	5-7	8-11	12-15	5-7	8-11	12-15
5	—	—	—	3	—	—	—	—	—	10	—	—
7	—	3	—	3	—	—	—	—	—	13	—	—
9	3	13	—	8	25	—	—	3	—	43	53	—
11	—	30	—	5	28	—	—	7	—	—	83	—
13	—	15	38	—	13	56	—	21	39	10	67	20
15	—	10	65	—	8	80	—	7	87	—	60	40

The contrast in the English-speaking countries with the previous Tables 14.3 and 14.4 is marked. The actual teaching age lags far behind the time the children say they would wish to receive some help. Although most voice the need in terms of the primary school years, the earliest most receive any assistance is in secondary school (12 to 15 years). The Swedish children, on the other hand, have their expectations satisfied by 9 years of age, a sizeable group claiming some instruction in the years 5 to 7 years, i.e. Swedish pre-school.

It is interesting, in view of claims by many adolescents who have left school to have received no sex education during their schooling (Schofield, 1968 and 1976; National Council, 1979; Holmes *et al.*, 1968), to see these claims made by a sizeable proportion of teenagers in this study (see Table 14.6). As we have pointed out elsewhere, a great deal depends upon what children recognise or identify as sex education in school, and the process of selective memory has to be considered in viewing these figures. Nevertheless, in the English-speaking countries sizeable groups claimed to have received no sex education by the age of 13 years, and by 15 years there were 23 per cent of the Australians and 15 per cent of the English making such claims. This may indicate several factors, apart from the operation of selective memory. The first is that these children's parents may not have granted permission for their children to attend sex education classes. The second is that the lessons were so few in number − a single film or a few talks by a visiting doctor or nurse educator − that these children were unintentionally absent. The third, reflecting a common practice in many English-speaking school systems, of having sex education competing as an option with other attractive activities such as sport, home economics or craft work.

TABLE 14.6   *Percentages of those claiming to have received no sex education at school by country and age-year (N = 838)*

Age-year	Australia	England	North America	Sweden
5	95	95	84	87
7	87	95	93	87
9	67	65	97	43
11	67	63	90	13
13	53	30	46	3
15	23	15	7	—

When these figures in Table 14.6 are compared with previous responses over the whole sample, 81 per cent of all children (the figures for each country were almost identical) wanted sex education at schools but only 41 per cent claimed to have received it, 39 per cent in Sweden and England, 35 per cent in Australia and 30 per cent in the North American sample. These overall figures, however, are misleading since they include younger age groups most of whom had little opportunity to receive sex education. When the years 9 to 15 only are taken the following contrasts are evident in Table 14.7. These figures indicate a serious gap between what these children feel is desirable and what they claim to have received. It reinforces what is evident in Table 14.4. The only country near to the target, as it were, set by the children, is Sweden. This is even more obvious when in Table 14.8 the teenage figures are separated from the rest. Swedish teenagers' target generally is in step with what is provided, with Australia the least satisfactory, and in the English-speaking countries the English teenagers being somewhat more generously catered for.

TABLE 14.7 *Comparative percentages between 9 to 15 years who state sex education should be taught in school, and those claiming to have received it by country (N = 564)*

Statement	Australia	England	North America	Sweden
Sex education should be taught in school	84	86	88	92
Have received some sex education in school	47	57	40	85

TABLE 14.8 *Comparative percentages between teenagers who state sex education should be taught in school and those claiming to have received it by country (N = 284)*

Statement	Australia	England	North America	Sweden
Sex education should be taught in school	95	94	96	100
Have received some sex education in school	62	77	73	98

Nevertheless, whatever the explanations for the incongruent percentages between what children want and what they claim to receive, the facts do not appear to fit well with the factor of earlier sexual maturing reviewed in chapter 2. In this respect the children appear to have a more realistic grasp of what is needed than those who provide sex education.

Sources of sex education

In trying to discover what were the main sources of sex information, two types of questions were asked. The first type concerned specific persons, would you ask your parents, a teacher, and friends about sex? The second series of questions covered a more general range of sources, 'Where did you learn most of these things, about sex, for yourself?' and the result was a much wider range cited than the three kinds of persons explored in the first question. The results therefore had two dimensions, one specific and the other much broader.

Asking parents about sex

These questions about parents, teachers, and friends, often thought to be the most common source of sex information or instruction (see Farrell, 1978) were asked, to see what confidence children had in eliciting information they felt they needed, from those adults and children with whom they most frequently associated. It takes some confidence and a sense of trust to ask questions about sex from anyone, as the children frequently testified. Many tempered their remarks with an 'it depends' qualification, suggesting innocuous or safe questions were acceptable but that they would hesitate to ask more serious questions. 'My dad will kill me if I asked him about sexual intercourse', said an 11-year-old Australian boy, 'but asking about babies is O.K.'.

TABLE 14.9   *Percentages of responses to 'Would you ask your parents about sex?' by country and age-year (N = 838)*

Age-year	Australia		England		North America		Sweden	
	Yes	No	Yes	No	Yes	No	Yes	No
5	85	15	92	8	87	4	70	23
7	87	13	90	10	97	3	80	13
9	87	13	77	23	80	20	80	20
11	87	13	82	18	87	13	83	17
13	77	23	77	23	94	6	87	13
15	75	25	80	20	84	16	80	20

Consequently the answers to the general question about parents (see Table 14.9) may be misleading. The proportion is very large of those who would appear to have enough confidence in parents to ask questions about sex, but more than half of them expressed reservations indicating some diffidence and inhibitions. 'Sometimes they get very nervous about it', says a perceptive 7-year-old (North American boy); 'I wouldn't tell anyone, or ask anyone, 'cos it's supposed to be a secret. They don't want to tell anyone' (Australian 5-year-old girl); 'I'd rather not tell them. It'd be rude' (English boy, 7 years); 'They wouldn't tell you. You're too young to know this. You'd get a smack' (Australian boy,

9 years); 'My mum won't tell me. She says I'm too young and she won't tell me until I'm 13' (English girl, 9 years); 'My dad hasn't got time. He's always listening to the radio and we're not allowed to talk' (North American boy, 11 years); 'No. (Q) They'd probably ask me why. Dad would probably go against it until I'm older' (Australian boy, 13 years); 'Not usually. We don't talk about it in the family. It would have to be very serious' (North American girl, 13 years); 'They'd not really listen, even if we did ask, and we'd all be embarrassed' (English boy, 15 years); 'No. I've got to live with them. What will they think of me if I ask these questions?' – yet this North American boy aged 15 can talk about sex to his girlfriend and *her mother*!

A truer picture emerges when the question is asked, 'Which parent would you ask (about sex)?' Very few insisted both parents could be asked but named one or the other. The totals of those selecting mother are presented in Table 14.10. These are overwhelmingly girls in the English-speaking countries, at all age levels. The figures for boys are no greater than 56 per cent (North American 7-year-olds), but more often as low as 10 per cent to 25 per cent. English boys tended to have some confidence in asking mother up to 13 years of age. The Swedish pattern is very different, the 5-year-old boys actually more mother-confident than the girls at that age, but the picture is then reversed in all other age groups to a marked degree, although the disparity is not usually so great between the sexes as in the English-speaking countries.

TABLE 14.10 *Percentages of children stating they would ask mother questions about sex by country, age-year and sex (N = 838)*

Age-year	Australia		England		North America		Sweden	
	Boys	Girls	Boys	Girls	Boys	Girls	Boys	Girls
5	50	85*	50	80	31	73	40	27
7	15	80*	45	95*	56	100*	20	40
9	50	75	40	90*	20	93*	20	60
11	20	85*	40	90*	27	93*	40	67
13	10	80*	35	85*	25	94*	20	93*
15	15	80*	–	80*	31	100*	33	47

(* The frequencies are statistically significant for girls, see Table B.9 Appendix B.)

The reasons given are varied: 'Your mum has babies and dads don't. Doctors only talk to Mum. Dads don't know much' (Australian boy, 5 years); 'My mum's a nurse, so she knows all about it' (North American girl, 7 years); 'My mum would know. She's had babies and gone through

305

having periods. She's more reasonable and takes it seriously' (English girl, 11 years); 'Mum's more understanding. She listens. I'd be a bit jumpy but I think she'd understand. Dad would just think I'd been mucking around' (Australian boy, 13 years). Some children report that their mothers are pregnant and they are allowed to feel the baby as it moves inside the mother.

In contrast Table 14.11 reveals widespread lack of confidence in asking fathers questions about sex, almost entirely among girls of all ages in all countries. But the number of boys opting to ask their fathers is also low, increasing in a few countries in the teenage years; for example, 40 per cent of Australian 13-year-old boys and 45 per cent English 15-year-old boys. If less than half the boys can ask their mothers, and less than a quarter their fathers, whom can they ask? The Swedish boys in particular have little confidence in asking their fathers. A naive 5-year-old boy (American) says, 'My dad makes babies at the factory. He's older and he knows more about babies. (Q) Because he can make a banana split'. Some judiciously say: 'You ask father about men and mother about women' (Australian boy, 9 years); 'My dad's not so keen on sex, he'd tell us off. My brother, he's doing sex lessons at school, and he tells me. He says, "Ask me, it's natural" ' (English boy, 9 years); 'I'd feel it not right to ask him. Too scared. I'm not sure what he'd say' (Australian boy, 13 years); 'We've talked quite frequently, Dad and I, ever since the first sex education film at school. But he didn't like it when I did ask' (English boy, 15 years).

TABLE 14.11 *Percentages of children stating they would ask father questions about sex by country, age and sex (N = 838)*

Age-year	Australia		England		North America		Sweden	
	Boys	Girls	Boys	Girls	Boys	Girls	Boys	Girls
5	25	5	15	10	15	9	13	—
7	15	5	15	—	13	—	20	—
9	10	—	15	—	7	—	—	—
11	25	—	10	—	27	—	7	—
13	40	—	15	—	25	—	—	—
15	15	—	45	5	13	—	—	—

Asking teachers about sex

In replying to, 'Would you ask your teacher about sex?' most younger children would have experienced only one class teacher with them most of the day, whereas at 12 or after most of the older ones had moved into a more subject-oriented curriculum with specialist teachers in greater numbers in the various subjects. Many of the older children therefore qualified their answers in terms of what subject the teacher taught. Hygiene, science, and physical education, or if sex education is taught these kinds of teachers might be asked. But the major doubt is whether teachers can be trusted not to gossip or joke about you with other teachers in the school if you do ask sex questions. Table 14.12 gives the figures. In the English-speaking countries the response is more positive in the early years but then declines after 7 or 9 years with a little gain at 13 and 15 years, presumably as more specialist teachers are encountered. The Swedish figures are consistently negative, which is surprising when sex education is so universal. But one Swedish boy reports, 'In the sex classes everyone sits quietly. There's a silence at the end. No one asks questions'.

TABLE 14.12 *Percentages of children responding to 'Would you ask a teacher questions about sex?' by country and age-year (N = 838)*

Age-year	Australia		England		North America		Sweden	
	Yes	No	Yes	No	Yes	No	Yes	No
5	33	67	52	48	54	33	10	50
7	45	53	43	57	56	37	17	67
9	13	87	33	67	27	73	20	60
11	28	70	28	70	23	77	27	63
13	28	72	33	67	24	76	23	63
15	32	68	33	67	39	61	20	70

There are no wide sex differences except at 9 years in all countries; the boys in Australia and North America are more trusting of the teachers, and the girls in England and Sweden less so. The younger children's reasons generally reveal monocentric and limited perceptions: 'Teachers don't know about babies' (English girl, 5 years); 'They don't work at hospitals, so they don't know about it' (English girl, 7 years); 'Sometimes they don't answer, or say "No"'. On the other hand, if a teacher is known to have had a baby, she will be asked by 5-year-olds, while other 5- and 7-year-olds think 'they know everything, so I'd ask them' (Australian boy, 7 years); 'Only if it was a nurse teacher', says a North American 7-year-old girl, in a system where nurse educators are employed; 'She might get angry and put you in a corner', says another 7-year-old (Australian boy); 'If I were a teenager I'd ask in special classes' (North American boy, 7 years); 'It's not the thing teachers want to tell people. They're a bit strict and teachers are too busy anyway' (English girl, 7 years).

The older age groups reflect increasing awareness of taboos and limited views of teachers: 'It's too personal and some would object to it. You might get the strap for being rude' (Australian boy, 9 years); 'That's not what she's supposed to be doing. She's supposed to be helping children work' (North American girl, 9 years); 'I'd ask if we were being taught about it in class, or after seeing a TV film, or if they're talking about sex in animals. If it comes up naturally' (English boy, 11 years); 'Only a Guidance teacher. He'd not avoid questions and he'd be free and candid, not like most teachers' (North American boy, 11 years); 'They might accidentally slip it out at staff meetings and it gets out to other kids' (Australian boy, 13 years); 'I don't like teachers. I don't trust them, they tell other teachers' (English girl, 13 years); 'It would be kind of weird, them knowing about you and seeing you every day' (North American boy, 15 years); 'Teachers can't handle it either, like parents. If you ask in class they call you an idiot and treat you as one' (Australian girl, 15 years); 'So many teachers don't seem to be human. Maybe younger teachers; student teachers are easier to talk to' (English girl, 15 years).

The overall picture painted by the children is one of naive ideas of teachers' limited roles, reflections of fierce or overbusy teachers, and later of suspicion that sex is too personal to be trusted to teachers who might gossip. The older the children the more important trusting becomes, very few in the teenage years willing to trust teachers, unless they are specialists in some way.

Asking your friends about sex

Children who would not ask their friends about sex give two major reasons, 'They wouldn't know either' and 'They'd laugh at me, and tell it all round the school'. These negative responses are in the majority (see Table 14.13) in the English-speaking countries, declining somewhat during the teenage years but with 50 per cent still negative among the English 15-year-olds. The Swedish picture shows more positive responses from 11 years onwards with 73 per cent of 15-year-olds having no hesitation in asking their friends about sex.

Dickinson (1978) observed from his study of Texan teenagers, that while parents were still the preferred source of sex information, friends as a preferred source increased in frequency during adolescence. His stress upon the importance of this for North American boys is supported in part by our study.

Many children with positive answers qualified their replies: 'Only the question I think they'd know' (Australian boy, 5 years); 'Only if they were girls. Girls know more stuff' (North American girl, 7 years); 'I'd only ask older ones about 10, there's no point in asking little children' (English girl, 7 years). The 9 to 11 year groups refer to trust

308

TABLE 14.13 *Percentages of children responding to 'Would you ask your friends questions about sex?' by country and age-year (N = 838)*

Age-year	Australia		England		North America		Sweden	
	Yes	No	Yes	No	Yes	No	Yes	No
5	40	58	40	60	17	63	7	53
7	18	80	30	70	30	70	43	53
9	23	77	20	78	13	83	17	73
11	38	58	30	65	23	77	57	33
13	45*	55	48	52	46	54	60	27
15	68	32	50	50	58	42	73**	10

(*Boys' responses significantly more frequent: ** Girls' responses significantly more frequent: see Appendix B, Table B.9.)

and best friends and not feeling silly talking with someone of the same age. The teenagers have developed more intense and personal friendships which are reflected in their replies: 'They're the next most important people to me after my parents' (North American girl, 13 years), 'Not straight out but bring it up in conversation and see what they say. You stand the risk of getting laughed at, but that's where you find out most' (Australian boy, 15 years who was negative regarding parents and teachers). An English 15-year-old boy who'd responded negatively to parents and teachers also, reports 'As long as I did it in a joking way, but there'd not be anyone if I wanted serious advice'; 'I wouldn't be embarrassed' (she had said 'No' to parents and teachers) 'Because they might have had sexual intercourse' (Swedish girl, 15 years).

English 5- and 7-year-old boys were more inclined to ask their friends than girls in their age cohorts, but 13- and 15-year-old Swedish girls (73 per cent and 93 per cent respectively) and 15-year-old English girls (65 per cent) and North American girls (67 per cent) are much more inclined to ask friends of their own sex, than do the boys. The intensity of teenage girl friendship shows through in many of their answers.

'Where did you learn most of these things for yourself?'

The previous section explored whom children would feel confident in asking questions about sex. This was followed by a much wider query, since asking questions is only a part of any person's sex education. Comparing both sets of responses, the more specific with the broader 'sources' below, little correspondence can be seen in some areas between questions asked and major sources of information. Indeed, by listening carefully and by overhearing adult conversations many children appeared to pick up a great deal of information as well as misinformation. The children were encouraged to answer this question in terms of receiving 'the most information'. Less than 4 per cent of the total sample failed to respond, many children giving more than one source of sex information. In all, 805 out of 838 children gave 1,351 responses, about equal proportions in each country, covering about 12 different categories. These were combined to make 7 major categories. The results in each category, arranged in order of choice frequency, are set out in Table 14.14. These results are not strictly comparable with Farrell (1978, p. 56), Gagnon and Simon (1973) and others since our question was on sources of 'most information', rather than source of 'first learning'. The results, however, appear to be somewhat similar, with parents, especially mother, being the prime source. Two categories, teachers and lessons at school on the one hand, and media sources on the other provide the remaining major sources of sex information. Parents, teachers and media between them supply about 80 per cent of children with their major sources.

TABLE 14.14   *Percentages of responses 'Where did you learn most about sex' by country (N = 838)*

Sources of information	Australia	England	North America	Sweden
Parents				
Mothers	23.2	22.3	32.3	15.1
Fathers	2.8	3.6	2.2	0.3
Both parents	8.8	5.2	8.6	19.6
Teachers				
and school lessons	19.2	28.1	19.4	31.6
Media				
TV, films, books, encyclopedias, magazines	26.8	20.0	17.6	20.6
Friends	8.3	8.8	7.9	8.2
Siblings				
Brothers and sisters (including other family)	4.8	6.8	5.0	1.4
Picked it up				
The street and playground	5.1	4.9	6.5	3.1
Medical				
Medical and others	1.0	0.3	0.7	–

The figures in Table 14.14 were consistent in some measure with the three questions asked previously, but illuminate how misleading Table 14.9, about asking sex questions of parents can be. While parents,

310

particularly mothers, are the major source, others are almost as important (if the frequency of response is a reliable indicator). Father's role as information giver is seen in perspective when the figures are compared with Table 14.11 and teachers when compared with Table 14.12. Friends and siblings, on the other hand, appear to play a very minor role as agents for 'most information'. It is of interest to look at mothers, teachers and media, the three major sources, separately in a little more detail. Table 14.15 giving 'mother' responses, when analysed by age-year and in terms of sex differences, indicates the same-sex bias towards mother on the part of girls, evident in Sweden although not as strong as in the English-speaking countries, as can be seen in Table 14.10.

TABLE 14.15 Percentages of responses giving mother as a major source of sex information by country, age-year and sex (N = 838)

Age-year	Australia		England		North America		Sweden	
	Boys	Girls	Boys	Girls	Boys	Girls	Boys	Girls
5	30	26	46	56	42	50	34	30
7	40	50	36	50	60	46	14	7
9	30	50	20	46	60	60	7	34
11	26	52	10	56*	34	80*	14	34
13	6	80*	20	56*	20	66*	14	46
15	10	66*	—	40*	12	76*	26	26

(*Girls' responses significantly more frequent than boys': see Table B.10, Appendix B.)

Choice of teachers, including 'lessons at school' (seen in Table 14.16), increases with age in all countries. This is to be expected as sex education programmes are introduced year by year. North American children respond rather later, reflecting the later introduction of sex education in schools. But this response also includes other teachers, such as physical education teachers, not only those taking official sex education classes. The discrepancy with Table 14.12 can be explained by the difference between willing to ask sex questions of teachers, and receiving sex information from them; one is active and the other may be passive.

The category of media, which children cited as television and films in most responses, also includes books, magazines and encyclopedias. One boy (North American, 11-year-old) said his father gave him old copies of *Playboy* magazine to look at. While the totals in Table 14.17 show more Australian children using this source and the North American children least, when broken down by age and sex the picture is somewhat

311

TABLE 14.16 *Percentages of responses giving teacher as a major source of sex information by country, age-year and sex (N = 838)*

Age-year	Australia		England		North America		Sweden	
	Boys	Girls	Boys	Girls	Boys	Girls	Boys	Girls
5	—	—	6	6	8	8	—	—
7	—	—	6	20	—	6	10	14
9	30	20	46	40	6	6	40	54
11	46	36	36	36	6	6	86	67
13	72*	26	70	100	48	60	100	86
15	67	80	92	92	100	100	94*	44

(*Boys' responses significantly more frequent than girls': see Table B.10, Appendix B.)

TABLE 14.17 *Percentages of responses giving media as a major source of sex information by country, age-year and sex (N = 838)*

Age-year	Australia		England		North America		Sweden	
	Boys	Girls	Boys	Girls	Boys	Girls	Boys	Girls
5	6	10	6	—	16	—	28	10
7	6	6	30	16	40*	—	28	33
9	66	56	46	40	48	26	28	34
11	66	86	76*	20	60	20	20	46
13	86	50	36	26	48	24	74*	20
15	60*	20	50	26	20	12	20	20

(*Boys' responses more significantly frequent than girls': see Table B.10, Appendix B.)

more complex as Table 14.17 indicates. Boys appear to report media sources as a major origin of sex information in the English-speaking countries more than girls, particularly from 9 to 13 years, Australian and English boys continuing to 15 years. This male emphasis is not seen in Sweden except among 13-year-old boys (74 per cent to 20 per cent), compared with Swedish girls of that age. These are probably the peak years for using school and public libraries and for parents to buy books, especially encyclopedias for their children. Many television programmes watched by children, as their comments indicate, are not designed as sex education programmes for the young, but often information is received when watching soap operas ('I learned about having babies from "Days of Our Lives" ') and police series ("Police Story" is when I first heard about rape'). Children hear the words and try to understand their meaning and the situations they portray in such programmes. Films and film-strips are sometimes used at school, often at PTAs (Parent-Teacher Associations) where parents are asked to bring their children, a familiar pattern in some American schools.

The overall picture shows the home as the dominant and most cited major source of information, with mother as the main informant, but as children grow older this is supplemented by the school, but not replacing the home as a major source of information. Media sources, however, appear to be as important as school, with some overlap between the two since television films and books are frequently available in home and school. Although questions and discussions do occur on sex topics between children and their friends and siblings, they do not appear in the children's minds as major sources from which they learn.

When results of the 'Would you ask your Mother (Teacher, Friends)?' questions are compared with these three persons cited as a major source of information about sex, by means of a chi-square test, some interesting facts emerge. There is, not unexpectedly, a close correspondence between willingness to ask mother questions about sex and mother cited as the major source of sex information. The results are highly significant in Australia, England and Sweden ($p < .001$) and markedly similar in North America. By contrast there is no apparent correspondence between asking father questions about sex and citing him as the major source of sex information.

In the remaining persons (teachers and friends) there was considerable discrepancy between those who were willing to ask sex questions and those citing the questioned persons as a major source of sex information. For example, of the 88 English children who were willing to ask teachers sex questions, only 44 cited them as major sources of sex information. Of the 92 Australian children who said they would ask their friends questions about sex, only 23 cited friends as a major source of sex information. We postulate that this infers that questions might be asked of teachers and friends, but the feedback is disappointing in most cases. Otherwise we presume the matching of both 'asking' and 'sources' would be roughly similar.

What children want to know about sex and what they receive

Two final questions were asked about sex education to compare what it was the children wanted to know about sex, and what they recalled having received. The first, not set within a school context, was the general question, 'What is the most important thing a boy(girl) needs to know about sex?' The actual phrasing was adjusted to the respondent's

313

sex, age and previous terminology used, so that older respondents were asked in relation to sex, and younger ones usually about babies, your own body, girls and boys, and growing up.

The second question, asked only of those who reported some kind of school-based sex education was, 'What are the most important things, about sex, you learned from these lessons?' The intention was to discover not only what the children themselves felt to be important but to compare these items with what they recollected of importance received in sex education at school. While the first question included most children, the second included only 41 per cent of the whole sample, 57 per cent of the 9- to 15-year-olds, and 78 per cent of the teenagers (13- and 15-year-olds).

No hierarchy of scores was devised since there was no purpose in producing a scale on this type of item. Instead the responses were coded into 5 categories and 13 sub-categories set out in Table 14.18. These were applicable to responses from both questions, 'What is the most important thing (about sex) a boy(girl) needs to know?' and, 'What are the most important things you actually learned in sex education at school?' In the following discussion it should be borne in mind that the emphasis in the second question was what is 'the most important' knowledge about sex, rather than what has been learned. For example when 'birth control' is cited as the most important sex information a boy should know, the boy concerned may not cite it among the most important information actually learned. That is to say, birth control may have been taught in some manner, but the same boy may not have rated it as 'the most important thing (about sex)' he had learned. There is, however, a strong probability that he would rate it as 'most important' in answer to both questions if, in fact, in his view he has been taught about it adequately. Another point to be considered in examining answers to the second question is, are the absences of many topics due to a respondent's selective memory, due to teachers' inability to teach certain topics either through lack of knowledge or inhibitions, or is it that the teaching has been haphazard, unsystematic, irregular and non-sequential?

Whatever the explanations, we shall look in turn at the categories mentioned by the majority of the children. The pre-sexual answers are excluded as irrelevant to this discussion due largely to younger children's generalised interpretations of learning. These kinds of answers are largely confined to the 5- and 7-year-olds.

How the body develops

How the body works and develops, and how it grows differently for the sexes is covered by Table 14.19. (Menstruation is treated as a

TABLE 14.18   *Categories of responses to 'most important thing to know about sex' and 'have learned about sex'*

Category	Sub-category and descriptions
Pre-sexual	*Generalised answers* 'What's bad for your teeth?'; 'About faith in God'; 'How strong my arms are'.
	Domestic answers 'How to get married'; 'How to help your wife'; 'What to eat'.
Developmental	*How the body works* 'How it develops'; 'What to expect and when'; 'The sex organs'.
	Differences in bodies of both sexes 'How sex organs develop'; 'Keeping clean and healthy'.
	Menstruation 'What to expect and what to do', reason for periods; personal hygiene for girls.
	Breasts 'How they develop'; 'What to expect'; 'What are they for?'
Coitus	*Sexual intercourse* 'What to expect and what to do'; 'How to do it'; 'The role of each sex'; masturbation and wet dreams; risk involved with coitus; venereal diseases.
	Birth-control 'What to do and when'; 'How to take care'; 'Abortion'.
	Conception 'How the seed comes'; 'Where to buy the seed'; 'How it happens'.
Babies	*Pregnancy* 'What happens?'; 'What to do'; gestation; how to ensure a healthy baby.
	Birth 'How it happens'; 'What to do?'; 'What to expect?'; 'Does it hurt?'.
Behaviour	*Parenthood* Responsibilities and skills in parenting; what being a mother or father involves.
	Courting and Premarital 'What to do and not, on dates'; 'How to keep out of trouble'; 'How to remain a virgin'.

separate section as can be seen below.) Responses in this category as the most important thing for a boy or girl to learn are present from 11 years onwards. Totals are rather similar across countries, with the exception of the North American 15-year-olds (55 per cent). There is some disparity in interest between the sexes on this item. When 'actually taught' is considered, most age groups, except in Sweden and Australia, experience a considerable 'shortfall'. The most marked deficiencies are

315

TABLE 14.19 *Percentages of responses in the body development category by country age-year and sex (N = 424)*

Age-year	Category	Australia		England		North America		Sweden	
		Boys	Girls	Boys	Girls	Boys	Girls	Boys	Girls
11	Need to know	30	25	15	40	20	40	33	47
	Most important, actually taught	5	15	10	15	7	7	33	47
13	Need to know	30	30	40	25	19	12	53	7
	Most important, actually taught	25	20	–	30	19	26	40	27
15	Need to know	25	30	20	40	69	40	20	27
	Most important, actually taught	20	35	25	20	38	27	27	40

in the English 11-year girls, 13-year boys and 15-year girls, and the North American 11 years of both sexes, and 15-year boys. In these countries and age groups there is a gap between what these children want and what they feel they received.

Menstruation

The majority of girls in all countries felt it most important that they should be instructed about menstruation (see Table 14.20), when to expect it, what to do when it does occur and why it happens. Australian girls were somewhat less concerned with its importance. However, by contrast, in all countries little seems to have been taught in this area, or it arrived too late, perhaps after menstruation had begun, that they no longer thought it important. Only a few boys thought it important to mention; most of them, Swedish boys at 13 years (27 per cent), rated menstruation as the most important thing they learned in sex education. Only a few girls felt breast development to be of any importance (20 per cent of Swedish 11-year-olds were the largest number) to know about, and only one reported this as the most important thing she learned in sex education. Consequently no separate section is included here.

Sexual intercourse

In contrast to menstruation it is boys who rate sexual intercourse as the most important topic they need to know about. There is a very pronounced sex difference in the Australian and English samples, a marked difference in the North American sample, except at 13 years

TABLE 14.20 *Percentages of responses in the menstruation category by country age-year and sex (N = 424)*

Age-year	Category	Australia		England		North America		Sweden	
		Boys	Girls	Boys	Girls	Boys	Girls	Boys	Girls
11	Need to know	–	55	–	70	7	53	–	47
	Most important, actually taught	–	10	–	15	–	–	–	20
13	Need to know	–	55	–	60	–	65	7	73
	Most important, actually taught	–	–	–	10	–	6	27	7
15	Need to know	–	50	–	70	–	67	20	80
	Most important, actually taught	5	10	–	20	–	20	–	20

(* See Table B.11, Appendix B for significant sex differences.)

TABLE 14.21 *Percentages of responses in the sexual intercourse category by country age-year and sex (N = 424)*

Age-year	Category	Australia		England		North America		Sweden	
		Boys	Girls	Boys	Girls	Boys	Girls	Boys	Girls
11	Need to know	30	5	50*	5	53*	7	47	33
	Most important, actually taught	10	–	15	–	7	–	40	13
13	Need to know	60*	15	60*	5	31	6	53	27
	Most important, actually taught	30	–	25	20	13	–	47	27
15	Need to know	60*	20	55*	10	38	20	53	13
	Most important, actually taught	15	5	25	15	38	20	73	33

(*Boys' frequencies of response are significantly more than girls': see Appendix B, Table B.11.)

where it is pronounced, and least discrepancies in the Swedish sample, although there are some marked differences at 15 years.

Discrepancies between what is considered they need to know and what was most important and actually taught, is again considerable in all English-speaking countries; in all ages in Australia for both sexes among 11-, 13- and 15-year-old English boys; and among North American 11- and 13-year-olds of both sexes. The Swedish expectations and realisations are well balanced.

Birth-control

Since there are only a handful of responses in this category at 11 years, the figures in Table 14.22 covering this category give only the teenagers' results. The figures of what they need to know at 13 years are too small to merit comment, except the Swedish sample is somewhat higher for boys. The 15-year-old boys in the English-speaking countries seem more concerned than girls about birth-control except that Australian 15-year-old girls seem more concerned than their male peers. These figures, however, are not statistically significant.

TABLE 14.22   *Percentages of responses in the birth-control category by country age-year and sex (N = 284)*

Age-year	Category	Australia		England		North America		Sweden	
		Boys	Girls	Boys	Girls	Boys	Girls	Boys	Girls
13	Need to know	–	5	10	–	6	12	20	13
	Most important, actually taught	–	–		–	–	6	13	13	13
15	Need to know	10	25	35	15	25	–	47	47
	Most important, actually taught	–	10	35	25	13	13	60	53

There appears to be little provision at 13 years, except in Sweden, of information about birth-control. In Australia and North America there is a shortfall at 15 years, with apparently provision meeting expectation with the English of both sexes, a slight shortfall for 15-year-old American boys, and a small 'overkill' in Sweden at 15 years. Apart from Sweden there appears overall to be little expectation and little consequent teaching on birth-control, perhaps a realistic recognition of social taboos operating very effectively for both students and teachers.

Conception

There is no clear pattern of trends with country, age or sex in this category as can be seen in Table 14.23. Children do express a need to know about conception – the origin of babies – well before 13 years, when the expectation generally is matched by what is actually taught. This balance is beginning to be apparent at 9 years in Sweden and clearly so at 11 years, well ahead of the English speaking countries.

Pregnancy and gestation

Interest in what happens during pregnancy and how the process of

TABLE 14.23   *Percentages of responses in the conception category by country age-year and sex (N = 704)*

Age-year	Category	Australia		England		North America		Sweden	
		Boys	Girls	Boys	Girls	Boys	Girls	Boys	Girls
7	Need to know	5	10	30	5	6	–	7	40
	Most important, actually taught	–	–	–	–	–	–	7	–
9	Need to know	25	45	20	40	20	33	7	33
	Most important, actually taught	15	5	20	5	7	–	–	43
11	Need to know	20	35	55	20	40	7	40	60
	Most important, actually taught	5	10	35	15	13	–	60	40
13	Need to know	25	25	30	15	50	24	27	20
	Most important, actually taught	35	20	50	30	25	24	27	27
15	Need to know	25	5	30	5	13	27	20	13
	Most important, actually taught	25	10	25	30	44	40	40	20

gestation affects mother and baby is viewed in all countries as essential knowledge by a fair proportion of children (see Table 14.24). In Australia girls evince much more concern overall than boys, but only English 9-year-old girls reveal this, at other ages both sexes being equal. At 13 North American boys appear more concerned than girls, whilst in Sweden, apart from a discrepancy at 11 years, both sexes appear equally concerned. The only difference, however, which is statistically significant is Australian 11-year-olds, where girls more frequently show a need to know about what happens during pregnancy. At other ages both sexes are about the same in the frequency of their responses.

Boys' expectations appear to be met generally except 13-year-old North American boys, and 9-year-old North American and Swedish boys. Australian girls at 9 and 11 years appear to experience a shortfall, as do English and North American girls at 9. Apart from 9 years the Swedish expectations and what is provided seems well matched.

The birth process

Children's curiosity about how a baby is actually born is infrequent until about 9 years (see Table 14.25) but the interest is not sustained in terms of rating it as important knowledge. Australian girls are much

319

TABLE 14.24 *Percentages of responses in the pregnancy-gestation category by country age-year and sex (N = 564)*

Age-year	Category	Australia		England		North America		Sweden	
		Boys	Girls	Boys	Girls	Boys	Girls	Boys	Girls
9	Need to know	25	45	20	40	20	27	20	20
	Most important, actually taught	15	10	30	15	7	–	–	27
11	Need to know	10	60	25	10	20	13	40	60
	Most important, actually taught	15	10	25	15	13	–	40	47
13	Need to know	10	25	10	15	36	18	27	27
	Most important, actually taught	15	20	45	30	6	26	27	27
15	Need to know	5	25	5	15	19	20	33	27
	Most important, actually taught	15	20	15	35	38	40	53	27

more concerned than any other group, apart from the Swedish children, but there is a sharp decline with age in voicing this as an important area to know. The need therefore appears to be met, except in the case of the North American children who receive little sex education before 12 years. The most consistent picture is the Swedish sample from 11 years onwards when expectations appear to match achievement.

Pre-marital and courting behaviour

So few children remarked on the importance of parenting skills and having received any instruction in this area that the results do not merit presentation. However, some responses under the pre-marital and courting behaviour category were evident from 11 years onwards. One would expect teenagers to consider this area as of some importance but there is little evidence of this in Table 14.26, except for a sizeable proportion of American 11- and 13-year-old boys and English 15-year-old boys. There is no evidence, however, that the majority of any age group thought it worthy of mention as the most important item learned at school in sex education.

No children seemed aware of the importance of knowing about venereal diseases, perhaps of some weight in view of the figures for gonorrhoea reviewed in chapter 2. The major concern of boys is how to do 'it', namely sexual intercourse, and that of the girls to be informed about menstruation before it happens. These expectations like many others did not appear to be met if recollection is a guide. Overall, the

TABLE 14.25   *Percentages of responses in the birth process category by country age-year and sex (N = 564)*

Age-year	Category	Australia		England		North America		Sweden	
		Boys	Girls	Boys	Girls	Boys	Girls	Boys	Girls
9	Need to know	20	30	15	20	27	27	13	7
	Most important, actually taught	10	0	5	–	–	–	–	13
11	Need to know	5	40	15	–	–	–	33	40
	Most important, actually taught	15	5	15	10	–	–	40	33
13	Need to know	10	25	5	10	–	6	20	27
	Most important, actually taught	10	5	25	25	6	12	27	40
15	Need to know	–	5	–	10	6	7	13	13
	Most important, actually taught	–	–	15	10	6	13	40	13

TABLE 14.26   *Percentages of responses in the pre-marital and courting behaviour category by country age-year and sex (N = 424)*

Age-year	Category	Australia		England		North America		Sweden	
		Boys	Girls	Boys	Girls	Boys	Girls	Boys	Girls
11	Need to know	10	10	–	–	33	13	–	–
	Most important, actually taught	–	–	5	5	–	–	–	–
13	Need to know	15	5	–	5	25	12	–	–
	Most important, actually taught	–	5	–	10	6	18	7	–
15	Need to know	10	5	25	10	–	13	–	–
	Most important, actually taught	–	5	5	10	–	–	–	–

picture would be characterised as too little given too late. Where sex education is concerned, the programmes may be geared to what adults consider suitable for children rather than what children consider they need to know.

Summary and discussion

Children's views were sought on whether sex education should occur,

321

where and at what age it should take place. What were their sources of sex information and in whom they had confidence to ask questions about sex were also investigated. Finally, what children wanted to know about sex was compared with what they recollected receiving.

The great majority of children in all countries felt they should be taught about sex, a slightly smaller proportion, but still the overwhelming majority of children, asserting that sex education should take place at school. Opposition was voiced mainly by the very young. Most of the children wanted sex education to be given in the primary school years (5 to 11). Some age groups of Swedish children asserted it should begin in pre-school but many English and North American teenagers felt it should be deferred until secondary schooling (12 to 16). When this was compared with the age at which they had received sex education in school, a considerable gap was evident, with less than 50 per cent on average having received any instruction at school on sexual matters before the age of 12. In contrast the figures for Sweden were 85 per cent. Even a sizeable proportion of teenagers claimed to have had no sex education in school, ranging from 38 per cent in Australia to 27 per cent in North America. Sweden by comparison had 2 per cent. These claims may be due to selective memory, absenteeism, lack of parental permission to attend classes, no systematic provision of sex education or sex education as a school option. 'I never took human relations. I did ball games instead' (Australian boy, 15 years) illustrates the last point.

Confidence in asking questions about sex was very strong towards mothers, especially among girls, less so among boys, and very weak towards fathers, few girls daring to ask their fathers, and only slightly more boys. From 9 years on children have developed a marked reluctance to ask teachers about sex, including Sweden with formalised sex instruction at a much earlier age. Girls generally had less hesitation in asking their friends about sex than boys. Children had mixed feelings about asking friends, fearing them as a source of ridicule or gossip. Overall, large numbers mirrored an awareness that even with those most trusted, caution had to be exercised. A sizeable proportion, particularly boys, felt they could not ask parents, teachers or friends.

Mothers, teachers and the media were named by 80 per cent as the major sources of 'most sex information' children had received, in that order of frequency. The home is still the dominant source of sex information, mothers in particular, with schools gradually supplementing this source and the media a strong third.

What children thought the most important areas of sex they should know about was compared with what they recollected having received. What they 'need to know' covered a wide range but did not include knowledge of venereal diseases or parenting skills and only minimally courtship behaviour. High on the list for girls was menstruation, and for boys, how to perform coitus. There was a contrast between what they wanted and what the provision appeared to be. Apart from Sweden, most age groups experienced a 'shortfall' of information the children wanted in most areas, the greatest deficiency being birth-control information. In view of the earlier maturing of teenagers the picture in the English-speaking countries appears to be characterised by too little too late.

Whatever the explanations for the incongruent percentages between what children want and what they claim to receive, the facts do not appear to fit well with several well-established developments in the sexual life and behaviour of the young in the English-speaking countries included in this study. These are the secular trend in physical growth (Tanner, 1978; Ljung *et al.*, 1974), the earlier sexual activity of the young (Schofield, 1968; Venner, 1972; Collins, 1974), and the greater risk of pregnancy and of venereal infection by young adolescents (National Council, 1979; Hunt, 1976).

In the light of children's needs, expressed by themselves, however imperfectly, it is evident to us that home, school and media co-operatively should provide clear information, within the context of human need and human relations, at a much earlier age than is practised currently. Parent education in how to be sex educators of their own children, especially fathers, should be a community concern. Perhaps the media is the most available and effective means in modern society for helping educate parents and their children. One fact is abundantly clear. Children perceive it is the adults who have hang-ups about sex, and adults who deliberately or unconsciously withhold the information and knowledge the children seek.

15 Clothes and nakedness

Obscured in the mists of prehistory, humans long ago began to wear clothes, first by adapting vegetation and later, as an adjunct of hunting, using the hides or skins of animals. There are two possible explanations, instrumental and expressive (Roach and Eicher, 1965). The first is that in colder climates the principal reason was protection from cold, and in any climate possible protection from injury or disease, such as wounds from thorns and insects. In this instrumental theory, as humans became less hairy, by necessity they had to find substitute protection. The second theory, involving an expressive function, is that the origins of human life possibly beginning in warmer climates, clothing was initially used for decorative purposes with some ancillary protective use, becoming ritualised and used as recognition signals of rank or tribal membership. Whatever the theory, at some period clothing took on sexual significance (Flugel, 1930; Frazer, 1936). In the 'attraction' hypothesis adornment was used to emphasise the sexual parts and enhance the sexual attractions of the wearers (Cordwell and Schwarz, 1979). It is postulated that only in later civilization and in some cultures nakedness was seen to be sexually provocative and so was discouraged by social taboos and their accompanying sanctions. Thus as social restraints about nakedness developed, becoming part of the mores and folkways, they were often justified by myths, such as Adam and Eve hiding their nakedness. Shame and guilt about sexual nakedness consequently became linked to morality and religion, a powerful authoritarian link. Humans in modern Western societies have acquired such associations and certainly children reflect them in their behaviour and sexual thinking.

It was interesting in the light of racial recapitulation theories of child development to explore what reasons children might advance for the wearing of clothes, to see what moral levels of reasoning were used to justify it, and to discover particularly children's view on nakedness.

In their survey of American mothers and the patterns of child-rearing observed in American families, Sears, Maccoby and Levin (1957) illustrate the key position of the mother enforcing 'modesty training', their term for nudity taboos (p. 181). When mothers explained why running around nude was forbidden, they often referred to the danger of catching cold (p. 188). In other words the moral reasons were not given to the children, but borrowed sanctions were used. Another characteristic of mothers noted was how many families seemed to cope without using any names for the sexual organs, using vague terms like 'it' or 'there', so avoiding labelling of parts of the body which should be covered.

Evidence of these taboos has been also illustrated from British society in the study by Newson and Newson (1968) where mothers by varied sanctions saw themselves as regulators of acceptable socio-sexual behaviour, particularly in the area of nudity. Such widely accepted authorities as Gesell and Spock have for thirty years urged greater tolerance in such matters as nudity in rearing children, to little effect as Finkelhor (1980) points out. Around 40 per cent of the American college students interviewed by Finkelhor recall warnings, scoldings and punishments by their parents, mother in particular, about nudity. He also reports considerable conflict of over 65 per cent of the students with their mother about nudity, and over 70 per cent with their father. The result was that by the age of twelve 86 per cent of boys reported being embarrassed at being seen naked by a sister, and 58 per cent of girls being seen naked by a sister. While 40 per cent of boys of that age were embarrassed at being seen naked by a brother, 94 per cent of girls reported embarrassment at being seen naked by a brother (p. 17). Since familial conflict and embarrassment about nudity would appear to be so evident, in our study the children were asked three questions: 'Suppose we all lived in a nice warm place or climate, should we need to wear clothes?'; 'Why should this be so?' (What are the reasons for saying 'Yes' or 'No'); 'Some people feel shy or funny about (revealing) certain parts of the body, why should this be so?'

As in all previous questions there were variations of wording for the younger or slower children, but after the trial interviews the questions formulated above appeared to have little ambiguity for children of all ages. In the third question, for example, there was no need to mention sexual parts by name or even by inference, since very few children did not make the identification or inference for themselves.

'Should people wear clothes, even in warm climates?'

The simple positive and negative answers to this question are tabulated in Table 15.1 and reveal some interesting differences. The North American

TABLE 15.1 *Percentages* of 'Yes/No' responses to 'Do we need to wear clothes in a warm climate?' by country and age-year (N = 838)*

Age-year	Australia		England		North America		Sweden	
	Yes	No	Yes	No	Yes	No	Yes	No
5	60	40	40	60	71	29	23	73
7	60	40	43	57	50	50	27	73
9	58	42	40	60	83	17	37	60
11	43	57	50	50	73	27	33	67
13	53	47	60	40	73	27	53	40
15	50	50	55	45	81	19	40	53

(* Zero scores are not included.)

children appear to be most adamant about the wearing of clothes and the Swedish children the least, both interestingly living in very cold winter climates. Only at 13 years is the need to wear clothes affirmed by most children (53 per cent) but in all other Swedish age groups the majority respond negatively. The majority of English children move from negative to positive at the age of 11 years, reflecting growing awareness of the implications, whereas the Australian children are fairly evenly balanced between positive and negative. Overall there appears to be a move towards the more positive need to wear clothes by the teenage cohorts across all countries, perhaps reflecting awareness of pubertal growth and its sexual significance. This is apparent from most of the answers of the 13- and 15-year-olds.

These figures, however, obscure sex differences, the differentiated responses being evident in Table 15.2. The Australian boys are the more consistently positive than Australian girls about the need to wear clothes. English boys show a similar pattern until 9 years but the girls are more positive at 11 and 15 years. The girls in the North American sample are more dominant from 9 years on, with teenage girls in particular, more than 82 per cent affirming the need to wear clothes. Apart from the 5-year-olds there are few major sex differences in the Swedish responses but 67 per cent of Swedish 13-year-old girls assert the need to wear clothes compared with 40 per cent of boys. If these figures can be taken as an indicator of sexual inhibitions of some kind, and it is not necessarily assumed that they are, then the North American children are the most inhibited about nakedness and Swedish children the least, with certain sex differences occurring particularly in some teenage girls' cohorts.

TABLE 15.2 *Percentages of 'Yes' responses to 'Do we need to wear clothes in a warm climate?' by country age-year and sex (N = 838)*

Age-year	Australia		England		North America		Sweden	
	Boys	Girls	Boys	Girls	Boys	Girls	Boys	Girls
5	80	40	45	35	85	55	47	–
7	65	55	55	30	56	43	33	20
9	80	35	45	35	73	93	33	40
11	40	45	45	55	67	80	33	33
13	60	45	65	55	63	82	40	67
15	70	30	40	70	75	87	40	40

Reasons for people wearing or not wearing clothes

To see whether or not racial recapitulation theories were reflected in the reasons given, the responses were examined to discover if they could be scored on some kind of evolutionary-social realism scale. Various categories were tried and eventually this concept was rejected, because while 'recapitulatory' answers were clearly in evidence they did not fit any hierarchical order. Kohlberg's (1969) three levels and six stages of moral thinking did, however, with some adaptation, appear to provide a suitable framework for scoring the two remaining questions which covered why people need to wear clothes (in a warm climate), and why some people feel shy or funny about (revealing) certain parts of the body. The criteria for scoring both these questions are set out in Table 15.3.

The criteria actually cover both kinds of reasons for 'Yes' and 'No' answers, reasons for wearing and not wearing clothes, since the same levels of thought are employed to justify positive and negative answers. There were few 'don't know' answers because once they had responded 'Yes' or 'No' to the first question, the children felt the need to defend their choice. A few were conditional in their replies, 'It depends on the people, and how cold it is at nights'. Some switched their position from 'No' to 'Yes', not thinking that wearing shorts or a bikini could be classified as clothing. Examples of some responses to the question on clothes are given below.

Pre-conventional answers (scores 1 and 2)

'Yes, because policemen might lock you up, and your father would give you a hiding. At home it's O.K. in the bath when you want to get clean' (English boy, 5 years); 'My mom says you shouldn't do

327

TABLE 15.3   *Criteria for scoring 'Why should people wear clothes?'*
and 'Why should people be embarrassed?' (adapted from
L. Kohlberg, 1969)

Levels	Stages	Category and description
	0	*Unscoreable* Don't know, no response, 'just so' or nonsense.
Pre-conventional	1	*Punishment and obedience* Avoid punishment and defer to power. Physical consequences decide regardless of meaning or value.
	2	*Instrumental relativist* What instrumentally satisfies one's own needs; hedonistic dominated by self-centred pragmatism.
Conventional	3	*Good boy; nice girl* What pleases or is approved by others; conformity to stereotypes of majority or natural behaviour; living in others' expectations.
	4	*Law and order* Authority fixed rules and maintenance of social order for their own sake; doing one's duty; showing respect for authority.
Post-conventional, autonomous or principled	5	*Social contract by consensus* Utilitarian overtones; awareness of relativism of personal values; law may be changed on rational considerations of social utility; free agreement is binding.
	6	*Universal ethical principle* Conscience; self-chosen principles appealing to consistency, universality and comprehensive application; reciprocity and equality of individuals.

that. She says it's not right to go around with nothing on' (Australian girl, 7 years); 'Yes, because you'd get badly sunburnt. You need to wear T shirts. You'd go black after two or three years. (Q) Then you'd be mistaken for an aborigine and you couldn't get a job then. Then there are the mossies (mosquitoes)' (Australian boy, 9 years); 'No, it'd be too hot and sweaty to wear anything. We could have our paddling pool filled' (North American girl, 7 years); 'Yes, they'd get dirty and scratched and maybe get an infection' (Swedish boy, 7 years).

Conventional answers (scores 3 and 4)

'You can't go around bare naked. You've got to wear bathers.
It's rude, and people would laugh' (Australian boy, 7 years); 'You
couldn't walk up the street naked. I mean, everyone would stare
at you. It's not nice. It wouldn't matter if there were only girls.
If there were boys they'd be rude about it' (English girl, 9 years);
'No, if you're a baby, it's all right to be naked. But if it were hot
and you had to go to school, you'd need to wear clothes. (Q) The
others would laugh. It's just normal to wear clothes. Everyone does'
(North American girl, 11 years); 'Yes, if they weren't wearing
clothes, crowds would come to watch. (Q) It's self-respect, when
you see natives running around with no clothes on, they don't
know any better. We do' (North American boy, 13 years); 'Yes,
you can't simply be all naked. That is not educated' (Swedish boy,
13 years); 'Yes, because we wouldn't dare show our genitals to each
other' (Swedish girl, 13 years); 'It's rude. You can go only to certain
beaches so they can get tanned all over. They're showing all their
personal things. It's got to be kept under control' (Australian boy,
15 years).

Post-conventional answers, autonomous or principled responses
(scores 5 and 6)

'No. Because everyone's the same. If it was hot, you wouldn't need
to wear clothes, because everyone's the same. (Q. Men and women?)
It wouldn't matter if everyone agreed to it' (Australian girl, 9 years);
'We didn't use to wear clothes because it was so hot. Then the ice
age came and people invented clothes to keep warm and keep our
privacy' (English boy, 11 years); 'Yes, but not if everyone agreed to
be naked' (Swedish boy, 15 years); 'Some believe you shouldn't
wear clothes, like nudists, and some believe you should. People
should be free to choose' (North American boy, 13 years); 'I don't
think you should be ashamed of your bodies. They are all the same.
Adam and Eve didn't wear clothes. (Q) That's an old fashioned
story' (North American girl, 13 years); 'Everyone's the same, and it's
no use hiding it. The only reason for clothes is warmth, so they
could be discarded if it's warm. It depends on what sort of person
you are. If you don't want to show your body off, it's up to you'
(Australian girl, 15 years); 'Most moral laws would inhibit it. The
concept of shame has been put in people's minds, and this has
restricted them' (English boy, 15 years); 'It's not shameful to be
naked, but it's usually wise to wear clothes' (English girl, 15 years).

TABLE 15.4 *Percentage scores on 'Why should people wear clothes?' scale, Kohlberg's 6 stages by country and age-year (N = 838)*

Age-year	Australia						England						North America						Sweden					
	1	2	3	4	5	6	1	2	3	4	5	6	1	2	3	4	5	6	1	2	3	4	5	6
5	2	66	15	3	3	—	3	90	5	—	—	—	—	75	17	—	—	—	3	87	3	—	—	—
7	—	55	30	10	3	—	—	85	8	3	3	—	—	57	30	3	—	—	—	70	13	3	7	—
9	—	72	20	3	—	5	—	85	13	—	—	—	—	70	20	3	3	—	—	80	13	7	—	—
11	—	52	5	10	15	13	—	52	18	7	15	7	—	40	13	17	23	7	—	33	40	3	20	—
13	—	36	10	8	23	23	—	62	10	13	10	5	—	24	24	15	30	7	—	30	50	3	3	—
15	—	5	5	10	52	28	—	50	17	5	18	10	—	29	16	10	26	19	—	20	23	7	47	3

(* Zero scores not included.)

The scoring on the Kohlberg six stages is set out in Table 15.4. The difficulties of scoring are reflected in these results since very few children conveyed punishment and obedience meanings in their responses, and it was difficult to differentiate at the top end of the scale between scores 5 and 6, the social contract by consensus category and the universal ethical principle category. Large numbers of older children often inferred universalisms but these were not easy to identify. Scorer reliability at 0.81 reflected this scoring problem. While the results are reasonably symmetrical, revealing a scaled sequence of scores with increasing age, the distribution of scores is not clear enough to see a hierarchy in six sequential stages. The highest scores are not achieved by the majority of 15-year-olds, so that universal principles are not sufficiently grasped in relation to the reasons why people wear clothes. It may be, of course, that the area is so new and unexpected that it raises cognitive problems. While clothes and nakedness are familiar to children as an area of experience, to explore reasons for their manifestation may be so unfamiliar that children regress cognitively in order to solve the problem presented. However, Table 15.5 presents a clearer picture, when the six stages are reduced to the three levels of pre-conventional, conventional and post-conventional thinking.

TABLE 15.5 *Percentage scores on 'Why should people wear clothes?' scale, Kohlberg's 3 levels by country and age-year (N = 838)*

Age-year	Australia			England			North America			Sweden		
	1	2	3	1	2	3	1	2	3	1	2	3
5	68	18	3	90	5	–	75	17	–	90	3	–
7	55	40	3	85	10	3	57	33	–	70	17	7
9	62	23	5	85	13	–	70	23	3	80	20	–
11	53	15	28	52	25	23	40	30	30	33	43	20
13	37	18	45	62	23	15	24	39	37	30	50	7
15	5	15	80	50	22	28	29	29	42	20	30	50

(Zero scores not included: 1 = pre-conventional; 2 = conventional; 3 = post-conventional.)

The Australian scores scale in reasonable symmetry, pre-conventional thinking giving way to conventional at about 11 years and post-conventional thinking dominating (80 per cent) at 15 years. The North American scores follow a similar pattern. The English scores, however, continue to reflect pre-conventional thinking throughout all age levels and only 28 per cent achieve post-conventional thinking at 15 years. The Swedish scores show a symmetrical pattern, pre-conventional to 9 years,

331

conventional thinking at 11 years and post-conventional thinking at 15 years, although barely achieved as a trend at 50 per cent. In comparative terms it is evident that in the ranking of post-conventional thinking at 15 years in highest scores, Australia (80 per cent) is highest, Sweden (50 per cent) and North America (42 per cent) are moderate and England (28 per cent) is the lowest.

The mean scores for each country set out in Table 15.6 reveal this differentiation, only Australian 15-year-olds achieving a mean score of 4.93 on a 6-point scale. The differences can be seen clearly on the graph (Figure 15.1) of mean scores for this item.

TABLE 15.6   *Mean scores on 'Why should people wear clothes?' scale, Kohlberg's 6 stages by country and age-year (N = 838)*

Age-year	Australia	England	North America	Sweden
5	2.08	1.95	2.00	1.87
7	2.52	2.15	2.16	2.27
9	2.45	2.08	2.30	2.27
11	3.10	3.08	3.44	3.00
13	3.83	2.85	3.71	2.47
15	4.93	3.20	3.88	3.90

These mean scores, however, obscure several differences between the sexes. Swedish girls of 7 years, Australian girls of 11 years and English girls of 15 years score much higher than the boys in the same age cohorts; while English 7-year-old boys, and North American and Swedish 15-year-old boys score much higher than the girls in the same age cohorts. Across countries differences are therefore mainly visible at the 15 year level. Only two of these differences are statistically significant, as Appendix B, Table B.25 indicates. There are no main effects of sex resulting from ANOVA (see Appendix D, Table D.1).

Reasons for some people feeling embarrassed

The third question put to the children about clothes and nakedness raised the question of embarrassment about revealing sexual parts of the body, when naked. The exact question was, 'Some people feel shy or funny about certain parts of the body. Why should this be so?' We have already indicated that 'certain parts of the body' did not need to be named, since children knew what was meant immediately. In fact, answers to the previous question normally provided an opportunity to ask this follow-up question naturally. The word 'embarrassment' was not understood by many younger children, the words 'shy' or 'funny' being substituted as more appropriate. The words 'some people' was

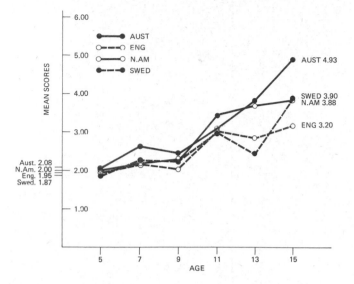

Figure 15.1 Mean scores of responses to 'Why should people wear clothes?' scale by country and age-year

also a deliberate phrasing after the trial interviews, since older children would argue that not *all* people are shy about these matters. The question put in its final form calls for some generalisations about personal motives, social pressures and conventional practices, so that the Kohlberg criteria, as set out in Table 15.3, were thought to be appropriate in scoring these responses. Some answers, based upon these criteria, are set out below. While many are similar to responses to the previous item, there are some marked differences, particularly in reference to modesty, privacy and exposure of the sex organs.

Pre-conventional answers (Scores 1 and 2)

'They don't know people. Visitors come to my house and I'm shy' (Australian girl, 5 years); 'Because windows might be showing and some people might see you, and mummy might smack you' (North American boy, 7 years); 'They don't want to be seen. They'd maybe get into trouble with mum or dad. Anyway, they might get hurt' (English girl, 9 years).

Conventional answers (Scores 3 and 4)

'They don't want to show them. (Q) Those parts are smelly and ugly. And you'd be showing off. You'd wear something over them.

333

TABLE 15.7 Percentage* scores on 'Why should people be embarrassed?' scale, Kohlberg's 6 stages by country and age-year (N=838)

Age-year	Australia						England						North America						Sweden					
	1	2	3	4	5	6	1	2	3	4	5	6	1	2	3	4	5	6	1	2	3	4	5	6
5	3	40	13	—	—	—	—	20	38	—	—	—	—	38	25	—	—	—	—	26	30	3	—	—
7	—	23	40	13	—	—	—	20	40	—	3	—	3	23	53	—	—	—	—	20	40	13	—	—
9	—	15	40	28	5	—	3	10	45	20	5	3	—	20	40	23	3	—	—	10	63	10	—	—
11	—	8	23	35	23	3	—	10	18	30	23	3	—	13	17	47	17	—	—	3	50	27	17	3
13	—	13	23	30	23	—	—	10	18	58	10	3	—	18	24	30	27	—	—	3	43	30	23	—
15	—	8	18	38	23	10	—	3	23	53	18	3	—	7	10	45	27	3	—	—	37	27	33	—

(* Zero scores are not included.)

(Q) They'd not like to show their dinkle' (English boy, 7 years); 'Because others would laugh at them. It's not funny to me. Why, my mum takes her clothes off and I'm taking a nap and I peep and I don't laugh' (North American boy, 7 years); 'Maybe they don't like their body, they think they look awful. They have lots of freckles on them, and maybe their bust is too small or too large' (English girl, 11 years); 'Girls and boys are different and they'd be shy at seeing each other. If it's just men its O.K.' (Australian boy, 9 years); 'It's in the interests of privacy. You don't show your sex organs. (Q Why not?) We like to reserve certain things to ourselves' (Australian girl, 13 years); 'Everyone wears clothes now and they think it's rude to show the privates. They probably a long time ago made a rule which spread. (Q) Don't know the original reason, but you've got to accept it' (English boy, 11 years); 'No. I'm not beautiful enough and I feel safer with clothes on. You may have too big breasts and be an early maturer, and you don't want to be teased' (Swedish girl, 15 years).

Post-conventional (Scores 5 and 6)

'After several generations, people wouldn't be embarrassed, like the Africans they're not' (English boy, 11 years); 'You were born with nothing on. There's no reason to be embarrassed. But if people haven't gone naked for a long time, since civilisation, it could be regarded as wrong' (Australian boy, 11 years); 'They're ashamed because they are taught it's rude to show the parts of a man and woman. They're told they are private parts. And many people don't understand their sex organs and won't show them' (North American girl, 15 years); 'Boys might have an erection or girls might have a period. It would be embarrassing. Normally we don't go to a formal dance with nothing on. But it's been going on so long, because Europeans started in a cold place' (Australian boy, 15 years).

The results of the scoring on this item are set out in Table 15.7. The same problems of scoring were evident here as for the previous question, since only a few scored in the lowest category, and the highest scores of universalisms were difficult to detect, even by inference. There is no clear scaling on a symmetrical pattern although scores do increase perceptibly with age. In the English-speaking countries stage 4 appears to be achieved by the largest percentage at 15 years – the law and order argument – with Sweden showing the highest scores at 15 years, 33 per cent at the social contract by consensus stage.

However, when the scores are collapsed from the six stages to Kohlberg's three levels the pattern is much clearer (see Table 15.8).

The conventional arguments dominate in all countries from 7 years onwards, very markedly from 9 years of age, with a much lower proportion of high scores than in the previous question. What depresses the scores is the large number of 'don't knows' at the younger age levels, and also an unusual proportion at other ages. Again, one may argue that this is one indication of level of difficulty; the question may be too unfamiliar and children either cannot answer or regress cognitively in order to resolve the problem at a lower level. It is probable in these circumstances that conventional thinking will tend to dominate.

TABLE 15.8   *Percentages* of responses on 'Why should people be embarrassed?' scale, Kohlberg's three levels by country and age-year (N = 838)*

Age-year	Australia			England			North America			Sweden		
	1	2	3	1	2	3	1	2	3	1	2	3
5	38	15	–	20	38	–	33	25	4	27	33	–
7	25	50	–	20	40	3	20	53	–	20	53	–
9	15	68	5	10	65	8	20	63	3	10	73	–
11	8	58	25	10	48	25	13	63	17	3	73	23
13	12	53	23	10	73	15	18	55	26	3	73	23
15	8	53	35	3	75	20	7	55	26	–	63	33

(*Zero scores are not included. 1 = pre-conventional; 2 = conventional; 3 = post-conventional.)

This is evident when the mean scores are examined (see Table 15.9 and its graphic presentation in Figure 15.2). Since this is based upon the 6-point scale (Kohlberg's 6 stages), no age group in any country, not even at the 15 year level, attains a mean score of 4.00. The nearest is the Australian 15-year-olds (3.90) with the North American 15-year-olds at 3.53 mean score. The difficulty of the item may well also be related to the influence of sexual inhibitions in discussing matters directly relating to the sex organs.

Considerable sex differences are evident in practically every age group in the English-speaking countries where boys consistently and markedly achieve higher scores than the girls (the exception is the Australian 15-year-old where boys and girls score equally). These sex differences are evident also in the Swedish sample where 13- and 15-year-old boys achieve markedly higher scores than the girls in those age groups. The one exception in Sweden is the opposite direction where the 7-year-old Swedish girls score significantly higher than Swedish 7-year-old boys. We would identify these as genuine sex differences, confirmed by ANOVA results (see Appendix D) not apparently affected

TABLE 15.9 *Mean scores on 'Why should people be embarrassed?'*
scale by country and age-year (N = 838)

Age-year	Australia	England	North America	Sweden
5	1.18	1.53*	1.44*	1.57
7	2.15*	1.73*	2.04*	2.13*
9	2.85*	2.75*	2.70*	2.50
11	3.50*	3.20*	3.47*	3.67
13	3.25*	3.68*	3.69*	3.73
15	3.90	3.85*	3.53	3.83

(*Significant sex differences: see Table B.26, Appendix B.)

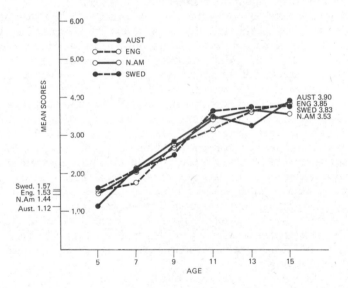

Figure 15.2 Mean scores on 'Why should people be embarrassed?'
Kohlberg's 6 stage scale by country and age-year

by interviewer differences, revealing we believe a greater willingness by
boys to explore the problem of why nakedness would embarrass some
people. Even so, male mean scores in only a few age cohorts achieve
more than 4.00 (the highest is 4.20 scored by 15-year-old Swedish and
English boys) drawing attention to the difficulty of this item for even
the oldest children in the sample.

Summary and discussion

Three areas were explored in relation to the wearing of clothes and nakedness, to see what proportions of children would regard clothing as necessary in a very warm climate, what reasons they would advance to justify the wearing or not wearing of clothes, and to explore children's explanations of feelings of embarrassment or guilt in revealing sex organs when in a state of nakedness. Kohlberg's three levels of pre-conventional, conventional and post-conventional thinking were used as scoring criteria. Most children in the English-speaking countries asserted that clothes were necessary, even in very warm climates, the most insistent being the North American children and the least being the Australian. The majority of Swedish children from 5 to 11 asserted that clothing would not be necessary in such circumstances. Some sex differences were noted in some countries.

Both questions involving the giving of reasons for the wearing of clothes and why people felt shy or embarrassed at being naked, were difficult for children, scores being low on the first question and even lower on the second. While Kohlberg's six stages were not seen in sequential stages, his three levels were quite clearly in evidence; on the wearing of clothes post-conventional thinking became evident at 15 years with Australian children the highest (80 per cent). On the embarrassment at nakedness question those achieving post-conventional thinking at 15 years were much lower at 15 years; the highest being Australian children (35 per cent) and the lowest the English (20 per cent). When subjected to Pearson's product-moment correlation, the correlation between the two sets of scores was significant at 0.85, despite a large number of zero scores in the second question. The modal score for all countries from 7 years was that of conventional thinking. Genuine sex differences were in evidence, boys of practically all ages scoring significantly higher than girls on the 'embarrassment' question in English-speaking countries, and also at the Swedish 13- and 15-year levels.

Several interesting issues are raised by the results reported. The first is that the opinions of the English-speaking children differ considerably from the Swedish children in asserting clothes are necessary even in very warm climates. The most insistent are the North American children, the least being the Australian. The rank order of opinions — North America, England, Australia — reflect a gradation of climate, especially in winter, among the 5- to 11-year-olds possibly indicating a 'protectionist theory' for the wearing of clothes. The Swedish exception, where winters are as severe and mild summers are relatively short, would appear to indicate that cultural influence may be stronger than climate, supporting current anthropological theories (Cordwell and Schwarz,

1979). In Sweden sex education is compulsory in all schools from the age of 8, and the social acceptance of a more open approach to sex, illegitimacy and related matters may well influence children's judgments. This cultural difference is not so evident when the reasons for wearing clothes, and why people should feel embarrassed when naked, are examined. In all four countries reasons are dominantly 'protectionist' and in terms of Kohlberg's stages dominantly conventional. It is clear that the questions were difficult for children, scores being low on the first question and even lower on the second. While Kohlberg's six stages were not seen in sequential stages, his three levels were quite clearly in evidence; on the wearing of clothes post-conventional thinking became evident at 15 years with Australian children the highest (80 per cent) and the English the lowest (28 per cent). On the embarrassment at nakedness question those achieving post-conventional thinking at 15 years were much lower; the highest being Australian children (35 per cent) and the lowest the English (20 per cent). When subjected to Pearson's product-moment correlation the correlation between the two sets of scores was significant at 0.85, despite a large number of zero scores in the second question. The modal score for all countries from 7 years onwards was that of conventional thinking. Interestingly this is one of the few items where the main effects of country are not significant (see ANOVA results, Table D.3). This low-level thinking about sexual dilemmas has been noted in other studies (Gilligan *et al.*, 1971) and is evident in other sections of this current study.

The picture revealed by the children's perceptions in this area illustrates societies where the wearing of clothes is rationalised on moral grounds, and nakedness, particularly sexual nakedness, is still strongly tinged with guilt. While younger children do reflect an innocence about the issues raised, older children are well aware of the need for conformity and the social sanctions to be faced if the 'natural' naked state were to be taken too far. Teenagers, particularly, show sensitivity to physical and sexual abnormalities, sometimes imagined, and reflect an overwhelmingly conventional law-and-order morality, with a poor grasp of universal ethical principles even at 15 years of age. While Swedish children appear to be less inhibited about nakedness, their thinking levels in matters relating to clothes and nakedness show no higher scores than the children in the English-speaking samples.

It was obvious from many children's responses that low-level thinking was conveyed primarily through parents' modesty training, and that the need for personal body privacy is a strongly inducted value in the four societies in this study. Finkelhor's (1980) findings and those of other studies cited are substantiated by these results. Whether children are less embarrassed by nakedness, or even the thought of it, than previous generations, cannot be deduced from the evidence produced here. It does indicate, however, that the sex education process in home or school has to overcome well-entrenched adult mythologies and rationalisations which prevent children from understanding, accepting and even enjoying the physical body and its sex organs as natural and normal.

16　Children's understanding of sexual vocabulary

As has been noted in chapter 9, children do have a sexual vocabulary of their own, whose terms are not 'clinically correct' words, to identify in particular the sex organs. The anatomically accurate vocabulary is often regarded as 'rude', so substitute words, which we have called sexual pseudonyms, are invented for private conversation presumably allowable in restricted circles. As Wilson has pointed out so succinctly, 'The domination of language in this sphere, as in others, cannot be overestimated, we can only think and talk in available words...' (1965, p. 111). Recognising the distinction just outlined as 'an appalling fission in our language', Wilson comments (ibid.),

> On the one hand there exist clinical words or polite euphemisms ('anus', 'vagina', 'sleeping with', 'orgasm'): on the other there exist the words in common usage (the reader may supply these for himself). The former are totally unreal to anyone except a biologist or doctor; the latter are forbidden in public usage. This means, virtually, that it is impossible to talk straight.

During the trial interviews, whilst the interview schedule was being revised, the factor of sexual vocabulary was evident to the investigators. It became very clear that unless a common vocabulary can be used in thinking about and discussing sexual matters, then communication in this area is bound to be limited. Ten important sexual words were therefore added to the interview, to see if the children were familiar with them ('Have you heard the word...?') and understood their meaning ('Can you tell me what it means?'). The choice of this vocabulary list may well be criticised, since many important words were excluded because of limitations of time. Some were excluded because they would be covered in the course of the interview, and some because in the investigators' judgment they transgressed what might be acceptable

341

to parents. Among these were words involving homosexuality and masturbation, the latter causing such embarrassment during the trial interviews when added to that vocabulary list, it had to be excluded, a sad indication in itself of the state of communication about sexuality. The authors recognise that another ten words could be justified for inclusion and do not claim their list to be comprehensive or exhaustive, but it is sufficiently wide to test out children's comprehension of the meaning attached to 'key' words. One major purpose was to see what differences, if any, there were between the various countries, particularly Sweden where most of the words listed are used as part of the accepted vocabulary in sex education programmes.

The children, almost at the end of the interview, were told, 'Here are some words children (students) are sometimes taught about in lessons. For each word tell me if you've ever heard it before, and tell me what you think it means.' The words were then read out one at a time, the interviewer writing down verbatim the response, encouraging the children to attempt a definition or enlarge upon their response if it was not clear. The vocabulary list is set out below:

Pregnancy
Conception
Stripping
Rape
Venereal disease
Uterus
Puberty
Virgin
Contraception
Abortion

To help the children, without providing clues, some slight variations were given such as 'pregnant', or 'to conceive'. Only the first two words were asked of the 5- and 7-year-olds, since an increasing level of difficulty was observed after the first two words which the younger children could not deal with at any meaningful level. Children from 9 to 15 were asked all 10 words; with the Australian sample there was one additional word 'rooting' which will be discussed towards the end of this chapter.

The criteria for scoring the words were standard, outlined in Table 16.1. Each word, however, had its own criteria for scores 3 and 4, which were drawn up after discussions with biologists and sexologists. The general descriptions are set out in Appendix B, and the specific criteria are discussed as each word in the vocabulary is introduced.

TABLE 16.1   *Criteria for scoring sexual vocabulary items*

Score	Code	Category
0	–	Not asked (younger children were asked only limited vocabulary).
1	–	Don't know; no response; can't remember.
2	TI	Totally inappropriate, including all 'nonsense' answers.
3	PA	Partially appropriate; not meeting all criteria required.
4	FA	Fully appropriate. Meets all required criteria.

The meaning of pregnancy

The criteria for score 3 was 'the physical state of a mother carrying an embryo, foetus or baby' and criteria for score 4 would include one of the following features: location in the womb, reference to the gestation period of approximately nine months, foetal growth, or the outcome of a fertilised egg. Technically correct terms were not taken into account as long as the meaning was clear. Also included in the FA (Fully Appropriate answer – score 4) was any literal, non-sexual meaning, 'being full' or 'satiated'. Below some examples are given to illustrate the categories.

Totally inappropriate answers (TI: Score 2)

'It's like a place, like a restaurant' (Australian boy, 7 years); 'It's when you pray to God to give you a baby' (North American girl, 5 years); 'A German word for saying "Be Quiet!"' (English boy, 5 years).

Partially appropriate answers (PA: Score 3)

'Mum's going to have a baby real soon. You're pregnant, the baby's expected' (North American boy, 9 years); 'When your stomach gets bigger and there's a baby inside' (Swedish girl, 11 years); 'To carry a baby, that's all' (English boy, 9 years).

Fully appropriate answers (FA: Score 4)

'When the lady is in the 9 months carrying a baby' (Australian boy, 13 years); 'The period when the sperm and egg unite until the baby is born' (English girl, 15 years); 'The baby is carried by the mother, a baby is started. Literally it means something is full of something' (North American boy, 15 years).

The scores for pregnancy are set out in Table 16.2. Only partially and fully appropriate percentages of scores are included, to obtain a clearer picture. At first glance it would appear that most children in the English-speaking countries seem to have a general idea of what pregnancy means at 7 years in the English and North American and at 9 years in the Australian sample, whereas in the Swedish sample this generalised meaning is never present in any substantial proportion, except at 11 years (33 per cent). The Swedish children clearly move to a fully appropriate meaning at the age of 11 years, whereas this is only attained by about 50 per cent at 15 years of age in the English and North American samples. In the Australian sample only 38 per cent at 15 years achieve a fully appropriate meaning compared with Sweden's 87 per cent. The time-lag in the Swedish sample may be explained by official school age not beginning until 7 years and the subsequent increase due to continued usage of the word 'pregnancy' during sex education lessons. The results are surprisingly low in view of the fact that all children in the sample had at least one younger sibling and had been present in the family situation when mother was pregnant.

TABLE 16.2 *Percentages of partially and fully appropriate responses on 'meaning of pregnancy' by country and age-year (N = 838)*

Age-year	Australia		England		North America		Sweden	
	PA	FA	PA	FA	PA	FA	PA	FA
5	30	–	35	–	21	–	–	–
7	37	3	60	8	60	–	7	–
9	77	18	77	13	87	3	7	20
11	80	20	82	18	83	13	33	50
13	73	27	55	45	70	30	17	77
15	62	38	48	50	48	52	13	87

(Only scores 3 and 4 are included: PA = partially appropriate; FA = fully appropriate.)

The mean scores for each age cohort are set out in Table 16.3 which clearly illustrates the Swedish 'catching up' at 11 years, and their higher scoring at 13 and 15 years. There are no marked sex differences in scores except among the English 7-year-olds, where girls in this cohort score significantly higher than boys. This may be accounted for by the fact that girls as future child-bearers may be more motivated than boys, although one would expect this to be so across all age cohorts if it represented a genuine sex difference.

TABLE 16.3   *Mean scores on 'meaning of pregnancy' responses by country and age-year (N = 838)*

Age-year	Australia	England	North America	Sweden
5	1.45	1.73	1.60	–
7	1.85	2.48*	2.19	0.27
9	3.10	2.95	2.84	1.04
11	3.20	3.18	3.07	3.03
13	3.28	3.45	3.30	3.70
15	3.38	3.48	3.52	3.87

(*Girls score significantly higher: see Table B.26, Appendix B.)

The meaning of conception

The criterion for partially appropriate answers (score 3) was 'When a baby is started' and seen as related to sexual intercourse. Fully appropriate answers (score 4) were scored on more specific terms; 'the act of fertilisation of the mother's egg by father's sperm' or 'the implantation of a fertilised egg in the wall of the womb'. Also included in the highest score was the non-sexual intellectual concept, rarely given by respondents, of 'thinking up an idea'. Some examples of scoring at the three levels (TI, PA and FA levels) are given below:

Totally inappropriate answers (Score 2)

'Is it a fluoride?' (English boy, 9 years); 'Is it to tell the future?' (North American girl, 11 years); 'I think it means "instead of"' (Australian boy, 11 years); 'It sounds like contraception, but I don't really know' (English girl, 15 years).

Partially appropriate answers (Score 3)

'Actually having sex, what you've done before to make the baby come' (Australian boy, 13 years); 'When the mother just starts to have a baby, or is it stopping the baby? No that's contraception' (North American girl, 13 years); 'Something to do with having sex and getting a baby' (English girl, 11 years); 'Yes, something to do with the flowers and the bees, beginning a new life' (Swedish boy, 9 years).

Fully appropriate answers (Score 4)

'Where the actual baby is made, when the sperm and egg meet' English boy, 15 years); 'Fertilisation, the moment the baby is

345

started during sexual intercourse' (North American girl, 15 years);
'It's when the man fertilises the woman's egg with his sperm'
(Swedish girl, 15 years).

Table 16.4 sets out the results and indicates how limited knowledge
of the meaning of this word is in the English-speaking samples. Partially
appropriate answers marginally begin to occur only at 11 years but are
very sparse even among the teenagers. At 15 years the Australian sample
have the highest proportion (40 per cent) with the North American and
English samples 27 per cent and 25 per cent respectively of fully appropriate answers. The Swedish children are much further ahead at every
age from 7 years on, almost all (93 per cent) achieving full understanding
of the word by 15 years.

TABLE 16.4　*Percentages of partially and fully appropriate responses
on 'meaning of conception' by country and age-year
(N = 838)*

Age-year	Australia		England		North America		Sweden	
	PA	FA	PA	FA	PA	FA	PA	FA
5	–	–	–	–	–	–	–	–
7	–	–	–	–	–	–	10	20
9	–	–	3	–	3	–	13	23
11	10	–	–	8	3	3	27	57
13	13	3	–	8	–	6	37	53
15	5	40	25	25	13	27	3	93

(Only scores 3 and 4 are included: PA = partially appropriate; FA = fully
appropriate.)

This can be seen more clearly when the mean scores are examined
(see Table 16.5). In the English-speaking countries sex differences are
noted in the Australian 9- and 11-year cohorts, in the North American
11-year cohort, and the English 13-year-old cohort, where the boys
score significantly higher than the girls. In the Swedish sample the 9-,
11- and 13-year cohorts show the girls' scores significantly higher than
the boys'. This may reflect some cultural differences in understanding
the word 'conception' on the part of the sexes but the evidence is
inconclusive.

The meaning of stripping

Vocabulary from this word onwards were asked only of the 9- to 15-
year-olds, as explained previously. The criterion for a general but
partially appropriate score on stripping was 'the removing of apparel

TABLE 16.5   *Mean scores on 'meaning of conception' responses by country and age-year (N = 838)*

Age-year	Australia	England	North America	Sweden
5	–	–	–	0.30
7	–	–	–	1.37
9	1.13*	1.03	1.14	1.84**
11	1.30*	1.33	1.27*	3.30**
13	1.45	1.43*	1.25	3.30**
15	2.55	2.48	2.22	3.84

(* Boys score significantly higher; ** Girls score significantly higher: see Table B.27, Appendix B.)

to be naked or partially naked'. To qualify for score 4, fully appropriate, an added feature had to be present such as 'removing in a sexually provocative manner', or 'the forcible removal of clothing for sexual stimulation'. The common usage for stripping, removing a covering from an object, such as paint or the bark of a tree, was included in the definition. Some examples of answers at the various levels (TI, PA and FA) are given below:

Totally inappropriate answers (Score 2)

> 'It's when you strip on a sheet of ice or in the mud and fall over' (North American boy, 9 years); 'When you use the wrong word by mistake' (English girl, 11 years).

Partially appropriate answers (Score 3)

> 'Taking off all your clothes' (Australian boy, 9 years); 'Take off your clothes and get into other clothes or get into the bath' (English girl, 9 years); 'When a man strips clothes off a lady. (Q) Don't know' (North American boy, 11 years); 'Taking all your clothes off and walks around outside' (Australian girl, 13 years).

Fully appropriate answers (Score 4)

> 'A stripper. A lady is fully dressed and starts taking things off slowly 'til it's rude' (English boy, 11 years); 'When you take your clothes off, girls that is, men get thrills of it' (Australian girl, 15 years); 'A girl that undresses in a teasing way, on a stage, accompanied by music. In a sex club' (Swedish boy, 15 years); 'A man and a woman undress each other before sex, it's kind of exciting' (North American boy, 13 years).

347

The results are set out in Table 16.6. While the more generalised meaning is understood by most 9-year-olds, its sexual meaning in the English-speaking countries is not fully grasped by many of the respondents even at 15 years. The highest proportion of scores are the English (23 per cent) and the lowest the North American (10 per cent) among 15-year-olds. The latter is interesting in view of the fact that only a few blocks from some of the schools used in this study were well advertised (with neon signs) lunch-time strip clubs for workers from the nearby factories. The proportions of Swedish 9-year-olds with an understanding of the word's sexual meaning at 9 years (27 per cent) exceeds that of older age groups in the English-speaking countries, and the percentage of the highest scores is over 70 per cent among Swedish 13- and 15-year-olds.

TABLE 16.6 *Percentages of partially and fully appropriate responses on 'meaning of stripping' by country and age-years 9 to 15 (N = 564)*

Age-year	Australia		England		North America		Sweden	
	PA	FA	PA	FA	PA	FA	PA	FA
9	90	5	75	8	67	7	–	27
11	82	18	92	8	77	20	40	40
13	82	18	77	23	76	18	3	77
15	80	20	77	23	87	10	23	73

(Only scores 3 and 4 are included: PA = partially appropriate; FA = fully appropriate.)

TABLE 16.7 *Mean scores on 'meaning of stripping' responses, by country and age-years 9 to 15 (N = 564)*

Age-year	Australia	England	North America	Sweden
9	2.93	2.68	2.56	1.20
11	3.18	3.07	3.14	2.87
13	3.18	3.23	3.06	3.20
15	3.20	3.18	3.03	3.64*

(* Boys score significantly higher than girls: see Table B.27, Appendix B.)

The higher scoring by Swedish children is again illustrated in Table 16.7. When the mean scores are perused the Swedish slower start is obvious as is also the catching up and higher scores in the later age groups. The only significant sex differences in scoring are in the Swedish 15-year-old sample where the boys achieve much higher scores than the girls. This may be explained in terms of boy's awareness that the word is related to sexual excitement, and thus may be more motivated to retain the meaning of the word. The majority of both boys and girls in Sweden tended to associate stripping as a female activity for the purposes of exciting the male.

The meaning of rape

Rape may be defined as the forcing of a person for the purpose of sexual intercourse or penetration against his or her will. In scoring partially appropriate (PA) answers, the criterion used was if the answer contained one of the following: seizure of a person by violence or the act of carnal knowledge or sexual intercourse. Fully appropriate (FA) answers included seizure by violence and a sexual act committed against the victim's will. Total or partial removal of clothing may be included, but were not counted as an integral part of an FA answer. Some examples of the scoring are given below:

Totally inappropriate answers (Score 2)

'To go into someone's house, take all the clothes off the dresser, and steal them' (Australian boy, 9 years); 'If a child is asleep inside the house, someone can go in and take the child' (English girl, 9 years); 'When someone makes someone pregnant' (North American boy, 9 years).

Partially appropriate answers (Score 3)

'Taking off your clothes, like it's a fight. Like a guy does it to anyone' (North American boy, 9 years); 'When a drunk, a boy, tries to take a girl's clothes off and she doesn't want to' (English girl, 11 years); 'A man ties up ladies and stabs them or mainly beats them or rips their clothes' (Australian boy, 9 years); 'When someone tries to make you pregnant' (Swedish girl, 11 years).

Fully appropriate answers (Score 4)

'Like a peeping Tom, a sex maniac grabs a girl and makes her do things she don't want to, like sex. I seen it on TV' (Australian boy, 9 years); 'When a man sexually abuses a lady and she doesn't want to. It was in "All in the Family" ' (North American girl, 11 years); 'When a man forces a woman to take off her clothes, and tries to make love. He doesn't know her. He might hit her' (English boy, 15 years); 'When a strange man forces someone to have sexual intercourse. It needn't be a stranger' (Swedish girl, 15 years);

'When a guy has sex with a lady who doesn't want to, or a guy doing it to another guy — it's in the paper a lot. (Q) Ladies don't rape guys. They aren't strong enough' (North American boy, 13 years).

The results of the scoring are set out in Table 16.8. In the English-speaking samples partially appropriate answers are given by the majority by 11 years and at 13 years the majority move up to fully appropriate responses. The Australian samples show the greater proportion of teenagers scoring at the fully appropriate level. The Swedish sample at 11 years indicates 47 per cent fully appropriate level of answers and 87 per cent at this level by 13 years. By 15 years the English-speaking countries have caught up with Sweden, and all Australian 15-year-olds are at the fully appropriate level of answer. We would postulate that this fairly high level of knowledge in all countries, compared with other words on the vocabulary list, is largely due to widespread publicity in the media, not only in news items but in TV drama series, as some of the responses suggest. There were clearly significant sex differences in the English-speaking countries in that all boys in the teenage groups scored significantly higher than teenage girls, in addition English 9- and North American 11-year-old boys scored significantly higher than the girls in those cohorts (see Table B.27, Appendix B).

TABLE 16.8 *Percentages of partially and fully appropriate responses on 'meaning of rape' by country and age-years 9 to 15 (N = 564)*

Age-year	Australia		England		North America		Sweden	
	PA	FA	PA	FA	PA	FA	PA	FA
9	43	5	28	3	10	7	3	10
11	60	25	45	38	63	10	23	47
13	23	73	33	65	30	64	13	87
15	—	100	13	87	13	87	13	86

(Only scores 3 and 4 are included: PA = partially appropriate; FA = fully appropriate.)

To determine if any respondents realised that rape could be committed by either sex on the other, by homosexuals or lesbians on a member of the same sex, or if multiple gang rape existed, as distinct from the 'man on woman' stereotype, an additional question was asked of those who gave a fully appropriate answer. (This additional question was not asked in Sweden.) The results are set out in Table 16.9 showing the percentage of all responses made which conveyed additional understanding beyond the stereotyped 'man on woman'

TABLE 16.9   *Percentages of those who define 'rape' as not confined to man on woman by country and age-years 9 to 15 (N = 444)*

Age-year	Australia	England	North America	Sweden
9	3	3*	3	
11	3	10	3	not asked
13	28*	20*	27*	
15	40*	23*	26*	

(* Boys score significantly higher than girls.)

concept. By the teenage years about 1 in 4 had gained this more inclusive concept, the highest proportion (40 per cent) among Australian 15-year-olds.

The mean scores are not included since they were somewhat distorted by the omission of Sweden. However, in the English-speaking countries in all age groups with two exceptions, boys score significantly higher than girls in understanding the full meaning of rape. The two exceptions are North American 9-year-olds and Australian 11-year-olds, where the boys exceed the girls' scoring but not significantly. In the Swedish sample, boys score significantly higher than girls at 11 years and exceed girls' scores at 13 and 15 years. We postulate genuine sex differences in the understanding of the word rape. This may be explained in terms of girls' repugnance and natural unwillingness to recognise an event which might happen to them. In this sense a boy may be more detached and less inhibited to learn and retain the meaning of the word.

The meaning of venereal disease

The initials VD were used in putting the question first, the full words 'venereal disease' being then added if there was no comprehension. The singular, 'disease', was used as the popular form, although the plural 'diseases' is more technically correct.

Partially appropriate answers were scored, if they described sexual intercourse as the cause, or if 'uncleanness', 'too much' sex or 'too many' sexual partners were cited as causes. If they named the major diseases, syphilis and gonorrhoea, these alone constituted only a partially appropriate answer. Similarly scored were answers describing VD's effects on babies or future fertility. A fully appropriate answer had to include the following: VD is caused by sexual intercourse with an infected person and in addition *either* the symptoms are usually on or in the sex organ(s) *or* the major diseases are named. Some examples of responses are given below:

Totally inappropriate answers (Score 2)

'I've heard of disease where you cough a lot and have the measles' (English boy, 9 years); 'It's an affection [*sic*] disease. (Q) Having a baby they get sick and have a disease' (Australian girl, 9 years).

Partially appropriate answers (Score 3)

'A type of cancer caused by sex at too young an age' (North American boy, 13 years); 'A disease you get from dirty toilets, that's what my Mum says. At school, in an English language class on "Abbreviations" a boy asked what VD was and the teacher got cross and wouldn't tell him' (English girl, 11 years); 'A disease so you can't wee wee' (Swedish boy, 9 years); 'It's an inflammation in the sex organs' (Swedish girl, 11 years); 'A disease you can get through sexual intercourse or through petting' (Swedish girl, 15 years).

Fully appropriate answers (Score 4)

'When men and women have a disease after sexual intercourse with several men and women who've got the germs. It's a disease on the sex parts of the body' (Australian boy, 11 years); 'Vagina diseases which a woman has when an old man has sexual intercourse with her and passes it on to her. (Q) Syphilis and gonorrhoea' (North American girl, 13 years); 'Diseases, for instance, syphilis and gonorrhoea. You only get it through sexual intercourse with someone infected' (Swedish boy, 15 years).

The results are to be seen in Table 16.10 which indicates a paucity of knowledge by the age of 13 years and only a generalised partially appropriate knowledge at 15 years. There is little difference between countries, with a slightly greater proportion of Swedish 13-year-olds scoring at the partially appropriate level (57 per cent) and a slightly higher proportion of English 15-year-olds at the partially appropriate level (85 per cent). The mean scores illustrate the similarities between countries (see Table 16.11). There are some differences between the sexes, the English 9-year-old boys and Australian boys at 15 years scoring significantly higher than the girls. Overall, however, there appears to be no genuine sex differences, the boys and girls equally sharing ignorance. In view of the high incidence of gonorrhoea in all four countries, reported in chapter 2, this lack of knowledge appears to be quite serious. It confirms other research findings, particularly reports of infected young persons interviewed (Holmes, Nicol and Stubbs, 1968).

TABLE 16.10   *Percentages of partially and fully appropriate responses on 'meaning of venereal disease' by country and age-years 9 to 15 (N = 564)*

Age year	Australia		England		North America		Sweden	
	PA	FA	PA	FA	PA	FA	PA	FA
9	–	–	–	–	3	–	3	–
11	15	–	3	–	17	–	33	–
13	43	3	53	–	52	–	57	3
15	70	20	85	10	77	20	70	20

(Only scores 3 and 4 are included: PA = partially appropriate; FA = fully appropriate.)

TABLE 16.11   *Mean scores of responses on 'meaning of venereal disease' by country and age-years 9 to 15 (N = 564)*

Age-year	Australia	England	North America	Sweden
9	1.13	0.98*	1.10	0.30
11	1.35	1.10	1.47	1.34
13	2.00	2.13	2.06	2.14
15	3.03*	3.00	3.13	2.97

(*Boys scoring significantly higher than girls: see Table B.27, Appendix B.)

The meaning of uterus

Partially appropriate scores were given where one of the following answers was given: a female organ, another name for 'womb', an organ which receives sperm following coitus, or any vague description of where the baby is during a pregnancy. A fully appropriate answer had to contain the two facts that the uterus is a female organ and it accommodates the embryo during pregnancy. Although other factors may be included in the definition both these two basics had to be included. Examples of the various levels of responses are presented below:

Totally inappropriate answers (Score 2)

'It's something in your body. (Q) The boy's body. Is it the sacks?' (North American boy, 11 years); 'It's a tunnel somewhere in Switzerland' (English girl, 9 years); 'Something to do with your penis or something' (Australian boy, 11 years).

Partially appropriate answers (Score 3)

'Where the baby's developing' (Australian boy, 11 years); 'One of the places in a girl near your "wound"' (Australian girl, 11 years); 'It's part of a lady's body' (North American girl, 13 years); 'The tube leading from the womb to the ovaries' (English girl, 13 years); 'In the lady between the hips, it's in the opening of the female's vagina' (English boy, 13 years); 'The textbook word for womb. It's in the woman isn't it?' (Swedish boy, 15 years).

Fully appropriate answers (Score 4)

'The place inside the female where the egg develops into a child. The womb' (Australian girl, 15 years); 'Where the baby lies in the mother's stomach. It's just above the vagina. Where the foetus develops' (Swedish boy, 15 years).

The results of the meaning of the word 'uterus' are to be seen in Table 16.12. In the English-speaking countries there is no real grasp of its meaning until 13 years and then only at the partially appropriate level. There is little progress to fully appropriate answers by 15 years. In contrast the Swedish sample reveals a much greater proportion of partially appropriate and fully appropriate answers from the age of 9 years with almost a majority understanding the word by 13 years. This probably reflects the use of the word over several years of sex education in school, but even in describing it many Swedish children still use the word 'stomach' to describe the uterus. Ninety-three per cent of Swedish children at 15 years understand its full meaning.

TABLE 16.12 *Percentages of partially and fully appropriate responses to 'meaning of uterus' by country and age-years 9 to 15 (N = 564)*

Age year	Australia		England		North America		Sweden	
	PA	FA	PA	FA	PA	FA	PA	FA
9	3	–	–	–	–	–	13	23
11	15	–	10	–	–	–	33	43
13	35	5	48	3	27	12	7	73
15	70	13	68	13	71	23	3	93

(Only scores 3 and 4 are included: PA = partially appropriate; FA = fully appropriate.)

The high scoring contrast can be seen in the mean scores (see Table 16.13) at the 13-year level and again at the 15-year level. There is only

TABLE 16.13   *Mean scores of responses on 'meaning of uterus' by country and age-years 9 to 15 (N = 564)*

Age year	Australia	England	North America	Sweden
9	1.08	0.93	1.23	1.77
11	1.35	1.23	1.50	3.13
13	1.85	2.18	2.00	3.44
15	2.78	2.75	3.09	3.90

one age group where the scores differ between the sexes, the Swedish 11-year-olds where girls score higher than boys but not significantly. This, however, is insufficient to establish any overall sex differences in understanding the word uterus, although one might expect girls to know the name of a vital part of their own anatomy more than the boys. It is astonishing that so many 15-year-old girls in particular, in the English-speaking countries, are so vague about the meaning of 'uterus'.

The meaning of puberty

'Puberty' was scored as partially appropriate when any primary or secondary characteristics were described as indicating a time when the body or person matured. These descriptions alone were not enough to qualify for a fully appropriate score. The criteria for this were both the description and the biological significance of puberty, namely 'The age or period of growth at which the sex organs in both male and female mature to make reproduction possible'. The latter part emphasising puberty as the time when reproduction, procreation, mating became possible was the essential ingredient of the definitions, however imperfectly expressed. Some examples of the scoring on these criteria can be seen below:

Totally inappropriate answers (Score 2)

'Is it something to do with eggs?' (Australian girl, 11 years); 'It's something to do with pregnancy, the time of the year the man releases the eggs' (English boy, 13 years).

Partially appropriate answers (Score 3)

'When people get hairs on their vagina and penis' (North American girl, 11 years); 'When you become a teenager and quarrel with your parents' (Swedish girl, 9 years); 'When a child becomes a teenager, and you start to take on adult features' (Australian boy, 13 years); 'Growing from child into adulthood, the physical and mental changes

355

from 13 years to 18 years. (Q) You get hair on sex parts' (English boy, 13 years); 'Your first period, when you've reached woman-hood' (Australian girl, 15 years).

Fully appropriate answers (Score 4)

'I think it's at 11, 12 or 13. It's the time you could have babies. Before that kids could have intercourse but no sperm and no eggs' Australian boy, 13 years); 'The age of biological change when you can have babies' (North American girl, 13 years); 'The age when you are sexually mature, girls menstruate and boys produce sperm' (Swedish girl, 15 years).

The distribution of scores can be seen in Table 16.14. In the English-speaking countries there is no real grasp of the meaning of puberty until 13 years and then only at the partially appropriate level. Progress to fully appropriate answers does not occur even at 15 years. In contrast the Swedish sample reveals a much greater proportion of partially and fully appropriate answers from the age of 11 years, with almost a majority understanding the word's meaning by 15 years. This probably reflects the use of the term 'puberty' over several years of sex education in school. The high scoring contrast can be seen in the mean score table (Table 16.15) particularly at the 13-year level and again at the 15-year level. There is one age group where the scores differ between the sexes: the Swedish 15-year-olds where the girls have significantly higher scores than the boys. It is odd, to say the least, that so few teenagers in the English-speaking countries can identify correctly the period of life they are passing through and voice its biological significance.

The meaning of virgin

Partially appropriate answers were scored where there was a general meaning given, where 'virgin' was vaguely seen as an unmarried person, or where it describes only a female who has not had sexual intercourse. This was a quite frequent assertion despite follow-up questioning. A fully appropriate answer was scored where either sex could be clearly identified as sexually inexperienced, that is, not to have had sexual intercourse. Included in this fuller meaning was any answer indicating inexperience in any activity such as 'virgin soldier' or 'virgin land', even if there was no sexual connotation involved. Some illustrations of typical responses are given below:

Totally inappropriate answers (Score 2)

'I think it's a story, a tale or something' (Australian boy, 11 years);

356

TABLE 16.14 *Percentages of partially and fully appropriate responses on 'meaning of puberty' by country and age-years 9 to 15 (N = 564)*

Age-year	Australia		England		North America		Sweden	
	PA	FA	PA	FA	PA	FA	PA	FA
9	–	–	–	–	–	–	3	–
11	8	–	5	–	–	–	37	17
13	43	3	63	3	55	9	77	20
15	88	5	88	3	94	3	57	43

(Only scores 3 and 4 are included: PA = partially appropriate; FA = fully appropriate.)

TABLE 16.15 *Mean scores of responses on 'meaning of puberty' by country and age-years 15 to 19 (N = 564)*

Age-year	Australia	England	North America	Sweden
9	1.03	0.93	1.10	0.27
11	1.23	1.13	1.23	2.17
13	1.93	2.35	2.39	3.17
15	2.90	2.83	2.97	3.44*

(* Girls scoring significantly higher than boys: see Table B.26, Appendix B.)

'A woman who believes in God, isn't her name Mary?' (English girl, 9 years); 'A little boy that's been looked after by parents' (North American girl, 9 years); 'I think it's the nationality of a person' (Australian boy, 11 years); 'Two ladies who get together' (North American boy, 13 years); 'There's a song ". . . she sailed a virgin, she sailed the sea". It's about love and sex' (English girl, 11 years); Is it a religion? Some people are virgins, they believe in what they want to believe' (North American boy, 13 years); 'Like a prostitute, she sells sex' (Australian girl, 13 years).

Partially appropriate answers (Score 3)

'When a lady hasn't made love' (Australian girl, 11 years); 'When a woman hasn't had sexual intercourse. (Q) I don't think it could be a man' (English boy, 13 years); 'In the Bible it says the baby was born to a virgin, probably someone who's not married' (North American girl, 11 years); 'A girl with her hymen intact' (Swedish girl, 15 years).

Fully appropriate answers (Score 4)

'When a boy or girl has not had sexual intercourse with someone' (Swedish girl, 15 years); 'If you've never had a root. (Q) A guy or a girl' (Australian girl, 11 years); 'A man who's always looking for a lady, and a lady who's always looking for a man. They haven't had it off with anyone yet' (English boy, 13 years).

The distribution of scores on the meaning of 'virgin' can be examined in Table 16.16. This is clearly a word more understood than most other words in the sexual vocabulary list by the English-speaking groups. Even so, the majority achieve the full both-sex meaning only by 15 years. The contrast with Sweden is again noticeable, the total percentage at 13 years with fully appropriate answers (70 per cent) being greater than the English (63 per cent) and North Americans (61 per cent) at 15 years. With 93 per cent of Swedish 15-year-olds achieving the highest score the disparity with the English-speaking groups is very apparent.

TABLE 16.16   *Percentages of partially and fully appropriate responses to 'meaning of virgin' by country and age-years 9 to 15 (N = 564)*

Age-year	Australia		England		North America		Sweden	
	PA	FA	PA	FA	PA	FA	PA	FA
9	—	—	5	—	3	—	3	3
11	10	8	8	15	13	—	20	13
13	20	48	35	38	27	39	3	70
15	17	83	28	63	29	61	3	93

(Only scores 3 and 4 are included: PA = partially appropriate; FA = fully appropriate.)

This is also evident when examining the mean scores in Table 16.17, particularly when comparing the teenage groups by country. There are no sex differences to report in mean scores except in Sweden, the 11-year-old girls scoring noticeably higher than the boys, the 13-year-old boys scoring noticeably higher than the girls but the results are not statistically significant. There are no general sex differences across countries.

The meaning of abortion

Although this area was explored earlier in the interview in the section 'Not having babies' and reported in chapter 13, and the meanings of 'abortion' and 'contraception' were asked at the conclusion of that

CHILDREN'S UNDERSTANDING OF SEXUAL VOCABULARY

TABLE 16.17 *Mean scores of responses on 'meaning of virgin' by country and age-years 15 to 19 (N = 564)*

Age year	Australia	England	North America	Sweden
9	1.08	1.38	1.34	0.70
11	1.70	1.83	1.60	1.67
13	2.95	2.90	2.86	3.17
15	3.87	3.50	3.49	3.90

discussion, the results are reported here since exactly the same questions were asked as for the other words on the sexual vocabulary list.

'Abortion' was scored as a partially appropriate answer when a vague explanation was given that it was something to do with ending a pregnancy; the definition given not meeting the three criteria for scoring a fully appropriate response. A partially appropriate response may meet one or two of these criteria but does not meet all of them. A fully appropriate response had to have all of the following ingredients: the termination of a pregnancy before it reached full term, resulting in the death of the embryo, foetus or baby. The method used, if described, was disregarded. Some examples of the types of answers are presented below.

Totally inappropriate answers (Score 2)

'Yes, you adopt one' (Australian girl, 9 years); 'It's something to do with a child after it's born' (English boy, 15 years); 'Maybe when the baby's at a certain stage, they call it that word' (North American girl, 11 years); 'It's when you going to have a baby' (North American boy, 9 years).

Partially appropriate answers (Score 3)

'An operation to dispose of a baby' (Australian boy, 13 years); 'The baby's killed. A needle piercing it kills it' (English girl, 15 years); 'Have an operation — the woman has — to stop eggs in her womb' (North American boy, 13 years); 'When the foetus is removed' (Australian girl, 15 years); 'The doctor does something so you can't have the baby. (Q) Don't know' (English boy, 11 years); 'It's an operation. The girl is cut like a cat being neutered, to take out the eggs' (North American boy, 11 years).

Fully appropriate answers (Score 4)

'Yes. One can kill the baby before the 12th week. One can use a saline solution' (Swedish girl, 15 years); 'When the foetus is taken

359

out of the placenta before it reaches 3 months. They suck it out with a vacuum. It dies' (Australian girl, 15 years); 'Speeding up the birth process long before it's due, so the baby is born dead' (English boy, 13 years); 'Abortion is to kill the baby before it comes out. They give it a drug. They say ladies fall over and that can kill the baby before time' (North American girl, 11 years).

The scores as set out in Table 16.18 show that the generalised meaning of abortion at a partially appropriate level is achieved in the English-speaking samples by 13 years and earlier, at 11 years, in the Swedish sample. Little more than 20 per cent achieve the highest score at 15 years in the English-speaking countries, while at the same age in Sweden 57 per cent score at the highest level. This topic is included in the syllabus in Sweden and pupils will have become familiar with the word and presumably more aware of its meaning.

TABLE 16.18 *Percentages of partially and fully appropriate responses to 'meaning of abortion' by country and age-years 9 to 15 (N = 564)*

Age-year	Australia		England		North America		Sweden	
	PA	FA	PA	FA	PA	FA	PA	FA
9	5	–	–	–	–	3	33	–
11	33	3	38	5	40	3	60	30
13	73	5	60	10	67	15	77	20
15	75	20	75	20	71	23	43	57

(Only scores 3 and 4 are included: PA = partially appropriate; FA = fully appropriate.)

TABLE 16.19 *Mean scores of responses on 'meaning of abortion' by country and age years 15 to 19 (N = 564)*

Age-year	Australia	England	North America	Sweden
9	1.35	1.10*	1.14	1.24
11	1.85	2.03	2.13	3.10
13	2.75	2.70	2.92*	3.13
15	3.15	3.10	3.16	3.57

(* Boys' score significantly higher than girls'.)

The figures giving mean scores in Table 16.19 illustrate this higher scoring from 11 years onwards, and the English-speaking 15-year-olds beginning to catch up. There are two age groups where scores differ significantly on this item, all in favour of boys, these being 9-year-old

English boys and 13-year-old North American boys. These do not, however, constitute a sufficient number to generalise about sex differences in response to this question.

When we compare these observations with the results of 'knowledge of abortion' scale in chapter 13, it is at once apparent that children's awareness of the possibility and process of abortion is in advance of their understanding of the vocabulary of abortion. This illustrates the fact that knowledge of a process is not dependent upon knowing the correct words, a truism aptly illustrated in this case. In other words, children know about the abortion process at 11 years whereas their knowledge of the meaning of the word itself was barely achieved by 15 years.

The meaning of contraception

This term was chosen rather than 'birth-control' because birth-control in itself is descriptive. It was also noted in the trial interviews, and subsequently in the later interviews, that in discussing 'not having babies' that the children rarely used 'birth-control' voluntarily to describe the means taken to prevent the 'starting' of a baby. Consequently 'contraception' was selected as more suitable for inclusion in the sexual vocabulary list.

Partially appropriate answers were scored when only a generalised statement was made about preventing a baby from starting, or where mention was made only of one method or device for preventing conception. The fully appropriate answers were judged on the meeting of the three following criteria: that before or during sexual intercourse the prevention of pregnancy or conception occurs by any practice, method or device. All three criteria had to be met. If only one or two were met then a partially appropriate response was scored. Some examples are set out below.

Totally inappropriate answers (Score 2)

'It's a washing powder, isn't it?' (Australian boy, 9 years); 'It means joining or something, joining cells together when the baby gets bigger' (English girl, 9 years); 'I've heard of "ception" and "cont" but not both together. Is it the name of the doctor who brought it?' (North American boy, 11 years); 'A tube of sperm and a woman can start a family without a man' (Australian girl, 13 years); 'Is it the food that goes in a baby? It might mean male or female organs' (English boy, 13 years).

Partially appropriate answers (Score 3)

'To stop a baby being born' (Australian boy, 9 years); 'It's the same

361

as a Durex or the pills' (English boy, 13 years); 'Use constraptions to stop the man's penis getting up the vagina' (North American girl, 13 years); 'Something mother or father takes if they don't want to have a baby' (North American girl, 15 years).

Fully appropriate answers (Score 4)

'Mother takes pills to stop the production of the eggs in the ovaries, so it's safe for sperm to come in and to have sex' (English boy, 13 years); 'Durex for men, a kind of rubber thing he puts on his penis, so it stops the sperm reaching the egg during intercourse. There's a pill for women. It kills the sperm as they enter the vagina' (Australian boy, 15 years); 'Cut off the opening in a woman, at a certain point, so there's a blockage the sperm can't get through in making love' (North American girl, 15 years).

The results of scoring on the meaning of contraception can be examined in Table 16.20. Understanding of the word is poorly grasped even at 15 years, with the exception of the English sample (83 per cent) and the Australian (60 per cent) in achieving most fully appropriate answers. The lowest scores are in the North American sample at 32 per cent, although Sweden is surprisingly low at 40 per cent. The North American figures are also surprising in the light of results on the 'not having babies' discussion and scores on the 'knowledge of contraception' scale. This, however, did not score vocabulary meaning, but focussed upon what people could do if they did not want to start a baby. The children were not asked the generic name of 'not having baby activities' or its meaning. It is possible, therefore, to have knowledge of practice without knowledge of labels or their meanings.

The Swedish results we suspect may be affected by translation, the high figures at 13 years signifying a high proportion of those with partially appropriate answers, which in the normal Swedish distribution would yield a progressively higher score as in Figure 13.1. Table 16.21 gives the mean scores for the meaning of contraception. Within these three discrepancies of scores between the sexes can be seen, English 13-year-old boys scoring significantly higher than the girls, and English and Swedish 15-year-old girls scoring significantly higher than the boys. There is not sufficient evidence to deduce any general sex differences on this item.

The meaning of rooting

This word, an Australian colloquial term or pseudonym for sexual intercourse, was given to only the Australian respondents to see how widespread its use was, and also to ascertain how Australian teenagers

TABLE 16.20 *Percentages of partially and fully appropriate responses to 'meaning of contraception' by country and age-years 9 to 15 (N = 564)*

Age-year	Australia		England		North America		Sweden	
	PA	FA	PA	FA	PA	FA	PA	FA
9	3	–	–	–	–	–	3	7
11	–	3	–	–	–	–	23	23
13	23	3	8	28	–	–	53	40
15	28	60	10	83	23	32	57	40

(Only scores 3 and 4 are included: PA = partially appropriate; FA = fully appropriate.)

TABLE 16.21 *Mean scores of responses on 'meaning of contraception' by country and age-years 15 to 19 (N = 564)*

Age-year	Australia	England	North America	Sweden
9	1.13	1.05	1.07	0.40
11	1.23	1.10	1.10	1.70
13	1.58	2.03*	1.03	3.22
15	3.40	3.70*	2.45	3.30*

(* Significant differences in mean scores between the sexes: see Table B.27, Appendix B.)

in particular defined it. It was impossible, when devising the interview schedule without an intimate knowledge of colloquial terms in the other countries, to find the English, American or Swedish equivalents. Consequently, no equivalent question was asked in the non-Australian samples, and 'rooting' scores are not included in the total sexual vocabulary scores, presented in the next section.

Partially appropriate answers were scored where there was a botanical reference to trees or plants, or vaguely connected with sexual intercourse. A fully appropriate answer was where it is seen as a slang or synonym for sexual intercourse, even if another slang term is used. Some answers at the three levels are given below.

Totally inappropriate answers (Score 2)

'When you're growing up' (boy, 9 years); 'When someone's dirty. (Q) Don't know' (girl, 9 years); 'Undressing and that, showing your roots' (boy, 11 years).

Partially appropriate answers (Score 3)

'When teenagers kiss' (boy, 9 years); 'Flowers roots and plants root, pulling out roots from the ground' (girl, 9 years); 'You're taking off a girl's clothes and kissing her and that' (boy, 11 years); 'When a lady and a man want to have a baby' (girl, 11 years).

Fully appropriate answers (Score 4)

'Mating. They all say it in our grade 4' (boy, 9 years); 'Having a baby by putting the penis in the vagina' (girl, 11 years); 'How they have the baby. The lady sticks the vagina in the man's penis' (girl, 9 years); 'Yes [laughs] It's having sex, placing joey in lady's hole' (boy, 13 years); 'Slang for having sex' (girl, 15 years).

Growing sexual awareness at 11 years is seen in the results (Table 16.22) where 53 per cent grasp its full meaning, increasing to 95 per cent who get the highest score by 15 years. This is very evident in the mean scores set out in Table 16.23, where more boys in the earlier years appear to have greater knowledge of the word 'rooting' than do the girls. By 15 years there is no sex difference.

TABLE 16.22 *Australian scores in percentages on 'meaning of rooting' by age-years (9 to 15) (N = 160)*

Age-year	Don't know can't say	Totally inappropriate	Partially appropriate	Fully appropriate
9	55	3	20	20
11	32	5	10	53
13	13	1	10	77
15	5	–	–	95

There is insufficient evidence here to discuss any significance between understanding of sexual pseudonyms and correct or clinical terms. It is obvious, however, that whatever word is used it is capable of being misunderstood or partially misunderstood in terms of meaning. This would appear to be particularly true of sexual words.

Total vocabulary scores

The scores of all ten words, excluding the word 'rooting', were added together to form a total vocabulary score, since each word was scored on generally standard levels (see Figure 16.1) with the major categories and scores being equivalent for each word. In the case of one word, 'rape', where a score of more than 4 had been added to indicate a more

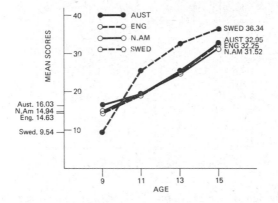

Figure 16.1   Mean scores from 9 to 15 years of age on sexual vocabulary totals by country

comprehensive meaning than 'man raping woman', the scores in excess of 4 were not added to the totals. The scores of all ten words were equivalent in the level of understanding and could therefore be totalled and the aggregates used statistically.

TABLE 16.23   *Australian mean scores on 'meaning of rooting' by age-years (9 to 14) and sex   (N = 160)*

Age-year	Boys	Girls	Total mean scores
9	2.20	1.80	2.00
11	3.15	2.50	2.88
13	3.90	3.15	3.53
15	3.85	3.85	3.85

The mean scores of the totals are tabulated in Table 16.24, where the maximum total possible was 40 points (10 words with maximum score of 4 for each word). The low scores at 5 and 7 years are explained by the fact that only the scores of two words, 'pregnancy' and 'conception', were used for these age groups, compared with the full ten used for the 9- to 15-year cohorts.

In the English-speaking countries the mean scores from 9 years onwards are very similar, with the Australian sample scoring the highest of the 9- and 15-year-olds, and the English sample at 13 years. The Swedish mean scores by contrast start very low at 9 years, move ahead of the English-speaking countries at 11 years, roughly approximate to the 15-year mean scores of the others at 13 years, and are clearly

365

TABLE 16.24   *Mean scores on the total vocabulary by country and age-year (N = 838)*

Age-year	Australia	England	North America	Sweden
5	1.45	1.73	1.60	0.57
7	1.90	2.48	2.19	1.97
9	16.03	14.63	14.94	9.54
11	19.37	19.18	19.37	25.33
13	25.20	26.30	24.95	32.50
15	32.95	32.25	31.52	36.34

(The maximum in the total vocabulary score is 40.)

significantly higher at 15 years. This picture can be seen visually in Figure 16.1 for ages 9 to 15 years. The overall higher scores in Sweden may be explained by longer and more sustained use of correct terminology in sex education programmes from the age of 8 years. The time lag at 9 years is possible while this process has not yet taken effect but is plainly visible by the age of 11. An added reason may be a wider and more open use of correct sexual words in Swedish society generally. The low scores by the younger age groups in Sweden may be explained by the age of compulsory schooling, beginning later than the English-speaking countries, at 7 years and that children in that year will have received little or no systematic sex education.

Certain sex differences are discernible when boys' and girls' mean scores are separated, as in Table 16.25. Boys score significantly higher than girls in five of the English-speaking cohorts as indicated in the table. The incidence is high enough, however, to postulate significant sex difference in the understanding of key words on a total vocabulary score, and is confirmed in ANOVA results (see Appendix D, Tables D.1, D.5 and D.6). In the Swedish sample girls at 9 and 11 years score higher than Swedish boys in those cohorts, but the results are not statistically significant. Both sexes in Sweden achieve similar mean scores at 13 and 15 years, with boys slightly but not significantly higher. There may be cultural differences to explain this, between Sweden and the English-speaking countries, the latter countries perhaps still reflecting male dominance and perpetuating the stereotype of males as the main initiators of sex activity.

Socio-economic status, as assessed by the children's father's occupation, reveals main effects at a significant level (see Table D.4 in Appendix D), although only at the .05 level. This is also confirmed from a three way interaction analysis between S.E.S., age year and country (Table D.10). This would appear to indicate that in all countries, including Sweden, class may affect an understanding of the sexual

TABLE 16.25 *Mean scores of 9 to 15 years on total vocabulary by country sex and age-year (N = 564)*

Age-year	Australia		England		North America		Sweden	
	Boys	Girls	Boys	Girls	Boys	Girls	Boys	Girls
9	16.90*	15.15	15.75*	13.50	15.60	14.27	7.67	11.40
11	19.50	19.25	19.80	18.55	20.67	18.07	23.33	27.33
13	27.35*	23.05	28.20*	24.40	26.25	23.65	32.60	32.33
15	33.95*	31.95	32.50	32.00	32.63	30.40	36.60	36.07

(* Boys score significantly higher than girls: see table B.27, Appendix B.)

vocabulary listed, the scores indicating the higher the socio-economic status the higher the scores. The significance noted, however, is somewhat marginal and no firm conclusions can be made on this point.

Summary and discussion

In the context of comparing correct clinical sexual terminology with words in common usage, the meanings of two sexual words were asked of all respondents, and ten were asked of the 9- to 15-year-olds. The limitation of two words to the younger age levels was justified in terms of ascending order of difficulty. The responses were scored in three major categories – totally inappropriate, partially appropriate and fully appropriate answers. All words were carefully defined and scored in terms of insight into their sexual meaning.

Overall, Swedish children scored significantly higher than their English-speaking peers, their total vocabulary score revealing much greater grasp of the meaning of the words except in the two words 'VD' (venereal disease) and 'contraception'. This higher scoring from 9 years onwards was attributed to systematic usage of these correct words in a suitable context of meaning during sex education in school, and possibly more open use of these terms in Swedish society.

The words most widely grasped in terms of meaning were 'rape' and 'virgin', those moderately grasped were 'pregnant' and 'conception', although the latter was grasped by only 40 per cent of Australian and 25 per cent of English 15-year-olds. 'Contraception' was an in-between with 83 per cent of English and 60 per cent of Australian 15-year-olds grasping its full meaning, but only 32 per cent of North Americans and 40 per cent of Swedes in that age group. The latter group may be explained by translation difficulties or interviewer differences.

Lowest of all were understanding of the meaning of 'uterus', 'puberty', 'VD', 'abortion' and 'stripping'. It was surprising to discover how many

15-year-old girls did not know the correct name for a vital part of their own anatomy, and how few teenagers understood the name for the current period of their development. Lack of insight into venereal disease was universally evident in all countries, a serious indicator in view of its dangers for earlier maturing teenagers.

The question may be asked, How important is the correct usage or understanding of sexual vocabulary? The results do report in the case of 'contraception' that children understand the process earlier without being able to define the meaning of the word. We would suggest that the use of correct vocabulary from the beginning, and some explanations of meaning will help the young to understand the 'processes' earlier. Linguistically, it surely retards development to use 'bow-wow' instead of 'dog', when the correct term can be used in the first instance. Much sexual vocabulary used by children and adults is equivalent to this baby language. If 'penis' rather than 'joey', and 'vagina' instead of 'beaver' are used from the beginning of learning about the human body, the words are seen in context and can develop further meaning over the years. More importantly, correct usage can minimise the aura of taboo and 'dirty talk' associations children have when judging what words to use. To suggest that the correct words are rude is absurd and a distorted outcome of years of adult prevarication and inhibition.

Our interpretation of the much higher scores on total sexual vocabulary, achieved at an earlier age by Swedish children, is that if the correct words are constantly used in a meaningful context, they are more likely to be sequentially and consistently part of the adult's way of communicating sexual matters to children and school programmes provide a systematic exposure to their meaning over the years of schooling. Swedish educators seem to have overcome, at least partially, what Delys Sargeant in her investigation into Australian sex education provision (1975) points out as 'The difficulty of teaching a subject in which the valid living language may be interpreted as offensive, or may be forbidden' (p. 117).

17 Summary and discussion of the results

The aims of this study, as set out at the beginning of chapter 3, were to estimate the extent of children's sexual knowledge in four countries, to assess their sexual understanding at various ages, and to identify and examine what processes of thought they use in trying to explain biological functions, their own growing bodies and varying aspects of sexuality which impinge upon their experience. Whether these aims have been realised and, if they have, to what extent, is for the reader to decide. It may, however, be better decided by examining a summary of the results and trying to gain an overview of some kind of the total picture.

A useful beginning is to examine the three scales devised – the Piagetian Scales, the Biological Realism Scales and the Sexual Vocabulary scales – and to see what variables appear to have affected the results. Then, since a large number of areas are not covered by the scales, we shall try to present an overview of children's sexual thinking, looking at the main contradictions, problems and issues which arise from the findings. Finally, we shall summarise what appears to us to be the major findings of the research.

Interpreting the combined scales

One of the major interests in interpreting the results has been to make comparisons between the countries involved in the study, particularly within the English-speaking countries and between these and Sweden. The comparison with Sweden is especially valuable since a firmly established system of compulsory sex education from the age of 8 years is a distinct feature of that country's provision for its children. The combined scales specifically lend themselves to these comparisons and it is appropriate that they are presented first.

Three combinations of scores were made to devise three major groups of questions which were designated as three scales — The Piagetian scales, the Biological Realism scales, and the Sexual Vocabulary scales. The items making up each scale are set out below and the scales are discussed in turn. By presenting these three scales of combined items it is possible to discern differences between countries and to show how certain variables appear to have affected the results much more effectively than examining individual items.

Piagetian scales	Biological Realism scales	Sexual Vocabulary scales
Best time to be alive	Body differences — baby	Pregnancy
Why people marry	Body differences — puberty	Conception
Origin of babies	Origin of babies	Stripping
Gestation process	Birth exit	Rape VD
Wearing clothes	Reasons for birth	Uterus
Nakedness and embarrassment	Gestation process	Puberty Virgin Contraception Abortion

There were two requirements necessary to justify the combining of items to make up the three scales. The first was that the scores in all items should be structured similarly so that the totals were not affected by one score to a greater or lesser extent than others. Since initially some of these items had scores of slightly different value, these had to be 'collapsed' so that equivalence was achieved. For example, the Piaget items were collapsed to three, the Biological Realism items to five and all Sexual Vocabulary items to four levels. The second requirement was that they covered the same 'universe', either in criteria for scoring or in the content covered overall by the items in the scale. In the Piagetian scale the common 'universe' was the 'operational' framework for evaluating the levels of thinking demonstrated. On the other two scales, the 'universe' was the biological content of the Biological Realism scales, and the meaning of sexual words for the Sexual Vocabulary scales.

Examining the mean scores and reliability coefficients in Table 17.1 it will be seen that there is a high reliability for all the combined scores in every country. The lowest alpha of 0.78 for Sweden on the Piagetian scales and the highest of 0.96 in all countries on the Sexual Vocabulary scales are within an acceptable range of reliability. Overall the Sexual Vocabulary scales have the highest reliability.

TABLE 17.1   *Combined scales: mean scores and reliability coefficients*

	Australia	England	North America	Sweden
Piagetian scales (6)	X̄ = 10.73 Alpha = 0.82	X̄ = 10.51 Alpha = 0.82	X̄ = 11.15 Alpha = 0.83	X̄ = 10.94 Alpha = 0.78
Biological Realism scales (6)	X̄ = 18.81 Alpha = 0.86	X̄ = 18.60 Alpha = 0.86	X̄ = 18.31 Alpha = 0.87	X̄ = 20.03 Alpha = 0.87
Sexual Vocabulary scales (10)	X̄ = 23.38 Alpha = 0.96	X̄ = 23.34 Alpha = 0.96	X̄ = 22.69 Alpha = 0.96	X̄ = 25.93 Alpha = 0.96

In examining the mean scores, the order of highest to lowest scores on the Piagetian scales are North America, Sweden, Australia and England, the two latter countries being very close together. The order for the Biological Realism scales is Sweden, Australia, England and North America, again with the Australian and English scores very close together. The order for the Sexual Vocabulary scales is Sweden, England, Australia and North America, the two middle countries once more with mean scores almost identical. Although the mean score differences appear to be small, they represent quite considerable disparities when the number of items and the number of children involved in each of the combined scales are considered.

The order from highest to lowest is interesting. Sweden is consistently high, coming second highest on the Piagetian scales and highest on the other two scales. The North American scores vary, highest on the Piagetian scales, and lowest both on the Sexual Vocabulary scales and on the Biological Realism scales. The very close similarity in all three combined scales of the Australian and English scores is most noticeable and may be accounted for by the closer educational and cultural traditions of these two countries.

The reasons to account for the order of mean scores, presented above, are not self evident. We would postulate that Sweden's consistently higher results may well be due to familiarity with the content of the items and with the correct language used, due to a much longer and more sustained sex education. The more open attitudes to sexuality in Swedish society permeating families as well as schools may also be an important factor. These overall results are consistent with the earlier and higher scoring of Swedish children seen in evaluating many of the items in previous chapters.

The North American children appear to have the least and the longest delayed sex education provision of all the four countries in the study. Since they may be least familiar with the content of the questions on the Piagetian scales, it is interesting that the North American scores are highest on these scales. It should be noted, however, that these scales are the least sexual in content, containing three out of the six items not overtly sexual to the child, namely 'The best time to be alive', 'Why people marry' and 'Why people wear clothes'. It may be that the answers to these relatively less sexual questions were not helped by familiarity with sexual matters or understanding of biological process or vocabulary. On the other hand the Biological Realism scales do appear to depend heavily upon familiarity with content and may so account for the North American lowest scores in this area.

The catching up of the North American teenagers in many items may be accounted for by possibly more intense social interest and activity, and earlier boy/girl relationships and dating habits of teenagers in Canada and the United States. As we have pointed out in an earlier chapter (10), it may also be that because information is received later and sexual motivation is greater with the onset of puberty that North American teenagers achieve a spurt of sexual learning between 13 and 14 years of age. Within the English-speaking countries the English sample reflects uneven results in the development of sexual thinking. This may be explained by the fact that within these countries the English system tends to encourage some sex education at the top end of the elementary schools. Earlier differential scores over their Australian and North American peers, however, are not continued in the teenage years. There is some evidence from other chapters that the English teenagers are not as advanced socially in terms of heterosexual friendships as their North American and Australian peers, which may be an important factor. Early cognitive stimulation in terms of sexual knowledge combined with teenage inhibitive behaviour and attitudes in the British sample may well 'equalise' the delayed cognitive stimulation in terms of sexual knowledge and earlier teenage sexual interests in the North American sample. These explanations, however, are advanced only tentatively and need to be pursued by more comparative studies of the kind conducted by the authors.

The Australian and English scores are consistent in two ways, being closely similar in all three combined scales and occupying a low position together on the Piagetian scales and the sexual vocabulary scales. The close similarity between the two samples' scores has been posited as due to the close educational and cultural traditions of Australia and England. The relatively higher, second place, scores on the Biological Realism scales may reflect their order of earlier sex education provision than is apparent in the North American schools. The similar placing for the Australian and English children, on the Sexual Vocabulary scales may be accounted for by the same reasons as those for the Biological Realism scales.

Differences between Sweden and the English-speaking countries should be seen in the light of the differential refusal rate of parents to have their children interviewed, mentioned previously. Twenty per cent of English-speaking parents refused, compared with only 5 per cent of the Swedish. This may not only be an indicator of a more permissive and open-minded society on sexual matters, but the higher refusal rate probably loads the samples in favour of the English-speaking groups. The Australian, English and North Americans would tend to be self-selected more in favour of open-minded families prepared to have their children questioned and more accessible to sex information, with a greater proportion of negative, inhibited and non-communicative families excluded than in Sweden. Thus the discrepancies between Sweden and the other countries may well be much greater than is reported by these results. In this sense the earlier and higher scores by Swedish children would appear to vindicate the earlier introduction of sex and human relations programmes early in the elementary stage of schooling.

Table 17.2 sets out the reliability of scores for the three combined scales. It will be seen from these results that the mean scores in every combined scale reveal a clear sequence of increasing scores with increasing age. In discriminating between ages and within all ages the Sexual Vocabulary scales do so consistently, in part explained by the fact that the 5- and 7-year-olds were not included in the calculations. The Piagetian scales do discriminate well between ages, but not too well within the 5-year age groups. The reliability improves a little from 7 to 13 years but is low again at 15 years. The Biological Realism scales are similar to the Piagetian scales, being less reliable at the extremes and more reliable in the middle age range of 7, 9 and 11 years.

The Piagetian combined scales in particular are worth examining in some detail country by country. When the mean scores are looked at in Table 17.3 the level of difficulty posed by the questions becomes apparent. If the score of 6 represents the pre-operational level, the score of 12 represents the concrete operational level and the score of 18 for the formal operational level, then what we call operational time lag is evident in Figure 17.1. Although the children have moved beyond the mean score of pre-operations (6) by the age of 7, concrete operations have barely been achieved by the age of 11, with the Australian and English children not quite achieving this even then. And at 15 years formal operations are not achieved in the mean scores shown; only what can be termed transitional-to-formal operations are in evidence.

This operational time lag may be accounted for in various ways. Unfamiliarity with content or the nature of the questions may be one. How often is a child faced with a reasoning problem comparing the various satisfactions of being alive at different periods of life, and are

TABLE 17.2 *Combined scales: mean scores and reliability coefficients across all countries and within age groups*

	Piagetian (6)	Biological (6)	Vocabulary (10)
Maximum score	6 × 3 = 18	6 × 5 = 30	10 × 4 = 40
Age-year			
5	X̄ = 6.40 Alpha = 0.32	X̄ = 11.02 Alpha = 0.56	
7	X̄ = 8.09 Alpha = 0.42	X̄ = 13.56 Alpha = 0.63	
9	X̄ = 9.82 Alpha = 0.41	X̄ = 17.23 Alpha = 0.71	X̄ = 13.95 Alpha = 0.68
11	X̄ = 12.10 Alpha = 0.47	X̄ = 22.01 Alpha = 0.59	X̄ = 20.50 Alpha = 0.72
13	X̄ = 13.30 Alpha = 0.41	X̄ = 23.80 Alpha = 0.36	X̄ = 26.53 Alpha = 0.72
15	X̄ = 14.82 Alpha = 0.24	X̄ = 25.32 Alpha = 0.21	X̄ = 32.68 Alpha = 0.59
Overall	X̄ = 10.80 Alpha = 0.80	X̄ = 18.90 Alpha = 0.85	X̄ = 23.41 Alpha = 0.96

TABLE 17.3 *Piagetian combined scales: mean scores by age-year and country*

Age-year	Australia	England	North America	Sweden
5	5.98	6.53	6.58	6.67
7	8.38	7.55	7.97	8.53
9	9.83	9.90	9.43	10.10
11	11.68	11.80	12.40	12.77
13	13.25	12.98	14.24	12.77
15	15.28	14.30	14.94	14.77
X̄ *	10.73	10.51	11.15	10.93

(* Maximum total possible 18.)

children ever introduced to questions about marriage? Areas such as the wearing of clothes are accepted at a conventional level, as the results indicate, and the conception of human life and ensuing gestation process are certainly unfamiliar areas for younger children.

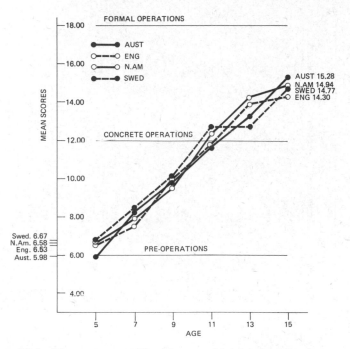

Figure 17.1   Mean scores on Piagetian combined scales by country and age year

Another reason for the operational time lag on the Piagetian scales may be a reflection of social immaturity. This includes the limitations of not having lived long enough to understand the complexity of human relationships, ignorance of the satisfactions and disappointments to be experienced at life's various stages, and unawareness of internal, unseen biological processes. Yet another reason may be the factor of inhibition and social taboo particularly related to problems which have an overtly sexual content.

It is probable that all three reasons combined – unfamilarity with content, social immaturity and social taboos – may account for the operational time lag visible in these results. Whatever the reasons they illustrate the variability of operational thinking and caution required when discussing ages and stages in cognitive development. The facile statement that children in general achieve concrete operational levels of thinking by 7 or 8 years of age, and formal operational levels by 11 or 12 years of age is seen to be both oversimplified and unrealistic. These ages may be relevant where first hand tangible experiences may be accumulated and reasoned about over a long period of time, particularly

TABLE 17.4 Analyses of Variance on the three combined scales

Independent variable	Dependent variable	All countries	Australia	England	North America	Sweden
Other sex in family	Piagetian	***	***	NS	NS	NS
	Biological Realism	***	***	*	NS	**
	Vocabulary	***	***	***	NS	*
Sex differences (boys)	Piagetian	***	**	***	**	*
	Biological Realism	**	NS	***	NS	*
	Vocabulary	NS	NS	NS	NS	NS
Father's occupation	Piagetian	NS	NS	*	NS	NS
	Biological Realism	NS	NS	*	NS	NS
	Vocabulary	NS	NS	NS	NS	NS
Mother's occupation	Piagetian	***	***	***	**	NS
	Biological Realism	***	***	***	***	NS
	Vocabulary	***	***	***	**	**
Size of family	Piagetian	***	***	**	NS	NS
	Biological Realism	***	*	***	NS	NS
	Vocabulary	***	***	***	NS	NS
Birth order	Piagetian	*	NS	NS	NS	NS
	Biological Realism	NS	NS	*	NS	NS
	Vocabulary	***	*	***	NS	NS
Ability	Piagetian	***	NS	*	*	***
	Biological Realism	***	NS	NS	*	***
	Vocabulary	***	NS	NS	*	***

(* = p < .05; ** = p < .01; *** = p < .001; NS = Not significant.)

in mathematics, where schooling provides some kind of sequential teaching. They are certainly not relevant in the much more complex area of sexual biology and human relationships affected strongly by moral associations as Gilligan et al. (1971) report. The time lag reported in this study supports Gilligan's, Kohlberg's and their colleagues' findings when testing the moral reasoning of adolescents about sexual and social dilemmas.

Variables affecting the results

Many other factors may have affected the results of the three combined scales presented in the previous section. Some were controlled for and may be seen as independent variables. Among these were the presence of a sibling of the other sex in the family (other sex in family), sex differences, socio-economic status (as indicated by father's and mother's occupations), size of family, birth order, and abilities. Studies in cognitive development generally tend to consider and if possible control for many of these variables. Any study into such an area as children's sexual thinking should in our view control for such factors as size of family and birth order. The presence or absence of a sibling of the other sex during a child's upbringing would seem to be a rather important factor also.

The results of Analyses of Variance on the three combined scales in relation to these variables are summarised in Table 17.4. The most surprising result is that father's occupation does not appear to be a significant factor in any of the scales. The one exception is the English sample where on the Piagetian and Biological Realism scales there is some indication of its significance, where $p < .05$. It is obvious from these English results that the higher a father's occupation is scored, the higher on these two scales are his children's scores. If we assume that social prestige of father's occupation is an indicator of socio-economic status, then it would be expected that the English sample would show a greater influence of father's occupation, since of the four countries England has the most rigid class structures. References to Appendix D will indicate that socio-economic status (SES), as measured by father's occupation does appear to have a significant main effect upon the sexual vocabulary totals result (Table D.4 and D.10). These are the results of different computations and are only marginally significant. The general evidence would appear to be very slender to justify substantial class differences in the children's responses to the sexual vocabulary items. It is certainly not supported in the Piagetian and Biological Realism totals.

The influence of mother's occupation

Equally surprising is the dominance of mother's occupation as a factor influencing children's scores. In all countries combined and in all three scales in the English-speaking countries the significance is at a very high level (p < .001 or .01). The mother's occupation was not scored on a prestige-type scale as was the case with father's occupation, but classified as home duties (score 1), part-time work or study (score 2), and full-time work or study (score 3). The results appear to indicate that a mother's part-time or full-time occupation may encourage greater insights, better interaction with her children and stimulate more mental energy which may arise from the wider social contacts and less frustration than being involved only in home duties. It may be true conversely that such a mother also invites greater stress by being required to do two jobs, but this cannot be inferred from the results. The fact that the Swedish children's scores appear to be unaffected by mother's occupation can be explained by examining Tables A.5 and A.6 (see Appendix A). The percentages of Swedish mothers involved in full-time jobs or study is much greater at any age level of childhood than in the English-speaking countries. The best indicator of this is the mean score of mother's occupation (Table A.6) which in Sweden is 2.35 on a maximum score of 3.00 compared with the nearest mean score of 1.89 for the English mothers.

This almost universal tendency for Swedish mothers to work outside the home, if part-time and full-time work are combined, does not argue that this factor is unimportant in Sweden. Rather it suggests that, since almost all the children experience mothers who have other than home duties, it does not affect the scores of Swedish children significantly. In the English-speaking countries where there is a greater variety of mother's occupation, it is an important factor, scores 2 and 3 being the determining factor of higher scores, whereas score 1 (home duties) is not. The picture of a stay-at-home mother devoting all her attention to her husband and particularly the children, stimulating their thinking and answering their questions, is not substantiated by these results. This is especially interesting since many children, particularly girls, find mother the major source of sex information and are less reluctant about asking their mothers about sex (see chapter 14).

The influence of family size

Size of family is shown as highly significant in all countries combined, revealing on all three combined scales the larger the family the higher the score of the children. The larger family probably presents greater and more frequent observations of other children, possibly of the other sex, more discussion and perhaps stimulated curiosity about sexual matters and maybe more exchange of information. The fact that in the Swedish and North American samples this factor does not appear to be significant can be explained by two reasons. The first is that the formula for significance was very rigorously observed (p < .05) and the results for these two countries did not quite achieve this level, almost but not quite. The other reason to be seen in Table 3.4 is that the percentages of 'large' families is smaller in the Swedish and North American samples than in the other two countries. In addition Table 3.3 indicates that Sweden has the smallest mean size of family, 2.57 compared with Australia's 3.26 in the samples taken.

The influence of siblings-of-other-sex in family

The factor of other-sex-in-family, the presence of a sibling of the other sex, occurring in the families of 65 per cent of the children in this study, has already been noted (see Table 9.1). This is a significant factor in all countries combined, on all the scales. As already observed, this presents an in-built family opportunity for first-hand observation of sex differences and other sexual matters which those children (35 per cent), having only a same-sex sibling, do not have. The non-significance of this factor in the North American sample, in particular, related to having somewhat smaller families, and in Sweden is perhaps counterbalanced by the nature of the sample. It is interesting that the scores on the Piagetian scales in three countries do not appear to be influenced by this factor. This is not surprising since the Piagetian scales contain less overtly sexual situation questions, compared with the Biological Realism and the Sexual Vocabulary scales.

The influence of birth order

Birth order is not seen to be a significant factor in the results of the Combined scales although in all countries combined and in two specific countries, Australia and England, the results are significant on the Sexual Vocabulary scales. As Table 3.5 indicates, Australia has the highest mean birth order (1.82) which indicates a wider spread of birth positions, namely more children, not the first born in the family. Understanding the meaning of sexual vocabulary may well be related to this birth order and size of family, since communications on these matters may be affected. However, the non-significant results in other countries may be due to variations in the sample.

The influence of sex differences

Sex differences have been noted throughout this study and are reported extensively in Appendices B and D. These include differing emphases of reasons for sexual intercourse by boys and girls, differing views on the reasons for marriage, on birth-control, abortion, rape and other matters.

The greater attachment of girls to romantic love and of boys to companionship have been noted as also the considerable anxiety about menstruation expressed by girls, and about how to do it (sexual intercourse) by boys. Despite the fact that babies are biologically more important to girls, boys often score significantly higher than girls in matters related to conception, gestation and childbirth, although in some areas both sexes reveal a considerable shared ignorance.

As an independent variable, the results set out in Table 17.4 show that the sex factor does appear to be highly significant across all countries on the Piagetian scales, boys demonstrating significantly higher operational levels of thinking. As we have observed, these scales are the least overtly sexual in content, and may reflect male role-expectations of exploring, questioning and problem solving, compared with female role expectations of a more passive non-enquiring intellectual kind. The sex factor is also present, although not as strong, in the Biological Realism scales. Boys tend to score higher on those items specifically sexual in nature and which require more scientific explanations. This is evident over all countries and is significant only in the English and Swedish samples. It appears to support a role-expectation of boys as 'more scientific' than girls, although some school traditions have tended to see the physical sciences as the boys' domain and the biological sciences as the girls' domain. On the Sexual Vocabulary scales, understanding the meaning of sexual words, the sex factor is not significant.

These overall results, however, have to be viewed cautiously in the light of girls' better performance in certain specific items reported earlier. Nevertheless, to be a boy does appear to be advantageous in the development of sexual thinking.

The influence of ability

The remaining independent variable is that of ability, as estimated by the children's teachers. This factor is seen to be significant in all countries together on all the Combined scales. This is consistent with other studies in cognitive development which have found a strong relationship between ability and scores on Piaget-type tests in particular. It is noticeable that within individual countries it is the Piagetian-scales which are the most frequently significant in terms of ability. The 'all countries' highly significant results (where $p < .001$) are strongly affected by the Swedish results which in turn may be affected by variations in the sample (see Table 3.7), the absence of estimates of 5-year-olds' abilities (see Table A.7, Appendix A) or by unreliability in the teachers' estimates. Ability is, however, still an important factor which is related to general vocabulary, problem solving and other factors which might affect children's scores on the three Combined scales.

SUMMARY AND DISCUSSION OF THE RESULTS

Overall view of variables affecting scores on the Combined scales

The discussion of the results to be seen in Table 17.4 shows the strong influence of a working mother, membership of a larger family, particularly with other-sex-siblings, and above average ability in high scoring on the three Combined scales. On the other hand, a stay-at-home mother, membership of a small family of no more than two children with no sibling of the other sex, and below-average ability would seem to be disadvantagous in scoring on the Combined scales. We would observe that since family size is shrinking in Western industrialised countries and thus opportunities become less for being reared in a large, both-sex family, the resulting disadvantages may have to be supplemented by other institutions, particularly the school. It would appear to support the case made by the vast majority of the children that sex education should begin in the primary or elementary schools.

An overview of children's sexual thinking

While the three Combined scales discussed above are useful indicators of certain aspects of children's sexual thinking, they cover only 21 questions out of a total of 63. This section is intended to provide an overview of the main outcomes of this study in terms of all the items used to describe children's sexual thinking. There were some interesting findings concerning children's perceptions of ageing and of their thinking and judgments about the best time to be alive. These findings are fully discussed in chapters 4 and 5 and are largely disregarded here, not because they are unimportant, but because the focus is to summarise those matters which directly impinge upon children's perceptions of their sexual world.

The myth of a latency period

If we begin with their judgments about ageing, what impresses about the children's sexual thinking is that only 4 per cent of them, mostly teenagers, saw fit to mention sexual characteristics of old people and these were negativisms, with emphasis upon the slowing down of sexual activities or 'being past it'. The complete silence on the part of the remaining 96 per cent presents a sexless view of old age, which is unrealistic. There is a similar, almost total silence about sexuality in children's reasons for choosing the best time to be alive. This is evident even among teenagers who do not, with few exceptions, list sexual reasons for choosing adolescence or young adulthood. Again, in providing reasons for why people get married, only 4.5 per cent of the children gave sexual answers. While it may be that sexuality is inferred, disguised or sublimated in other reasons such as socio-biological responses

381

('so they can have children') or emotional-dependence replies ('because they love one another'), nevertheless there is only a minimal reference to sexuality.

The same phenonemon is evident in children's discussion of their parents' characteristics as men and women, particularly the differences the children report between mother and father. While there is recognition of overt physical and sexual differences between a mother and a father on the part of most children, a substantial number of them, even during the teenage years, fail to report these differences. Some discussion took place in previous chapters about the unwillingness of children, reported in previous studies, to recognise their parents as sexually active beings. One of the reasons advanced to explain this unwillingness is the fear of incest within the family.

Much of the evidence summarised so far would appear to support the Freudian theory of a latency period. This theory is comprised of two parts. Firstly, that there is a latency period between 5 or 6 years and 11 or 12 years of age when children's sexual interests and activities cease to develop and are supposed to become sublimated into other activities. And secondly, that this is due to the Oedipal situation in the family, namely incestuous desires on the part of the child towards the parent of the other sex, terminated abruptly by castration fears for such forbidden desires and behaviour.

The evidence does not support the theory of a latency period, although it does indicate a growing awareness by children of social taboos about sexuality, particularly in relation to the sexuality of their parents. We would expect two features to occur if a latency period is to be substantiated. Firstly, the inhibitions or 'silence' about sexuality noted earlier would tend to ease off at about 11 years of age. This, however, does not occur since the inhibitions and silences, in the items discussed so far, continue in the teenage years. They can be accounted for simply by the results of continuous conditioning over many years, similar inhibitions being exhibited by many adults for the whole of their lives.

The second feature of a latency period theory would be a reasonable sexual awareness at about the age of 5 years, and little evidence of a 'development' of interest and knowledge before puberty is reached. This is not so, since in every question discussed involving the child's recognition of sexuality — differences between newborn babies, differences between girls and boys at puberty, how babies are made, and countless others — children at 7 and 9 were not less inhibited than their peers at 5. The youngest age group revealed poorer levels of sexual comprehension certainly but, far from being repressed and ceasing to develop in psycho-sexual terms, the so-called latency period children revealed increasing knowledge and willingness to discuss their knowledge.

Furthermore, there is no reason to accept any deep-seated psycho-pathological reasons to explain the inhibitions about sex that children do reveal. The Oedipal situation as a norm of development remains unsubstantiated and sexual inhibitions may be explained by non-Freudian social learning theory, particularly where moral sanctions in Western-type industrialised democratic societies are so apparent.

It is important to emphasise the latency period as a myth, because latency is an impediment to the desirable early provision of sex education in home and school during the years 5 to 11, the need for which is seen by the children (see chapter 14).

Relationships between men and women

Children perceive early in their development that a special relationship exists between men and women, even though they do not clearly perceive this relationship as overtly sexual in nature. Like any concept, the fuller and more complex meanings take time and experience to mature. Just as sorting and counting are the beginnings of mathematical concepts, so primitive ideas about marriage and relationships between the sexes form the foundations for later psychosexual insights.

Our findings indicate some variations between the perceptions of boys and girls in this respect. Girls tend to support the view of romantic love as the basis for a relationship between a man and a woman, while boys tend to see friendship and companionship as more basic. This is more marked in relation to the older respondents, mostly teenagers, when asked about why should people want to make love apart from having children. Boys substantively agreed that pleasure and enjoyment were the essentials, whereas girls saw coitus as an expression of love. When asked their preference to be a girl or a boy, girls gave predominantly sexual reasons for choosing to be girls, while boys chose predominantly recreational and activity reasons for wanting to be boys. When choosing friends, boys gave the major reason as sharing recreational activities and interests whereas the girls' emphasis was upon compatibility of feeling.

It was obvious to the authors, even at the data collecting stage, that mothers and fathers were regarded by the children as influential models. This was very obvious when choice of a favourite parent was made. The girls most strongly identified with their mothers, and although the boys chose mother in the earlier years they were more likely to choose their fathers later. Each sex tended to reinforce their same-sex parent favour-itism during the teenage years, in our view as sex-identity models in preparation for emerging heterosexual friendships and as a preliminary to courtship. It is interesting that both sexes find parents' attitudinal sympathy and support to be much more important in the teenage years than physical care and comfort, and personal services.

Relationships between men and women include distinctive roles and shared roles, and the family reflects as a microcosm of society the parents as role models for their children. The evidence from the children indicated a conventional sex-typed acceptance of roles in the family, domestic roles being generally complementary, mother inside (cooking, cleaning) and father outside (repairing, garden, motor car). While there is a sex bias towards mothers in child-care roles there is also a dominant one for fathers in leisure roles. Fathers are seen by the children as worthy of higher status employment than their mothers, and teenagers in particular view their fathers primarily in authority-leadership roles. Shared roles are perceived by only 3.8 per cent of the entire sample, North America being the only group which had a sizeable percentage (17 per cent at 9 years; 19 per cent at 15 years) of those seeing their parents as sharing roles. This indicates a powerful conservative force, illustrating the slowness of social change to sex-typing of a more egalitarian nature.

Choice of gender identity

As previously noted in chapter 8, boys and girls, given a choice as to whether they wish to be a boy or a girl, tend overwhelmingly to choose their own sex. The girls, however, show a greater degree of uncertainty, sometimes choosing to be a boy particularly around the age of 13 years, the time most of them are experiencing menstruation. This is no doubt due also to increased awareness of the limited roles of mother, as discussed in the last section, and the social advantages for leisure that fathers and boys enjoy. The choice of friends takes the same course as gender choice, except that in the teenage years there is a considerable increase of heterosexual choices. A slower interest in heterosexual friendship amounting to a retardation level was noted in the English teenagers. This accompanied high scores in aversion to the other sex in both English boys and girls. Generally children in all countries expressed negativisms about the other sex particularly in the years 7 to 11, more girls showing hostility to boys than vice versa.

The results suggest to us two basic needs of children. One is for them to be educated in social as well as sexual matters about being a boy and a girl, the stress being upon role sharing rather than role differentiation, and egalitarian views of the sexes rather than the acceptance of dominant sexist assumptions. The other need of children is the encouragement of the continuance of heterosexual friendship patterns experienced and enjoyed by younger children, and the lessening of social pressures to choose the same-sex friends. If teachers and parents were made more aware of the consequences of strong sex aversions, the resulting virtual exclusion of the other sex friendship at a vital period of development and possibly continuing projection of these aversions into the 'sex war', then some co-operative effort between home and school might be practicable.

Perceiving physical differences in babies and adolescents

Strong taboos appear to operate which inhibit children from recognising or identifying physical and sexual differences between the sexes. In the English-speaking countries this leads to a retardation of thinking regarding sex differences in babies, in that most children are pre-sexual in their identification of sex differences up to 9 years of age. A sizeable number are what we called 'transitional sexual' even at 11 years, although the teenagers generally are able to make accurate sex distinctions. Identification of sex differences during pubertal growth is also more retarded and even evident among teenagers, who should be aware of sex differences in the period they themselves are passing through. The fact that many 13-year-olds have not achieved fully sexual answers indicates the strength of inhibition in this area.

The taboos are illustrated by the wide-spread use of sexual pseudonyms, many respondents being unwilling to use the correct terms for the sex organs, even when they know them. The poor scores of the English-speaking countries on the meaning of sexual words (chapter 16) provide another example of inhibitions leading to non-comprehension of some important words, even in the teenage years. That the meanings of 'uterus', 'puberty', 'abortion' and 'VD' should not be understood at 15 years by so many, we regard as a serious deficit. It is no wonder that even the most elementary biological processes are not understood when no adequate vocabulary is available to children. Accordingly we have recommended the correct usage of sexual terms from the very beginning by adults when talking to children about sexual matters. In this way taboos would be lifted, inhibitions would be minimised and the 'dirty talk' associations many children have for correct words could be removed.

The procreative process

How children perceived the origin of babies revealed a clear progression in Piagetian terms, but on biological criteria while large numbers of children had grasped 'the facts' by 11 years of age, that is the origin of babies was the outcome of sex between a man and a woman, a large proportion were at this stage at 13 years, and could not explain or provide a satisfactory theory to illuminate the facts. One feature of the results is that earlier predictions that children are unable to grasp conception and gestation being inside the mother are shown to be false. The fact that many children are rather late (11 years) in recognising the sexual role of mothers and fathers is due, we maintain, not to any inherent difficulty in the problems posed, but to the considerable secrecy and inhibition still attached to the subject. Some children at 5 years in all four countries were telling us 'the facts', and in Sweden providing explanations for the facts from the age of 7 years.

Another feature of these results is that children are misled and confused by many of the analogies used to explain the origin of babies. Seed in soil, eggs and chickens, and sperm as tadpoles, provided at preoperational and even concrete operational levels, appear to be taken so literally that they retard understanding for some time. Similarly the vague use of stomach or tummy to indicate uterus or womb appears to block the child's thinking. And the new medical mythologies invented by children and reinforced by the mystique of the doctors, nurses and hospitals lead to further misunderstanding.

Sexism in the form of expected roles for each sex also appear. In the non-sexual stage of procreation mother is seen to be the more active, but once sexuality is recognised, the father is seen by most children as the initiator and dominant figure in coitus. Again Swedish children are somewhat different in their perceptions.

The six forms of children's explanations of the origin of babies, suggested by Bernstein (1978), were validated in our sample, although not in a clear progression. These were identified in a slightly different form as the geographers (the only explanation is that the baby is inside the mother), the manufacturers (it is made outside and put inside the mother by non-sexual means), the agriculturalists (the seed-in-the-soil analogy taken literally), the reporters (who know the facts but cannot explain them), the miniaturists (theorists who believe the baby is fully formed in miniature in either the sperm or egg) and the realists (who have a reasonably accurate theory of fertilisation and fusion). In our view many of these stages could be eliminated, or may occur for a more limited period in childhood, given sensible and sensitive explanations from non-secretive, uninhibited adults.

The gestation process appears to be much more difficult for the English-speaking children to comprehend. A realistic estimate of the length of gestation is not the norm until 11 years of age, and an understanding of gestation itself, what happens developmentally in the uterus and how the foetus survives in relation to the mother, is not comprehended adequately by most children, even at 15 years. We suspect that human biology is given too low a priority in secondary schools so that sequential teaching in this subject is inadequate. A similar conclusion may be reached about how children perceive the actual birth process and what are the causes and mechanisms of childbirth. There is considerable vagueness and mythology which makes this area unnecessarily confusing for the children. The medical mythologies referred to earlier are apparent here. Many of the manufacturers see the seed as inserted by the doctor by operating on the mother (this explains why she has to visit him so early in pregnancy) who cuts her open to insert the seed. Childbirth is cutting her open and extracting the baby once it has grown large enough. Thus the manufacturers and the agriculturalists, who see the mother as a greenhouse-cum-incubator, strongly adhere to the Caesarean as the normal process of childbirth.

Other agriculturalists see the birth exit as through the anus (Freud's cloacal theory is well supported by our evidence from 5- and 7-year-olds) and is all of a piece with the digestive fallacy, since the baby is made from the special food mother eats, and since all food is evacuated through the anus that is where the baby comes out.

Of all the biological problems posed to the children in this study the genetic determination of sex was the most difficult. Sexual transmission of the sex determinants is not clearly grasped until 13 years in the English-speaking groups, but any real concept of genetic transmission is only beginning to be perceived by 15 years. It appears to us that given good human biology teaching in sequential order at an earlier age, these difficult ideas could be grasped earlier (as in Sweden) but probably not much earlier than 13 years. A higher form of formal operations apears to be necessary to hypothesise adequately on this topic.

Birth-control knowledge

Children become aware about the age of 9 years that it is possible not to have babies by parents taking certain steps to prevent it. In the non-sexual cognitive period, when sexuality is not perceived as essential for procreation, it is felt that nothing can be done or the manufacturers and agriculturalists simply do not continue their activities. Once sexual intercourse is seen as a cause, the abstention from sex is seen as one method of birth-control, but by 11 years one partner or the other (one-sex devices) is perceived as being able to do something. Awareness of both-sex devices is not normally known until 13 years and in some groups (Australian girls, for example) not until 15 years. This is in contrast to Swedish 9-year-old girls and 11-year-old Swedish boys who have some knowledge of what each sex might do, and devices to use.

This is a serious time-lag, in our view, in the English-speaking countries. The evidence on earlier maturing and estimates about earlier full sexual activity by teenagers indicates that information about contraception devices and birth-control generally should be made available at 11 years at the latest. The evidence also indicates this to be a taboo area in sex education, and where information is given it is provided too late in many cases, since sexual intercourse may have been experienced already, with all its attendant risks. It should not, however, be seen as an emergency panic measure to avoid teenage pregnancies or venereal infection, but as a long-term preparation which every growing child approaching puberty has a right to know.

The earlier introduction of birth-control knowledge is supported by Rubin and Kirkendall (1969) who write, 'Psychiatric thinking suggests that the best time for the youngster to receive factual information about such subjects is the period in which his emotions in respect to that information are dormant or less involved'.

When in the teenage years subjects such as birth-control are continued in the context of human relations, and accompanied by moral and religious education, the choices open to the developing adolescents are known and can be examined and discussed. To refuse information or to discuss birth-control, when teenagers know increasingly that contraceptive devices exist, however vague their knowledge, is to practise hypocrisy which adolescents rightly discern to be typical of so many of their dealings with adults.

Knowledge of abortion

In the stage that children see birth-control as pre-sexual they revealed a knowledge of the post-natal disposal of babies. More than 30 per cent showed awareness of giving away, fostering, adopting and institutionalising of unwanted babies once they were born, although no direct question was asked about this. In all countries children were generally aware of abortion, although not necessarily the name, as a process for disposing of unwanted babies before birth. At 7 and 9 years Swedish children appeared to be aware in much greater proportion than children in the English-speaking countries. What was most striking about the children's knowledge of abortion from 11 years onwards were the indirect indications that girls regarded the process disapprovingly or with some revulsion. Nevertheless, we see no reason to leave children of 11 years and older in such a partial state of knowledge and every reason, in the proper setting of human relations, to educate them more about abortion and to discuss its meaning. If birth-control is presented, abortion is an accompanying converse side of the picture as one of the possible consequences of unwanted pregnancies.

Those who would protest on moral grounds that matters such as these should not destroy the innocence of childhood should read the evidence presented in chapter 2, and the general results of this study. Children by the age of 11 years are far from ignorant about birth-control and abortion. In our view partial knowledge is more dangerous a state on these topics than complete knowledge. Moralists should consider the immorality of silence and opposition to information, which may help children avoid the very moral dangers about which some moralists so loudly and negatively admonish society.

How children perceive sex education

The first important feature to note is the overwhelming evidence that children do wish to receive sex information, explanations and knowledge both from their parents and during their schooling. The vast majority wish to see sex education in the pre-pubertal period, in primary (elementary) school. Some Swedish age groups assert that sex education is best begun in pre-school. Yet the current practice is quite the opposite, except in Sweden where 85 per cent of the children claim to have received some sex education in primary school. In the English-speaking samples less than 40 per cent on average of children at 11 years said they had received any sex education in school up to that time. But sizeable groups of teenagers claim they had no sex education at all in school, including 38 per cent in Australia and 27 per cent in North America, compared with Sweden's 2 per cent.

This raises a social question of the first importance. If parents refuse permission for their children to attend sex education classes, and do not provide adequate sex education in the home – as the evidence from considerable numbers of children indicates – then has society any responsibility to ensure the children are informed and educated in what the children themselves see to be an important area? And what are the rights of the children in this respect? Sweden has solved the problem by the introduction of compulsory sex education for all children from the age of 8 years. Although there are clauses and limited exceptions to this law, the Swedish parliament has deemed children's rights to be of greater importance and of higher priority than those of parents. This is not to argue that the Swedish example is the best to follow, nor that all is sexually perfect in Sweden as a result. We do suggest that wider provision be given at an earlier age than is customary in the English-speaking countries' school systems, together with other measures which would enable parents to be better sex educators of their own children.

In terms of content children felt strongly that they should know about the origin of babies, conception, pregnancy, child-bearing and childbirth and related matters. Most children expressed the need to know about their own body development, particularly sexual changes which occur, the older girls emphasising strongly the need to be prepared for menstruation and to know why it occurs. Older boys, by contrast, felt they needed to know about coitus; what it is, how to do it and how to behave. Considerable anxiety was expressed by teenagers in both these areas. Contraception was also a major concern. What was not seen as a need was help in knowing about courting behaviour, parenting skills or venereal disease. Indeed the vast majority of teenagers in all countries appeared to be blissfully ignorant about venereal infection, despite its widespread incidence and the greater vulnerability of young people.

389

The contrast between what the children felt they needed to know and what they said they received, was considerable in almost every area of sex education identified. But the greatest shortfall between need and provision was in the area of birth-control, which we could character-ise as 'too little, too late'.

The results of other items analysed in chapter 14 show, however, that the home is regarded by children as the most important major source of sex information, especially mother. Father is not so regarded, girls particularly have no confidence in asking their fathers about sex, but both girls and boys have confidence in general in their mothers. There is a marked reluctance to ask teachers or friends about sex, mainly because of the fear of ridicule. Nevertheless when asked to name the most important source of sex information the children give mother, teachers and media sources, in that order. These account for 80 per cent of the responses, little importance being attached to friends, siblings, 'picking-it-up', medical or other sources.

Fears are frequently expressed that too much sex information will encourage sexual precocity in the young and lead to sexual promiscuity. An interesting study by Lewis (1973) found that where parents were the main source of sex education their maturing children were less prone to be promiscuous and had significantly engaged in premarital sexual intercourse less often. Rather than stimulate coital experience such sex education was seen as an effective deterrent and for girls especially as an agent of sexual socialisation.

All this indicates the pressing need to help parents to become more effective sex educators, particularly mothers, by providing short courses, suitable literature and perhaps media programmes children can watch with parents as their teachers. The home/school dyad should not be regarded as either/or sex education choices but as complementary services, mutually supportive and co-operating in choice of suitable content. The beginnings of co-operation have been attempted between the major sources of sex information, between parents and teachers and between teachers and the media, but not to our knowledge effectively involving all three. This, however, is a matter to be elaborated in detail in our second publication, 'Readiness for Sex Education'.

Clothes, nakedness and embarrassment

The exploration of reasons for why people wear clothes yielded some interesting results. If they can be regarded as indicators of sexual inhibitions, then in the childhood years Sweden is the least inhibited, followed closely by Australia, with North America the most inhibited. In the teenage years the picture is somewhat different, girls especially arguing for the sexual parts to be covered. The evidence is strong that teenagers in particular are fearful of revealing sexual abnormalities or atypical physical characteristics, many of them imaginary.

Kohlberg's three levels of moral thinking were clearly seen with the majority of children making conventional moral judgments. But there were wide differences between countries in reasons given for wearing clothes, only 28 per cent of the English 15-year-olds reaching post-conventional thinking compared with 80 per cent of the Australian 15-year-olds. This is not entirely a climatic factor since the Melbourne area is said to have 'English weather'. Sex differences were very evident in answers to 'why should people be embarrassed' by nakedness?, boys showing less concern and higher level responses than girls. Overall the results on the clothes and nakedness items reveal low level thinking and suggest the need in home and school sex education to inculcate healthier attitudes to the naked body as natural and normal.

The major findings of this study

1 Piaget's cognitive developmental stages are evident in sexual thinking, in terms of pre-operations, concrete operations and formal operations, with similar stages closely parallel to, but not identical with, the Piagetian stages, of non-sexual, transitional sexual and fully sexual stages of cognition.

2 Kohlberg's three levels of pre-conventional, conventional and post-conventional moral thinking are evident in certain items, although his six stages are not clearly seen in strict sequence.

3 Freud's cloacal theory of childbirth is well supported in the years from 5 to 7, but there is no evidence to support the Oedipal family situation as a normal process in family life or child development. The evidence against a latency period in children's sexuality is so strong as to merit the description of 'the myth of latency'.

4 Considerable time lags appear in most of the items which compose children's sexual thinking, revealing low level thinking and problem solving. These time lags are often so long that they could be described as representing a retardation in children's sexual thinking, except among Swedish children.

5 The evidence from the Swedish sample indicates that the retardation observed in the English-speaking children of this study may be due to cultural and educational differences and that children are capable of understanding quite complex biological concepts much earlier than was at first thought. Only two of the concepts examined — the causes of childbirth at a particular time, and the sex determination of babies — were judged to be appropriate at the secondary school level only.

6 Retardation of sexual thinking is postulated as due partly to

inadequate communication and adult inhibitions about using correct terminology and descriptions with children, the consequential usage of sexual pseudonyms by children, and the need to find suitable explanations for sexuality without adequate information. False analogies in sexual thinking appear to cause confusion and assist retarded thinking.

7 In the absence of adequate and systematic sex education, children invent their own explanations for biological and sexual processes often in the form of mythologies; medical mythologies being the dominant explanations in early to middle childhood.

8 Sex education is seen as necessary by the vast majority of children and should be provided in primary (elementary) schools, whereas the provision actually given to the majority appears to be in 'secondary schools only' — apart from Sweden — and often late in secondary schooling. In the English-speaking countries a sizeable proportion of teenagers report having received no sex education at school, while some of these report no help from their parents. A considerable shortfall exists between what the children want to know and what they claim to have received, which in their view is provided too late.

9 Tne home remains the most cited major source of sex information in the person of the mothers, with teachers and the media as secondary major sources. Children have considerable confidence in asking sex questions from mother, little confidence in asking them of fathers, friends or teachers, unless the latter are specialist teachers in sex education or related subjects. The indications are that parents, particularly mothers, need assistance in helping them to be more effective sex educators of their own children. Attention should also be directed to encouraging fathers to become more involved in their children's sex education.

10 The best conditions for well-developed sexual thinking would as reflected in evidence from our study appear to be upbringing in a family with at least one other-sex sibling in a family of three children or more, a well informed active mother who works or studies full-time, and a systematic school sex education programme in the primary school to follow the early years at home. Since the decreasing size of families makes several of these conditions inaccessible to the majority of children, supplementary sex education through other social agencies, schools in particular, becomes a pressing social need.

11 The time-lags and retardations reported should be seen in the context of the basic requirements for inclusion of children in this study, namely a two-parent family and at least one younger sibling. 65 per cent of the sample over-all were children who had an other-

sex sibling in the family, and 54 per cent came from families with more than two children.

12 The overall results should be viewed in the light of the practical background to this study described in detail in chapter 2. By far the most relevant would appear to be the factors of early maturing and the earlier onset of sexual activity.

The most comprehensive need which emerges from the results outlined above, a need still not met successfully, is a sequential series of specific programmes which involve home and school, parents and teachers, accompanied by appropriate resources, including the media. These programmes, however, should be based not upon adult intuition nor upon guesstimates of what children and teenagers can understand about sex at various ages, but upon what research demonstrates they are capable of understanding. The major contribution of this research has been, we believe, to suggest certain sequences upon which realistic programmes can be based than have been devised so far.

A comprehensive search of English, American and Scandinavian sources by the authors reveals that there is no shortage of certain types of resource material for children to learn about sex and sexuality; books, pictures, charts, three-dimensional models, films and many other aids for parents and teachers to use. Indeed, the choice is often bewildering. Despite this, there are many serious omissions and far too much well intentioned but misleading material, which while designed to enlighten may only add to children's confusions about sex.

What in our view is the greatest need is a conceptual structure for children's sexual thinking, to provide guidelines for programmes, and teaching materials which are developmentally, psychologically and socially sound. The authors have already begun to develop such a conceptual structure, which will be presented in *Readiness for Sex Education*, a sequel to the study dealt with in this volume.

Appendix A: Sample statistics and scorer reliabilities

TABLE A.1 *Size of family in percentages by country and age group*

Age	Australia	England	North America	Sweden
5 year				
Small	47.5	70	70.8	76.7
Medium	52.5	30	29.2	23.3
Large	–	–	–	–
7 year				
Small	30	65	46.7	66.7
Medium	70	35	50.0	33.3
Large	–	–	3.3	–
9 year				
Small	47.5	67.5	53.3	53.3
Medium	50.0	30	43.3	46.7
Large	2.5	2.5	3.3	–
11 year				
Small	22.5	45	33.3	56.7
Medium	67.5	50	66.7	40.0
Large	10.0	5	–	3.3
13 year				
Small	20	30	39.4	53.3
Medium	70	62.5	60.6	43.3
Large	10	7.5	–	3.3
15 year				
Small	22.5	25	32.3	43.3
Medium	60.0	70	61.3	56.7
Large	17.5	5	6.5	–
Totals				
Small	31.7	50.4	44.9	58.3
Medium	61.7	46.2	52.8	40.6
Large	6.7	3.3	2.2	1.1

(Small = 2 children; Medium = 3–5 children; Large = 6 children or more.)

TABLE A.2   *Frequency of birth order*

Year		1	2	3	4	5
5 AUS (40)		27	10	3	0	0
ENG (40)		33	7	0	0	0
N.AM (24)		21	3	0	0	0
SW (30)		25	4	1	0	0
7 AUS (40)		24	10	3	3	0
ENG (40)		34	4	2	0	0
N.AM (30)		14	10	5	1	0
SW (30)		22	6	1	1	0
9 AUS (40)		28	8	3	1	0
ENG (40)		32	7	0	1	0
N.AM (30)		20	7	2	1	0
SW (30)		19	9	2	0	0
11 AUS (40)		20	10	2	6	2
ENG (40)		28	6	3	3	0
N.AM (30)		15	8	5	2	0
SW (30)		19	8	2	1	0
13 AUS (40)		16	16	6	2	0
ENG (40)		20	10	7	3	0
N.AM (33)		20	10	3	0	0
SW (30)		24	5	0	1	0
15 AUS (40)		17	10	9	0	4
ENG (40)		22	10	6	2	0
N.AM (31)		19	7	2	2	1
SW (30)		19	9	1	0	1

(1 = 1st born, oldest; 2 = 2nd born, etc.)

TABLE A.3   Mean scores* of father's occupation by country, age and sex

Year	Australia			England			North America			Sweden		
	Boys	Girls	Total	Boys	Girls	Total	Boys	Girls	Total	Boys	Girls	Total
5	46.70	46.60	46.65	45.10	52.05	48.58	39.31	40.91	40.11	43.07	43.87	43.47
7	44.80	50.10	47.45	52.25	44.95	48.60	39.63	50.21	44.92	50.60	45.07	47.84
9	45.55	52.40	48.96	43.60	50.00	46.80	42.20	45.93	44.01	44.07	44.27	44.17
11	49.00	49.90	49.45	46.20	42.80	44.50	43.93	44.80	44.37	48.53	41.33	44.93
13	45.05	44.75	44.90	45.70	48.30	47.00	45.88	42.47	44.18	39.80	49.40	44.45
15	49.65	43.25	46.45	49.90	51.65	50.78	44.13	39.07	41.60	46.73	49.33	48.03
Entire population			47.31			47.71			43.25			45.74

(* Scores are based upon the Standard International Occupational Prestige Scale: Treiman, 1977.)

TABLE A.4 *Percentages of father's occupation in four categories by country and age-year*

	Australia	England	North America	Sweden
Very low	16.6	18.3	10.7	15.0
Low	41.3	40.8	25.8	33.3
Middle	30.0	32.5	43.3	34.4
Upper	12.1	8.4	20.2	17.3

(Very low = 13-33; Low = 34-43; Middle = 44-57; Upper = 58-79)

TABLE A.5 *Percentages of mother's occupation in three categories by country and age-year*

Year	Australia			England			North America			Sweden		
	1	2	3	1	2	3	1	2	3	1	2	3
5	57	14	29	84	3	13	70	20	10	27	23	50
7	73	15	12	53	14	33	56	29	15	17	40	43
9	42	31	28	33	6	61	70	20	10	27	37	37
11	40	26	34	38	19	43	53	7	40	20	33	47
13	55	18	27	25	15	60	59	19	22	3	40	57
15	35	10	55	26	15	59	48	10	42	3	33	64

(1 = home duties only; 2 = part-time job or study; 3 = full time job or study)

TABLE A.6 *Mean scores of mother's occupations**

	Australia	England	North America	Sweden
$\bar{X}$	1.63	1.89	1.59	2.35
SD	1.05	1.09	0.92	0.82
Variance	1.10	1.18	0.85	0.69
N	240	240	178	180

(* Score 1 = home duties only; Score 2 = part-time job or study; Score 3 = full time job or study)

TABLE A.7   *Frequency of ratings by teachers of interviewed pupils*

Year			1	2	3	4	5
5	AUS	(40)	2	3	22	13	0
	ENG	(40)	0	1	17	21	1
	N.AM	(24)	2	1	11	9	1
	SW	(30)	–	–	–	–	–
7	AUS	(40)	0	9	17	11	3
	ENG	(40)	0	7	13	17	3
	N.AM	(30)	0	6	13	8	3
	SW	(30)	1	4	13	9	3
9	AUS	(40)	1	6	13	15	5
	ENG	(40)	0	8	16	12	4
	N.AM	(30)	0	3	15	10	2
	SW	(30)	1	3	16	7	3
11	AUS	(40)	1	4	19	11	5
	ENG	(40)	2	8	7	16	7
	N.AM	(30)	2	3	12	7	6
	SW	(30)	0	5	8	12	5
13	AUS	(40)	0	3	19	16	2
	ENG	(40)	2	8	16	11	3
	N.AM	(33)	1	2	12	13	5
	SW	(30)	0	2	21	7	0
15	AUS	(40)	2	4	18	12	4
	ENG	(40)	4	5	15	14	2
	N.AM	(31)	0	4	11	10	6
	SW	(30)	0	7	13	6	4

(Since some countries use standardised tests to assess ability, other countries do not, and the tests vary enormously, teachers' estimates of ability are taken. These were in 5 categories: 1 = well below average; 2 = below average; 3 = average; 4 = above average; 5 = well above average. Swedish kindergarten teachers felt unable to make any estimates of their 5-year-olds' abilities.)

TABLE A.8   *Analyses of Variance to assess main effects of country*

Independent variable	d.f.	Mean squares	F	Significance
Family size	3	18.072	13.15	***
Residual	834	1.375		
Birth order	3	7.148	6.43	***
Residual	834	1.111		
Father's occupation	3	808.959	5.89	***
Residual	834	137.424		

TABLE A.8 (*cont.*)

Independent variable	d.f	Mean squares	F	Significance
Mother's occupation	3	23.176	23.68	***
Residual	834	0.979		
Ability estimates	3	16.452	14.41	***
Residual	834	1.141		

(*** = p < .001)

TABLE A.9   *Three-way Analyses of Variance to assess interactions between country and age-year*

Independent variable		d.f.	Mean squares	F	Significance
Size of family					
by:	Country	3	18.255	14.61	***
	Age-year	5	20.136	16.21	***
Two-way interactions					
Country – age-year		15	1.926	1.54	NS
Residual		814	1.249		
Birth order					
by:	Country	3	7.168	6.75	***
	Age-year	5	8.458	7.97	***
Two-way interactions					
Country – age-year		15	1.354	1.28	NS
Residual		814	1.133		
Father's occupation					
by:	Country	3	816.250	5.93	***
	Age-year	5	97.975	0.71	NS
Two-way interactions					
Country – age-year		15	134.228	0.98	NS
Residual		814	137.725		
Mother's occupation					
by:	Country	3	23.885	27.25	***
	Age-year	5	15.063	17.19	***
Two-way interactions					
Country – age-year		15	1.836	2.09	**
Residual		814	0.876		
Ability					
by:	Country	3	15.954	19.60	***
	Age-year	5	12.939	15.89	***
Two-way interactions					
Country – age-year		15	14.969	18.39	***
Residual		814	0.814		

(*** = p < .001; ** = p < .01; NS = not significant)

TABLE A.10 *Some scorer reliabilities in percentages and Pearson product moment correlations*

Item description	Percentage agreement	Scorer 1 X̄ score	Scorer 2 X̄ score	r
Origin of babies	84.8	3.43	3.41	0.95
Role of mother	85.7	3.41	3.40	0.92
Role of father	91.5	3.47	3.41	0.95
Reasons for birth	77.0	2.52	2.51	0.91
Sex determination	85.9	2.74	2.63	0.91
Contraception scale	84.0	3.43	3.46	0.95
Abortion scale	84.6	1.25	1.17	0.81
Adoption scale	72.0	0.58	0.56	0.86
Pregnancy vocabulary	94.0	2.79	2.78	0.96
Conception vocabulary	93.2	1.53	1.51	0.92
Stripping vocabulary	94.1	3.05	3.01	0.87
Rape vocabulary	91.2	3.34	3.32	0.96
VD vocabulary	79.3	1.86	1.61	0.75
Uterus vocabulary	93.4	1.81	1.82	0.93
Puberty vocabulary	97.5	1.84	1.83	0.98
Virgin vocabulary	94.4	2.35	2.40	0.96
Contraception vocabulary	88.5	2.29	2.30	0.91
Abortion vocabulary	93.7	1.77	1.74	0.94
Why wear clothes	80.7	2.76	2.88	0.81
Embarrassment	79.3	2.80	2.79	0.89

Appendix B: Results of testing for significant sex differences

Although there were marked sex differences in responses to many items, only those meeting the rigorous statistical requirement $p < .05$ are included here.

To assist clarity of presentation the chi-square test results are presented first (Tables B.1 to B.11), and the t-test results are presented second (Tables B.12 to B.27).

Chi-square tests for significant sex differences

All tables are 'corrected' where small numbers are involved. Fisher's exact test is occasionally used. In all tables * = $p < .05$; ** = $p < .01$; *** = $p < .001$.

TABLE B.1 *Significant sex differences in perceiving parents*

Question	Response	Country	Age	N	Corrected chi-square	d.f.	Signif.	Sex bias
Parental differences	Physical non-sexual	SWED	9	30	Fisher's	—	0.030	* B
	Overt sexual	SWED	9	30	Fisher's	—	0.007	** G
	Overt sexual	ENG	15	40	4.949	1	0.026	* B
	Overt sexual	SWED	15	30	Fisher's	—	0.013	* B
	Functional and social	ENG	5	40	3.906	1	0.048	* G
	Attitudinal	AUS	15	40	3.840	1	0.050	* G
	Attitudinal	SWED	15	30	Fisher's	—	0.011	* G
Mother's distinctive roles	Domestic — inside	AUS	11	40	10.230	1	0.001	** B
	Domestic — inside	AUS	13	40	4.103	1	0.043	* B
	Domestic — inside	SWED	15	30	9.187	1	0.002	** G
	Child-care	SWED	15	30	5.208	1	0.023	* B
	Leisure	ENG	7	40	3.906	1	0.048	* G
Father's distinctive roles	Domestic — outside	N.AM	15	31	4.779	1	0.029	* B
	Domestic — outside	SWED	13	30	5.208	1	0.023	* G
	Domestic — outside	SWED	15	30	6.806	1	0.009	** G
	Child-care	ENG	15	40	4.103	1	0.043	* B
	Child-care	SWED	15	30	3.840	1	0.050	* B
	Leisure	AUS	15	40	3.906	1	0.048	* B
	Leisure	ENG	15	40	4.902	1	0.027	* B

Favourite parent	Mother	N.AM	5	24	6.063	1	0.014	*	G
	Mother	N.AM	7	30	3.593	1	0.050	*	G
	Mother	AUS	7	40	3.840	1	0.050	*	G
	Mother	N.AM	11	30	11.250	1	0.001	***	G
	Mother	ENG	11	40	8.901	1	0.003	**	G
	Mother	ENG	13	40	8.182	1	0.004	**	G
	Mother	ENG	15	40	5.833	1	0.016	*	G
Reasons for favourite: mother	Personal services	SWED	9	30	3.840	1	0.050	*	G
	Supportive	SWED	9	30	4.261	1	0.039	*	G
	Supportive	SWED	13	30	8.352	1	0.004	**	G
Reasons for favourite: father	Gift provider	SWED	9	30	3.840	1	0.050	*	G
	Personal services	SWED	5	30	3.840	1	0.050	*	B
	Personal services	AUS	7	40	5.161	1	0.023	*	B
	Personal services	AUS	11	40	6.533	1	0.011	*	B
	Personal services	AUS	15	40	5.833	1	0.016	*	B
	Teacher – induction	AUS	5	40	4.103	1	0.043	*	B
	Teacher – induction	AUS	7	40	11.396	1	0.001	***	B
	Teacher – induction	SWED	9	30	3.840	1	0.050	*	G
	Teacher – induction	ENG	13	40	4.103	1	0.043	*	B
	Teacher – induction	ENG	15	40	5.833	1	0.016	*	B
	Teacher – induction	AUS	15	40	3.906	1	0.048	*	B
	Supportive	SWED	15	30	9.187	1	0.002	**	G

TABLE B.2   Significant sex differences in choice of gender identity (boys)

Question	Response	Country	Age	N	Corrected chi-square	d.f.	Signif.	Sex bias
Choice of	Boys	AUS	5	40	26.189	1	<0.001	*** B
gender identity		AUS	7	40	29.192	1	<0.001	*** B
(self)		AUS	9	40	26.189	1	<0.001	*** B
		AUS	11	40	22.500	1	<0.001	*** B
		AUS	13	40	14.436	1	0.001	*** B
		AUS	15	40	29.192	1	<0.001	*** B
		ENG	5	40	36.100	1	<0.001	*** B
		ENG	7	40	25.664	1	<0.001	*** B
		ENG	9	40	29.192	1	<0.001	*** B
		ENG	11	40	20.051	1	<0.001	*** B
		ENG	13	40	10.800	1	0.001	*** B
		ENG	15	40	22.727	1	<0.001	*** B
		N.AM	5	24	16.783	1	<0.001	*** B
		N.AM	7	30	13.274	1	0.001	*** B
		N.AM	9	30	11.250	1	0.001	*** B
		N.AM	11	30	13.333	1	0.001	*** B
		N.AM	13	33	16.307	1	0.001	*** B
		N.AM	15	31	9.307	1	0.002	** B
		SWED	5	30	19.200	1	<0.001	*** B
		SWED	7	30	22.634	1	<0.001	*** B
		SWED	9	30	19.200	1	<0.001	*** B
		SWED	11	30	22.634	1	<0.001	*** B
		SWED	13	30	14.354	1	0.001	*** B
		SWED	15	30	22.634	1	<0.001	*** B

TABLE B.3 *Significant sex differences in choice of gender identity (girls)*

Question	Response	Country	Age	N	Corrected chi-square	d.f.	Signif.	Sex bias
Choice of	Girls	AUS	5	40	26.189	1	<0.001	*** G
gender identity		AUS	7	40	29.192	1	<0.001	*** G
(self)		AUS	9	40	26.189	1	<0.001	*** G
		AUS	11	40	19.649	1	<0.001	*** G
		AUS	13	40	14.436	1	0.001	*** G
		AUS	15	40	29.192	1	<0.001	*** G
		ENG	5	40	36.100	1	<0.001	*** G
		ENG	7	40	25.664	1	<0.001	*** G
		ENG	9	40	29.192	1	<0.001	*** G
		ENG	11	40	20.051	1	<0.001	*** G
		ENG	13	40	10.800	1	0.001	*** G
		ENG	15	40	22.727	1	<0.001	*** G
		N.AM	5	24	16.783	1	<0.001	*** G
		N.AM	7	30	13.274	1	0.001	*** G
		N.AM	9	30	11.250	1	0.001	*** G
		N.AM	11	30	13.333	1	0.001	*** G
		N.AM	13	33	16.307	1	0.001	*** G
		N.AM	15	31	9.307	1	0.002	** G
		SWED	5	30	19.200	1	<0.001	*** G
		SWED	7	30	22.634	1	<0.001	*** G
		SWED	9	30	19.200	1	<0.001	*** G
		SWED	11	30	22.634	1	<0.001	*** G
		SWED	13	30	14.354	1	0.001	*** G
		SWED	15	30	16.806	1	<0.001	*** G

TABLE B.4 Significant sex differences in reasons for choice of gender identity

Question	Response	Country	Age	N	Corrected chi-square	d.f.	Signif.	Sex bias	
Reasons for choice of gender identity self	Recreational	AUS	13	40	8.438	1	0.004	**	B
		AUS	15	40	8.182	1	0.004	**	B
		ENG	5	40	6.827	1	0.009	**	B
		ENG	13	40	5.385	1	0.020	*	B
		N.AM	15	31	5.591	1	0.018	*	B
		SWED	7	30	6.563	1	0.011	*	B
		SWED	11	30	5.714	1	0.017	*	B
		SWED	13	30	9.187	1	0.002	**	B
	Behaviour – temperament	ENG	9	40	3.840	1	0.050	*	G
	Sexual	AUS	5	40	5.161	1	0.023	*	G
		AUS	9	40	8.901	1	0.003	**	G
		AUS	15	40	7.293	1	0.007	**	G
		ENG	5	40	5.385	1	0.020	*	G
		ENG	7	40	4.103	1	0.043	*	G
		ENG	11	40	6.533	1	0.011	*	G
		ENG	15	40	16.900	1	<0.001	***	G
		N.AM	7	30	5.242	1	0.022	*	G
		N.AM	9	30	6.806	1	0.009	**	G
		SWED	5	30	4.261	1	0.039	*	G
		SWED	9	30	6.708	1	0.010	**	G
		SWED	11	30	5.714	1	0.017	*	G
		SWED	15	30	3.840	1	0.050	*	G

TABLE B.5 Significant sex differences in reasons for choice of friends

Question	Response	Country	Age	N	Corrected chi-square	d.f.	Signif.	Sex bias
Reasons for choice of friend (boys)	Identity of activities	AUS	7	40	14.436	1	<0.001	*** B
		AUS	9	40	15.360	1	<0.001	*** B
		AUS	11	40	7.293	1	0.007	** B
		AUS	13	40	6.533	1	0.010	* B
		AUS	15	40	15.360	1	0.001	*** B
		ENG	5	40	25.664	1	<0.001	*** B
		ENG	7	40	22.500	1	<0.001	*** B
		ENG	9	40	20.907	1	<0.001	*** B
		ENG	11	40	15.360	1	<0.001	*** B
		ENG	13	40	13.297	1	0.001	*** B
		ENG	15	40	10.800	1	0.001	*** B
		N.AM	5	24	6.565	1	0.011	* B
		N.AM	7	30	9.381	1	0.002	** B
		N.AM	9	30	10.848	1	0.001	*** B
		N.AM	11	30	12.150	1	0.001	*** B
		N.AM	13	33	5.475	1	0.019	* B
		N.AM	15	31	4.779	1	0.029	* B
		SWED	5	30	4.800	1	0.029	* B
		SWED	13	30	5.208	1	0.023	* B

(cont. . .)

Table B.5 (cont...)

Question	Response	Country	Age	N	Corrected chi-square	d.f.	Signif.	Sex bias
Reasons for choice of friend (girls)	Identity of activities	AUS	9	40	6.533	1	0.011	*	G
		ENG	5	40	22.222	1	0.001	***	G
		ENG	7	40	8.812	1	0.004	**	G
		ENG	9	40	20.051	1	<0.001	***	G
		ENG	11	40	9.643	1	0.002	**	G
		ENG	15	40	3.906	1	0.048	*	G
		N.AM	7	30	5.363	1	0.021	*	G
		N.AM	9	30	5.714	1	0.017	*	G
		N.AM	11	30	7.350	1	0.007	**	G
		SWED	5	30	6.708	1	0.010	**	G
		SWED	9	30	4.261	1	0.039	*	G
	Identity of feeling	AUS	9	40	6.234	1	0.013	*	G
		ENG	7	40	3.906	1	0.048	*	G
		ENG	9	40	10.800	1	0.001	**	G
		ENG	11	40	9.176	1	0.003	**	G
		ENG	13	40	25.664	1	<0.001	***	G
		ENG	15	40	4.950	1	0.026	*	G
		SWED	7	30	10.159	1	0.002	**	G
		SWED	11	30	7.350	1	0.007	**	G
	Sexual attraction	AUS	13	40	6.533	1	0.011	*	B

TABLE B.6 *Significant sex differences in aversion to other sex*

Question	Response	Country	Age	N	Corrected chi-square	d.f.	Signif.	Sex bias	
Aversion	Aversion to other sex	AUS	5	40	3.333	1	0.050	*	G
		SWED	7	30	11.250	1	0.001	***	G
		SWED	13	30	8.352	1	0.004	**	G
		SWED	15	30	5.208	1	0.023	*	G

TABLE B.7 *Significant sex differences in correct terms for describing the sex organs*

Question	Response	Country	Age	N	Corrected chi-square	d.f.	Signif.	Sex bias	
Sex organs	Correct description	SWED	15	30	5.208	1	0.023	*	G

TABLE B.8 *Significant sex differences in reasons for coitus*

Question	Response	Country	Age	N	Corrected chi-square	d.f.	Signif.	Sex bias	
Reasons for coitus	Enjoyment	AUS	13	40	8.182	1	0.004	**	B
		N.AM	11	30	3.840	1	0.050	*	B
		SWED	13	30	8.352	1	0.004	**	B
	Expression of love	ENG	13	40	4.514	1	0.037	*	G
		N.AM	15	31	3.934	1	0.047	*	G
		SWED	13	30	5.714	1	0.017	*	G

TABLE B.9 Significant sex differences in asking sex questions of mother, father and friends

Question	Response	Country	Age	N	Corrected chi-square	d.f.	Signif.	Sex bias	
Sex education: 'Would you ask mother?'	Yes	AUS	5	40	4.103	1	0.043	*	G
		AUS	11	40	14.436	1	<0.001	***	G
		AUS	15	40	14.436	1	<0.001	***	G
		ENG	7	40	9.643	1	0.002	**	G
		ENG	9	40	8.901	1	0.003	**	G
		ENG	11	40	8.901	1	0.003	**	G
		ENG	13	40	8.438	1	0.004	**	G
		ENG	15	40	23.438	1	<0.001	***	G
		N.AM	7	30	5.731	1	0.017	*	G
		N.AM	9	30	13.575	1	<0.001	***	G
		N.AM	11	30	11.250	1	0.001	***	G
		N.AM	13	33	13.725	1	<0.001	***	G
		N.AM	15	31	13.122	1	0.001	***	G
		SWED	13	30	13.575	1	<0.001	***	G
'Would you ask father?'	Yes	ENG	15	40	6.533	1	0.011	*	B
'Would you ask friends?'	Yes	AUS	13	40	7.656	1	0.006	**	B
		SWED	15	30	6.436	1	0.040	*	G

410

TABLE B.10 *Significant sex differences in citing major sources of sex information*

Question	Response	Country	Age	N	Corrected chi-square	d.f.	Signif.	Sex bias	
Sex education	Mother major source of information	AUS	13	40	20.051	1	<0.001	***	G
		AUS	15	40	10.667	1	0.001	**	G
		ENG	11	40	7.294	1	0.007	**	G
		ENG	13	40	3.840	1	0.050	*	G
		ENG	15	40	7.656	1	0.006	**	G
		N.AM	11	30	4.687	1	0.027	*	G
		N.AM	13	33	5.369	1	0.021	*	G
		N.AM	15	31	11.648	1	0.001	***	G
	Teacher major source of information	AUS	13	40	6.416	1	0.011	*	B
		SWED	15	30	4.261	1	0.039	*	B
	Media major source of information	AUS	15	40	3.840	1	0.050	*	B
		ENG	11	40	8.182	1	0.004	**	B
		N.AM	7	30	4.428	1	0.035	*	B
		SWED	13	30	6.563	1	0.011	*	B

TABLE B.11 *Significant sex differences in expressed needs for information in sex education classes*

Question	Response	Country	Age	N	Corrected chi-square	d.f.	Signif.	Sex bias
Sex education: 'What do you need to know?'	Pre-sexual	ENG	7	40	14.405	1	0.001	*** G
	Menstruation	AUS	11	40	12.539	1	<0.001	*** G
		AUS	13	40	12.539	1	<0.001	*** G
		AUS	15	40	10.800	1	0.001	*** G
		ENG	11	40	18.571	1	<0.001	*** G
		ENG	13	40	14.405	1	<0.001	*** G
		ENG	15	40	18.571	1	<0.001	*** G
		N.AM	11	30	5.714	1	0.017	* G
		N.AM	13	33	12.754	1	0.001	*** G
		N.AM	15	31	12.840	1	<0.001	*** G
		SWED	11	30	6.708	1	0.010	** G
		SWED	13	30	11.250	1	0.001	*** G
		SWED	15	30	8.533	1	0.004	** G

Sexual intercourse	AUS	13	40	6.827	1	0.009	**	B
	AUS	15	40	5.104	1	0.024	*	B
	ENG	11	40	8.025	1	0.005	**	B
	ENG	13	40	11.396	1	0.001	***	B
	ENG	15	40	7.294	1	0.007	**	B
	N.AM	11	30	5.714	1	0.017	*	B
Conception	ENG	11	40	3.840	1	0.050	*	B
	SWED	9	30	5.208	1	0.023	*	G
Pregnancy	AUS	11	40	8.901	1	0.003	**	G
Birth process	AUS	11	40	5.161	1	0.023	*	G
Pubertal body growth	ENG	13	40	4.902	1	0.027	*	G

Sex education: most important item learned

T-tests for significant sex differences

(In all tables * = p < .05; ** = p < .01; *** = p < .001)

TABLE B.12 Significant sex differences in 'Causes of Ageing' scores

Variable	Country	Age	N	Sex	Mean score	S.D.	T. value	2 tail prob.	Signif.	Sex bias
Causes of ageing	ENG	5	20 20	B G	1.60 0.90	0.995 0.778	2.47	.018	*	B
	AUS	7	20 20	B G	2.45 0.95	1.191 0.605	5.02	< .001	***	B
	ENG	7	20 20	B G	2.30 1.40	1.418 0.821	2.46	.019	*	B
	N.AM	7	16 14	B G	1.94 0.86	1.063 0.770	3.15	.004	**	B
	AUS	9	20 20	B G	3.20 1.75	0.834 1.020	4.92	< .001	***	B
	ENG	9	20 20	B G	3.45 1.10	1.191 1.021	6.70	< .001	***	B
	N.AM	9	20 20	B G	2.80 1.53	1.424 1.125	2.70	.012	*	B
	AUS	11	20 20	B G	3.50 2.15	0.761 1.461	3.67	.001	***	B
	ENG	11	20 20	B G	3.20 2.00	1.152 1.338	3.04	.004	**	B

N.AM	11	15	B	3.93	0.799	5.05	<.001	***	
		15	G	2.13	1.125				B
ENG	13	20	B	4.00	1.076	4.14	<.001	***	
		20	G	2.30	1.490				B
ENG	15	20	B	4.10	0.912	4.57	<.001	***	
		20	G	2.40	1.392				B
N.AM	15	16	B	4.00	0.816	4.47	<.001	***	
		15	G	2.20	1.373				B

TABLE B.13 *Significant sex differences on 'Best time to be alive' scores*

Variable	Country	Age	N	Sex	Mean score	S.D.	T. value	2 tail prob.	Signif.	Sex bias
'Best time to be alive'	N.AM	7	16	B	2.38	0.719	-2.72	.011	*	
	N.AM		14	G	2.93	0.267				G
	SWED	9	15	B	2.67	1.175	-2.71	.011	*	
			15	G	3.60	0.632				G
	SWED	13	15	B	3.27	0.961	-3.28	.003	**	
			15	G	4.33	0.816				G

TABLE B.14 *Significant sex differences on 'Why people marry' scores*

Variable	Country	Age	N	Sex	Mean score	S.D.	T. value	2 tail prob.	Signif.	Sex bias
'Why people marry'	AUS	7	20	B	3.05	0.999	2.81	.008	**	B
			20	G	2.30	0.657				
	SWED	7	15	B	1.87	1.302	−2.20	.036	*	G
			15	G	2.73	0.799				
	SWED	9	15	B	2.40	1.056	−2.20	.036	*	G
			15	G	3.13	0.743				
	SWED	11	15	B	2.47	1.060	−3.47	.002	**	G
			15	G	3.67	0.816				
	SWED	13	15	B	2.80	0.676	−2.05	.050	*	G
			15	G	3.60	1.352				
	AUS	15	20	B	5.10	0.912	2.36	.023	*	B
			20	G	4.35	1.089				
	SWED	15	15	B	3.20	0.941	−2.46	.020	*	G
			15	G	4.27	1.387				

TABLE B.15 Significant sex differences in perceiving sex differences in newborn babies

Variable	Country	Age	N	Sex	Mean score	S.D.	T-value	2 tail prob.	Signif.	Sex bias
Sex difference of babies	ENG	5	20 20	B G	2.30 1.35	1.490 1.268	2.17	.036	*	B
	N.AM	5	13 11	B G	1.15 1.91	0.987 0.701	−2.12	.045	*	G
	SWED	5	15 15	B G	1.93 3.53	1.624 1.407	−2.88	.007	**	G
	SWED	9	15 15	B G	3.67 4.93	1.345 0.799	−3.14	.004	**	G

TABLE B.16 Significant sex differences in perceiving sex differences in puberty

Variable	Country	Age	N	Sex	Mean score	S.D.	T-value	2 tail prob.	Signif.	Sex bias
Sex difference in puberty	ENG	5	20 20	B G	2.00 1.00	1.338 1.170	2.52	.016	*	B
	SWED	5	15 15	B G	1.20 3.27	1.897 2.282	−2.70	.012	*	G
	ENG	7	20 20	B G	2.15 1.35	1.182 1.268	2.06	.046	*	B
	AUS	15	20 20	B G	5.20 4.25	1.436 1.517	2.03	.049	*	B
	N.AM	15	16 15	B G	5.63 3.73	0.806 1.751	3.91	.001	***	B

TABLE B.17 *Significant sex differences in 'Origin of babies' scores, and role of mothers and fathers in procreation scores*

Variable	Country	Age	N	Sex	Mean score	S.D.	T-value	2 tail prob.	Signif.	Sex bias
Origin of babies	ENG	5	20	B	2.05	0.686	2.30	.027	*	B
			20	G	1.55	0.686				
	ENG	9	20	B	3.65	1.089	2.46	.019	*	B
			20	G	2.60	1.569				
	SWED	9	15	B	3.53	1.407	−2.76	.010	**	G
			15	G	4.60	0.507				
	AUS	13	20	B	4.95	0.686	4.73	<.001	***	B
			20	G	3.90	0.718				
Mother's role in origin of babies	ENG	5	20	B	2.80	1.508	2.68	.011	*	B
			20	G	1.65	1.182				
	SWED	5	15	B	2.27	1.944	−2.46	.021	*	G
			15	G	3.67	1.047				
	ENG	7	20	B	3.30	1.218	2.12	.041	*	B
			20	G	2.45	1.317				
	ENG	9	20	B	4.35	1.040	4.44	<.001	***	B
			20	G	2.45	1.605				
	SWED	9	15	B	3.47	1.685	−3.15	.004	**	G
			15	G	4.87	0.352				
	ENG	11	20	B	4.00	1.518	2.92	.006	**	B
			20	G	2.30	2.296				

			Sex	N	Mean	SD	t	p	sig	
	N.AM	11	B	15	4.20	1.373	3.15	.004	**	B
			G	15	2.27	1.944				
	AUS	13	B	20	4.80	0.894	3.25	.002	**	B
			G	20	3.15	2.084				
	ENG	13	B	20	5.00	0.000	3.44	.001	***	B
			G	20	3.60	1.818				
	N.AM	13	B	16	4.81	0.544	2.71	.011	*	B
			G	17	3.35	2.090				
Father's role in origin of babies	ENG	7	B	20	2.65	1.565	2.24	.031	*	B
			G	20	1.55	1.538				
	ENG	9	B	20	4.20	1.399	2.63	.012	*	B
			G	20	2.85	1.814				
	SWED	9	B	15	3.87	1.767	−2.15	.040	*	G
			G	15	4.87	0.352				
	ENG	11	B	20	4.40	1.231	2.21	.033	*	B
			G	20	3.15	2.207				
	N.AM	11	B	15	4.47	1.302	2.20	.037	*	B
			G	15	3.13	1.959				
	ENG	13	B	20	5.00	0.000	2.50	.017	*	B
			G	20	3.95	1.877				
	N.AM	13	B	16	4.94	0.250	2.79	.009	**	B
			G	17	3.65	1.835				

TABLE B.18 *Significant sex differences in 'identifying birth exit' scores*

Variable	Country	Age	N	Sex	Mean score	S.D.	T-value	2 tail prob.	Signif.	Sex bias
Birth exit	SWED	5	15	B	1.87	1.407	−3.05	.005	**	
			15	G	3.20	0.941				G
	AUS	7	20	B	3.10	0.788	2.46	.019	*	
			20	G	2.20	1.436				B
	ENG	9	20	B	3.10	1.021	2.30	.027	*	
			20	G	2.10	1.651				B
	N.AM	9	15	B	2.93	1.100	2.77	.010	**	
			15	G	1.60	1.502				B

TABLE B.19 *Significant sex differences in 'gestation process' scores*

Variable	Country	Age	N	Sex	Mean score	S.D.	T-value	2 tail prob.	Signif.	Sex bias
Gestation process	AUS	5	20 20	B G	1.45 0.90	0.826 0.553	2.48	.018	*	B
	ENG	7	20 20	B G	2.50 1.30	1.192 0.979	3.48	.001	***	B
	N.AM	7	15 15	B G	2.44 1.36	0.964 0.633	3.57	.001	***	B
	SWED	7	15 15	B G	2.40 3.20	0.986 0.775	-2.47	.020	*	G
	ENG	9	20 20	B G	3.65 2.05	0.875 1.432	4.26	< .001	***	B
	AUS	11	20 20	B G	3.85 3.00	0.671 1.170	2.82	.008	**	B
	N.AM	11	15 15	B G	4.47 2.73	0.516 1.223	5.06	< .001	***	B
	AUS	13	20 20	B G	4.10 2.55	0.641 1.276	4.85	< .001	***	B
	ENG	13	20 20	B G	3.70 2.85	1.174 1.182	2.28	.028	*	B
	N.AM	13	16 17	B G	4.13 3.29	0.806 1.213	2.30	.028	*	B
	ENG	15	20 20	B G	4.30 3.25	0.801 1.118	3.41	.002	**	B

TABLE B.20 *Significant sex differences in 'birth necessity' scores*

Variable	Country	Age	N	Sex	Mean score	S.D.	T-value	2 tail prob.	Signif.	Sex bias
Birth necessity	AUS	7	20	B	2.45	0.887	2.87	.007	**	B
			20	G	1.65	0.875				
	ENG	7	20	B	3.00	0.858	3.64	.001	***	B
			20	G	1.80	1.196				
	SWED	7	15	B	1.67	0.976	−2.61	.014	*	G
			15	G	2.53	0.834				
	ENG	9	20	B	3.10	0.912	2.18	.036	*	B
			20	G	2.50	0.827				
	N.AM	11	15	B	3.93	0.799	3.58	.001	***	B
			15	G	2.87	0.834				
	AUS	13	20	B	4.05	0.887	2.71	.010	**	B
			20	G	3.10	1.284				
	N.AM	13	16	B	3.63	0.719	2.52	.017	*	B
			17	G	3.00	0.707				
	AUS	15	20	B	4.10	0.553	2.32	.026	*	B
			20	G	3.65	0.671				
	N.AM	15	16	B	4.06	0.772	2.07	.045	*	B
			15	G	3.47	0.834				

TABLE B.21 *Significant sex differences in the 'sex determination of babies' scores*

Variable	Country	Age	N	Sex	Mean score	S.D.	T-value	2 tail prob.	Signif.	Sex bias
Genetic determination of sex	ENG	5	20	B	1.90	0.912	5.89	< .001	***	B
			20	G	0.30	0.801				
	AUS	7	20	B	2.15	1.040	3.33	.002	**	B
			20	G	1.05	1.050				
	ENG	7	20	B	2.20	1.436	6.04	< .001	***	B
			20	G	0.15	0.489				
	N.AM	7	16	B	2.44	1.153	4.58	< .001	***	B
			14	G	0.50	1.160				
	AUS	9	20	B	2.75	1.517	2.90	.006	**	B
			20	G	1.40	1.429				
	ENG	9	20	B	3.30	1.261	4.32	< .001	***	B
			20	G	1.05	1.959				
	N.AM	9	15	B	2.40	1.352	3.67	.001	***	B
			15	G	0.67	1.234				
	AUS	11	20	B	2.35	1.725	2.08	.044	*	B
			20	G	1.20	1.765				
	ENG	11	20	B	3.95	0.945	5.15	< .001	***	B
			20	G	1.20	2.191				
	N.AM	11	15	B	3.67	1.113	4.22	< .001	***	B
			15	G	1.47	1.685				

(cont...)

Table B.21 (cont...)

Variable	Country	Age	N	Sex	Mean score	S.D.	T-value	2 tail prob.	Signif.	Sex bias
	AUS	13	20	B	4.30	1.922	3.98	<.001	***	
			20	G	1.75	2.124				B
	ENG	13	20	B	4.40	1.957	3.16	.003	**	
			20	G	2.05	2.685				B
	N.AM	13	16	B	4.50	1.673	3.20	.003	**	
			17	G	2.12	2.497				B
	ENG	15	20	B	5.50	1.573	3.12	.003	**	
			20	G	3.20	2.895				B
	SWED	15	15	B	6.33	1.113	2.39	.024	*	
			15	G	5.13	1.598				B

TABLE B.22 Significant sex differences in 'knowledge of contraception' scores

Variable	Country	Age	N	Sex	Mean score	S.D.	T-value	2 tail prob.	Signif.	Sex bias
Knowledge of contraception (highest score)	ENG	9	20	B	2.15	1.565	-2.10	.042	*	
			20	G	3.65	2.777				G
	SWED	11	15	B	6.73	0.458	2.52	.018	*	
			15	G	5.07	2.520				B
	SWED	15	15	B	7.00	0.000	2.65	.013	*	
			15	G	6.67	0.488				B

TABLE B.23 *Significant sex differences in knowledge of various contraceptive methods*

Variable	Country	Age	N	Sex	Mean score	S.D.	T-value	2 tail prob.	Signif.	Sex bias
Nothing can be done	ENG	9	20 / 20	B / G	3.00 / 0.00	0.470 / 0.000	2.85	.007	**	B
Abstention methods	AUS	9	20 / 20	B / G	0.20 / 0.55	0.401 / 0.510	-2.39	.022	*	G
	ENG	11	20 / 20	B / G	0.65 / 0.15	0.587 / 0.366	3.23	.003	**	B
No interference methods	ENG	15	20 / 20	B / G	0.05 / 0.40	0.224 / 0.598	-2.45	.019	*	G
Surgical methods	AUS	15	20 / 20	B / G	0.50 / 0.00	0.889 / 0.000	2.52	.016	*	B
One-sex devices	ENG	9	20 / 20	B / G	0.10 / 0.45	0.308 / 0.510	-2.63	.012	*	G
	AUS	15	20 / 20	B / G	0.15 / 0.50	0.366 / 0.607	-2.21	.033	*	G
	SWED	15	15 / 15	B / G	0.00 / 0.33	0.000 / 0.488	-2.65	.013	*	G
Both-sex devices	AUS	13	20 / 20	B / G	0.90 / 0.10	1.165 / 0.447	2.87	.007	**	B
	ENG	15	20 / 20	B / G	2.35 / 3.15	1.040 / 1.137	-2.32	.026	*	G
	SWED	15	15 / 15	B / G	4.33 / 2.40	0.724 / 1.882	3.71	.001	***	B

TABLE B.24 Significant sex differences in 'knowledge of abortion' scores

Variable	Country	Age	N	Sex	Mean score	S.D.	T-value	2 tail prob.	Signif.	Sex bias
Knowledge of abortion	ENG	9	20	B	1.65	1.755	2.70	.010	**	
			20	G	0.40	1.095				B
	N.AM	9	15	B	1.27	1.624	2.24	.033	*	
			15	G	0.27	0.594				B
	SWED	13	15	B	3.80	0.775	4.21	< .001	***	
			15	G	2.00	1.464				B
	SWED	15	15	B	3.33	1.234	3.83	.001	***	
			15	G	1.60	1.242				B

TABLE B.25 Significant sex differences on 'Why wear clothes?' scores

Variable	Country	Age	N	Sex	Mean score	S.D.	T-value	2 tail prob.	Signif.	Sex bias
'Why wear clothes?'	ENG	7	20	B	2.40	0.821	2.39	.022	*	
			20	G	1.90	0.447				B
	N.AM	15	16	B	4.56	1.315	2.67	.012	*	
			15	G	3.20	1.521				B

TABLE B.26 *Significant sex differences in reasons 'for embarrassment at being naked' scores*

Variable	Country	Age	N	Sex	Mean score	S.D	T-value	2 tail prob.	Signif.	Sex bias
Nakedness embarrassment	ENG	5	20	B	2.55	0.945	7.07	< .001	***	B
			20	G	0.50	0.889				
	N.AM	5	13	B	2.15	1.068	3.34	.003	**	B
			11	G	0.73	1.009				
	AUS	7	20	B	2.85	0.933	3.66	.001	***	B
			20	G	1.45	1.432				
	ENG	7	20	B	2.65	1.089	5.22	< .001	***	B
			20	G	0.80	1.152				
	N.AM	7	16	B	2.50	1.033	2.19	.037	*	B
			14	G	1.57	1.284				
	SWED	7	15	B	1.47	1.302	−2.84	.008	**	G
			15	G	2.80	1.265				
	AUS	9	20	B	3.40	0.754	2.84	.007	**	B
			20	G	2.30	1.559				
	ENG	9	20	B	3.55	0.945	3.90	< .001	***	B
			20	G	1.95	1.574				
	N.AM	9	15	B	3.33	1.113	2.97	.006	**	B
			15	G	2.07	1.223				
	AUS	11	20	B	4.20	0.894	3.30	.002	**	B
			20	G	2.80	1.673				

(cont...)

Table B.26 (cont...)

Variable	Country	Age	N	Sex	Mean score	S.D.	T-value	2 tail prob.	Signif.	Sex bias
	ENG	11	20	B	4.10	1.334	3.70	.001	***	
			20	G	2.30	1.720				B
	N.AM	11	15	B	4.07	0.799	2.80	.009	**	
			15	G	2.87	1.457				B
	AUS	13	20	B	3.85	1.089	2.60	.013	*	
			20	G	2.65	1.755				B
	ENG	13	20	B	4.00	0.795	2.04	.048	*	
			20	G	3.35	1.182				B
	N.AM	13	16	B	4.19	0.981	3.01	.005	**	
			17	G	3.18	0.951				B
	ENG	15	20	B	4.20	0.768	2.33	.025	*	
			20	G	3.50	1.100				B
	N.AM	15	16	B	4.13	0.719	2.15	.040	*	
			15	G	2.93	2.086				B

428

TABLE B.27 *Significant sex differences in 'understanding sexual vocabulary' scores*

Variable	Country	Age	N	Sex	Mean score	S.D.	T-value	2 tail prob.	Signif.	Sex bias
Meaning of pregnancy	ENG	7	20	B	2.15	1.040	-2.18	.035	*	G
			20	G	2.80	0.834				
Meaning of conception	AUS	9	20	B	1.25	0.444	2.52	.016	*	B
			20	G	1.00	0.000				
	SWED	9	15	B	1.20	1.146	-2.45	.021	*	G
			15	G	2.47	1.642				
	AUS	11	20	B	1.50	0.761	2.03	.050	*	B
			20	G	1.10	0.447				
	N.AM	11	15	B	1.53	0.915	2.26	.032	*	B
			15	G	1.00	0.000				
	SWED	11	15	B	2.93	0.884	-2.07	.047	*	G
			15	G	3.67	1.047				
	ENG	13	20	B	1.80	1.056	3.11	.004	**	B
			20	G	1.05	0.224				
	SWED	13	15	B	2.80	1.207	-3.03	.005	**	G
			15	G	3.80	0.414				
Meaning of stripping	SWED	15	15	B	4.00	0.000	2.75	.010	**	B
			15	G	3.27	1.033				
Meaning of rape	ENG	9	20	B	2.00	1.214	2.26	.029	*	B
			20	G	1.25	0.851				

(cont...)

Table B.27 (cont...)

Variable	Country	Age	N	Sex	Mean score	S.D.	T-value	2 tail prob.	Signif.	Sex bias
Meaning of rape (cont.)	N.AM	11	15	B	3.33	0.900	2.05	.050	*	B
			15	G	2.60	1.056				
	AUS	13	20	B	4.90	1.021	5.20	<.001	***	B
			20	G	3.30	0.923				
	ENG	13	20	B	4.35	1.226	2.17	.036	*	B
			20	G	3.60	0.940				
	N.AM	13	16	B	4.81	1.276	3.43	.002	**	B
			17	G	3.35	1.169				
	AUS	15	20	B	5.40	0.883	5.88	<0.001	***	B
			20	G	4.10	0.447				
	ENG	15	20	B	4.75	1.070	3.05	.004	**	B
			20	G	3.90	0.641				
	N.AM	15	16	B	4.94	1.124	3.69	.001	***	B
			15	G	3.80	0.414				
Meaning of VD	ENG	9	20	B	1.10	0.308	2.34	.025	*	B
			20	G	0.85	0.366				
	AUS	15	20	B	3.30	0.470	2.53	.016	*	B
			20	G	2.75	0.851				
Meaning of puberty	SWED	13	15	B	2.93	0.258	-3.18	.004	**	G
			15	G	3.40	0.507				

					Mean	SD	t	p		
Meaning of abortion	ENG	9	20	B	1.20	0.410	2.18	.036	*	B
			20	G	1.00	0.000				
	N.AM	13	16	B	3.25	0.577	2.92	.006	**	B
			17	G	2.59	0.712				
Meaning of contraception	ENG	13	20	B	2.50	1.469	2.35	.024	*	B
			20	G	1.55	1.050				
	ENG	15	20	B	3.45	0.999	−2.18	.035	*	G
			20	G	3.95	0.224				
	SWED	15	15	B	3.00	0.926	−2.20	.036	*	G
			15	G	3.60	0.507				
Total of vocabulary scores	AUS	9	20	B	16.90	2.634	2.18	.035	*	B
			20	G	15.15	2.434				
	ENG	9	20	B	15.75	1.713	2.31	.026	*	B
			20	G	13.50	4.007				
	ENG	13	20	B	28.20	5.550	2.39	.022	*	B
			20	G	24.40	4.430				
	AUS	13	20	B	27.35	4.133	2.93	.006	**	B
			20	G	23.05	5.094				
	AUS	15	20	B	33.95	2.625	2.11	.041	*	B
			20	G	31.95	3.316				

Appendix C: Biological criteria

Statements A to H were used as the basis for constructing 'biological realism' scales. These statements were adapted from textbooks on human biology and checked for accuracy by qualified biologists.

A Ageing (chapter 4)

The life of a human being starts with a collection of cells which develop the ability to work together as a co-ordinated whole. It ends when the cells lose this ability and work in isolation from each other.

A normal organism in the active state effects repairs so that it can sustain a series of injuries over a span of time, which would, if occurring simultaneously, have caused death.

Any operating organism must inevitably become impaired by use and accident. The gradual accumulation of defects constitutes old age or senescence. As these become more numerous, homeostatic mechanisms progressively deteriorate and the probability of death increases. The defects may occur in any part of the body.

Some biologists consider that the concept of 'wearing out' is inappropriately borrowed from static man-made machines and that they should not be applied to self-replacing living systems. However, environmental stress (i.e. wear) can be a contributory cause of senescence, as also can abuse of the organism (by over-exertion, drugs, over-eating or poor diet).

Whatever the basis of senescence may be, it is a necessary and inevitable stage in the human species, prior to death in which heritable factors (racial and individual) play a large part.

Declining powers in old age are due partly to irreversible changes in the body, as when the walls of the arteries become hardened and the flow of blood is thus restricted.

The decline is also partly due to less efficient adjustment to changes required, such as temperature, oxygen supply and in resisting disease or poisons. For example, digestion is impaired: there is less hydrochloric acid, trypsin and pepsin in the stomach. Temperature control is poor, due to poorer circulation, and keeping warm becomes a problem. Calcium is deposited in arteries and cartilage, leading to arteriosclerosis, so that less oxygen is available to the muscles. Bones, on the other hand, become decalcified and fracture more easily. Elasticity of tissue decreases, so that wrinkles are produced as a visible sign of ageing. (Sources: Young, J.Z. (1971) *An Introduction to the Study of Man.* Oxford: Clarendon Press; *Nuffield School Science*, vol. 3 (1974).)

B Pubertal differences between male and female (chapter 9)

Definition: Puberty is the age at which the sexual organs in the male and female mature, and reproductive functions may commence.

Girls	Boys
Primary sex characteristics	
Those characteristics considered to be of primary importance for the reproduction of the species	
menstruates usually monthly	penis and testicles grow larger
breasts enlarge	testicles become permanently descended
release of eggs from ovaries	sperm produced in testicles
	seminal emission or wet dreams, i.e. release of sperm occurs during sleep
Secondary sex characteristics	
Those characteristics associated with yet not considered to be essential to the primary sex characteristics	
growth of pubic hair and under-arm hair	growth of pubic hair, under-arm hair, facial and chest hair, i.e. on chin and upper lip
general rounding of contours of body	voice deepens, vocal cords lengthen, 'Adam's Apple' begins to grow
possible blushing and feelings of embarrassment	possible blushing and feelings of embarrassment

C Conception (chapter 10)

These statements seek to describe in simple terms

1 The male reproductive system.
2 The female reproductive system and female cycle.
3 The processes of intercourse, fertilisation and pregnancy.

1 Male reproductive system

1 The sperm-producing organs or testes are located in the scrotum.
2 Within the testes sperm cells develop in a series of highly coiled tubes and are then transported to another part of the testes for storage.
3 Accessory structures of the testes, the prostate gland and seminal vesicles produce the components which, with sperm, make up semen.
4 The average human male produces millions of sperm compared with each egg produced by the average human female.
5 If sperm are not discharged along the sperm duct and urethra they gradually die and are disposed of by certain testicular tissue.

2 Female reproductive system and female cycle

1 The egg-producing organs or ovaries are located deep in the female body in contrast to the male organs.
2 Each egg develops in a tiny sac-like structure called a follicle. As the follicle grows it becomes filled with fluid.
3 When the egg is ripe, that is, has developed sufficiently as to be almost ready for fertilisation, the follicle ruptures near the surface of the ovary and the tiny egg is carried out with the fluid. The release of the egg is called ovulation. This normally occurs monthly.
4 After leaving the ovary the egg is drawn into the widened funnel of the oviduct which leads into the thick walled muscular organ called the uterus.
5 Prior to ovulation the uterus is small with thick tissues and few blood vessels. After ovulation the uterus enlarges, the inner wall becomes thick, soft and moist with fluid and the blood supply is greatly increased.
6 When a fertilised egg enters the uterus it normally lodges in the soft uterine tissues and starts to develop. If after ovulation an unfertilised egg enters the uterus it does not become implanted in the tissues and usually the inner lining of the uterus breaks down and along with the unfertilised egg is passed out of the body via the vagina. The breakdown and discharge of this uterine tissue is the process known as menstruation.
7 After menstruation a new ovarian follicle begins to mature. The uterus is again prepared for the possible entry of a fertilised egg and the reproductive cycle is repeated.

3 Intercourse, fertilisation and pregnancy

(a) Intercourse

1 When the male becomes sufficiently sexually aroused through visual, tactile, auditory, olfactory and/or taste stimuli, or mental images such as fantasy, the penis becomes enlarged and erect through the increased pressure of blood in the penis.

2 If the stiffened penis is inserted into the female vagina, stimulated by rhythmic to-and-fro movements, ejaculation usually occurs. Ejaculation is the release of sperm and fluid which provides the medium for transporting the sperm.

(b) Fertilisation and pregnancy

1 Sperm are released from the penis near the cervix or the small narrow neck of the uterus.

2 By a lashing of their tails the sperm becomes sufficiently mobile to move into the fallopian tube or oviduct. Sperm can live for up to 48 hours.

3 If a mature egg is present, the sperm head enters the egg and the tail drops off. The nuclei of sperm and egg fuse. This process is called fertilisation. The fertilised egg is able to move to and implant itself in the thickened wall of the uterus. This process is the beginning of pregnancy and there is a temporary interruption of the female menstrual cycle.

4 Pregnancy normally lasts about 280 days. The embryo develops with the umbilical cord leading from the embryo's digestive tract to the placenta, which is a piece of tissue attached to the wall of the uterus. In the placenta exchange of nutrients, oxygen, carbon dioxide and dissolved waste materials occur. Normally there is no direct flow of blood between mother and embryo. The embryo develops human features and before the ninth month of pregnancy the baby's head is usually turned down towards the opening of the uterus.

D Gestation: Development in pregnancy (chapter 11)

This statement seeks to clarify in simple terms

(1) The nature of the baby's growth during pregnancy
(2) The baby's physical connection with the mother

1 The nature of growth

After conception the fertilised egg moves down the fallopian tube on its way to attaching itself to the womb. During this time it divides into two cells, then into four and further cell division increasing the complexity of the embryo. At birth the baby is composed of about 200 million cells.

After a few days the attachment of the embryo to the wall of the uterus occurs. The uterus lining has been prepared by thickening and an enriched supply of blood vessels and glands. The part to which the embryo becomes attached is called the placenta. Gradually a sac forms rather like a balloon filled with fluid, which protects the embryo, and an umbilical cord develops from the embryo's digestive tract to the placenta.

By the end of the first month development has been rapid – the embryo is now 10,000 times larger than the fertilised egg. The embryo has a rudimentary brain, liver, kidneys and digestive tract and a simple heart. The umbilical cord has begun to grow.

During the second month bone cells appear and all the organs of a human have developed in rudimentary form. This essential completion of the body pattern is used to mark the change from an embryo to a foetus.

By the end of the third month it is possible to tell the foetus' sex. It can kick, swallow and may breathe some of the amniotic fluid surrounding. In so doing it cannot choke for it is merely practice for breathing, since the foetus does not rely on breathing for its supply of oxygen.

In the fourth, fifth and sixth months there is considerable increase in size and solidity. The foetus is supported by the growth of more bone. A pattern of waking and sleeping develops.

By the seventh month development is normally sufficient to enable the baby to live if born.

2 *The physical connection between foetus and mother*

The placenta is the mass of tiny blood vessels and tissues attached to part of the lining of the uterus. It is linked to the growing foetus by means of the umbilical cord joined to the baby's digestive tract (through the navel). Through this supplies of oxygen and nutrients are received and carbon dioxide and dissolved waste materials are expelled, both necessary for the existence and growth of the baby.

The umbilical cord is kept sufficiently still to remain unknotted by the flow of the baby's blood through the cord. The mother and baby have separate unconnected blood streams, yet close enough to exchange contents through the process of diffusion.

E Childbirth (chapter 11)

1 *Pregnancy*

1 Pregnancy or the duration of internal development normally lasts about 280 days.
2 By the ninth month the baby is able to support itself outside the special environment of the womb and he/she begins to outgrow it. Its head is usually turned down toward the opening of the uterus.

2 *Childbirth*

1 Childbirth begins when the muscle layers of the uterus, initiated hormonally, start to contract and relax. These actions are known as labour. Initially, muscular activity of the uterus is strong enough to move the baby slowly toward the vagina.
2 Usually the fluid-filled sac, the amnion, surrounding the baby breaks and releases the fluid content. This is a sign that labour has started.
3 When the contraction of the muscles becomes stronger and more frequent, the baby is pushed through the vagina into the outer world. Thus the baby moves from an aquatic environment to a dry environment. The umbilical cord is cut and tied.

3 *Afterbirth*

1 After the birth of a baby, the muscle action of the uterus continues until it expels the placenta, commonly called 'the afterbirth'.

F The genetic determination of sex (chapter 12)

(1) Humans have 23 pairs of (or 46) chromosomes in the nuclei of their body cells. The exceptions to this are the gametes, that is, the egg in the female and the sperm in the male. Gametes have 23 single chromosomes in their nuclei, one from each pair. DNA is the chemical part of chromosomes from which inherited characteristics are built up.
(2) When an egg containing a set of 23 chromosomes fuses with a sperm containing another set of 23 chromosomes, the resulting cell is now diploid and has 46 chromosomes, that is 23 pairs. One pair of these 23 pairs determine the sex of the foetus.
(3) All female ova or eggs carry a chromosome which is called X. Half of the male sperm carry a chromosome which is called X and half carry a chromosome which is called Y. When an egg with its X chromosome is fertilised by a sperm bearing a Y chromosome, the baby is male — XY. When an egg with its X chromosome is fertilised by a sperm bearing an X chromosome, the baby is female — XX.

(4) Twins or multiple births may be in various forms:
  (i) *Identical twins* result from a separation of a single fertilised egg into 2 parts which then develop separately. They have identical genetic material and are of same sex and similar appearance.
  (ii) *Fraternal twins* are the result of 2 eggs being released, both being fertilised. The embryos usually have separate placentas and are no more alike than any other 2 children of the same parents.
  (iii) *Triplets and Quadruplets* are usually due to 3 or 4 separate eggs, each of which is fertilised, but may be identical due to early splitting of the egg followed by further splitting.

G Contraception (chapter 13)

This is the use of adaptive behaviour, equipment or chemicals to prevent conception.

Adaptive behaviour by abstention, withdrawal or use of safe periods is used to avoid the male sperm and female egg conjoining.

Equipment, such as the condom or the cap and an intrauterine device, is used to place an artificial barrier between the male sperm and the female or, in the case of the IUD, making the embryo less likely to implant within the uterus.

Chemicals include the use of the pill designed to prevent ovulation and/or to affect the growth of the uterus lining making the embryo less likely to implant in the uterus. Spermicides (foam, jellies, creams) alone or in conjunction with a cap (or diaphragm) are used to kill the sperm before it reaches the female egg.

Two further methods of birth control are sterilisation of either the man or woman, and induced abortion (although technically it may be argued that since abortion occurs after conception it is not strictly 'birth control').

Sterilisation of the woman may be by ovariectomy (i.e. the removal of the ovaries) or by tubal ligation, which is the cutting and tying of the fallopian tubes. It may also be by hysterectomy, the removal of the uterus. Sterilisation of the man can be by castration, the removal of his testes, but the less drastic vasectomy is most used, where the vas deferens is clamped or tied. This is the removal of that part of the tube by which sperm leaves the testes, by cutting and tying its ends, preventing the sperm from leaving the testes.

Abortion may be 'natural' or 'induced'. It is the termination or ending of a pregnancy before full term, rendering the embryo or foetus unable to function outside the mother's body.

Natural abortion appears to be a safeguard against the production of abnormal offspring and is often called a 'miscarriage'. It may be due to imbalance of hormones, injury to the mother or toxic substances produced by infection or drugs.

Induced abortion is a deliberate attempt to terminate a pregnancy by artificially causing injury or toxic conditions or by an operation performed through the vagina which removes the embryo or foetus. This may be done by scraping or 'vacuuming' the womb. Normally this is done within the first three months of a pregnancy but in unusual circumstances the law in some countries allows termination up to 28 weeks (just over 6 months or two-thirds of a full term).

Adoption once a child has been born, is the act of transferring all rights and responsibilities of parenthood from the natural parent(s) to the adoptive parents(s).

H Sexual vocabulary definitions (chapter 16)

Pregnancy	the physical state of a woman carrying an embryo, foetus or baby. It is the growth period during which this occurs.
Conception	the act of successful fertilisation of the female egg by the male sperm including the implantation of the fertilised egg in the wall of the uterus.
Rooting	a slang term for sexual intercourse (Australia only).
Stripping	the act of removing a covering completely such as a layer of paint or the bark of a tree. Sexually it refers to either the removing of clothes provocatively, or the forcible removing of clothes for sexual stimulation or the act of sex.
Rape	seizure by violence. Sexually its meaning is to attack a person for the purpose of sexual intercourse against that person's will. It may occur by a man raping a woman, a woman raping a man, male with male, female with female, or an act perpetrated on children. Stripping, beating, injury or murder are not necessary ingredients of rape.
Venereal disease	general term for those diseases which, as a rule, result from sexual intercourse with an infected person. Infection may occur from infected sources by other than sexual activity but rarely so, except in the case of syphilis, which may be congenital. The two most commonly known to the public are gonorrhoea, the most common; and syphilis, less common but most

serious. The symptoms are usually irritation of the skin on or around the sexual organs or discharge from the sex organs.

Uterus or womb   female organ of muscles elastic in nature, provided to accommodate the embryo or foetus during pregnancy, stretching as the baby grows. The cervix is the neck of the uterus jutting down into the vagina.

Puberty   the age or period of growth at which the sex organs in both male and female mature to make reproduction possible.

Virgin   a man or woman who has not had sexual intercourse (retained chastity or not had carnal knowledge). A broader meaning is one who is pure or inexperienced in a particular area (as in virgin land, or virgin soldier, i.e. inexperienced in battle). Its most popular association is religious, i.e. the Virgin Mary.

Appendix D: Analyses of variance of results

Three-way analyses of variance were applied to data which clearly scaled, the variables including 2(sex) × 6(age-year) × 4(country), and 4(father's occupation) × 6(age-year) × 4(country). In one item, 'The Causes of Ageing', only three countries' results were analysed — Australia, England and North America.

In all tables in this appendix $* = p < .05$; $** = p < .01$; $*** = p < .001$; and NS = Not Significant.

TABLE D.1 *Main effects of sex (2)*

Variable	d.f.	Mean squares	F	p	Significance
Causes of ageing	1	216.64	174.94	.001	***
Best time to be alive	1	1.12	2.46	.117	NS
Why people marry	1	0.05	0.05	.817	NS
Sex differences: newborn	1	7.66	4.03	.045	*
Sex differences: pubertal	1	3.77	1.90	.169	NS
Origin of babies	1	1.95	2.41	.121	NS
Mother's procreative role	1	94.73	50.27	.001	***
Father's procreative role	1	25.66	15.06	.001	***
The birth exit	1	2.34	2.19	.139	NS
Gestation process	1	84.83	84.18	.001	***
Birth necessity	1	12.33	14.98	.001	***
Genetic determination of sex	1	363.03	133.34	.001	***
Contraceptive knowledge	1	2.00	0.58	.446	NS
Abortion knowledge	1	0.14	0.34	.561	NS
Why wear clothes	1	4.20	3.27	.071	NS
Why embarrassment	1	174.09	119.31	.001	***
Sexual vocabulary: totals	1	140.05	12.08	.001	***
Piagetian items: totals	1	194.60	52.92	.001	***
Biological Realism: totals	1	405.69	33.29	.001	***

TABLE D.2 *Main effects of age-year* (6)

Variable	d.f.	Mean squares	F	p	Significance
Causes of ageing	5	84.60	68.32	.001	***
Best time to be alive	5	82.78	180.25	.001	***
Why people marry	5	113.00	121.34	.001	***
Sex differences: newborn	5	287.85	151.68	.001	***
Sex differences: pubertal	5	210.51	106.10	.001	***
Origin of babies	5	229.67	282.83	.001	***
Mother's procreative role	5	115.88	61.49	.001	***
Father's procreative role	5	214.46	125.88	.001	***
The birth exit	5	72.27	67.77	.001	***
Gestation process	5	121.45	120.50	.001	***
Birth necessity	5	68.70	83.49	.001	***
Genetic determination of sex	5	323.62	118.86	.001	***
Contraceptive knowledge	5	714.65	207.96	.001	***
Abortion knowledge	5	270.82	672.70	.001	***
Why wear clothes	5	82.50	64.35	.001	***
Why embarrassment	5	125.15	85.79	.001	***
Sexual vocabulary: totals	5	2355.73	31.61	.001	***
Piagetian items: totals	5	1635.28	444.73	.001	***
Biological Realism: totals	5	4692.80	385.09	.001	***

444

TABLE D.3 *Main effects of country (4)*

Variable	d.f.	Mean squares	F	p	Significance
Causes of ageing	2	0.24	0.19	.825	NS
Best time to be alive	3	4.31	9.37	.001	***
Why people marry	3	19.03	20.43	.001	***
Sex differences: newborn	3	14.13	7.45	.001	***
Sex differences: pubertal	3	4.79	2.42	.065	NS
Origin of babies	3	11.89	14.64	.001	***
Mother's procreative role	3	22.92	12.16	.001	***
Father's procreative role	3	27.52	16.15	.001	***
The birth exit	3	5.52	5.17	.001	***
Gestation process	3	9.96	9.88	.001	***
Birth necessity	3	0.04	0.05	.986	NS
Genetic determination of sex	3	38.63	14.19	.001	***
Contraceptive knowledge	3	66.88	19.46	.001	***
Abortion knowledge	3	6.30	15.65	.001	***
Why wear clothes	3	16.94	13.21	.001	***
Why embarrassment	3	0.55	0.37	.772	NS
Sexual vocabulary: totals	3	143.75	12.40	.001	***
Piagetian items: totals	3	8.31	2.26	.080	NS
Biological Realism: totals	3	140.84	11.56	.001	***

TABLE D.4 *Main effects of socio-economic status as assessed by father's occupation (4)*

Variable	d.f.	Mean squares	F	p	Significance
Causes of ageing	3	1.84	1.12	.339	NS
Best time to be alive	3	3.18	7.06	.001	***
Why people marry	3	0.33	0.33	.805	NS
Sex differences: newborn	3	5.50	2.87	.036	*
Sex differences: pubertal	3	2.07	0.99	.393	NS
Origin of babies	3	2.23	2.70	.045	*
Mother's procreative role	3	1.43	0.67	.571	NS
Father's procreative role	3	6.92	3.88	.009	**
The birth exit	3	0.74	0.67	.574	NS
Gestation process	3	0.69	0.58	.625	NS
Birth necessity	3	0.45	0.51	.674	NS
Genetic determination of sex	3	1.80	0.53	.660	NS
Contraceptive knowledge	3	9.76	2.87	.036	*
Abortion knowledge	3	0.36	0.91	.433	NS
Why wear clothes	3	0.88	0.67	.568	NS
Why embarrassment	3	0.98	0.58	.631	NS
Sexual vocabulary: totals	3	32.56	2.81	.039	*
Piagetian items: totals	3	5.27	1.28	.279	NS
Biological Realism: totals	3	27.06	1.99	.113	NS

TABLE D.5 *Two-way interactions between sex and age-year* (2 × 6)

Variable	d.f.	Mean squares	F	p	Significance
Causes of ageing	5	6.25	5.05	.001	***
Best time to be alive	5	1.14	2.48	.030	*
Why people marry	5	0.31	0.33	.893	NS
Sex differences: newborn	5	3.56	1.88	.096	NS
Sex differences: pubertal	5	7.31	3.68	.003	**
Origin of babies	5	1.48	1.82	.106	NS
Mother's procreative role	5	7.41	3.93	.002	**
Father's procreative role	5	3.70	2.17	.056	NS
The birth exit	5	1.95	1.83	.104	NS
Gestation process	5	2.00	1.98	.079	NS
Birth necessity	5	1.23	1.50	.189	NS
Genetic determination of sex	5	5.82	2.14	.059	NS
Contraceptive knowledge	5	2.06	0.60	.701	NS
Abortion knowledge	5	0.63	1.56	.169	NS
Why wear clothes	5	0.63	0.49	.783	NS
Why embarrassment	5	1.11	0.76	.578	NS
Sexual vocabulary: totals	5	48.02	4.14	.001	***
Piagetian items: totals	5	2.46	0.67	.647	NS
Biological Realism: totals	5	35.14	2.88	.014	*

TABLE D.6 *Two-way interactions between sex and country* (2 × 4)

Variable	d.f.	Mean squares	F	p	Significance
Causes of ageing	2	4.42	3.57	.029	*
Best time to be alive	3	3.77	8.21	.001	***
Why people marry	3	15.95	17.12	.001	***
Sex differences: newborn	3	8.61	4.54	.004	**
Sex differences: pubertal	3	9.46	4.77	.003	**
Origin of babies	3	1.30	1.61	.187	NS
Mother's procreative role	3	22.60	11.99	.001	***
Father's procreative role	3	12.52	7.35	.001	***
The birth exit	3	7.50	7.03	.001	***
Gestation process	3	12.94	12.84	.001	***
Birth necessity	3	9.41	11.43	.001	***
Genetic determination of sex	3	47.24	17.35	.001	***
Contraceptive knowledge	3	12.12	3.53	.015	*
Abortion knowledge	3	0.81	2.02	.110	NS
Why wear clothes	3	2.71	2.12	.097	NS
Why embarrassment	3	21.96	15.06	.001	***
Sexual vocabulary: totals	3	71.70	6.19	.001	***
Piagetian items: totals	3	87.99	23.93	.001	***
Biological Realism: totals	3	239.43	19.65	.001	***

TABLE D.7 *Two way interactions between age-year and country* (6 × 4)

Variable	d.f.	Mean squares	F	p	Significance
Causes of ageing	10	2.07	1.67	.084	NS
Best time to be alive	15	1.45	3.16	.001	***
Why people marry	15	1.18	1.27	.216	NS
Sex differences: newborn	15	8.96	4.72	.001	***
Sex differences: pubertal	15	5.35	2.70	.001	***
Origin of babies	15	5.18	6.40	.001	***
Mother's procreative role	15	3.30	1.75	.038	*
Father's procreative role	15	4.09	2.40	.002	**
The birth exit	15	2.52	2.36	.002	**
Gestation process	15	1.74	1.73	.041	*
Birth necessity	15	2.17	2.64	.001	***
Genetic determination of sex	15	12.46	4.58	.001	***
Contraceptive knowledge	15	9.01	2.62	.001	***
Abortion knowledge	15	1.47	3.66	.001	***
Why wear clothes	15	4.33	3.38	.001	***
Why embarrassment	15	1.40	0.96	.497	NS
Sexual vocabulary: totals	15	191.68	15.56	.001	***
Piagetian items: totals	15	9.41	2.56	.001	***
Biological Realism: totals	15	46.71	3.83	.001	***

TABLE D.8 *Two-way interaction between socio-economic status and age-year* (4×6)[1]

Variable	d.f.	Mean squares	F	p	Significance
Sex differences: newborn	15	3.25	1.69	.048	*
Contraceptive knowledge	15	6.23	1.83	.028	*
Abortion knowledge	15	0.80	2.01	.013	*

[1] Only the few significant results are listed. There were no significant two-way interactions between socio-economic status and country.

TABLE D.9 *Three-way interactions between sex, age-year and country* $(2 \times 6 \times 4)$[1]

Variable	d.f.	Mean squares	F	p	Significance
Causes of ageing	10	2.22	1.80	.058	NS
Sex differences: newborn	15	3.16	1.67	.053	NS
Sex differences: pubertal	15	3.58	1.81	.030	*
Origin of babies	15	2.30	2.83	.001	***
The birth exit	15	2.81	2.63	.001	***
Gestation process	15	2.09	2.08	.009	**
Birth necessity	15	1.68	2.04	.011	*
Contraceptive knowledge	15	0.69	1.71	.044	*
Why wear clothes	15	2.10	1.64	.059	NS
Why embarrassment	15	3.10	2.13	.007	**
Sexual vocabulary: totals	15	18.05	1.56	.080	NS
Piagetian items: totals	15	6.52	1.77	.034	*
Biological Realism: totals	15	37.21	3.05	.001	***

[1] Only significant results, or near-significant results, are listed.

TABLE D.10 *Three-way interactions between socio-economic status, age-year and country* $(4 \times 6 \times 4)$[1]

Variable	d.f.	Main squares	F	p	Significance
Best time to be alive	45	0.68	1.51	.019	*
Why embarrassment	45	2.55	1.49	.022	*
Sexual vocabulary: totals	45	19.51	1.68	.004	**
Piagetian items: totals	45	5.77	1.41	.044	*
Biological items: totals	45	21.03	1.55	.013	*

[1] Only significant results are listed.

Bibliography

AHAMMER, I. M., and BALTES, P. B. (1972), 'Objective versus perceived difference in personality. How do adolescents, adults and older people view themselves and each other?', *Journal of Gerontology*, 27, pp. 46-51.

AHAMMER, I. M., and BENNETT, K. (1977), 'Viewing "Older People"': a comparative method – comparative sample approach', *Australian Journal of Psychology*, 29, 2, pp. 97-110.

ALLPORT, G. W. (1951), *The Individual and his Religion*, Constable, London.

American Psychologist (1979), Special Issue on 'Psychology and children – current research and practice', 34, 10, October.

AMES, L. B. (1946), 'The development of the sense of time in the young child', *Journal of Genetic Psychology*, 66, pp. 97-125.

AMIR, M. (1971), *Patterns in Forcible Rape*, University of Chicago Press, Chicago.

ANSELLO, E. (1978), 'Ageism: the subtle stereotype', *Childhood Education*, January, pp. 118-22.

ANTHONY, E. J. (1970), 'Behaviour disorders of childhood', in Mussen, P. (ed.), *Carmichael's Manual of Child Psychology*, Wiley, New York, vol. 2, pp. 667-764.

ARAFAT, I., and ALLEN, D. E. (1977), 'Venereal Disease: college students' knowledge and attitudes', *Journal of Sex Research*, 13, 3, August, pp. 223-30.

ARGYLE, M. (1958), *Religious Behaviour*, Routledge & Kegan Paul, London.

ARNOLD, C. B. (1972), 'The sexual behaviour of inner-city adolescent condom users', *Journal of Sex Research*, 8, 4, pp. 298-309.

AUSTIN, M. C., and THOMPSON, G. G. (1948), 'Children's friendships: a study of the bases on which children select and reject their best friends', *Journal of Educational Psychology*, 39, 2, pp. 101-16.

Australian Bureau of Statistics (1976), *Characteristics of the Population: State, Territories and Australia (Preliminary)*, Catalogue No. 2209.0, 1976 Census. Government Printer, Canberra.

451

Australian Bureau of Statistics (1979), *Australian Demographic Statistics Quarterly*, Catalogue No. 3101.0, June, Government Printer, Canberra.

Australian Bureau of Statistics (1979), *Catalogue of Publications*, Catalogue No. 1101.0, Australian Government Printer, Canberra.

Australian Bureau of Statistics (1979), *Population and Vital Statistics: December Quarter 1978*, Catalogue No. 3212.0, Government Printer, Canberra.

Australian Bureau of Statistics (1979), *Year Book, Australia*, No. 63, Government Printer, Canberra.

Australian Bureau of Statistics (1980), *Divorces Australia 1978*, Catalogue No. 3007.0, Government Printer, Canberra.

BALTES, P. B., and NESSELROADE, J. R. (1972), 'Cultural change and adolescent personality development; an application of longitudinal sequences', *Developmental Psychology*, 7, pp. 244-56.

BARNUM, P. (1977), 'Discrimination against the aged in young children's literature', *Elementary School Journal*, 77, pp. 301-8.

BAUMRIND, D., and BLACK, A. E. (1967), 'Socialization practices associated with dimensions of competence in pre-school boys and girls', *Child Development*, 48, pp. 187-94.

BEARD, R. M. (1960), 'An Investigation of Concept Formation among Infant School-Children', unpublished Ph.D. thesis, University of London.

BEE, H. L. (1974), *Social Issues in Developmental Psychology*, Harper & Row, New York.

BELL, R. R. (1966), 'Parent-child conflict in sexual values', *Journal of Social Issues*, 22, pp. 34-44.

BENNINGA, J. S. (1975), 'The relation of self concept to moral judgement in young children', US Educational Resources Information Centre, Report No. ED 139542.

BERELSON, B., and STEINER, G. A. (1964), *Human Behavior. An Inventory of Scientific Findings*, Harcourt Brace & World, New York.

BERNSTEIN, A. C. (1973), 'The Child's Concepts of Human Reproduction', Ph.D. dissertation, University of California, Berkeley.

BERNSTEIN, A. C. (1978), *The Flight of the Stork*, Delacorte Press, New York.

BERNSTEIN, A. C., and COWAN, P. A. (1975), 'Children's concepts of how people get babies', *Child Development*, 46, 1, March, pp. 77-91.

BERRY, J. W., and DASEN, P. R. (1974), *Culture and Cognition: Readings in Cross Cultural Psychology*, Methuen, London.

BETTELHEIM, B. (1965), 'The problem of generations', in Erikson, E. (ed.), *The Challenge of Youth*, Doubleday, New York.

BETTELHEIM, B. (1969), *Children of the Dream*, Macmillan, New York.

BIGELOW, B. J. (1977), 'Children's friendship expectations; A cognitive-developmental study', *Child Development*, 48, 1, pp. 246-53.

BIGELOW, B. J., and LA GUIPA, J. J. (1975), 'Children's written descriptions of friendships: a multidimensional analysis', *Developmental Psychology*, 11, 6, pp. 857-8.

BILLER, H. B. (1968), 'A multiaspect investigation of masculine development in kindergarten age boys', *General Psychology Monographs*, 78, pp. 89-138.

Biological Sciences Curriculum Study (1963), *Biological Science, Molecules to Man*, Houghton Mifflin, Boston.

BOEHM, L. (1957), 'The development of independence: a comparative study', *Child Development*, 28, pp. 85-92.

BOVET, P. (1928), *The Child's Religion*, Dent, London.

BREASTED, M. (1971), *Oh, Sex Education!*, New American Library, New York.

BREESE, R. (1978), 'The application of Piagetian theory to sexuality: a preliminary exploration', *Adolescence*, 13, 50, pp. 269-78.

BREMBERG, S. (1977), 'Pregnancy in Swedish teenagers. Perinatal problems and social situation', *Scandinavian Journal of Social Medicine*, 5, pp. 15-19.

BRINDLEY, C., CLARKE, P., HUTT, C., ROBINSON, I., and WETHLI, E. (1973), 'Sex differences in the activities and social interactions of nursery school children', in Michael, R. P. and Crook, J. H. (eds.), *Comparative Ecology and Behavior of Primates*, Academic Press, New York.

BRISLIN, R. W., and BAUMGARDNER, S. (1971), 'Non-random sampling of individuals in cross cultural research', *Journal of Cross-Cultural Psychology*, 2, pp. 397-400.

BRISLIN, R. W., LONNER, W. J., and THORNDIKE, R. M. (1973), *Cross-Cultural Research Methods*, Wiley, New York.

BRITTAIN, C. V. (1963), 'Adolescent choices and parent-peer cross-pressures', *American Sociological Review*, 28, 3, pp. 385-91.

BRODERICK, C. (1966), 'Sexual behaviour among pre-adolescents', *Journal of Social Issues*, 22, pp. 6-21.

BRONFENBRENNER, U. (1960), 'Freudian theories of identification and their derivatives', *Child Development*, 31, pp. 15-40.

BROPHY, B. (1968), *Black and White: A Portrait of Aubrey Beardsley*, Jonathan Cape, London.

BROVERMAN, I. K., VOGEL, S. R., BROVERMAN, D. M., CLARKSON, F. E., and ROSENKRANTZ, P. S. (1972), 'Sex role stereotypes: a current appraisal', *Journal of Social Issues*, 28, pp. 59-78.

BROWN, D. G. (1956), *The It Scale for Children*, Psychological Test Specialists, Grand Forks, North Dakota.

BROWN, D. G. (1957), 'Masculinity — feminity development in children', *Journal of Consulting Psychology*, 21, 3, pp. 197-202.

BROWN, D. G. (1958), 'Sex role development in a changing culture', *Psychological Bulletin*, 55, 4, pp. 232-42.

BROWN, G., and DESFORGES, C. (1979), *Piaget's Theory*, Routledge & Kegan Paul, London.

BROWN, J. A. C. (1961), *Freud and the Post Freudians*, Penguin, Harmondsworth.

BROWN, W. J., DONOHUE, J. F., AXNICK, N. W., BLOUNT, J. H., EWEN, N. H., and JONES, O. G. (1970), *Syphilis and Other Venereal*

Diseases, Vital and Health Monographs, American Public Health Association, Harvard University Press, Cambridge, Mass.

BROWNMILLER, S. (1976), *Against Our Will: Men, Women and Rape*, Penguin, Harmondsworth.

BRUNER, J. S. (1966), 'On cognitive growth', in Bruner, J. S., Olver, R. R., and Greenfield, P. M. (eds.), *Studies in Cognitive Growth*, Wiley, New York.

BUCK-MORSS, S. (1975), 'Socio-economic bias in Piaget's theory and its implications for cross-cultural studies', *Human Development*, 18, pp. 35–49.

BURGESS, A. W., GROTH, A. N., HOLDSTROM, L. L., and SGROI, S. M. (1978), *Sexual Assault of Children and Adolescents*, Lexington Books, Lexington, Mass.

BURNS, B. (1976), 'The emergence and socialization of sex differences', *Merrill-Palmer Quarterly*, 22, 3, pp. 229–54.

CALDERONE, M. S. (1969), 'The development of healthy sexuality', in Powers, G. P., and Baskin, W. (eds.), *Sex Education in a Changing Culture*, Peter Owen, London.

CAMPBELL, D. T. (1969), 'Reforms as experiments', *American Psychologist*, 24, pp. 409–29.

CARTWRIGHT, A. (1970), *Parents and Family Planning Services*, Routledge & Kegan Paul, London.

CARTWRIGHT, A. (1976), *How Many Children?* Routledge & Kegan Paul, London.

CATTELL, R. B. (1938), *Psychology and the Religious Quest*, Nelson, London.

CHASEN, B. (1977), 'Towards eliminating sex role stereotyping in early childhood classes', *Child Care Quarterly*, 6, 1, Spring, pp. 30–41.

CHURCHILL, E. M. (1958), 'The number concepts of young children', *Research and Studies*, 17 and 18, Institute of Education, University of Leeds.

CLARK, A. H., WYON, S. M., and RICHARDS, M. P. (1969), 'Free-play in nursery school children', *Journal of Child Psychology and Psychiatry*, 10, pp. 205–16.

CLARK, LeM. (1968), 'The range and variety of questions people ask about sex', in Vincent, C. E. (ed.), *Human Sexuality in Medical Education and Practice*, C. C. Thomas, Springfield, Ill., pp. 552–65.

CLAUTOUR, S. E., and MOORE, T. W. (1969), 'Attitudes of 12-year-old children to present and future life roles', *Human Development*, 12, pp. 221–38.

COLE, M., and BRUNER, J. S. (1971), 'Cultural differences and influences about psychological processes', *American Psychologist*, 26, pp. 867–76.

COLE, M., GAY, J., CLICK, J. A., and SHARP, D. W. (1971), *The Cultural Context of Learning and Thinking*, Methuen, London.

COLE, M., and SCRIBNER, S. (1974), *Culture and Thought: A Psychological Introduction*, John Wiley, New York.

COLLINS, J. K. (1974), 'Adolescent dating intimacy: norms and peer expectations', *Journal of Youth and Adolescence*, 3, 4, pp. 317-27.

COLLINS, J. K., KENNEDY, J. R., and FRANCIS, R. D. (1976), 'Insights into a dating partner's expectations of how behavior should ensue during the courtship process', *Journal of Marriage and the Family*, May, pp. 373-78.

COLTHAM, J. B. (1960), 'Junior School Children's Understanding of Some Terms Commonly used in the Teaching of History'. Unpublished Ph.D. thesis University of Manchester.

COMFORT, A. (1972), *The Joy of Sex*, revised edition, Quartet Books, London.

CONGALTON, A. A. (1969), *Status and Prestige in Australia*, Cheshire, Melbourne.

CONN, J. H. (1947), 'Children's awareness of the origin of babies', *Journal of Child Psychiatry*, 1, pp. 140-76.

CONN, J. H. (1951), 'Children's awareness of sex differences', *Journal of Child Psychiatry*, 2, pp. 82-9.

CONNELL, R. W. (1971), *The Child's Construction of Politics*, Melbourne University Press, Melbourne.

COOMBS, R. H. (1968), 'Acquiring sex attitudes and information in our society', in Vincent, C. E. (ed.), *Human Sexuality in Medical Education and Practice*, C. C. Thomas, Springfield, Illinois.

CORDWELL, J. M. and SCHWARZ, R. A. (1979) (eds.), *The Fabrics of Culture: The Anthropology of Clothing and Adornment*, Mouton, The Hague.

COWAN, P. A. (1978), *Piaget with Feeling. Cognitive, Social and Emotional Dimensions*, Holt, Rinehart & Winston, New York.

Current Sweden (1974), 'The State Commission on Aspects of Sex and Personal Relationships', no. 43.

DALLAS, D. M. (1972), *Sex Education in School and Society*, National Foundation for Educational Research, Windsor.

DANIEL, A. (1979), 'It depends on whose housewife she is: Sex work and occupational prestige', *Australian and New Zealand Journal of Sociology*, 15, 1, pp. 77-81.

DANZIGER, K. (1957), 'The child's understanding of kinship terms: a study in the development of relational concepts', *Journal of Genetic Psychology*, 91, pp. 213-32.

DASEN, P. R. (1972), 'Cross cultural Piagetian research. A summary', *Journal of Cross-cultural Psychology*, 3, 1, pp. 23-9.

DASEN, P. R. (1975), 'Concrete operational development in three cultures', *Journal of Cross-cultural Psychology*, 6, 2, pp. 156-72.

DASEN, P. R. (1977) (ed.), *Piagetian psychology: Cross-Cultural Contributions*, Gardner Press, New York.

D'AUGELLI, J. F., and D'AUGELLI, A. R. (1977), 'Moral reasoning about sex', *Journal of Social Issues*, 3, 2, pp. 49-50.

DICKINSON, G. E. (1978), 'Adolescent sex information sources: 1964-1974', *Adolescence*, 13, 52, pp. 653-8.

455

DORLAND, N. (1948), *The American Medical Dictionary*, W. B. Saunders, London.

DRAPER, E. (1965), *Birth Control in the Modern World*, Penguin, Harmondsworth.

DUNCAN, B., and DUNCAN, O. D. (1978), *Sex typing and social roles*, A research report in collaboration with McRae, James, Academic Press, New York.

DUNCAN, O. D. (1961), 'A sociometric index for all occupations', in Reiss, A. J. (ed.), *Occupations and Social Status*, Free Glencoe Press, New York, pp. 109–38.

DUNNELL, K. (1976), *Family Formation*, A survey carried out on behalf of the Population Statistics Division of the Office of Population Censuses and Surveys, HMSO, London.

EDELMAN, M. S., and OMARK, D. R. (1973), 'Dominance hierarchies in young children', *Social Science Information*, 12, 1, pp. 103–10.

EDER, D., and HALLINAN, M. T. (1978), 'Sex differences in children's friendships', *American Sociological Review*, 42, April, pp. 237–50.

ELKIND, D. (1962), 'Children's conception of brother and sister: Piaget replication study V', *Journal of Genetic Psychology*, 100, pp. 129–36.

EPPEL, E. M., and EPPEL, M. (1966), 'Adolescent values and teenage values', in Raison, T. (ed.), *Youth in New Society*, Hart-Davis, London.

ERIKSON, E. H. (1959), *Identity and the Life Cycle*, Psychological Issues, Monograph 1, International University Press, New York.

ERIKSON, E. H. (1963), *Childhood and Society*, Penguin, London.

EYSENCK, H. J., and WILSON, G. D. (1973), *The Experimental Study of Freudian Theories*, Methuen, London.

Fact Sheet on Sweden (1979), 'Equality between Men and Women in Sweden', The Swedish Institute, January, FS 82.

FARRELL, C. (1978), *My Mother Said . . . The Way Young People Learned about Sex and Birth Control*, Routledge & Kegan Paul, London.

FAUST, B. (1975), 'Offensiveness', *The Australian Science Teachers Journal*, 21-2, pp. 33–9.

FINKELHOR, D. (1979), *Sexually Victimized Children*, The Free Press, New York.

FINKELHOR, D. (1980), 'The sexual climate in families', Unpublished paper, Family Violence Research Laboratory, University of New Hampshire, Durham, pp. 1–30.

FLUGEL, J. C. (1930), *The Psychology of Clothes*, Hogarth Press, London.

FLUGEL, J. C. (1945), *Man, Morals and Society*, Duckworth London.

FOGELMAN, K. (1976) (ed.), *Britain's 16-year-olds*, National Children's Bureau, London.

FOOT, H. C., CHAPMAN, A. J., and SMITH, J. R. (1980) (eds.), *Friendship and Social Relations in Children*, John Wiley, New York.

FORD, C. S., and BEACH, F. A. (1951), *Patterns of Sexual Behaviour*, Harper & Row, New York.

FRANCOEUR, A. K., and FRANCOEUR, R. T. (1974), *Hot and Cool Sex*, Harcourt, Brace & Jovanovich, New York.

FRASER, S. E. (1972) (ed.), *Sex, Schools and Society*, Aurora Publishers, New York.

FRASER, S. E. (1977), 'Family planning and sex education: the Chinese approach', *Comparative Education*, 13, 1, pp. 15-27.

FRAZER, J. G. (1936), *The Golden Bough*, supplementary volume, Macmillan, London.

FREUD, S. (1957), 'On narcissism: an introduction', *Complete Psychological Works of Sigmund Freud*, Standard edition, vol. 14, pp. 73-102, Hogarth, London, First published 1914.

FREUD, S. (1963), 'On the sexual theories of children' in Reiff, P. (ed.), *The Collected Papers of Sigmund Freud*, Collier Books, New York, First published 1908.

FREUD, S. (1966), 'The dissolution of the Oedipus complex', *Complete Psychological Works of Sigmund Freud*, Standard edition, vol. 19, Hogarth, London, First published 1924.

FREUD, S. (1966), 'An outline of psychoanalysis', *Complete Psychological Works of Sigmund Freud*, Standard Edition, vol. 23, Hogarth, London, First published 1940.

FREUD, S. (1975), 'The sexual life of human beings', *Introductory Lectures on Psychoanalysis*, Penguin, Harmondsworth.

FREY, F. (1970), 'Cross-cultural survey research in Political Science', in Holt, R., and Turner, J. (eds.), *The Methodology of Comparative Research*, The Free Press, New York, pp. 173-264.

FRIEDMAN, C. (1972), 'Unwed motherhood – a continuing problem', *American Journal of Psychiatry*, 3, 129, pp. 85-9.

FRIJDA, N., and JAHODA, G. (1966), 'On the scope and methods of cross-cultural research', *International Journal of Psychology*, 1, pp. 110-27.

GAGNON, J. H. (1968), 'Sexuality and sexual learning in the child', in Vincent, C. E. (ed.), *Human Sexuality in Medical Education and Practice*, C. C. Thomas, Springfield, Illinois.

GAGNON, J. H., and SIMON, W. (1973), *Sexual Conduct*, Hutchinson, London.

GARDINER, P. (1969), *Measuring Readiness for High School Biology. Teachers Guide for Biology Readiness Test Materials*, Australian Council for Educational Research, January, Melbourne.

GEBHARD, R. H. (1977), 'The acquisition of basic sex information', *Journal of Sex Research*, 13, 3, pp. 148-69.

GILL, D. G., ILLESLY, R., and KOPLIK, L. H. (1970), 'Pregnancy in teenage girls', *Social Science and Medicine*, 3, pp. 549-74.

GILL, D. G., REID, G. D. B., and SMITH, D. M. (1971), 'Sex Education – press and parental perceptions', *Health Education Journal*, March, pp. 2-10.

GILLIGAN, C., KOHLBERG, L., LERNER, J., and BELENSKY, M.

457

(1971), 'Moral reasoning about sexual dilemmas', *Technical Report to the US Commission on Obscenity and Pornography*, vol. 1, pp. 145–73.

GLICK, J. (1975), 'Cognitive development in cross-cultural perspective', in Horowitz, T. D. *et al.* (eds.), *Review of Child Development Research*, University of Chicago Press, Chicago, pp. 595–654.

GOGGIN, J. E. (1975), 'Sex differences in the activity level of pre-school children as a possible precursor of hyperactivity', *Journal of Genetic Psychology*, 127, pp. 75–81.

GOLDE, P. G., and KOGAN, R. A. (1959), 'A sentence completion procedure for assessing attitudes to old people', *Journal of Gerontology*, 14, pp. 355–63.

GOLDMAN, R. J. (1964), *Religious Thinking from Childhood to Adolescence*, Routledge & Kegan Paul, London.

GOLDMAN, R. J. (1965a), *Readiness for Religion*, Routledge & Kegan Paul, London.

GOLDMAN, R. J. (1965b), 'The application of Piaget's schema of Operational Thinking to religious story data by means of Guttman Scalogram', *British Journal of Educational Psychology*, 35, 2, pp. 158–170.

GOLDMAN, R. J. (1969), *Angry Adolescents*, Routledge & Kegan Paul, London.

GOLDMAN, R. J. (1971), 'A concept for teacher education' in *Concepts in Teacher Education*, Ontario Teachers Federation, Toronto.

GOLDMAN, R. J., and GOLDMAN, J. D. G. (1980), *Children's Conceptualisation of Development*. A comparative study of children aged 5 to 15 years in Australia, England, North America and Sweden. Centre for the Study of Urban Education, La Trobe University, Melbourne, Australia.

GOLDMAN, R. J., and GOLDMAN, J. D. G. (1981a), 'How children view old people and ageing', *Australian Journal of Psychology*, 33, 3.

GOLDMAN, R. J., and GOLDMAN, J. D. G. (1981b), 'Children's perceptions of clothes and nakedness', *Genetic Psychology Monographs*, 104, 2, pp. 163–85.

GOLDMAN, R. J., and GOLDMAN, J. D. G. (1981c), 'What children want to know about sex', *Australian Science Teachers Journal*, 27, 2, pp. 61–9.

GOLDMAN, R. J., and GOLDMAN, J. D. G. (1981d), 'Sources of Sex Information for Australian, English, North American and Swedish children', *Journal of Psychology*, 109, pp. 97–108.

GOLDMAN, R. J., and GOLDMAN, J. D. G. (1981e), 'Children's Concepts of Why People Get Married', *Australian Journal of Sex Marriage and Family*, August, 2, 3, pp. 105–18.

GOLDMAN, R. J., and GOLDMAN, J. D. G. (1982a), *Readiness for Sex Education*, Routledge & Kegan Paul (in press).

GOLDMAN, R. J. and GOLDMAN, J. D. G. (1982b), 'How children perceive the origin of babies and the roles of mothers and fathers in procreation', *Child Development* (in press).

GOLDMAN, R.J. and GOLDMAN, J.D.G. (1982c), 'Children's perceptions of length of gestation period, the birth exit, and birth necessity explanations', *Journal of Biosocial Science* (in press) 14.

GOLDMAN, R.J., and GOLDMAN, J.D.G. (1982d), 'Children's understanding of sexual vocabulary', *Journal of Sex Research* (in press).

GOLDMAN, R.J.,and GOLDMAN, J.D.G. (1982e), 'Children's perceptions of parents and their roles', *Sex Roles* (in press).

GOLDTHORPE, J.H. and HOPE, K. (1964), *The Social Grading of Occupations: A New Approach and Scale*, Clarendon, Oxford.

GOODENOUGH, D.R. (1974), 'Articulation of the body concept', in Witkin, H., Dyk, R.B., and Faterson, H.F. *Psychological Differentiation*, John Wiley, New York, pp. 115-33.

GOODNOW, J.J. (1969), 'Problems in research on culture and thought', in Elkind, D., and Flavell, J.A. (eds.), *Studies in Cognitive Development*, Oxford University Press, New York, pp. 439-62.

GREEN, R. (1975) (ed.), *Human Sexuality: A Health Practitioners Text*, Williams and Wilkins, Baltimore.

GREENFIELD, P.M. (1976), 'Cross-cultural research and Piagetian theory: paradox and progress', in Riegel, K., and Meacham, J. (eds.), *The Developing Individual in a Changing World*, Mouton, The Hague.

GRUENBERG, B.C. (1926) (ed.), *Guidance of Childhood and Youth: Readings in Child Study*, Child Study Association of America, Macmillan, New York.

GUEST, P.M., and GURVICH, M. (1979), *Divorce in Australia*, Sun Books, Melbourne.

HAIMES, L.J. (1973),*Sex Education and the Public Schools*, Lexington Books, Lexington, Mass.

HAMPSON, J., and MONEY, J. (1955), 'Idiopathic sexual precocity', *Psychosomatic Medicine*, 17, pp. 1-35.

HARPER, J.H., and COLLINS, J.K. (1972a), 'The secular trend in the age of menarche in Australian schoolgirls', *Australian Paediatric Journal* 8, pp. 44-8.

HARPER, J.H., and COLLINS, J.K. (1972b), 'The effects of early and late maturation on the prestige of the adolescent girl', *Australian and New Zealand Journal of Sociology*, 8, pp. 83-8.

HARTUP, W.W. (1962), 'Some correlates of parental imitation in young children', *Child Development*, 33, pp. 85-96.

HARTUP, W.W., (1964), 'Friendship status and the effectiveness of peers as reinforcing agents', *Journal of Experimental Child Psychology*, 1, 2, pp. 154-62.

HARTUP, W.W. (1970), 'Peer interaction and social organization', in Mussen, P.H. (ed.), *Carmichael's Manual of Child Psychology*, vol. 2, Wiley, New York.

HARTUP, W.W. (1978), 'Children and their friends', in McGurk, H. *Issues in Childhood Social Development*, Methuen, London, pp. 130-70.

HASS, A. (1979), *Teenage Sexuality: A Survey of Teenage Sexual Behaviour*, Macmillan, New York.

HASS, P. H. (1974), 'Wanted and unwanted pregnancies: a fertility decision-making model', *Journal of Social Issues*, 30, 4, pp. 125–65.

HERON, A. (1974), 'Cultural determinants of concrete operational behaviour', in Dawson, J. L. M., and Lonner, W. J., *Readings in Cross-Cultural Psychology*, Hong Kong University Press, Hong Kong, pp. 94–101.

HESS, B. (1972), 'Friendship', in Riley, M. W., Johnson, M., and Foner, A. (eds.), *Aging and Society*, vol. 3, Russel Sage Foundation, New York.

HESS, R. D., and SHIPMAN, V. C. (1965), 'Early experience and the socialisation of cognitive modes in children', *Child Development*, 36, pp. 869–86.

HINSIE, L. E., and SHATZKY, J. (1947), *Psychiatric Dictionary*, Oxford University Press, London.

HOFFMAN, L. W. (1972), 'Early childhood experiences and women's achievement motives', *Journal of Social Issues*, 23, pp. 129–55.

HOLMES, M., NICOL, C., and STUBBS, R. (1968), 'Sex attitudes of young people', *Educational Research*, National Foundation for Educational Research, 11, pp. 38–42.

HOLMSTEDT, M. (1974) (ed.), *Second Seminar on Sex Education and Social Development in Sweden, Latin America and the Caribbean, April, 1972*, Stockholm Institute of Education, University of Stockholm, Stockholm.

HOLSTROM, L. L., and BURGESS, A. W. (1978), *The Victim of Rape: Institutional Reactions*, John Wiley, New York.

HOROWITZ, L., and GAIER, E. L. (1976), 'Adolescent erotica and female self concept development', *Adolescence*, XI, 44, pp. 497–508.

HUNT, W. B. (1976), 'Adolescent fertility, risks and consequences', *Population Reports, Series J*, US Department of Health, Welfare and Education, 10, July, pp. 157–76.

HUSEN, T. (1967), *International Study of Achievement in Mathematics: A Comparison of 12 Countries*, vol. 1, Wiley, New York.

HUTT, C. (1978a), 'Sex role differentiation in social development', in McGurks, H., *Issues in Childhood Social Development*, Methuen, London, pp. 171–203.

HUTT, C. (1978b), 'Biological bases of psychological sex differences', *American Journal of Diseases of Children*, 132, pp. 170–7.

HYDE, H. (1971), 'A Review of Sex Education in Sweden, United Kingdom, Ceylon and Guatemala'. M.Ed., Science Education thesis, University of London.

IRVINE, S. H. (1970), 'Affect and construct: a cross-cultural check on theories of intelligence', *Journal of Social Psychology*, 80, pp. 23–30.

IRWIN, J. (1976), 'Survey into sexual knowledge, attitudes and behaviour in first year university students and teachers college students', in Stewart, R. A. C. (ed.), *Adolescence in New Zealand*, vol. 1, Heinemann, Auckland.

JACKSON, L. (1952), *A Test of Family Attitudes*, Methuen, London.
JAHODA, G. (1970), 'A cross-cultural perspective in psychology', *The Advancement of Science*, 27(1), 14, pp. 57–70.
JOHNSON, M. M. (1963), 'Sex role learning in the nuclear family', *Child Development*, 23, pp. 319–33.
JOHNSON, M. M. (1975), 'Fathers and Mothers and sex typing', *Sociological Inquiry*, 45, 1, pp. 15–26.
JOSEPH, J. (1961), 'A research note on attitudes to work and marriage of six hundred adolescent girls', *British Journal of Sociology*, 12, pp. 176–183.
Journal of Social Issues, (1979), 'Children of Divorce', 35, 4, pp. 1–187.
JUHLIN, L. (1968), 'Factors influencing the spread of Gonorrhoea', *Acta Derm-Venereol*, 48, pp. 75–82, Uppsala.
KAHANA, B., and KAHANA, E. (1970), 'Grandparenthood from the perspective of the developing grandchild', *Developmental Psychology*, 3, 1, pp. 98–105.
KANTNER, J. F., and SELNIK, M. (1972), 'Sexual experience of young unmarried women in the United States', *Family Planning Perspectives*, 4, 4, pp. 9–18.
KELLY, J. G. (1979), *Adolescent boys in High School; a psychological study of coping and adaptation*, Lawrence Erlbaum, Hillsdale, New Jersey.
KINSEY, A. C. (1953), *Sexual Behaviour in the Human Female*, Sanders, Philadelphia.
KINSEY, A. C., POMEROY, W. B., and MARTIN, C. E. (1948), *Sexual Behaviour in the Human Male*, Sanders, Philadelphia.
KIRKENDALL, L. A. (1968), 'Sex Education', in Vincent, C. E. (ed.), *Human Sexuality in Medical Education and Practice*, C. C. Thomas, Springfield, Illinois.
KLEIN, M. (1963), *The Psycho-Analysis of Children*, Hogarth, London. First published 1932.
KLINE, P. (1972), *Fact and Fantasy in Freudian Theory*, Methuen, London.
KOBASIGAWA, A. (1968), 'Inhibitory and disinhibitory effects of models on sex-inappropriate behavior in children', *Psychologia* 11(1–2), pp. 86–96.
KOHLBERG, L. (1966), 'Cognitive stages and preschool education', *Human Development* 9, pp. 5–17.
KOHLBERG, L. (1969), *Stages in the Development of Moral Thought and Action*, Holt, Rinehart & Winston, New York.
KOHLBERG, L., and ULLIAN, D. Z. (1974), 'Stages in the development of psychosexual concepts and attitudes', in Friedman, R. C., Richart, R. M., and Van de Wiele, R. L. *Sex Differences in Behavior*, Wiley, New York.
KOHLBERG, L., and ZIGLER, E. (1967), 'The impact of cognitive maturity on the development of sex role attitudes in the years 4–8', *Genetic Psychology Monographs*, 75, pp. 89–165.
KONOPKA, G. (1976), *Young Girls: A Portrait of Adolescence*, Prentice-Hall, Englewood Cliffs, N.J.

KORNER, A. F. (1969), 'Neonatal startles, smiles, erections and reflex sucks as "related" to state, sex and individuality', *Child Development*, 40, pp. 1039-53.

KREITLER, H., and KREITLER, S. (1966), 'Children's concepts of sexuality and birth', *Child Development*, 37, pp. 363-78.

KROEBER, A., and KLUCKHOHN, C. (1952), *Culture*, Papers of the Peabody Museum, 47, 1.

KULKA, R. A., and WEINGARTEN, H. (1979), 'The longterm effects of parental divorce in childhood and adult adjustment', *Journal of Social Issues*, 35, 4, pp. 50-78.

Laboratory of Comparative Human Cognition (1979), 'Cross cultural psychology's challenge to our ideas of comparative human cognition', *American Psychologist*, 34, 10, pp. 827-33.

LACEY, De P. (1970), 'A cross-cultural study of classificatory ability in Australia', *Journal of Cross Cultural Psychology*, 1, 4, pp. 293-304.

LAMB, M. E. (1976), *The Role of the Father in Child Development*, Wiley, New York.

LAMB, M. E. (1979), 'Paternal influences and the father's role', *American Psychologist*, 34, 10, pp. 938-43.

LANGFORD, P. E. (1975), 'The development of the concept of development', *Human Development*, 18, pp. 321-32.

LANGLOIS, J. H., GOTTFRIED, N. W., BARNES, B. M., and HENDRICKS, D. E. (1978), 'The effect of peer age on the social behavior of preschool children', *Journal of Genetic Psychology* 132(1), pp. 11-20.

LERNER, R. M., and BRACKNEY, B. E. (1978), 'The importance of inner and outer body parts' attitudes in the self concept of late adolescents', *Sex Roles*, 4, 2, pp. 225-38.

LESSER, G., and KANDEL, D. (1968), 'Cross-cultural research; advantages and problems', in Holt, R., and Turner, J. (eds.), *The Methodology of Comparative Research*, The Free Press, New York.

LE VINE, R. A. (1970), 'Cross-cultural study in child psychology', in Mussen, P. A. (ed.), *Carmichael's Manual of Child Psychology* 3rd. edition, Vol. II, Wiley, New York, pp. 559-612.

LEWIS, R. (1973), 'Parents and peers: socialisation agents in the coital behaviour of young adults', *Journal of Sex Research*, 9, pp. 156-70.

LINNER, B. (1971), *Sex and Society in Sweden*, Random House, New York.

LINNER, B. (1977), 'No illegitimate children in Sweden', *Current Sweden*, The Swedish Institute, No. 157, April.

LINNER, B. (1978), 'The new handbook on instruction in sex and personal relationship in the Swedish schools', *Current Sweden*, No. 183, February.

LIPSET, S. M. (1963), 'The value patterns of democracy – a case study in comparative analysis', *American Sociological Review*, 28, 4, pp. 515-31.

LJUNG, B. O., BERGSTEN-BRUCEFORS, A., and LINDGREN, G. (1974), 'The secular trend in physical growth in Sweden', *Annals of Human Biology*, 1, pp. 245-56.

LLOYD, B.B. (1972), *Perception and Cognition from a cross-cultural perspective*, Penguin, Harmondsworth.
LLOYD, B.B., and ARCHER, J. (1976), *Exploring Sex Differences*, Academic Press, New York.
LODWICK, A.R. (1958), 'An investigation of the question whether the inferences that children draw in learning history correspond to the stages of mental development that Piaget postulates', Unpublished Advanced Diploma thesis, University of Birmingham.
McCABE, M.P., and COLLINS, J.K. (1979), 'Sex role and dating orientation', *Journal of Youth and Adolescence*, 8, 4, pp. 407-25.
McCANCE, C., and HALL, D.J. (1972), 'Sexual behavior and contraceptive practice of unmarried female undergraduates at Aberdeen University', *British Medical Journal*, 2, pp. 694-700.
MACCOBY, E.E. (1967) (ed.), *The Development of Sex Differences*, Tavistock Publications, London.
McCONAGHY, M.J. (1979), 'Sex role contravention and sex education directed toward young children in Sweden', *Journal of Marriage and the Family*, November, pp. 893-904.
McDONALD, G.W. (1979), 'Determinants of adolescent perceptions of maternal, and paternal power in the family', *Journal of Marriage and the Family*, 41, 4, pp. 757-70.
McDONALD, G.W. (1980), 'Parental power and adolescents' parental identification: A reexamination', *Journal of Marriage and the Family*, 42, 2, pp. 289-96.
McDOUGALL, W. (1922), *An Introduction to Social Psychology*, Methuen, London. First publication 1908.
McGREW, W.C. (1972), *An Ethological Study of Children's Behavior*, New York, Academic Press.
MACHTLINGER, V.J. (1976), 'Psychoanalytic theory: pre-oedipal and oedipal phases, with special reference to the father', in Lamb, M.E. (ed.), *The Role of the Father in Child Development*, University of Wisconsin, Madison, Wisconsin, pp. 278-305.
MANNARINO, A.P. (1980), 'The development of children's friendships', in Foot, H.C., Chapman, A.J., and Smith, J.R. (eds.), *Friendship and Social Relations in Children*, Wiley, Chichester, pp. 45-63.
MARTINSON, F.M. (1976), 'Eroticism in infancy and childhood', *Journal of Sex Research*, 12, 4, pp. 251-62.
MASLOW, A.H. (1963), 'The need to know and the fear of knowing', *Journal of Genetic Psychology*, 68, pp. 111-25.
MASTERS, W.H., and JOHNSON, V.E. (1966), *Human Sexual Response*, Churchill, London.
MASTERS, W.H., and JOHNSON, V.E. (1970), *Human Sexual Inadequacy*, Churchill, London.
MASTERS, W.H., and JOHNSON, V.E. (1975), *The Pleasure Bond: A New Look at Sexuality and Commitment*, Little Brown, Boston.
MEDEA, A., and THOMPSON, K. (1974), *Against Rape*, Farrar, Straus & Giroux, New York.

MEHL, L. E., BRENDSEL, C., and PETERSON, G. H. (1977), 'Children at birth: effects and implications', *Journal of Sex and Marital Therapy*, 3, 4, Winter, pp. 274–79.
MELSTED, L. (1979), 'Election year '79. Swedish Family Planning', *Current Sweden*, The Swedish Institute, No. 225, June (2).
MEYER, A. W. (1939), *The Rise of Embryology*, Stanford University Press, Palo Alto.
MILLER, J. P. (1978), 'Piaget, Kohlberg and Erikson: developmental implications for secondary education', *Adolescence*, 13, 50, pp. 237–50.
MODGIL, S. (1974), *Piagetian Research: a Handbook of Recent Studies*, National Foundation for Educational Research, Windsor.
MONEY, J. (1976), 'The development of Sexology as a discipline', *Journal of Sex Research*, 12, 2, pp. 83–87.
MONEY, J., and EHRHARDT, A. A. (1972), *Man and Woman, Boy and Girl*, The Johns Hopkins University Press, Baltimore, Maryland.
MONGE, R. H., DUSEK, J. B., and LAWLESS, J. (1977), 'An evaluation of the acquisition of information through a sex education class', *Journal of Sex Research*, 13, 3, pp. 170–84.
MONTGOMERY, B. (1979), 'Teaching children about sex', in Griffin, M., and Hudson, A. (eds.), *Children's Problems. A Guide for Parents*, Circus Books, Melbourne.
MOORE, J. E., and KENDALL, D. C. (1971), 'Children's concepts of reproduction', *Journal of Sex Research*, 7, pp. 42–61.
MOORE, S. G. (1967), 'Correlates of peer acceptance in nursery school children', in Hartup, W. W. and Smothergill, N. L. (eds.), *The Young Child*, vol. 1, Washington: National Association for the Education of Young Children.
MORIARTY, A. E., and TOUSSIENG, P. W. (1976), *Adolescent Coping*, Grime and Stratton, New York.
MORTON, R. S. (1971), *Sexual Freedom and Venereal Disease*, Peter Owen, London.
MURDOCK, G. P. (1969), *Outline of World Cultures*, 4th edition, HRAP Press, New Haven, Conn.
MURDOCK, G. P., and PROVOST, C. (1973), 'Measurement of social complexity', *Ethnology*, 12, pp. 379–92.
MURPHY, L. B. (1962), *The Widening World of Childhood*, Basic Books, New York.
MURPHY, L. B. and MORIARTY, A. E. (1976), *Vulnerability, coping and growth, from infancy to adolescence*, Yale University Press, New Haven.
MURRAY, H. A. (1943), *The Thematic Apperception Text Manual*, Harvard University Press, Cambridge, Mass.
MUSSEN, P. H., CONGER, J. J., and KAGAN, J. (1979), *Child Development and Personality*, Harper & Row, New York, pp. 494–555.
National Council of One Parent Families (1979), *Pregnant at School*, UK Report, September, National Council of One Parent Families, London.

National Swedish Board of Education, (1976), 'Self perception of children starting school', *School Research Newsletter*, April.

National Swedish Board of Health and Welfare (1978), 'Living Together – a Family Planning Project on Gotland, Sweden 1973–76', Committee on Health Education, Stockholm.

NEEDHAM, J. (1934), *A History of Embryology*, Cambridge University Press, New Haven, Conn.

NEWMAN, B. M. (1979), 'Coping and Adaptation in Adolescence', *Human Development*, 22, pp. 255–62.

NEWSON, J., and NEWSON, E. (1968), *Four Years Old in an Urban Community*, Allen & Unwin, London.

NEWSON, J., NEWSON, E., RICHARDSON, D., and SCAIFE, J. (1978), 'Perspectives in sex-role stereotyping', in Chetwynd, J., and Hartnett, O. (eds.), *The Sex Role System*, Routledge & Kegan Paul, London.

Nuffield Secondary Science Project, (1979), vol. 3. Barker, J. A. (ed.), Longman, York.

OAKDEN, E. C., and STURT, M. (1922), 'The development of the knowledge of time in children', *British Journal of Psychology*, 12, pp. 309–36.

OSOFSKY, H. J. (1971), 'Adolescent sexual behaviour: current status and anticipated trends for the future', *Clinical Obstetrics and Gynaecology*, 14, pp. 393–408.

PEEL, E. A. (1960), *The Pupil's Thinking*, Oldbourne, London.

PEEL, E. A. (1971), *The Nature of Adolescent Judgement*, Wiley-Interscience, New York.

PEIFER, M. R. (1971), 'The effects of varying age-grade status of models on the imitative behavior of six-year-old boys'. Unpublished doctoral dissertation, University of Delaware.

PIAGET, J. (1926), *The Language and Thought of the Child*, Routledge & Kegan Paul, London.

PIAGET, J. (1928), *Judgement and Reason in the Child*, Routledge & Kegan Paul, London.

PIAGET, J. (1930), *The Child's Conception of Causality*, Routledge & Kegan Paul, London.

PIAGET, J. (1932), *The Moral Judgement of the Child*, Routledge & Kegan Paul, London.

PIAGET, J. (1951), *The Child's Conception of the World*, Routledge & Kegan Paul, London. First published 1929.

PIAGET, J. (1951), *The Child's Conception of Physical Causality*, Routledge & Kegan Paul, London. First published 1927.

PIAGET, J. (1966), 'The need and significance of cross-cultural studies in genetic psychology', *International Journal of Psychology*, 1 (1), pp. 3–13.

PIAGET, J. (1971), *Biology and Knowledge*, Edinburgh University Press, Edinburgh. First published in French 1967.

PIAGET, J. (1971), *The Child's Conception of Time*, Ballantine, New York. First published 1946.

PIAGET, J. (1972), 'A structural foundation for tomorrow's education', *Prospects*, Quarterly Review of Education, UNESCO II, 1, pp. 12–27.
PIAGET, J. (1978), *Behaviour and Evolution*, Random House, New York. First published 1976.
PIAGET, J. and INHELDER, B. (1966), *The Psychology of the Child*, Basic Books, New York.
PLUMMER, K. (1975), *Sexual Stigma*, Routledge & Kegan Paul, London.
POCS, O., and GODOW, A. (1977), 'Can students view parents as sexual beings?' *Family Coordinator*, 26, 1, pp. 31–6.
POLLARD, A. H. (1970), 'Demographic aspects of ageing', in Sax, S. (ed.), *The Aged in Australian Society*, Angus & Robertson, Sydney.
PRAWAT, R. S., JONES, H., and HAMPTON, J. (1979), 'Longitudinal Study of Attitude Development in Pre, Early and Later Adolescent Samples', *Journal of Educational Psychology*, 71, 3, pp. 363–9.
PRICE-WILLIAMS, D. R. (1969) (ed.), *Cross-cultural Studies. Selected Readings*, Penguin Books, Harmondsworth.
RABIN, A. I. (1965), *Growing Up in the Kibbutz*, Springer, New York.
RAINWATER, L. (1968), 'Sexual behaviour and family planning in the lower class', in Vincent, G. E. (ed.), *Human Sexuality in Medical Education and Practice*, C. C. Thomas, Springfield, Illinois.
RAUH, J. L., JOHNSON, L. B., and BURKET, R. L. (1973), 'The reproductive adolescent', *Pediatric Clinics of North America*, 20, p. 1005.
REISS, I. L. (1960), *Premarital Sexual Standards in America*, Free Press of Glencoe, New York.
REISS, I. L. (1967), *The Social Context of Premarital Sexual Permissiveness*, Holt, Rinehart & Winston, New York.
REISS, I. L. (1970), 'Premarital sex as deviant behaviour', *American Sociological Review*, 35, 1, pp. 78–87.
REST, J., TURIELE, E., and KOHLBERG, L. (1969), 'Level of moral development as a determinant of preference and comprehension of moral judgements made by others', *Journal of Personality*, 37, 2, pp. 219–52.
ROACH, M. E., and EICHER, J. B. (1965), *Dress, Adornment and the Social Order*, John Wiley, New York.
ROBERTS, D. F., and DANN, T. C. (1975), 'A twelve year study of menarcheal age', *British Journal of Preventive Social Medicine*, 29, pp. 31–9.
ROBSON, J. (1978) (ed.), *Parents, Children and Sex, A New Sex Education Guide for Parents*, A Family Life Guide Book, Family Life Movement of Australia, North Strathfield, N.S.W.
ROGERS, R. S. (1974), *Sex Education: Rationale and Reaction*, Cambridge University Press, Cambridge.
ROKEACH, M. (1960), *The Open and Closed Mind*, Basic Books, New York.
ROSENMAYER, L., and ALLERBECK, K. (1979), 'Social life-time of youth and historical epochs', *Current Sociology*, 27, 2/3, pp. 59–78.
RUBIN, I., and KIRKENDALL, L. A. (1969) (eds.), *Sex in the Adolescent Years*, Fontana Books, New York.

466

RUBIN, I., and KIRKENDALL, L. A. (1970) (eds.), *Sex in the Child-hood Years*, Association Press, New York.

RUBIN, J. Z., PROVENZANO, F. J., and LURIA, Z. (1974), 'The eye of the beholder; parents' views on sex of newborns', *American Journal of Orthopsychiatry*, 44, pp. 512-19.

RUSSELL, J. (1979), 'Fathers! Incompetent or reluctant parents?' *Australian and New Zealand Journal of Sociology*, 15, 1, pp. 57-65.

SADKER, M., SADKER, D., and MILLER, D. (1977), *Now upon a time – a Contemporary View of Children's Literature*, Harper & Row, New York.

SANTROCK, J. W. (1970), 'Paternal absence, sex typing and identification', *Developmental Psychology*, 2, pp. 264-72.

SARGEANT, D. (1975), 'An innovation of inter-disciplinary in-service education in human sexuality', unpublished M.Ed. thesis, La Trobe University.

SAX, S. (1979), 'Priorities for Ageing Research', in *Ageing in Australia*, (ed.), Donald, J. M., Everitt, A. V., and Wheeler, P. J., Association of Gerontology, Sydney.

SCHERESKY, R. F. (1978), *Elementary School Children's Views of Occupational Roles*, Research Institute for Studies in Education, Iowa State University, Iowa.

SCHLOSSMAN, S., and WALLACH, S. (1978), 'The crime of precocious sexuality: female juvenile delinquency in the Progressive Era (1900-20)', *Harvard Educational Review*, 48, pp. 65-94.

SCHOFIELD, M. (1968), *The Sexual Behaviour of Young People*, Penguin, Harmondsworth.

SCHOFIELD, M. (1976), *Promiscuity*, Gollancz, London.

SCHULZ, E. D., and WILLIAMS, S. R. (1968), *Family Life and Sex Education*, Harcourt, Brace & World, New York.

SEARS, R. R., MACCOBY, E. E., and LEVIN, H. (1957), *Patterns of Child Rearing*, Harper & Row, New York.

S.E.I.C.U.S. (1970), *Sexuality and Man*, Charles Scribner, New York.

SELMAN, R. L., and JAQUETTE, D. (1977), 'Stability and oscillation in interpersonal awareness: a clinical-development analysis', in Keasey, C. B. (ed.), *The Nebraska Symposium on Motivation*, vol. 25, University of Nebraska Press, Lincoln, Neb.

SELNIK, M., and KANTNER, J. F. (1972), 'The probability of premarital intercourse', *Social Science Research*, 1, pp. 335-41.

SERPELL, R. (1976), *Culture's Influence on Behaviour*, Methuen, London.

SHARPE, S. (1978), *Just Like a Girl. How Girls Learn to be Women*, Penguin, Harmondsworth.

SHAVELSON, R. J., HUBNER, J. J., and STANTON, G. C. (1976), 'Self-concept: validation of construct interpretations', *Review of Educational Research*, 46, 3, pp. 407-41.

SILVERN, L. E. and RYAN, V. L. (1979), 'Self-rated adjustment and sex-typing on the Bem Sex-Role Inventory: Is masculinity the primary predictor of adjustment?' *Sex Roles*, 5, 6, pp. 739-763.

467

S.I.O.P.S., Standard International Occupational Prestige Scale. (See Treiman, D.J.)

SLABY, R. G. and FREY, K. S. (1975), 'Development of gender constancy and selective attention to same-sex models', *Child Development*, 46, 4, pp. 849–56.

SMYTH, C. J. F. (1976), 'Exnuptial births in New Zealand', in Stewart, R. A. C. (ed.), *Adolescence in New Zealand*, Heinemann, Auckland, vol. I, pp. 122–35.

Social Trends (1980), Central Statistical Office, London.

SPANIER, G. B. (1977), 'Sources of sex information and premarital behaviour', *Journal of Sex Research*, 13, 2, pp. 73–88.

SPANIER, G. B. (1978), 'Sex educational and premarital sexual behaviour among American college students', *Adolescence*, 13, 52, pp. 659–74.

Stanford-Binet Intelligence Scales (1937), Terman, L. M., and Merrill, M. A., Houghton Mifflin, Boston.

Statesman's Year Book (1979), Macmillan, London.

STEPHENS, W. N. (1962), *The Oedipus Complex Hypothesis: Cross-cultural Evidence*, Free Press of Glencoe, New York.

STERNGLANZ, S. H., and SERBIN, L. A. (1974), 'Sex role stereotyping in children's TV programs', *Developmental Psychology*, 10, pp. 710–15.

STEVENSON, H. W., PARKER, T., WILKINSON, A., BONNEVAUX, B., and GONZALEZ, M. (1978), 'Schooling, environment and cognitive development, a cross-cultural study', *Monograph of Society for Research in Child Development*, 43, 3, no. 175.

STEWART, R. A. C. (1976), *Adolescence in New Zealand*, Heinemann, Auckland, vols. I and II.

STOREY, D. (1977), 'Gray power; an endangered species? Ageism as portrayed in children's books', *Social Education*, October, pp. 528–32.

STRODTBECK, F. (1969), 'Consideration of meta methods in cross-cultural studies', *American Anthropology*, 66, pp. 223–29.

SUEHSDORF, A. (1964), (ed.), *What to tell your children about sex*, Allen & Unwin, London.

SUNDSTRÖM, K. (1976), 'Young people's sexual habits in today's Swedish society', *Current Sweden*, Swedish Institute, July, 125.

Sweden: Fact Sheet on Sweden (1979), January No. Fs 82e/ohj.

Swedish National Board of Education (1977), 'Education in Living Together', Stockholm.

Swedish Statistical Yearbook (1979), Government publishers, Stockholm.

TANNER, J. M. (1961), *Education and Physical Growth*, University of London Press, London.

TANNER, J. M. (1978), *Foetus into Man*, Harvard University Press, Cambridge, Mass.

TAVRIS, C., and OFFIR, C. (1977), *The longest War: Sex Differences in Perspective*, Harcourt Brace & Jovanovich, New York.

THOMPSON, J. (1976), 'Fertility and abortion inside and outside marriage', *Population Trends*, Office of Population, Censuses and Surveys, HMSO, London, V.5, pp. 3-8.

THOMPSON, S. K. (1975), 'Gender labels and early sex role development', *Child Development*, 46, 2, June, pp. 339-47.

TIETZE, C., and MURSTEIN, M. (1975), 'Induced abortion: 1975 factbook', Reports on Population — *Family Planning*, 14, December.

TORRANCE, E. P. (1962), *Guiding Creative Talent*, Prentice-Hall, Englewood Cliffs, New Jersey.

TORRANCE, E. P. (1963), *Education and the Creative Potential*, University of Minnesota Press, Minneapolis.

TREIMAN, D. J. (1977), *Occupational Prestige in Comparative Perspective*, Academic Press, New York.

TROTTER, W. (1919), *Instincts of the Herd in Peace and War*, Unwin, London.

TURIEL, E. (1969), 'Developmental processes in the child's moral thinking', in Mussen, P., Langer, J., and Covington, M. (eds.), *New Directions in Developmental Psychology*, Holt, Rinehart & Winston, New York.

ULLIAN, D. Z. (1976), 'The development of conceptions of masculinity and feminity', in Lloyd, B. B., and Archer, J. *Exploring Sex Differences*, Academic Press, New York.

UNGER, R. K. (1979a), 'Toward a redefinition of sex and gender', *American Psychologist*, 34, 11, pp. 1085-94.

UNGER, R. K. (1979b), *Female and Male: Psychological Perspectives*, Harper & Row, New York.

VAILLANT, G. E. (1977), *Adaptation to Life*, Little, Brown, Boston.

VENNER, A. M., STEWART, C. S. and HAGER, D. L. (1972), 'The sexual behaviour of adolescents in middle America', *Journal of Marriage and the Family*, 34, November, pp. 696-705.

VERNON, P. E. (1969), *Intelligence and Cultural Environment*, Methuen, London.

VINCENT, C. E. (1968), *Human Sexuality in Medical Education and Practice*, C. C. Thomas, Springfield Ill.

WAGNER, N., FUJITA, B., and PION, R. (1973), 'Sexual behaviour in high school', *Journal of Sex Research*, 9, pp. 150-5.

WAINER, B., and WAINER, J. (1975), 'Pathways to abortion', *La Trobe Sociology Papers*, La Trobe University, Melbourne.

WAINER, J. (1979), 'Women and Abortion: A Sociological Study of the Decision and its Consequences', M. A. thesis, Department of Sociology, La Trobe University, Melbourne.

WALLACE, H. M., GOLD, E. M., GOLDSTEIN, H., and OGLESBY, A. C. (1973), 'A study of services and needs of teenage pregnant girls in the large cities of the United States', *American Journal of Public Health*, 63, 5.

WALLERSTEIN, J. S., and KELLY, J. B. (1974), 'The effects of parental divorce: the adolescent experience', in Koupernik, A. (ed.), *The Child in His Family: Children at Psychiatric Risk*, Wiley, New York.

469

WARD, W. (1973), 'Patterns of culturally defined sex-role preferences and parental imitation', *Journal of Genetic Psychology*, 122, pp. 337–43.

WAXMAN, S. (1976), *What is a Girl? What is a Boy?*, Widescope, Melbourne.

WEBSTER, B. (1972), *Report of the National Commission on Venereal Disease*, DHEW Publication, HSM, 72–8125, Washington, DC.

WESTIN-LINDGREN, G. (1976), 'Height, weight and menarche in Swedish urban school children in relation to socio-economic and regional factors', *Annals of Human Biology*, 3, pp. 501–28.

WESTIN-LINDGREN, G. (1979), *Physical and Mental Development in Swedish Urban School Children*, Studies in Education and Psychology, Stockholm Institute of Education, Stockholm.

WILLIAMS, J. E., et al. (1979), 'Sex-trait stereotyping in France, Germany and Norway', *Journal of Cross-cultural Psychology*, 10, 2, pp. 133–56.

WILSON, J. (1965), *Logic and Sexual Morality*, Penguin, Harmondsworth.

WILSON, J., WILLIAMS, N., and SUGARMAN, B. (1968), *An Introduction to Moral Education*, Penguin, Harmondsworth.

WISEMAN, J. P. (1976) (ed.), *The Social Psychology of Sex*, Harper & Row, New York.

WITKIN, H., DYK, R. B., FATERSON, H. F., GOODENOUGH, D. R., and KARP, S. A. (1974), *Psychological Differentiation*, Wiley, London.

WITTORP, B. (1977), 'Joint custody of the children of divorced and unmarried parents', *Current Sweden*, The Swedish Institute, February, 149, Stockholm.

WOOD, C., SHANMUGAM, N., and MEREDITH, E. (1969), 'The risk of premarital conception', *Medical Journal of Australia*, 2, pp. 228–32.

WRIGHT, H. (1968), *Sex and Society*, Allen & Unwin, London.

WRIGHT, M. R., and McCARY, J. L. (1969), 'Positive effects of sex education on emotional patterns of behaviour', *Journal of Sex Research*, 5, 3, pp. 162–69.

YANOW, E. R., and DAVIS, C. M. (1978), 'A cumulative index of the Journal of Sex Research: 1965–1977', *Journal of Sex Research*, 14, 3.

YORBURG, B. (1974), *Sexual Identity, Sex Roles and Social Change*, Wiley, New York.

YOUNG, J. Z. (1971), *An Introduction to the Study of Man*, Clarendon Press, Oxford.

ZONGKER, C. E. (1977), 'The self concept of pregnant adolescent girls', *Adolescence*, 12, 48, pp. 477–88.

Name index

NAME INDEX

Subject index